UNDERSTANDING
EMPLOYMENT LAW

LexisNexis Law School Publishing Advisory Board

UNDERSTANDING EMPLOYMENT LAW

Second Edition

Jeffrey M. Hirsch
Associate Professor of Law
University of North Carolina School of Law

Paul M. Secunda
Associate Professor of Law
Marquette University Law School

Richard A. Bales
Professor of Law and Director, Chase Center for Excellence in Advocacy
Northern Kentucky University, Salmon P. Chase College of Law

ISBN: 978–0–7698–5991–0 (print)
ISBN: 978–0–3271–8394–5 (eBook)

Library of Congress Cataloging-in-Publication Data

Hirsch, Jeffrey M.
   Understanding employment law / Jeffrey M. Hirsch, Associate Professor of Law, University of North Carolina School of Law, Paul M. Secunda, Associate Professor of Law, Marquette University Law School, Richard A. Bales, Professor of Law and Director, Chase Center for Excellence in Advocacy Northern Kentucky University, Salmon P. Chase College of Law. -- Second edition.
      pages cm
   Includes index.
   ISBN 978-0-7698-5991-0
1. Labor laws and legislation--United States. I. Secunda, Paul M. II. Bales, Richard A. III. Title.
   KF3455.B354 2013
   344.7301--dc23
 344.7301--dc23

Editorial Offices
121 Chanlon Rd., New Providence, NJ 07974 (908) 464-6800
201 Mission St., San Francisco, CA 94105-1831 (415) 908-3200
www.lexisnexis.com

MATTHEW◆BENDER

Dedications

JMH: To Lynn, Noah, and Naomi, with love

PMS: To Mindy, Jake, and Izzy, who continue to provide constant inspiration and support for all my work

RAB: With love to Dennis and Emma

Preface

Barely 30 years ago, what today is known as "employment law" was known as "master-servant law." The change of nomenclature is telling. Historically, "regulation" of the workplace amounted to little more than market forces and employer whims. The modern workplace, however, is governed by a complex and multifaceted legal framework that is continually evolving both as a result of federal and state statutes and as a result of decisions by state courts.

This book strikes a balance between comprehensiveness and selectivity. It provides the substantive material needed to succeed in practice and in the classroom and on final examinations, without overwhelming the reader with details that are unduly esoteric or tangential. The book begins with common-law employment doctrines such as employment at-will, employment contracts, employment torts, workplace privacy issues, and restrictive covenants. It then turns to federal and state statutory regulation of the workplace, covering topics such as compensation (including wage and hour legislation and unemployment insurance), employee benefits (including leave time, pensions, and health insurance), and workplace safety legislation.

Acknowledgments

The authors wish to acknowledge their intellectual debt to Steven Willborn, Stewart Schwab, John Burton, and Gillian Lester. Their LexisNexis casebook EMPLOYMENT LAW: CASES AND MATERIALS was the foundation upon which much of this UNDERSTANDING book was built.

Professor Bales thanks his co-authors, Jeff Hirsch and Paul Secunda, for their inspiration, gentle prodding, fine editing, and never-ending words of encouragement.

Professor Hirsch thanks his co-authors, Rick Bales and Paul Secunda, for their diligence, great editing, and, most importantly, good cheer throughout this project. He also is indebted to Steven Willborn for providing him the opportunity to take part in this project and to Leslia Caia and Casey Turner for their excellent research assistance.

Professor Secunda thanks his wonderful co-authors, Dean Joseph Kearney for his continual financial and institutional support of my work, and the authors of the Fifth Edition of the Willborn, Schwab, Burton & Lester book for providing a wonderful template for our own work.

Table of Contents

Table of Contents

Table of Contents

Table of Contents

Table of Contents

Table of Contents

Table of Contents

Table of Contents

Chapter 1

INTRODUCTION

§ 1.01 HISTORICAL OVERVIEW AND THE MULTI-LAYERED NATURE OF EMPLOYMENT LAW

[A] At-Will Employment

In 1877, treatise-writer Horace Gay Wood penned what has become the employment at-will rule: an employer or employee may unilaterally terminate the employment relationship at any time, for any reason, absent prior agreement to the contrary.[1] To make this formulation of the rule current, another caveat must be added: the termination cannot violate statutory law (such as federal antidiscrimination law) or common law (such as wrongful discharge in violation of public policy). With this caveat, Wood's rule provides the baseline for the American employment relationship. As a legal matter, an employer wishing to discharge an employee need not provide (or even have) a reason for discharge.

In the early 1900s, the Supreme Court seemed to constitutionalize the at-will rule. In *Adair v. United States*,[2] the Court struck down a federal statute prohibiting employers from discriminating against union members, declaring that federal legislation infringing on employers' unfettered right to fire is "an invasion of the personal liberty as well as of the right to property, guaranteed by [the Fifth] Amendment."[3] Similarly, in *Lochner v. New York*,[4] the Court struck as

---

[1] Horace Gay Wood, Master and Servant 283-84 (1877).

[2] 208 U.S. 161 (1908).

[3] *Id.* at 172.

unconstitutional a state law limiting the number of hours per week workers could work in bakeries. In subsequent cases, however, the Court upheld protective legislation for women, whose "physical structure and . . . performance of maternal functions place her at a disadvantage in the struggle for subsistence," especially "when the burdens of motherhood are upon her."[5] Thus, the Court held that there was some room — though not much — for states to enact statutes designed to protect employees.

An employee wishing to challenge a discharge must find a legal exception to the baseline rule that the discharge is permissible. Much of Employment Law is the study of those exceptions. The following sections provide an overview of both statutory and common law exceptions.

[B] Workers' Compensation

Apart from "protective" legislation for women, the first significant statutory regulation of the American workforce occurred in 1908, when the federal government passed a workers' compensation statute providing monetary benefits to certain federal employees injured on the job.[6] States began following the federal example in 1911, and by 1948, all states had some sort of workers' compensation system.[7] These state workers' compensation systems involved a trade-off: employees benefited from a no-fault system that enabled them to recover even when a tort suit would have been unsuccessful; employers benefited from limited liability, meaning that employees could recover only the benefits specified in the workers' compensation statute.

[C] New Deal Federal Legislation

The next major stage in the regulation of the American workplace occurred as part of the New Deal response to the Great Depression. The New Deal included three major pieces of workplace legislation that still exist today. The first was the Fair Labor Standards Act (FLSA),[8] passed in 1938. The FLSA sets a minimum wage, requires premium pay for overtime, and restricts the use of child labor. The FLSA is administered by the Department of Labor (DOL).

The second major piece of Depression-era workplace legislation was the National Labor Relations Act of 1935 (NLRA),[9] also known as the Wagner Act. The NLRA, administered by the National Labor Relations Board (NLRB), establishes (among other things) the right of employees to organize into unions, and requires employers to bargain collectively with employees through these unions. The NLRA and FLSA were considered to co-exist comfortably, with the FLSA setting a floor

---

[4] 198 U.S. 45 (1905).

[5] Muller v. Oregon, 208 U.S. 412, 421 (1918).

[6] Federal Employers' Liability Act, 45 U.S.C. §§ 51-60.

[7] ARTHUR WILLIAMS, JR. & PETER S. BARTH, COMPENDIUM ON WORKMEN'S COMPENSATION 13-18 (1973).

[8] 29 U.S.C §§ 201-19.

[9] Id. §§ 151-63.

beyond which employees could bargain through the framework of the NLRA.[10]

The third major Depression-era piece of workplace legislation was the Social Security Act of 1935,[11] which, among other things, created unemployment insurance. The statute created a hybrid federal-state program for collecting payroll taxes and administering unemployment benefits.[12]

[D]   Federal Antidiscrimination Legislation

It took nearly thirty years for Congress to enact another major piece of workplace legislation. In 1963, Congress passed the Equal Pay Act[13] as an amendment to the FLSA. The Equal Pay Act prohibits wage discrimination on the basis of sex. A year later, Congress passed groundbreaking legislation in the form of Title VII of the Civil Rights Act of 1964 (Title VII),[14] which prohibits workplace discrimination and retaliation on the basis of race, color, religion, sex, and national origin. Title VII is administered by the Equal Employment Opportunity Commission (EEOC) and enforced primarily through private lawsuits.

After Title VII, Congress passed two additional antidiscrimination statutes. The first was the Age Discrimination in Employment Act of 1967 (ADEA),[15] and the second was the Americans with Disabilities Act of 1990 (ADA).[16] Both of these statutes are administered by the EEOC and, like Title VII, enforced primarily through private lawsuits.

[E]   Federal Legislation Setting Workplace Standards

In addition to these antidiscrimination statutes, Congress also has passed several statutes setting minimum workplace standards. In 1970, Congress passed the Occupational Safety and Health Act (OSHA),[17] setting standards for workplace safety and health. In 1974, Congress passed the Employee Retirement Income Security Act (ERISA),[18] setting standards for pensions and welfare benefit plans such as employer-provided health insurance. In 1988, Congress passed the Worker Adjustment and Retraining Notification Act (WARN),[19] requiring employers with 100 or more employees to provide at least sixty days notice to employees who will be discharged because of a plant closing or mass layoff. In 1993, Congress passed the Family and Medical Leave Act (FMLA),[20] requiring employers with fifty or

---

[10] *See* J. JOSEPH HUTHMACHER, SENATOR ROBERT F. WAGNER AND THE RISE OF URBAN LIBERALISM 203-04 (1968).

[11] 42 U.S.C. §§ 301-1397jj.

[12] *See infra* § 13.02.

[13] 29 U.S.C. § 206(d).

[14] 42 U.S.C. § 2000e-2.

[15] 29 U.S.C. §§ 621-34.

[16] 42 U.S.C. §§ 12101-12213.

[17] 29 U.S.C. §§ 651-78.

[18] *Id.* §§ 1001-461.

[19] *Id.* §§ 2101-09.

[20] *Id.* § 2601.

more employees to permit their employees to take up to twelve weeks of unpaid leave to care for a new child, or to care for themselves or a family member with a serious health condition. In May 2008, President George W. Bush signed into law the Genetic Information Nondiscrimination Act ("GINA"),[21] which prohibits employers from discriminating on the basis of an employee's genetic information.

[F]   State Legislation and Common Law

As Congress has been expanding federal workplace legislation, states have been adding their own employment protections. On the legislative front, all states except Mississippi, Arkansas, and Alabama have enacted general antidiscrimination laws roughly parallel to the federal antidiscrimination laws. Many of these state laws forbid discrimination on grounds not covered by the federal laws. The New Jersey antidiscrimination statute, for example, forbids discrimination against transgendered employees;[22] the Kentucky statute forbids discrimination against smokers.[23]

Almost all states forbid retaliatory dismissal for filing a workers' compensation claim; some states do so by statute[24] and others through the common law. Most states have passed legislation protecting whistleblowers and establishing workplace safety regulation. In addition, many states restrict the use of drug testing in the workplace, and some have enacted statutes protecting employees from the adverse effects of corporate takeovers.

State courts also apply contract and tort principles to protect employees. For example, courts in many states use contract principles to bind employers to promises of tenure and progressive discipline made orally or in employee handbooks. Courts also use contract principles to enforce employee promises, including covenants not to compete, non-solicitation agreements, and invention agreements. Some states are applying the covenant of good faith and fair dealing to give employees a cause of action for wrongful discharge. Courts have additionally become increasingly receptive to the application of tort doctrines to the employment context, such as intentional infliction of emotional distress (for particularly egregious mistreatment of employees), invasion of privacy (especially for workplace searches and drug testing), and defamation (for giving false reasons for discipline or discharge, or in providing employment references). Finally, most states have adopted a public policy exception to employment at-will to protect employees who are discharged for refusing to commit an unlawful act, for exercising a statutory right, or for performing a public duty.

---

[21] Pub. L. No. 110-233, 122 Stat. 881 (2008) (codified in scattered sections of 26, 29, and 42 U.S.C.).

[22] N.J Stat. Ann. § 10:5.

[23] Ky. Rev. Stat. Ann. § 344.040.

[24] See, e.g., Tex. Lab. Code Ann. § 451.001.

§ 1.02   SCOPE OF THIS BOOK

This book covers most of the material described above. It does not, however, cover three important topics. The first is the NLRA. The NLRA usually is taught in a stand-alone Labor Law course. Students interested in learning more about the NLRA are directed to *Understanding Labor Law* by Douglas E. Ray, Calvin William Sharpe, and Robert N. Strassfeld. The second topic not covered by this book is antidiscrimination law. Antidiscrimination law usually is taught in a stand-alone Employment Discrimination course, although it often is taught in abbreviated form in the Employment Law course. Students interested in learning more about employment discrimination are directed to *Understanding Employment Discrimination* by Thomas R. Haggard. Third, workers' compensation law is not covered in this book, as this subject is also often covered in a separate course and mostly involves issues surrounding a specific type of statutory compensation system.

Although Employment Law, Employment Discrimination, Labor Law, and Workers' Compensation Law often are taught separately, they are closely interrelated. Cases interpreting Title VII and other employment discrimination statutes, for example, built upon a method of proving discrimination that originally was developed under the NLRA for dealing with employers who discriminated against workers on the basis of union membership or union activity. Similarly, when an employee files suit alleging employment discrimination, she almost always alleges several employment-related tort claims as well, if for no reason other than to try to avoid the damage caps imposed by federal antidiscrimination laws. Finally, employment discrimination cannot properly be understood without first understanding the background rule of employment at-will.

Because Employment Law, Employment Discrimination, Labor Law, and Workers' Compensation Law are so interrelated, students will benefit by taking courses on these topics concurrently or sequentially, or by taking courses that integrate elements from each of these studies of the employment relationship.

Chapter 2

LEGAL BOUNDARIES OF THE EMPLOYMENT RELATIONSHIP

SYNOPSIS

§ 2.01   EMPLOYEES VERSUS INDEPENDENT CONTRACTORS

[A]   Introduction

Employment law protects employees, aspiring employees, and former employees.[1] Employers, therefore, have a strong incentive to classify workers as something other than "employees" to avoid application of the laws regulating the employment relationship. One such classification is the "independent contractor."

The distinction between an employee and an independent contractor is pragmatically critical for two reasons.[2] First, as described above, classification as

---

[1] *Contracts — Independent Contractor Agreements — Ninth Circuit Finds That Misclassified Employees Are Eligible for Federally Regulated Employee Benefits*, 111 Harv. L. Rev. 609, 609 (1997).

[2] Brian A. Langille & Guy Davidov, *Beyond Employees and Independent Contractors: A View from*

an employee is a "gateway" or threshold decision entitling a person to the protection of employment laws. Second, most statutory attempts to define protected "employees" are, as described below, either vacuous or circular.[3]

[B] The Control Test

Historically, under the doctrine of respondeat superior, an employer was only liable for a tort committed by a worker over whom the employer exercised sufficient control.[4] The rationale was that an employer exercising control over its workers should be responsible to others for its workers' actions. This "control test" for establishing an employer's vicarious liability, which itself derived from the law of agency,[5] became the leading test for distinguishing employees from independent contractors.

The Internal Revenue Service (IRS) requires employers to pay employment taxes (federal unemployment insurance, Social Security, and Medicare) for, and to withhold taxes (income, Social Security, and Medicare) from, employees but not independent contractors. The IRS uses the control test to distinguish employees from independent contractors.[6] The IRS's articulation of the test, although not controlling in other employment-related contexts, provides a useful list of the common-law factors courts using the control test tend to consider. The IRS divides the common-law "control" factors into three categories.[7]

The first category is behavioral control. These factors focus on whether the employer has the right to direct and control the work, primarily by instructing the worker how to do the work. These factors include:

> when and where to do the work; what tools or equipment to use; what assistants to hire; where to purchase supplies and services; what work must be performed by a specified individual; and what order or sequence to follow.[8]

Another factor related to behavioral control is training: employees often receive training, while independent contractors usually do not.

The second category of IRS control factors is financial control. These factors include:

> [t]he extent to which the worker has unreimbursed business expenses (independent contractors are presumed to have more of these than employees); [t]he extent of the worker's investment (independent contrac- tors are presumed to invest more than employees in tools or other

---

Canada, 21 COMPARATIVE LAB. L. & POL'Y J. 7 (1999).

  [3] Langille & Davidov, *supra* note 2, at 16.

  [4] Myra H. Barron, *Who's An Independent Contractor? Who's An Employee?*, 14 LAB. LAW. 457, 459 (1999).

  [5] *See* RESTATEMENT (SECOND) OF AGENCY § 220(2).

  [6] 29 C.F.R. § 31.3121(d)-1(c)(2); Rev. Rule 87-41, 1987-1 C.B. 296.

  [7] I.R.S. Publication 15-A (Employer's Supplemental Tax Guide - Supplement to Circular E).

  [8] *Id.*

implements of the trade); [t]he extent to which the worker makes services available to others (independent contractors are presumed to offer their services to a wider market than employees); [h]ow the business pays the worker (independent contractors usually are paid a flat fee per job, whereas employees usually are paid an hourly, weekly, or annual wage); and [t]he extent to which the worker can make a profit or loss (independent contractors generally can whereas employees generally cannot).[9]

The third category of IRS control factors is the "type of relationship." These factors include:

> [w]hether the parties have a written contract describing the relationship they intend to create; [w]hether the business provides the worker with employment-like benefits (such as insurance, a pension, vacation pay, sick pay); [w]hether the relationship is expected to be permanent or indefinite (this indicates employment) versus for a specific project or period (this indicates independent contract); and [t]he extent to which the services performed by the worker are a key aspect of the business's regular activity (if so, the business is presumed to be more likely to retain the right to control the worker's activity).[10]

The control test has been justifiably criticized on two grounds. First, the test yields indeterminate results. The factors are unweighted and nondispositive, and not every factor will apply to every case. In most cases, some factors will lean toward employment status while other factors will lead toward independent contractor status; the test provides no decisional criteria for weighing the various factors.

Second, the control test has been criticized as rigid and formalistic — a one-size-fits-all test used without due regard for the many different contexts to which it is applied. There might, for example, be good reasons to classify a given worker as an employee for purposes of obtaining employment law protections, but to classify that same worker as an independent contractor for purposes of taxes and employer vicarious liability.[11]

The new Restatement of Employment sets forth a variation of the control test. Under the Restatement, an individual will be classified as an employee if he or she is acting, at least in part, to serve the employer's interests; the employer consents to receive the individual's work; and the work relationship effectively prevents the individual from rendering his or her services as part of an independent business.[12] "Services as part of an independent business" is defined as an individual, in his or her own interest, exercising entrepreneurial control over the manner and means that the services are performed.[13]

---

[9] *Id.*

[10] *Id.*

[11] Langille & Davidov, *supra* note 2, at 18.

[12] RESTATEMENT (THIRD) OF EMPLOYMENT LAW § 1.01(1) (2009).

[13] *Id.* § 1.01(2). "Entrepreneurial control" is defined as "control over important business decisions, including whether to hire and where to assign assistants, whether to purchase and where to deploy

[C] The Economic Realities Test

The economic realities test represents an attempt to correct the deficiencies of the control test. The test is used for some employment statutes (such as the FLSA), but not others (such as ERISA). The economic realities test is designed specifically for the employment law context — not the tax or vicarious liability tort context. In the employment law context, the "employee versus independent contractor" issue arises most frequently when a business argues that a particular statute does not apply because a worker is an independent contractor rather than an employee. The economic realities test attempts to resolve the issue consistently with the purpose of the employment statute, which is to protect and benefit certain types of workers.[14]

This purposive approach, therefore, is supposed to be the antithesis of the formalism represented by the control test. The very name of the test — economic realities — emphasizes its alignment with the legal realism movement which itself rejected formalism. Thus, Judge Frank Easterbrook of the Seventh Circuit Court of Appeals in the *Lauritzen* case to be discussed in more detail below, missed the point when he ridiculed the economic realities test by unflatteringly comparing it to an "economic fantasy" test.[15]

The economic realities test ideally should correct the formalism and indeterminacy of the control test in two ways. First, this purposive approach can account for the fact that employer control often is absent from situations that otherwise should clearly be defined as employment relationships, such as when the worker is a specialized professional, the work requires the use of discretion, or the work is performed outside the employer's premises.[16] Courts applying a purposive approach shift attention away from direct control mechanisms toward "bureaucratic" or "administrative" control mechanisms, such as the power to promote, discipline, or fire the worker.[17]

The second way the economic realities test should improve upon the control test is by focusing on economic dependency. In *National Labor Relations Board v. Hearst Publications, Inc.*,[18] the U.S. Supreme Court, interpreting the National Labor Relations Act, held that when particular workers "are subject, as a matter of economic fact, to the evils the statute was designed to eradicate,"[19] such as abject economic dependency, these workers should fall within the protection of the statute notwithstanding the "technical legal classification"[20] of the workers as independent contractors. This was so, the Court reasoned, because the classification of the workers as independent contractors derived from agency principles "unrelated to

---

equipment, and whether and when to service other customers." *Id.* § 1.01(3).

[14] Barron, *supra* note 4, at 460.

[15] Sec'y of Labor v. Lauritzen, 835 F.2d 1529, 1539 (7th Cir. 1987) (Easterbrook, J., concurring).

[16] Langille & Davidov, *supra* note 2, at 19.

[17] *Id.*

[18] 322 U.S. 111 (1944).

[19] *Id.* at 127.

[20] *Id.* at 128.

the statute's objectives."[21] Although Congress later rejected the application of this approach to the NLRA,[22] the approach nonetheless potentially helps concentrate employment law protections on the workers who most need them.

The Wage-Hour Administrator of the Department of Labor, applying the economic realities test to the Fair Labor Standards Act, summarized the test by stating that "an employee, as distinguished from a person who is engaged in a business of his own, is one, who as a matter of economic reality follows the usual path of an employee and is dependent on the business which he serves."[23] The Administrator listed six factors courts should consider in making this determination, the existence of which indicated employee status.[24] These six factors are:

1. A limited amount of the worker's investment in facilities and equipment;

2. The nature (close supervision) and degree of control (high) retained or exercised by the company;

3. The worker's limited opportunities for profit and loss;

4. The small degree of the worker's independent initiative, judgment, and foresight in open market competition with others required for the success of the operation;

5. A high degree of permanency of the work relationship; and

6. The broad extent to which the services are an integral part of the company's business.[25]

One need not be an employment law scholar to recognize these factors as remarkably similar to the factors used in the control test. Moreover, like the control test, the factors are unweighted and nondispositive.[26]

Unsurprisingly, in practice, the economic realities test often has proven as formalistic and indeterminate as the test it was designed to replace.[27] A case in point is *Secretary of Labor v. Lauritzen*,[28] in which the Seventh Circuit was required to determine whether migrant pickle pickers (technically, the workers were small-cucumber-pickers, because cucumbers do not become pickles until they are pickled) were employees protected by the FLSA or unprotected independent contractors. The court mechanically applied the facts to a version of the Wage-Hour Administrator's economic realities test and concluded that the workers were protected employees. Judge Easterbrook, concurring, criticized the indeterminacy

---

[21] *Id.*

[22] *See* MARC LINDER, THE EMPLOYMENT RELATIONSHIP IN ANGLO-AMERICAN LAW: A HISTORICAL PERSPECTIVE ch. 6 (1989).

[23] W&H Op. Letter, No. 832, June 25, 1968.

[24] *Id.*

[25] *Id.*

[26] *Id.*

[27] Langille & Davidov, *supra* note 2, at 22.

[28] 835 F.2d 1529 (7th Cir. 1987).

of the test, and for each factor of the test demonstrated how the facts could be applied to reach a different outcome (e.g., whereas the majority found the workers were dependent on the company in order to survive economically, Easterbrook pointed out that the workers had "broken the ties that bind them to one locale"[29] and moved frequently in search of ripening crops and better wages) or provided a counter-example to illustrate how the factor might cut the other way (e.g., lawyers, like migrant farmworkers, often possess little physical capital, yet nonetheless may not be employees of their clients under the FLSA).

Worse still, both the control and the economic realities tests are subject to employer manipulation.[30] Consider, for example, any company that sends its employees to customers' homes to provide services, such as a residential carpet-cleaner or utility meter-reader. Even when the carpet-cleaners are technically employees, the company seldom directly supervises them, because work is done away from company headquarters. However, consider what the company can do if it wants to avoid the application of employment laws to these carpet-cleaners. The company can fire them, terminate their retirement and health plans, eliminate sick and vacation pay, sell the trucks and other equipment to the former employees, and begin paying them a percentage of the revenue they bring in or by the amount of work performed rather than an hourly rate or salary. Presto! The former employees now are independent contractors — and the company no longer must worry about employment discrimination laws, wage and hour laws, retirement and benefit laws, and the like. Yet these independent contractors are in far more need of legal protection than they were when they were legally classified as employees.

[D]   Applying the Tests to Employment Laws

Employment statutes typically do not specify which test should be used to distinguish employees from independent contractors. Some statutes do not define the terms at all. For example, the Copyright Act, under which an employee's creation is likely to belong to the employer, but an independent contractor is presumed to retain a copyright in her work, does not define either "employee" or "independent contractor."[31] The Supreme Court, in *Community for Creative Non-Violence v. Reid*,[32] held that "[w]here Congress uses terms that have accumulated settled meaning under . . . the common law, a court must infer, unless the statute otherwise dictates, that Congress means to incorporate the established meaning of these terms." The Court therefore applied the common law control test.

Similarly, ERISA explicitly applies only to employees, but defines "employee" unhelpfully as "any employee or former employee of an employer."[33] In *Nationwide Mutual Insurance Co. v. Darden*,[34] the Supreme Court favorably cited

---

[29] *Id.* at 1542 (Easterbrook, J., concurring).

[30] Langille & Davidov, *supra* note 2, at 20-23.

[31] Copyrights and other intellectual property issues surrounding the employment relationship are discussed in more detail *infra* § 11.05.

[32] 490 U.S. 730 (1989).

[33] 29 U.S.C. § 1002(6).

[34] 503 U.S. 318 (1992).

Reid and again held that Congress's failure to provide a meaningful definition demonstrated its intent that the common law control test would apply.[35] In *NLRB v. United Insurance Co.*,[36] the Court applied the common law control test to the NLRA, in this case finding that Congress had expressly provided for this test.

The FLSA defines "employ" as "to suffer or permit to work."[37] The Supreme Court in *Darden* noted that this definition is broader than the definitions used in other employment statutes, and lower courts have consistently applied one or another version of the economic realities test to the FLSA.[38] The FMLA's definition of "employ" is the same as the FLSA's,[39] so most courts have applied the economic realities test to the FMLA.[40] The Supreme Court also has held that the economic realities test applies to the Social Security Act.[41]

Title VII, the ADEA, and the ADA define an "employee" as "an individual employed by an employer."[42] Lower courts have applied a "hybrid" approach by analyzing the economic reality of the relationship while focusing on control as the most important factor.[43] This approach, however, has been called into question by the Supreme Court's decision in *Clackamas Gastroenterology Associates, P.C. v. Wells*.[44] In this case, the Court had to decide whether physician-shareholders who owned the company were "employees" for purposes of reaching the fifteen-employee threshold required for the ADA to apply to a company, or whether instead they were "employers" who could not be counted. The Court held that the common law control test applied, and remanded for application of the test. It is unclear what effect this decision will have on future Title VII/ADEA/ADA cases requiring a distinction between employees and independent contractors. On the one hand, *Clackamas* is at least technically distinguishable, as there was no argument that the physicians were independent contractors. However, the case contains language quite dismissive of the economic realities test, and the Court equated the ADA's circular definition of employee with the similar definition in ERISA to which the Court in *Darden* had applied the common law control test. On balance, it seems likely that the Court is moving in the direction of applying the common law control test to Title VII, the ADEA, and the ADA.[45]

The distinction between employees and independent contractors is becoming increasingly important as the American economy shifts from manufacturing to

---

[35] For further discussion of coverage issues under ERISA, see *infra* § 14.02.

[36] 390 U.S. 254, 256 (1968).

[37] 29 U.S.C. § 203 (g).

[38] *See, e.g.*, Sec'y of Labor v. Lauritzen, 835 F.2d 1529 (7th Cir. 1987).

[39] 29 U.S.C. § 2611(3).

[40] *See, e.g.*, Nichols v. All Points Transp. Corp. of Mich., Inc., 364 F. Supp. 2d 621, 630 (E.D. Mich. 2005).

[41] United States v. Silk, 331 U.S. 704 (1947).

[42] 42 U.S.C. § 2000(e)(f) (Title VII); 29 U.S.C. § 630(b) (ADEA); 42 U.S.C. § 12111(4) (ADA).

[43] *See, e.g.*, Muhammad v. Dallas County Cmty. Supervision & Corrs. Dep't, 479 F.3d 377 (5th Cir. 2007).

[44] 538 U.S. 440 (2003).

[45] *See, e.g.*, Bogues v. Town of Trumball, 383 F. Supp. 2d 348, 353 (D. Conn. 2005).

service, as the workplace is reorganized to give workers more autonomy, and as employers increasingly manipulate the status of their workers to avoid employment regulation. As discussed below in § 2.02[C], employers are increasingly replacing traditional workers with contingent workers, many of whom are classified as independent contractors.

§ 2.02 COVERED EMPLOYEES

Just because a worker is an employee rather than an independent contractor does not necessarily mean the worker is covered by a given employment law. Some statutes specifically withhold coverage from certain employees, and employers can sometimes withhold certain employment benefits by contract. On the other hand, some statutes cover workers who are not employees, and sometimes workers can be joint employees of two or more employers.

[A] Exclusion by Statute

Some employment laws exclude certain employees from coverage. The longest list of exclusions can be found in the Fair Labor Standards Act.[46] The FLSA sets a minimum wage, requires payment of overtime for work exceeding forty hours per week, and forbids child labor. The statute, however, contains a long list of occupational exemptions.[47] The following, for example, are just some of the occupations exempt from both the minimum wage and overtime provisions:

- Executive, administrative, or professional employees;

- Employees of seasonal amusement or recreational establishments;

- Certain agricultural employees; and

- Casual babysitters or care givers.

Some occupations are exempt from the overtime provisions, but are subject to the minimum wage provisions, such as

- Certain agricultural employees;

- Taxicab drivers;

- Employees of motion picture theaters;

- Employees of small law enforcement or firefighting agencies;

- Employees engaged in processing green leaf tobacco, ginning cotton, or processing sugar.

Still other occupations are exempt from the FLSA's child-labor provisions. Children under fourteen, for example, may

- Work for their parents;

---

[46] 29 U.S.C. §§ 201-19.

[47] *Id.* § 213.

- Deliver newspapers;

- Be employed as actors or performers;

- Work on family farms.

The National Labor Relations Act similarly contains significant exclusions. For example, the NLRA expressly excludes "supervisors."[48] Courts and the National Labor Relations Board have defined this exclusion broadly, and have thereby excluded a large numbers of workers from the protection of the NLRA.[49] The NLRA similarly excludes agricultural workers.[50] The NLRB recently has interpreted the NLRA as excluding graduate student workers, but in the summer of 2012 invited amicus briefs on whether it should reverse course and instead consider graduate students covered employees under that statute.[51]

The Family Medical Leave Act covers only "eligible employees," which the Act defines as employees who has been employed (1) for at least twelve months by the employer and (2) for at least 1250 hours of service with this employer during the previous twelve months.[52] However, the Act excludes employees who work for an employer with less than fifty employees at the employee's worksite.

The preceding examples of employees excluded from statutory coverage are not exhaustive and are meant merely to show the importance of reading the different employment law statutes carefully to determine coverage issues.

[B] Exclusion by Contract

Many employment rights are non-waivable. A prospective employee may not, for example, contract with a prospective employer to submit to sexual harassment or discrimination, even in return for a wage premium.[53] Similarly, courts have held that employee agreements to waive FLSA minimum-wage and overtime rights are unenforceable.[54]

Some employment rights, however, are waivable. For example, the right to a jury trial may be waived by signing an arbitration agreement, even if an employment statute specifically provides for a jury trial.[55] Similarly, a waiver of the right to participate in an ERISA employee benefit plan is valid so long as the waiver is knowing and voluntary.[56]

---

[48] *Id.* § 152(11).

[49] NLRB v. Ky. River Comty. Care, Inc., 532 U.S. 706 (2001); Oakwood Healthcare, Inc., 348 N.L.R.B. No. 37 (2006).

[50] 29 U.S.C. § 152(3).

[51] Brown Univ., 342 N.L.R.B. No. 42 (2004); NYU v. UAW, Case 29-RC-012054, Notice and Invitation to File Briefs (June 22, 2012).

[52] 29 U.S.C. § 2611(2).

[53] *See* Alexander v. Gardner-Denver Co., 415 U.S. 36, 52 n.15 (1974); Rogers v. Gen. Elec. Co., 781 F.2d 452, 454 (5th Cir. 1986).

[54] *See, e.g.,* Dunlop v. Gray-Goto, Inc., 528 F.2d 792 (1976).

[55] Gilmer v. Interstate/Johnson Lane Corp., 500 U.S. 20 (1991).

[56] *See, e.g.,* Rodriguez-Abreu v. Chase Manhattan Bank, 986 F.2d 580, 587 (1st Cir. 1993).

A company and worker may not define the worker's relationship to the company as either an independent contractor or an employee merely by contractually labeling it as such. However, an employer may condition a worker's receipt of certain benefits on the worker's contractually defined status.

An example of both circumstances can be found in ERISA. ERISA imposes two requirements for a worker to participate in an ERISA plan.[57] First, the worker must be an employee under ERISA which, as discussed above, uses the common-law control test. Second, the worker must be contractually eligible to receive benefits under the terms of the plan itself.

An employer may define contractual eligibility (the second ERISA requirement for eligibility) in a number of ways. A health plan might, for example, provide different benefits and plan features for different groups of employees.[58] An ERISA plan might also exclude workers based on their status. For example, in *Wolf v. Coca-Cola Co.*,[59] a Coca-Cola ERISA plan specified that only "regular employees" were eligible for benefits under the plan; the plan specifically excluded temporary, seasonal, and leased employees. A leased employee[60] sued Coca-Cola, claiming she was entitled to benefits under the plan because she was an employee under the common-law control test. The Eleventh Circuit held that even if she was a common-law employee, she was not contractually eligible for benefits because the plan itself excluded her.

An employer may not, however, use a contract to make an end-run around a common-law or statutory definition of an employee (the first ERISA requirement for eligibility). For example, in *Vizcaino v. Microsoft Corp.*,[61] Microsoft employed both a "core" workforce of regular employees and a set of "freelancers" who performed the same work under the same supervisors. The freelancers, however, signed contracts stating that they were independent contractors, that they were ineligible for health and retirement benefits, and that they were receiving extra pay as a result of their status. The IRS audited Microsoft and determined that the freelancers fit the common law definition of employees, and therefore were subject to taxation. Several of the freelancers requested retroactive benefits, which Microsoft's plan administrator denied. The freelancers filed a class action against Microsoft for the benefits. By the time the case reached the Ninth Circuit, Microsoft had conceded that notwithstanding the freelancers' contractual designation as independent contractors, the freelancers were actually employees for both tax and ERISA purposes. The court therefore found that the first ERISA requirement for eligibility was satisfied. The court then held that because Microsoft's ERISA plan was contractually open to any "common law employee . . . on the United States payroll," the second ERISA requirement for eligibility was met also. The Microsoft case presumably would have been decided differently if

---

[57] *See* 29 U.S.C. § 3(7) (defining a plan participant as "any employee or former employee of an employer . . . who is or may become eligible to receive a benefit of any type from the [ERISA plan]").

[58] For a more detailed discussion of why such plan language is consistent with the non-discrimination provisions of the Health Insurance Portability and Accountability Act (HIPAA), see *infra* § 14.04[F].

[59] 200 F.3d 1337 (2000).

[60] *See infra* § 2.03[C] for further discussion of leased employees.

[61] 120 F.3d 1006 (9th Cir. 1997) (en banc).

Microsoft's plan had included a contractual exclusion of freelancers, as Coca Cola's plan did for leased employees.

Vizcainzo stands for the proposition that employers may not designate a worker's status for purposes of ERISA and other employment laws merely by contractually affixing a label. In other words, the contract is a means to an end, not an end in itself. An employer may use a contract to specify, for example, that a worker is responsible for setting her own hours, supplying her own equipment, and controlling the means of production — all factors that, if implemented in fact as well as on paper, would tend to lead a court to conclude that the worker is an independent contractor rather than an employee. Microsoft's failure in *Vizcainzo* was in poorly drafting the contracts with its freelancers, such that the IRS determined that the freelancers were employees notwithstanding the contractual designation as independent contractors. But even if the contracts had been more clearly drafted, that would not have changed the outcome of the case if Microsoft *in practice* treated the freelancers as employees.[62] If an employer wants the benefits of non-regulation that come from independent contractor status, then the employer must be willing to treat workers as independent contractors, by ceding to them control over when and how they do their work. This is the brake on what otherwise would be a full-throttle rush to replace employees wholesale with independent contractors.

[C]   Contingent Workers

In contrast to the long-term, relatively stable employment relationships that characterized the manufacturing-based economy of most of the twentieth century, an increasing share of today's employment relationships are "contingent."[63] Contingent workers have short-term contracts and no expectation of continued employment. They include independent contractors, temporary and leased workers, part-time and job-sharing workers, adjunct professors, and employees of temporary staffing agencies. Contingent workers receive few if any health care or retirement benefits, little or no training, and zero job security.

Though some highly skilled members of the workforce might benefit from contingent employment, the majority of contingent workers do not.[64] Companies, however, often profit from hiring contingent workers because it is even easier to dismiss them than it is to dismiss at-will employees, and easy dismissal gives companies maximum flexibility in responding to changes in demand for the company's product or service.[65]

While there is widespread consensus that the share of contingent workers as a percentage of the American workforce is growing significantly, there is little

---

[62] *See* WILLIAM SHAKESPEARE, ROMEO AND JULIET act 2, sc. 2 ("What's in a name? That which we call a rose [b]y any other word would smell as sweet.").

[63] KATHERINE V.W. STONE, FROM WIDGETS TO DIGITS: EMPLOYMENT REGULATION FOR THE CHANGING WORKPLACE 67 (2004).

[64] *See* Danielle Tarantolo, Note, *From Employment to Contract: Section 1981 and Antidiscrimination Law for the Independent Contractor Workforce*, 116 YALE L.J. 170, 172-78 (2006).

[65] Gillian Lester, *Careers and Contingency*, 51 STAN. L. REV. 73, 97 (1998).

agreement on how contingent workers should be counted. In a 2005 survey that has not been replicated as of 2012, the Bureau of Labor Statistics (BLS) reported that 4.1% of the workforce is contingent and that 10.7% of the workforce is in an "alternative [employment] relationship."[66] Many scholars, however, have criticized these numbers as too low and the BLS's definition of contingent as too narrow, and have instead suggested that contingent workers represent between 16 – 29% of the workforce.[67]

§ 2.03   COVERED EMPLOYERS

[A]   Statutory Exemptions

[1]   Certain Types of Employers

Employment statutes often exempt certain types of employers either from the definition of a covered employer or from being subject to some or all of the statutory provisions. For example, Title VII exemptions include:

- The federal government, which is not exempt from any of the prohibitions on discrimination, but is subject to different enforcement mechanisms than private-sector employers.[68]

- Native American tribes, and businesses on or near a Native American reservation that give hiring preferences to Native Americans — such preferences do not violate the prohibition on national origin discrimination.[69]

- Bona-fide tax-exempt private membership clubs such as fraternal lodges, swim clubs, and country clubs.[70]

- Religious institutions, which may discriminate on the basis of religion as to employees working on either religious or secular activities.[71]

Similarly, as discussed in § 2.02[A], the FLSA exempts family farms from that statute's child labor laws. This list is not exhaustive, as other employment law statutes also have similar exceptions.

---

[66] Bureau of Labor Statistics, U.S. Dep't of Labor, Contingent and Alternative Employment Arrangements 4, 1 (2005).

[67] See, e.g., Kathleen Barker & Kathleen Christensen, Contingent Work: American Employment Relations in Transition 306, 307 (1998).

[68] 42 U.S.C. §§ 2000e(b) 2000e-16(a).

[69] Id. §§ 2000e(b)(1), 2000e-2(i).

[70] Id. § 2000e(b).

[71] Id. § 2000e-1.

[2] The "Small Employer" Exemption

Most employment statutes contain an exemption for small employers. Some statutes define this exemption by the number of employees. For example, Title VII and the ADA require fifteen employees, the ADEA requires twenty, the FMLA requires fifty within seventy-five miles, and the WARN Act one hundred.[72] Parallel state statutes, especially antidiscrimination laws, often have lower employee thresholds. Other federal statutes define this exemption by the dollar volume of business. For example, the FLSA "enterprise" coverage generally applies only to employers with $500,000 or more in annual sales,[73] and the NLRB exerts jurisdiction only over retail businesses with annual sales exceeding $500,000 and over law firms with annual sales exceeding $250,000.

Should small employers be exempt from employment laws? The arguments for exemption are that (1) small employers do not have the resources to comply with the often paperwork-heavy requirements of employment laws, whereas large employers have the ability to do so through economies of scale; and (2) the government should give small employers a break at every opportunity in the hope that they will grow and become big employers. Arguments against the exemption are that (1) the exemption subverts the policy of the employment laws (e.g., employers exempt from Title VII employ more than 19 million American employees);[74] (2) if small employers are capable of complying with common law employment requirements and workers compensation statutes, they are capable of complying with other employment laws; (3) the vast majority of small employers (such as the corner auto shop) never grow into big employers; and (4) if anything, the government should promote big employers over small ones, because big employers are far more likely to pay premium wages and to offer health and retirement benefits.

[B] Joint Employees

Joint employees are employees of two or more closely related companies, such as contractors-subcontractors and franchisors-franchisees. These types of workers are employees of both companies for purposes of employment laws.[75] Under the FLSA, joint employment exists where (1) employers arrange to share a worker's services, (2) one employer is working in the interest of another employer in relation to the employee, or (3) the employers share control over the employee or a company employing an employee controls or is controlled by another company.[76]

For example, in *Zheng v. Liberty Apparel Co.*,[77] plaintiffs worked for several "Contractor Corporations" that assembled clothing for Liberty Apparel Company.

---

[72] 42 U.S.C. § 2000e(b) (Title VII); 42 U.S.C. § 12111(5) (ADA); 29 U.S.C. § 630(b) (ADEA); 29 U.S.C. § 2611(4) (FMLA); *id.* § 2101(a)(1) (WARN).

[73] 29 U.S.C. § 203(s).

[74] Richard Carlson, *The Small Firm Exemption and the Single Employer Doctrine in Employment Discrimination Law*, 80 ST. JOHN'S L. REV. 1197 (2006).

[75] *See, e.g.*, 29 C.F.R. § 825.106 (FMLA).

[76] *Id.* § 791.2(b).

[77] 355 F.3d 61 (2d Cir. 2003).

Plaintiffs alleged overtime and minimum wage violations of the FLSA. Both parties agreed that plaintiffs were employed by the Contractor Corporations, but disagreed over whether Liberty was a joint employer. The district court, finding that Liberty was not the plaintiff's joint employer, granted Liberty's motion for summary judgment. The Second Circuit, however, reversed and remanded, finding that the district court had failed to consider many of the factors pertinent to the economic realities test, such as:

(1)   whether Liberty's premises and equipment were used for the plaintiff's work;

(2)   whether the Contractor Corporations had a business that could or did shift as a unit from one putative joint employer to another;

(3)   the extent to which plaintiffs performed a discrete line-job that was integral to Liberty's process of production;

(4)   whether responsibility under the contracts could pass from one subcontractor to another without material changes;

(5)   the degree to which the Liberty Defendants or their agents supervised plaintiff's work; and

(6)   whether plaintiffs worked exclusively or predominantly for [Liberty].[78]

Other employment law statutes similarly provide that a worker may be a joint employee of two or more closely-related companies. For example, under federal employment discrimination laws, courts consider a variety of factors in determining whether joint employment exists, such as whether both companies participate in hiring, discipline, discharge, control of work assignments, training, and payroll.[79] Similarly, under the NLRA, leased employees (see below) are joint employees of the lessor and lessee, and both may be held liable for violation of the statute.[80]

The new Restatement of Employment Law would find a joint employment relationship where an individual is considered an employee[81] of two or more employers through the individual's services to each employer in either a separate or a single course of conduct.[82]

[C]   Leased Employees

In employee leasing, a lessor company hires workers and leases them to a lessee company. The lessee pays the lessor; the lessor pays the workers' wages, benefits, and payroll taxes. Some employers, especially small employers, may prefer this arrangement to direct employment because leased employment permits economies

---

[78] *Id.* at 72; *see also* Liu v. Donna Karan Int'l, Inc., 6 Wage & Hour Cas. 2d (BNA) 1142 (S.D.N.Y. 2001) (applying similar analysis).

[79] EEOC v. Sage Realty Corp., 87 F.R.D. 365 (S.D.N.Y. 1980).

[80] Dunkin' Donuts Mid-Atlantic Distrib. Ctr., Inc., v. NLRB, 363 F.3d 437 (D.C. Cir. 2004).

[81] *See supra* § 2.01[B].

[82] RESTATEMENT (THIRD) OF EMPLOYMENT LAW § 1.04 (2009).

of scale: a lessor providing workers to many small employers can more efficiently handle payroll, employment taxes, and retirement plans, and is in a better position to negotiate with health insurance companies for better (or less expensive) health insurance for workers.

This arrangement generally does *not* allow the lessee company to avoid employment laws. The IRS, for example, considers leased workers to be employees of the lessee if the lessee directs the workers as to the work to be done and how to do it.[83] The rule for leased employees is thus similar to the rule for employees and independent contractors: if a worker functions as an employee, the IRS will consider that person an employee regardless of the label the company attempts to affix. Similarly, EEOC regulations provide that for federal employment discrimination purposes, leased workers generally are employees of the lessee.[84]

---

[83] *See* 26 C.F.R. §§ 31.3401(c)-1(b), 31.3121(d)-1(c)(2), 31.3306(i)-1(b).

[84] EEOC Notice No. 915.002 (Dec. 1997).

Chapter 3

HISTORICAL FOUNDATIONS OF EMPLOYMENT AT WILL

SYNOPSIS

Modern American Employment Law traces its origins to efforts by English nobility to manipulate the labor market in the 1300s. Many of the themes surrounding early employment legislation resonate just as strongly today.

§ 3.01   ENGLISH ORIGINS

The 1349 Statute of Labourers[1] usually is considered the first Anglo-American employment statute. Parliament (consisting of the landowning class) passed this Statute after a recurrence of the plague decimated the English agricultural workforce. The reduced supply of farmworkers made it possible for the surviving farmworkers to demand higher wages, which they could back up by the threat of leaving to work for another lord or to work as an artisan in a nearby town. The Statute of Labourers attempted to correct what the lords perceived as a temporary economic imbalance by compelling service, fixing wages, and limiting labor mobility.

The 1562 Statute of Artificers[2] was similarly a response to a plague's reduction of the labor supply. This Statute, however, differed from the Statute of Labourers in several important ways; many of these differences reflect themes that are still critical to the study of employment law today. First, the Statute of Artificers noted that there were too many overlapping and often contradictory regulations governing wages and the hiring and firing of workers. Second, the Statute recognized the difficulty of attempting to set permanent workplace standards when economic

---

[1]   23 Edw. 3 (1349).

[2]   5 Eliz., c. 4 (1562).

conditions (such as the local supply of labor then, and an international supply of labor now) and the mode of production (from tenant farming to artisan[3] labor then, and from manufacturing to service now) were constantly changing. Third, the Statute attempted to shift the burden of caring for the poor from local parishes to employers — much like modern statutes that attempt to shift to employers the cost of providing health care, pensions, and disability insurance. Fourth, the Statute was a combination of both national and local regulation of the labor market, much as modern American employment law is a combination of state and federal regulation. Fifth, the Statute acknowledged the increasing prevalence of artisans, and imposed one-year employment contracts for these workers. Sixth, the Statute created a just-cause standard for terminating employment, foreshadowing the standard now used in virtually all union-negotiated collective bargaining contracts. Seventh, the just-cause standard applied both to employees seeking to quit and to employers seeking to discharge, introducing the concept of mutuality. Eighth, the Statute created an arbitration-like procedure for enforcing the just-cause standard, just as arbitration today is used to resolve contract disputes arising under collective bargaining agreements and, increasingly, to resolve statutory and common-law employment claims.[4]

In 1765, William Blackstone wrote in his Commentaries[5] that the length of employment should be presumed to be a year, "throughout all the revolutions of the respective seasons."[6] Four things should be noted about Blackstone's formulation of this rule. First, like the just-cause standard of the Statute of Artificers, it was mutual, as it applies both to "servants" and their "masters." Second, it was predicated on the presumption of a largely agricultural workforce. Third and relatedly, it was designed to avoid opportunism. Because farmworkers worked long hours during the growing season but little during winter, the workers were at risk of being discharged in late fall after the harvest, and the employer was at risk during summer and early fall of the workers leaving or demanding unreasonable wages. This incentive to behave opportunistically is common in employment relationships — consider the vulnerability of an employer who has just shared important trade secrets with an employee, or an employee who is on the verge of retiring and collecting a pension.

The fourth noteworthy thing about Blackstone's rule is that it was a default rule. A default rule, unlike an immutable rule, can be changed by the parties by agreement. The employment of domestic servants, for example, may not create the same opportunities for opportunism as the employment of farm labor, so the parties might by contract abandon the one-year rule and instead require a period of notice before the employment is terminated.[7] The American employment-at-will rule, discussed below, is similarly a default rule.

---

[3] Artisans were skilled craftspeople, such as blacksmiths, shoemakers, bakers, etc.

[4] *See supra* § 3.03.

[5] 1 WILLIAM BLACKSTONE, COMMENTARIES 413 (1765).

[6] *Id.*

[7] Jay M. Feinman, *The Development of the Employment At Will Rule*, 20 AM. J. LEGAL HIST. 118, 120-22 (1976).

§ 3.02   HORACE WOOD'S TREATISE

In 1877, Horace Gay Wood, a New York State treatise writer, wrote what is often credited as the first iteration of the American employment-at-will rule. In his treatise Master and Servant, he wrote:

> [T]he rule is inflexible that a general or indefinite hiring is prima facie a hiring at-will and if the servant seeks to make it out a yearly hiring, the burden is upon him to establish it by proof. . . . It is competent for either party to show what the mutual understanding of the parties was in reference to the matter; but unless their understanding was mutual that the service was to extend for a certain fixed and definite period, it is an indefinite hiring and is determinable at the will of either party.[8]

This rule — that absent a prior agreement, either the employer or the employee may terminate the employment relationship for any reason without notice — has been firmly entrenched as the default rule for American employment since the early 1900s.

[A]   Contrasting Approaches

Wood's rule should be contrasted with two alternative approaches to presuming the duration of employment. The first approach, which had evolved from Blackstone's presumption of a one-year term,[9] was the English practice of setting a notice period for terminating an employment contract. Employees generally prefer maximum notice of termination from their employers, so they can begin looking for a new job. Employers generally prefer giving minimal notice, so they can quickly adapt to changes in demand for the employer's goods or services, and to minimize the possibility that an about-to-be-fired employee will look for another job on the employer's time. This notice period often functioned as *de facto* severance pay.

The second approach, which had been adopted in some states, was to presume that the parties intended employment to last for the time indicated by the rate-of-pay — e.g., if the employer offered a job at a salary of $1000 per week, the presumption was that the parties intended a week-to-week employment contract.[10]

[B]   Flexibility

Wood described the at-will rule as "inflexible." In one sense, this is incorrect, for Wood also described the rule as a default rule and noted that parties to an employment arrangement were free to contract for a fixed term of employment.[11]

---

[8] HORACE GAY WOOD, MASTER AND SERVANT 283-84 (1877).

[9] An employment contract specifying the length of employment, or limiting the circumstances under which the employer may discharge the employee, is a definite-term contract. *See infra* § 5.01[A].

[10] *See, e.g.*, Winograd v. Willis, 789 S.W.2d 307, 309-10 (Tex. App. 1990).

[11] Mayer G. Freed & Daniel D. Polsby, *The Doubtful Provenance of "Wood's Rule" Revisited*, 22 ARIZ. ST. L.J. 551, 553 (1990).

In a different sense, however, Wood proved correct. As will be discussed below,[12] early judicial interpretations of the at-will rule made it very difficult for employees to demonstrate that the parties intended anything other than at-will employment. Moreover, the at-will rule was inflexible in the sense that although the parties could contract for fixed-term employment, they could not contract for an indefinite-term contract that limited the employer's ability to discharge. For example, a for-cause-only provision in an indefinite-term contract would not be judicially enforceable.

[C] As Legal Scholarship

When Horace Gay Wood wrote what now has become recognized as the employment-at-will rule, he was not claiming to have invented a new rule. He thought, instead, that he was accurately summarizing an existing majority rule. Scholars have since questioned whether Wood got the law right. Theodore J. St. Antoine, for example, has described the at-will rule as springing "full-blown . . . from [Wood's] busy and perhaps careless pen."[13]

The controversy centers on the four cases cited in Wood's footnote 4.[14] None have holdings directly on point. Two of the cases were employee victories — weak support for a legal rule giving employers an unfettered right to fire. One of the cases did not involve an employment contract at all, but rather a contract between the army and private company for the transportation of goods. The final case involved a bartender who lived on the premises; when he was fired, he challenged his eviction but not his discharge. At best, these cases provide weak support for a legal rule that quickly became the national norm.

[D] Explanations for the Rule

Horace Gay Wood was a prolific and well-respected law treatise writer of his time, and treatises then were a widely-used source of law. Nonetheless, it seems odd that one, perhaps careless, treatise writer would have such a profound effect on American employment law. Commentators have proposed several possible explanations.

One possible explanation is that the at-will rule was the product of a judiciary fixated on laissez-faire reasoning and freedom of contract. At-will employment became permanently ensconced as *the* American rule at about the same time the Supreme Court was, on property-rights grounds, invalidating multiple legislative attempts to regulate the employment relationship.[15] However, as described in the next subsection, courts often imposed at-will terms on parties who clearly had intended to contract for something other than at-will employment. As Professor Sanford Jacoby has explained, this refusal to consider party intent was anti-

---

[12] *See infra* § 4.03.

[13] Theodore J. St. Antoine, *You're Fired!*, 10 Hum. Rts. Q. 32, 33 (1982).

[14] For a thorough discussion of these cases and evaluation of the quality of Wood's scholarship, see generally Jay M. Feinman, *The Development of the Employment At Will Rule Revisited*, 23 Ariz. St. L.J. 733 (1991); Freed & Polsby, *supra* note 11.

[15] Lochner v. New York, 198 U.S. 45 (1905).

contractualist.[16] For this reason, Samuel Williston, the leading contract scholar of the time, considered the at-will rule a deviation from general contract principles.[17]

Professor Jay Feinman has argued that the at-will rule spread rapidly because economic conditions were ripe for it to do so.[18] Capital was becoming consolidated into large trusts and other corporate forms of organization; employers were increasingly asserting control over the manner of production at the expense of craft guilds; and products were increasingly mass-produced in factories instead of by artisans. At-will employment facilitated these transitions. However, as Professor Andrew Morriss points out, the first states to adopt at-will employment often were Western populist states, not the Northeastern states presumably dominated by capital and big business.[19] Extending this argument, Professor Richard Bales argues that the under-industrialized states first adopting the at-will rule likely did so to help attract capital; once the first under-industrialized states adopted the rule, other under-industrialized states followed to remain economically competitive with the early adopters and industrialized states ultimately adopted the rule to maintain their competitive advantage in the labor market.[20]

§ 3.03 HISTORICAL APPLICATION

Regardless of the reason, at-will employment became the American norm in the late 1800s and early 1900s. Courts imposed at-will employment with a vengeance, often under circumstances in which it was clear that both parties had intended to contract around the rule. An example is *Skagerberg v. Blandin Paper Co.*[21]

The plaintiff, R. Skagerberg, was an engineer who received an offer to teach at Purdue while he was also being recruited by Blandin. An officer of Blandin promised Skagerberg by phone that if he would reject the Purdue offer and agree to purchase the home of a Blandin superintendent, Blandin would give Skagerberg "permanent" employment at a fixed salary. Skagerberg followed up this phone call with a confirmation letter, again reciting that the job would "be a permanent one." Two years later, Blandin fired Skagerberg, and Skagerberg sued for breach of contract. The trial court dismissed the claim, and the Minnesota Supreme Court affirmed:

> The words "permanent employment" have a well-established meaning in the law. The general rule is well stated [ ]: "In case the parties to a contract of service expressly agree that the employment shall be "permanent" the law implies, not that the engagement shall be continuous or for any definite

---

[16] Sanford M. Jacoby, *The Duration of Indefinite Employment Contracts in the United States and England: An Historical Analysis*, 5 Comp. Lab. L.J. 85, 116-18 (1982).

[17] Samuel Williston, 1 The Law of Contracts 62 (1920).

[18] Feinman, *supra* note 7.

[19] Andrew Morriss, *Exploding Myths: An Empirical and Economic Reassessment of the Rise of Employment At-Will*, 59 Mo. L. Rev. 679, 681-82 (1994).

[20] Richard A. Bales, *Explaining the Spread of At-Will Employment as an Inter-jurisdictional Race to the Bottom of Employment Standards*, 75 Tenn. L. Rev. 453 (2008).

[21] 266 N.W. 872 (1936).

period, but that the term being indefinite the firing is merely at will.[22]

Two things are worth noting about this case. First, it is typical of cases for its time. When courts saw employment contracts containing durational words such as "permanent" or "continuous" or "career" or "lifetime," courts reflexively equated these words with "at-will" even when it was clear that at least one, and often both, of the parties had intended something different. Second, as with the *Skagerberg* case, most of these cases never made it to a jury, but were dismissed by the trial court on the modern equivalent of a Rule 12(b)(6) motion to dismiss.

Cases such as *Skagerberg* often relied on the misapplication of two contract doctrines. The first is consideration. The doctrine of consideration requires that both parties to a contract promise, or give up, something of at least nominal value. Under traditional contract doctrine, courts do not enquire into the relative value of the promises, but merely require that items or promises exchanged be of some value. Early (and some modern) employment-at-will cases, however, required employees claiming they had been offered long-term employment to prove they had provided some extra consideration, beyond the regular performance of their jobs, to support the "extra" promise of long-term employment. Generally, courts found such extra consideration only under two circumstances: when the employee agreed to give up an existing business, or when the employee agreed to release a claim for damages.

The second misapplied contract doctrine was mutuality of obligation. Courts applied this doctrine to forbid one party to an employment contract to terminate the contract under different standards than the other party. In other words, if the employer was bound for a year, the employee must also be bound for a year; if the employee could quit at-will, then the employer must be able to fire at-will. As with the doctrine of consideration, this application of the doctrine of mutuality to employment contracts was inconsistent with its use in other types of contracts.[23]

§ 3.04   MODERN APPLICATION

Today, at-will employment is the baseline legal rule in every American state except Montana, which in 1987 enacted the Wrongful Discharge from Employment Act.[24] Under this statute, after an employee has passed a probationary period, the employer cannot fire the employee absent "good cause," which the statute defines as "reasonable job-related grounds for dismissal based on a failure to satisfactorily perform job duties, disruption of the employer's operation, or other legitimate business reason."[25]

---

[22] *Id.* at 872.

[23] Clyde W. Summers, *The Contract of Employment and the Rights of Individual Employees: Fair Representation and Employment at Will*, 52 Fordham L. Rev. 1082, 1098-99 (1984) (noting that mutuality, "particularly in the form of mirrored obligations . . . , has never been considered essential to make promises binding").

[24] Mont. Code Ann. § 39-2-901.

[25] *Id.* § 39-2-903.

In the other 49 states, modern application of the at-will rule has been tempered by the gradual encroachment over the last 50 years or so on the at-will rule by federal and state employment statutes and by state common-law contract and tort doctrines. After the passage of Title VII of the Civil Rights Act of 1964, for example, an employer could no longer hire and fire on the basis of race.[26] Similarly, an employer that fires an employee for participating in jury duty is likely to find itself on the wrong end of a public policy tort suit.[27] Nonetheless, despite the many exceptions that have been carved out of the rule in recent years, the employment at-will rule remains the background legal rule covering the vast majority of employed American workers today.[28]

§ 3.05   EVALUATING THE AT-WILL RULE

Default legal rules usually are justified on three grounds. The first is that if they reflect the presumed intentions of most of the potential parties, they will avoid the transaction costs of individualized negotiation. This justification, however, does not seem to work well for the at-will rule. Although most employers no doubt prefer at-will employment, most employees do not. As evidence of this, consider that the first thing most employees bargain for after forming a union is a just-cause employment clause. Moreover, informational asymmetries distort employees' ability to bargain around the default rule. Empirical studies have consistently shown that most at-will employees erroneously believe they can be fired only for a good reason.[29] Just as Skagerberg thought he was negotiating for permanent employment even while his employer probably knew that courts would equate "permanent" with "at-will," most modern employees simply do not understand the baseline legal rule governing their employment.

A second justification for default legal rules is that they encourage parties who prefer to contract around a legal rule to reveal their true preferences during contract negotiations. This does not work, however, if most employees are ignorant of the baseline legal rule of at-will employment. Moreover, a prospective employee who tries to bargain with an employer for just-cause employment against a background of at-will employment is likely to be perceived by the employer as a slacker, and not hired at all. Finally, this justification could equally be served by a baseline legal rule of just-cause employment, which would force the employer to bargain with an employee for at-will employment.

A third justification for default legal rules is that they further a result seen as socially desirable. The at-will rule might be justified, for example, by the argument

---

[26]   42 U.S.C. § 2000e-(2)(a).

[27]   *See* Nees v. Hocks, 536 P.2d 512 (Or. 1975).

[28]   In retaining the at-will rule, the United States is an international outlier. *See* Convention Concerning Termination of Employment, International Labour Organization Convention No. 158 art. 4, Jun. 22, 1982, *available at* www.ilo.org/ilolex/cgi-lex/convde.pl?%20C158 ("The employment of a worker shall not be terminated unless there is a valid reason for such termination . . .").

[29]   *See, e.g.*, Pauline T. Kim, *Bargaining with Imperfect Information: A Study of Worker Perceptions of Legal Protection in at At-Will World*, 83 CORNELL L. REV. 105 (1997).

that the rule reduces the "transaction costs" to an employer of hiring and firing.[30] Such efficiency might arguably make the United States more competitive in a global labor market. On the other hand, the at-will rule has long been criticized as for the sweeping power it gives employers over employees.[31]

Regardless of the criticism, however, the at-will rule remains the baseline in forty-nine out of fifty American states. Reflecting this, the proposed RESTATEMENT (THIRD) OF EMPLOYMENT LAW § 2.01 (2009) adopts the at-will rule absent "a statute, other law or public policy, or . . . an agreement" to the contrary.

As of the date this book went to press, the Restatement of Employment Law is still somewhat of a work-in-progress. Most of the chapters have been approved by the membership and are citable as ALI tentative drafts. Two chapters have not yet been submitted to the ALI Council: Chapter 4 (Employer Liability for Harm to Employees) and Chapter 9 (Remedies). Two sections of Chapter 7 (Workplace Privacy and Autonomy) similarly have not been submitted. For an up-to-date description of the status of each chapter, see http://ali.org/index.cfm?fuseaction=publications.ppage&node_id=31.

This Understanding book will not attempt to cover the Restatement of Employment Law comprehensively. It will, instead, discuss the Restatement as it applies to interesting issues as they arise.

---

[30] *See, e.g.*, Yindee v. CCH Inc., 458 F.3d 599 (7th Cir. 2006) (noting, in opinion authored by Judge Easterbrook, that "poor personnel management receives its comeuppance in the market rather than the courts").

[31] *See, e.g.*, Lawrence E. Blades, *Employment at Will vs. Individual Freedom: On Limiting the Abusive Exercise of Employer Power*, 67 COLUM. L. REV. 1404 (1967).

Chapter 4

CONTRACT EROSIONS OF EMPLOYMENT AT WILL

§ 4.01 EXPRESS MODIFICATION OF AT-WILL CONTRACTS, WRITTEN AND ORAL

Because the employment at-will rule is a default rule, it can be changed by contract. The first way at-will employment typically is changed is by a contract between the employer and an *individual* employee. Such a contract may be written or oral, express or implied, definite-term or satisfaction. The second way at-will employment is typically changed is by a contract between the employer and *many* employees who are collectively represented by a union. Such a contract is called a collective bargaining agreement. This book focuses on the first way of changing at-will employment.[1]

[A] Definite-Term Contracts

If a written contract specifies the length of employment, or limits the circumstances under which the employer may discharge the employee, the employment is not at-will — the employer and employee must follow the terms of the contract. Oral contracts have the same effect, subject to the limitation imposed by the statute of frauds which is discussed below in § 4.01[C].

---

[1] For a thorough discussion of the second way of modifying an employment at-will arrangement in the unionized context, see generally Douglas E. Ray et al., Understanding Labor Law (3d ed. 2011).

A definite-term contract is a contract for a specified amount of time, or lasting until a specified date. An example of a written definite-term contract can be found in *Chiodo v. General Waterworks Corp.*[2] Vincent Chiodo owned a telephone company before he sold it to General Waterworks. A term of the sale was that General Waterworks would employ Chiodo for ten years at a specified annual salary. Three years later, General Waterworks fired Chiodo, and Chiodo sued for breach of contract. The court found that Chiodo had a "contract of employment for a stated term," and held that it was "assumed that the parties intended that [Chiodo] would conform to the usual standards expected of an employee [to provide] honest, faithful and loyal service in accordance with his ability."[3] General Waterworks proffered several reasons for firing Chiodo, but the court found those reasons pretextual, and ruled that Chiodo was entitled to his salary for the remaining seven years of the contract.

The *Chiodo* case demonstrates that employment contracts may be enforceable like other contracts. It also raises, but does not answer, three important issues.

The first issue is which standard of discharge should be implied into an employment contract that is silent on that issue. A well-drafted employment contract, for example, will specify the circumstances under which an employer is entitled to terminate the contract and discharge the employee (e.g., for the employee's conviction of a felony). Often, however, as in *Chiodo*, employment agreements do not. This does not, however, mean that General Waterworks would be obliged to keep Chiodo on the payroll even if Chiodo had embezzled huge sums of money. Most courts instead would imply a "just cause" standard into the term contract. An example is the *Chiodo* case itself, in which the court framed the issue as "whether [Chiodo]'s conduct constituted such justifiable cause for his discharge."[4] This is arguably not, however, what Chiodo had intended to bargain for — he may have intended that his right to employment (or at least to the paycheck that came with employment) be absolute.

A second issue raised by the case is: assuming the existence of a just-cause provision (either because the parties wrote it into the contract or because a court implied it), what does just cause mean? Some well-drafted employment contracts describe at length what will constitute just cause; most do not. One recurring issue is whether a business downturn constitutes just cause. Under such circumstances, each party tends to define "just cause" myopically, from its own point of view — the employer arguing that the business downturn provides a "good reason" for the discharge, and the employee arguing that just cause requires employee misconduct and that she or he did nothing wrong. Roger Abrams and Dennis Nolan have created a test for just cause by synthesizing a huge volume of cases arising under collective bargaining agreements,[5] but cases arising in the collective bargaining

---

[2]   413 P.2d 891 (Utah 1966).

[3]   *Id.* at 892.

[4]   *Id.*

[5]   Roger I. Abrams & Dennis R. Nolan, *Toward a Theory of "Just Cause" in Employee Discipline Cases*, 1985 DUKE L.J. 594, 611-12. Examples of conduct constituting just cause for discharge include irregular attendance, disobedience of reasonable work rules, poor quality and quantity of work, and conduct interfering with the employer's ability to carry on the business effectively.

context may arguably not apply to cases arising in the context of individual employment contracts.

A third issue is whether and with what consequence an employee may quit during a term contract — i.e., could Chiodo have quit in the middle of his ten-year contract? A court requiring Chiodo to specifically perform his employment contract might run afoul of the constitutional prohibition on involuntary servitude. Most courts, however, have held that employment contracts should be interpreted "symmetrically" and that employees, like employers, may terminate the employment contract for just cause.[6] This, however, raises the issue of what constitutes just cause for an employee's termination of an employment contract: a business upturn and a subsequent offer of a better-paying job? A job closer to home? A medical condition making it difficult for the employee to perform the original job? It also raises the issue of the damages to which the employer is entitled if it shows that the employee lacked cause to terminate the contract: The cost of hiring a replacement? Consequential damages to the job not being performed? In any event, employers seldom sue employees for breach of employment contract, both because potential damages usually are low and because developing a reputation for suing former employees makes it difficult to recruit future employees.

[B]   Oral Contracts

Most reported employment contract cases do not involve written employment contracts, but instead involve employees claiming that their employer gave them oral promises of job security. The difficulty courts have in dealing with claims predicated on an oral employment contract is illustrated by a trio of Michigan cases.

In *Toussaint v. Blue Cross Blue Shield of Michigan*,[7] one employee claimed his employer had told him he would be with the company "as long as [he] did [his] job," and another employee claimed his employer had told him "if he was 'doing the job' he would not be discharged." Both employees were fired and sued for breach of contract. The Michigan Supreme Court held that the alleged oral statements were sufficient for a jury to find that the employer had contracted with the employees to fire them only for cause. The court reasoned that the company could have "avoided the misunderstandings that generated this litigation" by "requiring prospective employees to acknowledge that they serve at the will or the pleasure of the company."[8]

Six years after *Toussaint*, a Michigan appellate court decided *Hetes v. Schefman & Miller Law Office*.[9] The employee alleged that despite the employer's pre-hiring

---

[6] *See, e.g.*, Handicapped Children's Educ. Bd. v. Lukaszewski, 332 N.W.2d 774 (Wis. 1983) (holding speech therapist liable for breach of employment contract after she resigned her job to take a competing job closer to home, but indicating she would not have been liable if she had resigned for a legitimate medical reason).

[7] 292 N.W.2d 880 (Mich. 1980).

[8] *Id.* at 891.

[9] 393 N.W.2d 577 (Mich. Ct. App. 1986).

promise that she would not be fired "as long as she did a good job," she was subsequently fired without cause. The trial court awarded summary judgment to the employer, but relying on *Toussaint*, the appellate court reversed, holding that the purported promise could support a jury finding that the employer had contracted for just-cause employment.

Five years after *Hetes*, the Michigan Supreme Court seemed to backtrack in *Rowe v. Montgomery Ward & Co.*[10] The employee, hired for a retail sales position, claimed the company had told her that sales representatives "had a job at Ward's" and "generally, as long as they generated sales and were honest . . . about the only way that you could be terminated would be if you failed to make your draw."[11] When the employee was fired, she sued for breach of contract. Here, in contrast to *Toussaint* and *Hetes*, the court found no oral contract. Oral statements of job security, the court held, "must be clear and unequivocal to overcome the presumption of employment at will." The court explained that the words "about" and "generally" in the employer's purported promise were too vague and general to create a contract, but instead appeared to be "merely intended to emphasize the number one priority of plaintiff's job — sales."

Employees asserting claims based on oral employment contracts have four problems. The first is that nearly every employee has heard language like that described in the above cases from his or her employer at one time or another. What the employer perceives as mere words of encouragement, or the hope that the employment relationship will be a long and productive one, often is taken by the employee as a legally enforceable promise. An employer could avoid such misunderstandings, as the *Toussaint* court suggested, by constantly reminding employees that they are employed at will and can be fired at any time with no notice and for no good reason, but that approach is unlikely to inspire loyalty and peak performance and more likely to inspire employees to update their resumes.

A second problem often faced by employees asserting oral contract claims is that many courts require the employee to show not only that the employer made contractual representations, but also that the employee furnished additional consideration, beyond mere continued employment, in reliance on those representations. Such additional consideration might include, for example, accepting the job offer in the first place, or forgoing other job opportunities.

A third problem is the difficulty of proving exactly what was said years afterward. In a typical case, for example, an employee might receive representations of job security in his pre-hiring interview, be fired five years later, and then be deposed or get to a jury two or three years after that. Indeed, in *Hetes*, the employee's only victory was in getting summary judgment reversed — the employee still had to convince a jury of the claim before he could recover damages.

A fourth problem often faced by employees asserting oral contract claims is the statute of frauds. The statute of frauds is discussed in the next section.

---

[10] 473 N.W.2d 268 (Mich. 1991).

[11] *Id.* at 274.

[C]   Statute of Frauds

The statute of frauds, among other things, nullifies oral contracts not performable within one year. It is the relic of a statute Parliament enacted in 1677 during the reign of King Charles II, and was intended to prevent unreliable or perjured testimony from supporting alleged oral promises.

Most courts interpret the statute of frauds narrowly, as barring only contracts that could not possibly be performed within one year, even if performance in fact outlasts a year. For example, in *Ohanian v. Avis Rent A Car System, Inc.*,[12] Robert Ohanian was a successful regional manager for Avis in California. Avis wanted Ohanian to take control of the northeastern region, and during negotiations over this transfer, Ohanian's supervisor told him that Ohanian's "future was secure in the company . . . unless he screwed up badly." Ohanian took the new position, moved to New York, and was fired a year and a half later. He sued for breach of an oral employment contract.

Avis defended by arguing that the statute of frauds made Ohanian's alleged oral contract unenforceable. The contract was not performable within a year, Avis argued, because the contract according to its terms would only terminate if Ohanian breached it (i.e., he "screwed up badly"), and breach was the antithesis of performance. The court, however, disagreed. Interpreting "screwed up badly" to mean "just cause," the court held that Avis would have had just cause to fire Ohanian if market conditions in the northeastern region had tanked and forced Avis to close that region. If that had happened, the just-cause employment contract with Ohanian would have been performed within one year. Therefore, the court concluded, the statute of frauds did not apply.

Before discussing in more detail how other courts apply the statute of frauds, it is worth noting two things about the *Ohanian* case. First, as the dissenting judge pointed out, the *Ohanian* case was in many ways the type of case for which the statute of frauds was specifically designed. There were only two witnesses to the alleged oral contract — Ohanian and his supervisor — and both had been fired by Avis within a few days of each other. This illustrates the practical difficulty employers often face defending employment suits — often the key witnesses themselves have been fired or disciplined. Of course, the flip side often is true as well — current employees, for obvious reasons, often are loath to testify against their employer (the phrase "biting the hand that feeds you" comes to mind). Second, Ohanian wins his case, but only by convincing the court that a business downturn constitutes just cause for which an employer can fire an employee under contract — a holding that is at best a pyrrhic victory for employees generally.

The statute of frauds is difficult to apply to employment cases, and courts (often within the same jurisdiction) are inconsistent. Part of the problem derives from a longstanding disagreement over the meaning of performance, termination, and excusable nonperformance.[13] If A promises to work for B for five years, A may die within a year. A's death is not performance, however, but excusable

---

[12] 779 F.2d 101 (2d Cir. 1985).

[13] John Edward Murray, Jr., Murray on Contracts § 72(C) (2001).

nonperformance — performance would require five years, which is impossible if A is dead. Many courts therefore would conclude that the contract is within the statute of frauds and unenforceable. Other courts, however, might interpret the contract as A promising to work for B for five years if A lives that long — that might be construed as alternative promises (to work for five years or to work until A dies); the latter promise would be performable within a year if A does in fact die. These courts would find the contract outside the statute of frauds and therefore enforceable.

Reported employment cases provide several variations on this theme. If an employee asserts a contract for employment "until retirement," most courts will refuse enforcement if the employee is young and therefore not within retirement age (but what if the employee were to win the lottery?). However, courts are split on how to handle employees who are within plausible retirement age. Courts similarly split on promises of "lifetime employment" — some courts reason that the possibility of the employee's early death makes the contract potentially performable within a year; other courts, as described above, treat death as excusable nonperformance. Likewise, courts are split on whether satisfaction contracts, such as the promise in *Hetes* that "I had a job as long as I did a good job," are enforceable under the statute of frauds. Finally, when an oral contract is for one year of employment, what the court defines as the start-date is critical to whether the contract is covered by the statute of frauds. If the start-date is the day the contract is made, the contract is performable within exactly one year and is enforceable; in contrast, if the start-date is the first day the employee starts work (usually at least a few days after the day the contract was made), the contract is not performable within a year of its making and therefore is unenforceable under the statute of frauds. Thus, there is no generalizable legal rule about whether the statute of frauds will apply to a particular oral contract — a good employment lawyer must carefully research the cases of the jurisdiction in which the employment dispute arises.

A final point is worth mentioning about the statute of frauds cases. On the one hand, it is easy for a fired employee to allege that he or she received an oral promise of lengthy employment, and such a promise is often difficult for an employer to disprove. The possibility that the employee will testify fraudulently — or at least "remember" the facts in a particularly favorable light after learning from his or her lawyer that he or she is otherwise an at-will employee subject to summary dismissal — is a real one. On the other hand, many of the cases are reminiscent of the old *Skagerberg*-type of case where the parties say "lifetime employment" and the court translates that as "at-will."[14]

§ 4.02   PROMISSORY ESTOPPEL

The contract theory of promissory estoppel enforces promises that induce reasonable reliance. The theory is particularly pertinent to the employment relationship, explains Professor Robert Hillman, because employers, through their communications, "seek to create the expectation of a stable, secure work environ-

---

[14] *See supra* § 4.03.

ment," and employees, "because of their general lack of contractual job security and their material and psychological investments in their jobs, . . . are prone to rely on those messages."[15]

A promissory estoppel claim can be divided into four elements: (1) a promise (2) which the promisor should reasonably expect to induce action or forbearance, (3) which does induce such action for forbearance, (4) resulting in injustice.[16] Promissory estoppel usually is a "second-best" claim — it is used when a straightforward breach of contract claim is untenable. This often occurs in the employment context when an employer makes a job offer (of at-will employment) to a prospective employee, the prospective employee resigns her current job and moves to the employer's place of employment, and then the employer rescinds the job offer at the last minute. Because the employer's original job offer was for at-will employment (i.e., there was no definite-term contract), most courts would say that the "offer" was illusory, as neither party was bound to anything — either party could have terminated the employment relationship on day one. An employer's promise of at-will employment is a meaningless promise that is unenforceable under a straightforward breach of contract claim. For this reason, employees turn to a claim of promissory estoppel.

For example, in *Grouse v. Group Health Plan, Inc.*,[17] John Grouse, pharmacist, quit one job and rejected another job offer because he had accepted an offer from Group Health Plan. After Grouse had given notice to his current employer but before he began the new job, Group Health hired another pharmacist. When Grouse reported for work, Group Health told him that there was no job available.

Grouse's employment with Group Health was to have been at-will. For this reason, the court found that "neither party is committed to performance and the promises are, therefore, illusory."[18] The court therefore rejected Grouse's breach of contract claim. However, the court concluded that Group Health knew Grouse had to resign his prior job to accept Group Health's offer, and held that it would be "unjust not to hold Group Health to its promise."[19] The court stated:

> What we [ ] hold is that under the facts of this case [Grouse] had a right to assume he would be given a good faith opportunity to perform his duties to the *satisfaction* of [Group Health] once he was on the job. He was not only denied that opportunity but resigned the position he already held in reliance on the *firm* offer which [Group Health] tendered him.[20]

Consider again the four elements of promissory estoppel. Although Grouse seemed to have met elements three and four (inducement and injustice), he arguably had not met elements one and two. Regarding the first element — a

---

[15] Robert A. Hillman, *The Unfulfilled Promise of Promissory Estoppel in the Employment Setting*, 31 Rutgers L.J. 1, 2 (1999).

[16] *See* Restatement (Second) of Contracts § 90.

[17] 306 N.W.2d 114 (Minn. 1981).

[18] *Id.* at 116.

[19] *Id.*

[20] *Id.* (emphasis added).

promise — recall that although the court characterized Group Health's promise as "firm" for purposes of the promissory estoppel claim, the court had characterized that same offer as "illusory" for purposes of the breach of contract claim.

Regarding the second element — reasonable reliance — employers typically argue that it is not reasonable for a prospective employee to rely on an (illusory) offer of at-will employment. However, as the *Grouse* court pointed out, this is a head-in-the-sand argument, because the employer knows the prospective employee must quit her current job before she can accept the employer's offer, and the employer presumably would not have made the offer in the first place if the employer did not believe there was at least some possibility that the prospective employee would accept it.

In holding that Group Health should have given Grouse an opportunity to perform the job to Group Health's satisfaction, the court appears to have converted the at-will employment for which the parties bargained into a one-way satisfaction contract of indefinite duration. Though the result in this case may be just, the case indicates that the doctrine of promissory estoppel may be incompatible with the doctrine of at-will employment.

Many promissory estoppel employment claims are brought by employees who relocate themselves and their families great distances to take a new job or promotion. Sometimes, instead of bringing the claim under a promissory estoppel theory, the plaintiff argues that the relocation constituted "additional consideration" sufficient to support an implied promise by the employer to discharge only for cause. An example is *Veno v. Meredith*.[21] Veno, a newspaper editor, quit a job in Newark and moved his family to Philadelphia to accept a new job there. He worked for the Philadelphia newspaper for eight years, all the while turning down other job offers. The newspaper fired him, however, after he printed a story criticizing a local judge. Veno sued, arguing that his move and his forbearance on other job offers constituted "additional consideration" to support a claim for just-cause employment. The court found that the move and forbearance were insufficient to support such a claim, both because those inconveniences are suffered by all employees who relocate for another job and because eight years had elapsed since the relocation. Other courts, however, use promissory estoppel or a theory of additional consideration to protect employees who move long distances and are summarily fired.[22]

Courts declining to protect employees after long-distance moves often conclude that it is unreasonable for an employee to relocate for an offer of at-will employment. Consider, however, that many new lawyers relocate and turn down competing offers when they take their first full-time law job, which almost invariably is at-will. What would be the likely outcome if one of these lawyers conditioned her acceptance of the employment offer on the employer's agreement to a just-cause employment contract?

The success rate of promissory estoppel claims is extraordinarily low, particularly in the employment setting. An empirical study by Professor Hillman found

---

[21] 515 A.2d 571 (Pa. Super. Ct. 1986).

[22] *See, e.g.*, Cashdollar v. Mercy Hosp., 595 A.2d 70 (Pa. Super. Ct. 1991).

that plaintiffs won about fifteen percent of non-employment promissory estoppel claims, but only about four percent of employment-related promissory estoppel claims.[23] Hillman concluded that "judicial veneration of the employment-at-will-rule" makes it very difficult for employees to succeed on these claims.[24]

§ 4.03   RELIANCE AND IMPLIED-IN-FACT CONTRACTS

Like promissory estoppel, arguing for an implied-in-fact contract is a second-best claim, used only when the facts cannot support a straightforward breach of contract claim. An implied-in-fact contract arises not from what the parties say to each other (whether orally or in writing), but rather from what the parties do.

An example is *Pugh v. See's Candies, Inc.*[25] Wayne Pugh, a 32-year employee of See's Candies, had started as a dishwasher and worked his way up to Vice President of Production and a member of the board of directors. Prior to his termination, See's enjoyed a record-setting year for which Pugh was largely responsible, and See's never gave Pugh any indication that his work performance was less than stellar. Nonetheless, when Pugh returned from a trip to Europe, See's fired him without explanation. Pugh sued for breach of contract.

The trial court dismissed the case, finding that Pugh's employment was at will. The California Court of Appeals, however, reversed, holding that an employer's conduct can give "rise to an implied promise that it [will] not act arbitrarily in dealing with its employees." Conduct creating such an implied-in-fact contract for Pugh included "the duration of [Pugh's] employment, the commendations and promotions he received, the apparent lack of any direct criticism of his work, the assurances [of job security] he was given, and the employer's acknowledged" practice of "not terminating administrative personnel except for good cause."[26] The court therefore remanded the case for further consideration of Pugh's contract claim. On remand, however, See's produced evidence at trial that it had had good cause to fire Pugh, the jury found for See's, and the court of appeals affirmed.[27]

For a time after *Pugh*, California courts focused on length of tenure as the primary factor in determining the existence of implied-in-fact employment contracts.[28] However, in *Guz v. Bechtel*,[29] the California Supreme Court retreated, reasoning that "a rule granting such contract rights on the basis of successful longevity alone would discourage the retention and promotion of employees."[30] Instead, explained the court, long tenure is one factor in the determination of an

---

[23] Hillman, *supra* note 15, at 7-8.

[24] *Id.* at 25-26.

[25] 171 Cal. Rptr. 917 (Cal. Ct. App. 1981).

[26] *Id.* at 917.

[27] Pugh v. See's Candies, Inc., 250 Cal. Rptr. 195 (Cal. Ct. App. 1988).

[28] *See, e.g.*, Cleary v. Am. Airlines, 168 Cal. Rptr. 722 (Cal. Ct. App. 1980) (upholding claim of employee fired after eighteen years of service); Foley v. Interactive Data Corp., 765 P.2d 373 (Cal. 1988) (upholding claim of employee fired after less than seven years of service).

[29] 8 P.3d 1089 (Cal. 2000).

[30] *Id.* at 1105.

implied-in-fact employment contract, but it cannot alone form such a contract.

Dean Stewart Schwab has argued that the *Grouse, Veno,* and *Pugh* cases collectively represent differentiated treatment of employees at varying stages of their work-life cycles.[31] Courts are most likely to protect employees, Schwab argues, when employees are most vulnerable, such as early in their careers when they move to take a new job and late in their careers after they have invested decades of work into a single company, and are less likely to protect mid-career employees who presumably are less vulnerable to employer exploitation.

Another way of viewing *Pugh* is that an employer can create an implied-in-fact employment contract through the use of enlightened personnel practices, such as a history of firing employees only for good reason, the adoption of a progressive disciplinary policy, and encouraging employee loyalty by treating employees fairly. If this is what *Pugh* stands for, then employment attorneys might well advise their corporate clients to fire a few employees at random every once in awhile and to otherwise regularly remind employees that they are employed at-will. This result, however, would be inconsistent with the California Supreme Court's rationale in *Guz* that the law should encourage, rather than discourage, employee-friendly personnel practices.

Many states have rejected *Pugh*-type claims as inconsistent with at-will employment.[32] Other states, however, follow the *Pugh* approach of considering many different factors, though these states differ on the relative weight given to each factor.

Long-term employees in the public sector may receive job security via the Due Process Clause of the U. S. Constitution. In *Board of Regents v. Roth*,[33] the United States Supreme Court rejected the due process claim of an assistant professor who was discharged after one year on the job. However, in *Perry v. Sindermann*,[34] decided the same day as *Roth*, the Court found that a professor who had completed ten one-year employment contracts for the State of Texas had a due process property right in his job. The Court explained that "[a] teacher . . . who has held his position for a number of years might be able to show from the circumstances of this service — and from other relevant facts — that he has a legitimate claim of entitlement to job tenure."[35]

§ 4.04 EMPLOYMENT MANUALS

Most large- and medium-sized employers distribute employment manuals to their employees. Employers do so for many reasons. First, these manuals promote consistency in the treatment of employees, which in turn both improves employee morale and decreases the likelihood of discrimination suits which often are

---

[31] Stewart J. Schwab, *Life-Cycle Justice: Accommodating Just Cause and Employment At Will*, 92 MICH. L. REV. 8 (1993).

[32] *See, e.g.*, Calleon v. Miyagi, 876 P.2d 1278 (Haw. 1994).

[33] 408 U.S. 564 (1972).

[34] 408 U.S. 593 (1972).

[35] *Id.* at 602.

predicated on inconsistent treatment. Second, the manuals help fulfill statutory notice requirements, such as the requirement that covered employers inform their employees of rights under the Family Medical Leave Act.[36] Third, the manuals can create a defense in other types of employment claims, such as when a manual creates an effective way for employees to internally report sexual harassment. Fourth, employment manuals efficiently communicate to employees basic information about the workplace, such as how vacation days are calculated. Fifth, some employers use handbooks as a loyalty-encouraging or union-avoidance strategy by conveying the sense that the employer is fair and empathetic toward employee concerns, and perhaps by giving the appearance of job security even if no such job security actually exists.

Employment manuals can create employment contracts in much the same way that employer speech or conduct can. However, the legal requirements for enforcing an employment manual as a contractual obligation vary from state to state. In some states, the employee must have read and relied upon the handbook; in other states, the employee need not even have known of the handbook's existence.[37]

A leading case dealing with employment manuals is the New Jersey Supreme Court case of *Woolley v. Hoffman-La Roche, Inc.*[38] Richard Woolley was an engineer who had worked for Hoffman-La Roche for nine years and been promoted twice. Shortly after his employment began, Hoffman-La Roche gave him an employment manual. The manual contained eight pages devoted to "termination." It listed five types of termination: "layoff," "discharge due to performance," "discharge, disciplinary," "retirement," and "resignation."[39] It did not list a category for discharge without cause. The preamble to the termination section of the employment manual stated that "[i]t is the policy of Hoffman-La Roche to retain to the extent consistent with company requirements, the services of all employees who perform their duties efficiently and effectively."[40]

Hoffman-La Roche fired Woolley, telling him only that the company "had lost confidence in him."[41] Woolley sued for breach of contract, arguing that the employment manual had created a just-cause employment contract. The lower courts disagreed, finding that Woolley's employment was at will, and granted summary judgment to Hoffman-La Roche. The New Jersey Supreme Court reversed and remanded the case for trial, holding that an employment manual may contractually convert at-will employment into just-cause employment. In so holding, the court rejected four arguments raised by Hoffman-La Roche.

First, Hoffman-La Roche argued that the employment manual never promised anything to Woolley. The court disagreed, finding that the manual arguably promised job security in two ways. The first was through express language — the

---

[36] 29 U.S.C. § 2601; *see infra* § 12.04.

[37] *Compare* Baron v. Port Auth., 271 F.3d 81 (2d Cir. 2001) (New York law), *with* Anderson v. Douglas & Lomason Co., 540 N.W.2d 277 (Iowa 1995).

[38] 491 A.2d 1257, *modified*, 499 A.2d 515 (N.J. 1985).

[39] *Id.* at 1259 n.2.

[40] *Id.*

[41] *Id.* at 1258.

language in the preamble to the termination section in which Hoffman-La Roche said it was company policy to retain efficient and effective employees. The second way the *Woolley* court found that the employment manual promised job security was by implication: by omitting "discharge without cause" from the types of termination, Hoffman-La Roche implied that it would not discharge employees except for cause. Other courts have similarly held that employment manuals can create a just-cause standard by implication. For example, manuals that provide an exclusive list of dischargeable offenses imply that employees cannot be fired for unlisted reasons;[42] manuals providing that new employees are "probationary" imply that once the probationary period is complete, employment is something other than at-will;[43] manuals committing the employer to a progressive discipline system imply that the employer will not fire employees inconsistently with that system.[44]

Hoffman-La Roche's second argument was that it had not *intended* to form a contract, and that without any "meeting of the minds," there was no contract. The court held that actual intent was unnecessary because Hoffman-LaRoche had displayed what Woolley could reasonably have interpreted as apparent intent. Hoffman-LaRoche distributed to nearly all employees "a document carefully prepared by the company with all the appearances of corporate legitimacy that one could imagine." The court held that the manual should be construed "in accordance with the reasonable expectations of the employees."

Hoffman-La Roche's third argument was that the employment manual was not contractual because it lacked consideration. The court, however held that the manual constituted an offer of a unilateral contract; Woolley's consideration was his continuation of work for Hoffman-La Roche when he had no legal obligation to do so. Note, however, that many courts do not consider a promise of continued employment (whether the "promise" originates from the employer or the employee) to be sufficient consideration to support a subsequent contract, because by definition either party may terminate at-will employment at any time.

Fourth, Hoffman-La Roche argued that the terms of the employment manual were too indefinite to form a contract. The court disagreed, finding that indefiniteness was a problem "of the employer's own making from which it should gain no advantage."

[A] Disclaimers

In the last paragraph of the *Woolley* decision, the court explained that Hoffman-La Roche could have avoided the creation of a contractual obligation by adding a disclaimer to its handbook:

> All that this opinion requires of an employer is that it be fair. It would be unfair to allow an employer to distribute a policy manual that makes the workforce believe that certain promises have been made and then to allow

---

[42] Austin v. Howard Univ., 267 F. Supp. 2d 22 (D.D.C. 2003).

[43] *See, e.g.,* Norris v. Filson Care Home Ltd., No. 89-CA-0599-MR, 1990 Ky. App. LEXIS 8 (Ky. Ct. App. Jan. 26, 1990).

[44] *See, e.g.,* Trombley v. Sw. Vermont Med. Ctr., 738 A.2d 103 (Vt. 1999).

the employer to renege on those promises. What is sought here is basic honesty: if the employer for whatever reason, does not want the manual to be capable of being construed by the court as a binding contract, there are simple ways to attain that goal. All that need be done is the inclusion in a very prominent position of an appropriate statement that there is no promise of any kind by the employer contained in the manual; that regardless of what the manual says or provides, the employer promises nothing and remains free to change wages and all other working conditions without having to consult anyone and without anyone's agreement; and that the employer continues to have the absolute power to fire anyone with or without good cause.[45]

Not all courts, however, agree that the mere inclusion of a disclaimer automatically "erases" otherwise-contractual language in an employment manual. The Tenth Circuit, for example, has stated that a disclaimer is merely one factor the court is to consider in determining whether an employment manual is a contract;[46] the D.C. Court of Appeals has held that a disclaimer "rationally at odds with other language" in the manual creates a jury question as to whether the manual is a contract.[47]

A disclaimer, to be effective, generally must meet three criteria.[48] First, it must be prominent, must not be buried in the fine print, should be placed at the front of the manual, and ideally should be set off by font, color, or border. Many employers require employees to sign an "acknowledgment form" stating yet again that employment is at will. Second, an effective disclaimer must be clear: it must be understandable by the average worker and devoid of legalese. Third, an effective disclaimer must be specific. It might state, for example, that (1) employment is at will, (2) the handbook is not a contract, and (3) the employer reserves the right to modify, at any time and with no notice, the terms of the handbook or of the employment relationship.

Bluntly reminding employees that they can be fired at any time for no good reason is inconsistent with the desire of most employers to create a "feel-good" employment manual that engenders employee loyalty. However, as one commentator has put it, "the more an employer tries to sugarcoat the language, the more likely it is that a judge or jury will find that the employer is bound by the contents" of the manual.[49] The best an employer can do is to remind the employee in warm and fuzzy language that she, too, has the unilateral right to terminate the employment relationship: "Just as you have the right to quit your job at any time for any reason, the Company may release you at any time for any reason."

---

[45] *Woolley*, 491 A.2d at 1271.

[46] *See, e.g.*, Toth v. Gates Rubber Co., No. 99-1017, 2000 U.S. App. LEXIS 14374 (10th Cir. 2000).

[47] Dantley v. Howard Univ., 801 A.2d 962 (D.C. 2002).

[48] Shawe & Rosenthal, Labor and Employment Law § 259.03[2][b][i] (2006).

[49] *Id.*

[B] Amendments

Employment manuals must be updated regularly to reflect changes in employment laws and workplace policies. Such updates generally are non-contractual, because they merely describe the new state of the law. However, sometimes an employer wishes to amend its manual in a way that negatively affects employees. For example, an employer might distribute a manual that the employer thought was non-contractual, a court might later decide that the manual was contractual (as in *Woolley*), and the employer might then wish to make the manual non-contractual. This raises the issue of whether, and how, an employer may amend a contractual employment manual.

If the manual contains a disclaimer reserving to the employer the unilateral right to rescind or modify the manual, the amendment is easy to accomplish. The employer simply must give employees adequate notice of the changes. If, however, the handbook contains no such language, then the employer may have to jump through contractual hoops to accomplish the amendment.

For example, in *DeMasse v. ITT Corp.*,[50] ITT's original employment manual specified that layoffs would be based on seniority. The manual did not contain either an at-will clause or a reservation-of-right-to-modify clause. ITT later issued a subsequent edition of the manual containing both an at-will clause and a reservation clause. Four years after ITT issued this new edition, ITT announced that layoffs would be based on performance rather than seniority. Ten days after that, the company began laying off employees.

Several laid-off employees who would have been retained if the layoffs had been seniority-based sued, arguing that their layoffs violated the contractual seniority provisions of the earlier edition of the employment manual. ITT argued that the subsequent edition replaced the old edition, and that it both transformed the status of the employees from contract-based to at will and gave ITT the unilateral right to modify the seniority provision. The court, however, disagreed. The court held that because the earlier edition of the employment manual had been contractual, it could only be modified in the traditional way that contracts are modified — by offer, acceptance, and consideration.

The court found that the subsequent edition of the employment manual did not contractually modify the earlier edition because it lacked both acceptance and consideration. Acceptance was lacking, the court found, because ITT had not specifically told its employees how the subsequent edition modified the earlier edition and did not bargain with employees for the modification. Consideration was lacking, the court found, because continued employment alone could not constitute sufficient consideration.[51]

Courts are inconsistent in how they handle amendments to employment manuals. Some, like the court in *DeMasse*, require employers to go the traditional

---

[50] 984 P.2d 1138 (Ariz. 1999).

[51] The *DeMasse* approach to acceptance and consideration is inconsistent with the *Woolley* approach. Woolley, who received his manual after a month on the job, neither bargained for the just-cause terms of the contract nor provided Hoffman-La Roche with any consideration beyond continued employment.

contract-modification route. Others take the position that a promise in an employment manual is binding on the employer only until the employer announces that it no longer wishes to be bound — that is, the promise is binding only until the employer says it is not. A third group of courts has held that an employer can unilaterally modify job-protection promises only "after a reasonable time, on reasonable notice, and without interfering with the employee's vested benefits."[52]

The new Restatement of Employment Law adopts a variation of this third approach. It provides that "[a]n employer may prospectively modify or revoke its binding policy statement by providing reasonable advance notice of the modified statement or revocation to the affected employees," and that these modifications and revocations "apply to all employees hired, and all employees who continue working, after the effective date of the notice of modification or revocation."[53]

Of course, the easiest way for an employer to avoid this issue is to include an effective disclaimer at the front end.

§ 4.05   CONTRACT DAMAGES

Employees seldom ask for or receive specific performance, such as reinstatement, as a remedy for an employer's breach of an employment contract.

The traditional remedy for breach of contract is expectation damages — the lost economic benefits of the contract. Expectation damages seek to put the injured employee in the same position the employee would have been in had there been no breach. Expectation damages in employment cases typically include back pay and benefits through the day of judgment, less any income the employee did earn or could have earned during that period by getting another reasonably comparable job (mitigation). Expectation damages may include front pay from the day of judgment forward, depending on the jurisdiction and the evidence on damages presented at trial. An employee may argue that front pay should be calculated all the way to the employee's expected retirement date, but most courts would consider damages that far into the future too speculative.

The traditional remedy in a promissory estoppel case is reliance damages rather than expectation damages. Reliance damages seek to put the injured employee in the same position the employee would have been in had she not relied on the employer's promise. For example, say Grouse was making $10 an hour at his original job, Group Health offered $15, and when that job evaporated Grouse could only find a job paying $8. Expectation damages would be $7 ($15-8), while reliance damages would be $2 ($10-8).

Courts seldom award emotional distress damages, punitive damages, or attorneys' fees in breach of contract cases. However, such damages generally *are* available in tort cases. Employment torts are covered in the next chapter.

---

[52] *See, e.g.*, Asmus v. Pac. Bell, 999 P.2d 71, 73 (Cal. 2000).

[53] Restatement (Third) of Employment Law § 2.06 (2009).

Chapter 5

TORT EROSIONS OF EMPLOYMENT AT WILL

§ 5.01   INTRODUCTION

Chapter 5 describes how the common law views the employment relationship as a private contract between an employer and employee. Sometimes, however, the employment relationship can affect third parties, including society as a whole. These "third party effects" provide the rationale for applying tort law to the employment relationship.[1] Whereas the focus in the preceding chapter was on how the parties intended to define the employment relationship, party intent is not the focus of employment torts. Instead, the law of employment torts focuses on ways

---

[1] STEVEN L. WILLBORN ET AL., EMPLOYMENT LAW: CASES AND MATERIALS 117 (5th ed. 2012); Stewart J. Schwab, *Wrongful Discharge Law and the Search for Third-Party Effects*, 74 TEX. L. REV. 1943, 1950–53 (1996).

that the employment relationship might harm third parties and, sometimes, the employee.[2]

In addition to this theoretical difference between employment contract law and employment tort law, there is an enormous practical difference as well. Tort remedies are far more generous than contract remedies (for example, tort remedies can include punitive damages), and tort remedies are not subject to the damage caps found in many employment discrimination statutes.[3] Moreover, torts may be asserted against employers too small to be covered by some employment statutes,[4] and against supervisors and co-workers in their individual capacities. For these reasons, employment torts often are an integral part of litigated employment cases, even in cases concerning primarily contract or discrimination claims.

§ 5.02 WRONGFUL DISCHARGE IN VIOLATION OF PUBLIC POLICY

The tort for wrongful discharge in violation of public policy may be the employment tort that best fits the "third-party effects" rationale. Examples include *Peterman v. Teamsters Local 396*,[5] in which an employee was fired for refusing his employer's request to commit perjury in testifying before the legislature, and *Nees v. Hocks*,[6] in which an employee was fired for participating in jury duty.[7] The public has an interest in truthful testimony to legislatures and in jury pools that are representative of the general population. Employees will be less likely to testify truthfully and serve on juries if they can be fired for doing so. The public policy tort allows the employee to serve the public interest notwithstanding the employer's displeasure. Moreover, the tort is not a default rule that the parties are free to alter by contract. Even if an employee signs an employment contract specifying that he or she can be fired for testifying truthfully or serving on a jury, the public policy tort would still apply.

[A] Defining Public Policy

Most states have recognized the tort of wrongful discharge in violation of public policy, though a few have not.[8] The states recognizing the tort typically define public policy in one of two ways.

---

[2] The tort rationale for protecting the employee himself or herself is that the public suffers harm indirectly when an employee is harmed in a manner protected by the tort.

[3] *See, e.g.*, 42 U.S.C. § 1981a(b)(3) (capping compensatory and punitive damages in Title VII cases).

[4] *See supra* § 2.03[A][2].

[5] 344 P.2d 25 (Cal. Ct. App. 1959).

[6] 536 P.2d 512 (Or. 1975).

[7] The employer had given the employee a letter to give the court asking that she be excused from jury duty. The employee gave this letter to the court clerk, but volunteered that she nonetheless would like to serve on jury duty.

[8] *See, e.g.*, Salter v. Alfa Ins. Co., 561 So. 2d 1050, 1053 (Ala. 1990).

The first way of defining public policy is to require that the policy be articulated in a constitution, statute, regulation, or judicial holding.[9] Some courts defining public policy this way require the employee to identify a particular law that would have been violated.[10] Other courts, however, require only that the employee identify a *policy* expressed in the law.[11] Similarly, some courts (both state and federal) have rejected federal law as a source of public policy in the application of the state public policy tort.[12] Other courts treat federal law on parity with state law,[13] and still other courts require a link between federal law and state public policy.[14] The myriad ways in which courts handle issues of public policy make clear that it is important to check the law of your jurisdiction before proceeding in this area of employment law.

The second way of defining public policy is much broader, and requires only that the employee articulate a public good or civic duty. An example is *Palmateer v. International Harvester Co.*,[15] in which the Illinois Supreme Court defined public policy as "what is right and just and what affects the citizens of the state collectively."[16]

[B] Pigeonholing Public Policy Claims

Successful claims for wrongful discharge in violation of public policy typically fall into one of four categories: refusing to commit an unlawful act, exercising a statutory right, fulfilling a public obligation, or whistleblowing.[17]

[1] Refusing to Commit an Unlawful Act

An example of a successful public policy claim brought by an employee fired for refusing to commit an unlawful act is the *Peterman* case discussed above,[18] in which an employee was fired for refusing to commit perjury. Other examples include an

---

[9] *See, e.g.*, Pierce v. Ortho Pharmaceutical Corp., 417 A.2d 505 (N.J. 1980).

[10] *See, e.g.*, Lucas v. Brown & Root, Inc., 736 F.2d 1202 (8th Cir. 1984) (upholding claim of employee who refused her foreman's sexual advances because acceding to the advances would have violated Arkansas anti-prostitution law). Texas courts define public policy even more restrictively. Violation of a civil law is insufficient; the employee may only invoke the public policy tort if the employee is "forced to choose between risking *criminal* liability or being discharged." Winters v. Houston Chronicle, 795 S.W.2d 723, 724 (Tex. 1990) (emphasis added).

[11] *See, e.g.*, Wagenseller v. Scottsdale Mem'l Hosp., 710 P.2d 1025, 1035 n.5 (Ariz. 1985) (upholding claim of employee fired for refusing to participate in skit that involved "mooning" audience of co-workers even though mooning might not be technical violation of indecent-exposure statute).

[12] *See, e.g.*, Guy v. Travenol Labs, 812 F.2d 911 (4th Cir. 1987) (applying North Carolina law); *see also* Nancy Modesitt, *Wrongful Discharge: The Use of Federal Law as a Source of Public Policy*, 8 U. PA. J. LAB. & EMP. L. 623 (2006).

[13] *See, e.g.*, Faulkner v. United Techs. Corp., 693 A.2d 293, 296-97 (Conn. 1997).

[14] *See, e.g.*, Peterson v. Browning, 832 P.2d 1280 (Utah 1992).

[15] 421 N.E.2d 876 (Ill. 1981).

[16] *Id.* at 878.

[17] WILLBORN ET AL., *supra* note 1, at 120.

[18] *See supra* § 6.02.

employee fired for refusing to defraud the employer's customers,[19] a truck driver fired for refusing to drive a truck that lacked a legally required inspection sticker,[20] and a deck hand fired for refusing to illegally pump bilges (wastewater) into open water.[21]

[2] Exercising a Statutory Right

The prototypical example of a statutory right that can underlie a public policy claim is the right to receive workers' compensation benefits for workplace injuries. For example, in *Frampton v. Central Indiana Gas Co.*,[22] an employer fired an employee shortly after the employee settled a workers' compensation claim. The employee sued, alleging the employer had retaliated against her for filing the claim. Though the workers' compensation statute did not expressly prohibit retaliation, the Indiana Supreme Court nonetheless reversed the trial court's dismissal of her case. The court reasoned that otherwise, employers would pressure employees to abandon workers' compensation claims, thereby undermining the statute.

Other statutory rights that courts have held to be protected by the public policy tort include occupational safety and health laws[23] and minimum wage laws.[24] Many statutes (including OSHA, the FLSA, and most state workers' compensation statutes) contain explicit anti-retaliation provisions.[25] Some courts have held that such statutory provisions displace the common-law remedy that would otherwise exist.[26] Other courts, however, reason that the two sources of employee protection can coexist and supplement each other both substantively and remedially.[27] The issue often is of great practical significance, because the tort remedies may significantly exceed the statutory remedies.[28]

[3] Fulfilling a Public Obligation

An example of a successful public policy claim brought by an employee fired for refusing to commit an unlawful act is the *Nees* case discussed above,[29] in which an employee was fired for participating in jury duty. Some courts include refusing to violate a professional code of ethics, and whistleblowing, as part of fulfilling a public obligation,[30] although other courts would classify those acts separately.

---

[19] McArn v. Allied Bruce-Terminix Co., 626 So. 2d 603 (Miss. 1993).

[20] Adams v. George W. Cochran & Co., 597 A.2d 28 (D.C. Ct. App. 1991).

[21] Sabine Pilot Serv. Inc. v. Hauck, 687 S.W.2d 733 (Tex. 1985).

[22] 297 N.E.2d 425 (Ind. 1973).

[23] D'Angelo v. Gardner, 819 P.2d 206 (Nev. 1991).

[24] Amos v. Oakdale Knitting Co., 416 S.E.2d 166 (N.C. 1992).

[25] *See, e.g.*, TEX. LAB. CODE ANN. § 451.001.

[26] *See, e.g.*, Wehr v. Burroughs Corp., 438 F. Supp. 1052, 1055 (E.D. Pa. 1977).

[27] *See, e.g.*, *Amos*, 416 S.E.2d 166.

[28] *See, e.g.*, Hodges v. S.C. Toof & Co., 833 S.W.2d 896 (Tenn. 1992).

[29] *See supra* § 6.02.

[30] *See, e.g.*, Smith v. Chaney Brooks Realty, Inc., 865 P.2d 170 (Haw. App. 1994).

[4]   Whistleblowing

[a]   Source of Legal Protection

A fourth category of public policy claims is whistleblowing. Laws protecting whistleblowers from employer retaliation derive from four sources. The first source is the tort of wrongful discharge in violation of public policy. An example is *Adler v. American Standard Corp.*,[31] in which the Maryland Court of Appeals framed the issue as whether an employee's discharge (ostensibly for reporting to upper management the payment of commercial bribes and the falsification of corporate records and financial statistics) "contravened some clear mandate of public policy."[32] The court held that the employee in that case had not adequately specified the statutes creating the public policy on which his wrongful discharge claim was based. Many courts invoking public policy to protect whistleblowers do so on the rationale that whistleblowing is tantamount to refusing to commit an illegal act.[33]

A second source of protections for whistleblowers is state statutory law. Approximately twenty states have enacted whistleblowing statutes that apply generally to private employers.[34] Most of these same states also recognize an overlapping tort for wrongful discharge in violation of public policy.[35]

A third source of laws protecting whistleblowers is federal statutory law. Many federal statutes — such as the Clean Air Act[36] — protect employees who report their employer's violation of those statutes. The Sarbanes-Oxley Act of 2002,[37] discussed in more detail below,[38] prohibits publicly traded companies from retaliating against employees who provide information or assist in an investigation of fraud or a violation of federal securities law. Most employment statutes contain anti-retaliation provisions protecting employees who participate in regulatory or judicial proceedings related to the statutes or who otherwise oppose employment practices made unlawful by the statutes.[39]

A fourth source of laws protecting whistleblowers is the Constitution, which in some cases protects public employee whistleblowers.[40]

---

[31] 432 A.2d 464 (Md. 1981).

[32] *Id.* at 471.

[33] *See, e.g.*, Johnson v. Kreiser's Inc., 433 N.W.2d 225 (S.D. 1988).

[34] Miriam A. Cherry, *Whistling in the Dark? Corporate Fraud, Whistleblowers, and the Implications of the Sarbanes-Oxley Act for Employment Law*, 79 Wash. L. Rev. 1029, 1045 (2004).

[35] *Id.*

[36] 42 U.S.C. § 7622.

[37] 18 U.S.C. § 1514A(a).

[38] *See infra* § 6.02[B][4][d].

[39] *See, e.g.*, 42 U.S.C. § 2000e-3(a) (Title VII).

[40] *See infra* § 8.02.

[b]   Scope of Legal Protection

As discussed above, states vary widely in how broadly they define public policy for purposes of the tort of wrongful discharge in violation of public policy. Federal and state whistleblowing statutes likewise vary widely in the scope of protection. Some statutes protect all employees;[41] others protect only public-sector employees or employees in certain occupations.[42] Some statutes, such as in New York, protects only whistleblowing on unlawful conduct that "creates a substantial and specific danger to the public health or safety,"[43] while other statutes, such as in New Jersey, do not require danger to public health or safety.[44]

Both courts applying the common-law public policy tort and courts applying state statutes differ on whether internal whistleblowing (e.g., to a supervisor or someone else "up the chain of command") is protected, or whether the tort/statute protects only external whistleblowing (e.g., to the police or regulatory agency). For example, in *Belline v. K-Mart Corp.*,[45] the Seventh Circuit held that internal whistleblowing is protected because a contrary rule would encourage employees to "bypass internal channels altogether and immediately summon the police."[46] However, in *Fox v. MCI Communications Corp.*,[47] the Utah Supreme Court refused to protect an internal whistleblower because such whistleblowing "ordinarily serves the private interest of the employer, not the public interest." In a later case, however, the court retreated from its categorical rule, stating that it would uphold wrongful discharge claims by internal whistleblowers, but only if the whistleblowing furthered a clear and substantial public policy.[48]

A case illustrating a narrow approach to whistleblower protection is *Wright v. Shriners Hospital for Crippled Children*.[49] Anita Wright was the Assistant Director of Nursing at a Shriners Hospital. When a survey team from the Shriners national headquarters visited the hospital and interviewed her, Wright criticized the medical staff of the hospital and complained that patients were receiving substandard care. Shortly afterward, the hospital administrator fired her.

Wright sued in tort for wrongful discharge in violation of public policy. A jury found liability and awarded damages of $100,000. The Massachusetts Supreme Court, however, reversed and ordered judgment in favor of the employer. The majority opinion defined public policy protection for whistleblowers narrowly to require articulation of a particular statute that would have been violated. The court held that Wright's citation of general statutes requiring adequate patient care, a

---

[41] *See, e.g.*, CONN. GEN. STAT. § 31-51m (covering an employee of "a person engaged in business who has employees").

[42] *See, e.g.*, MO. STAT. ANN. § 197.285 (covering hospital and ambulatory surgical center employees).

[43] N.Y. LAB. LAW § 740(2).

[44] N.J. STAT. ANN. 34:19-3.

[45] 940 F.2d 184 (7th Cir. 1991).

[46] *Id.* at 187.

[47] 931 P.2d 857 (Utah 1997).

[48] Ryan v. Dan's Food Stores, 972 P.2d 395 (Utah 1998).

[49] 589 N.E.2d 1241 (Mass. 1992).

professional code of ethics, and a narrow administrative regulation targeting nurses was insufficient. The dissent, however, defined public policy more broadly, and argued that "it must be the public policy of [Massachusetts] to protect, if not encourage, hospital employees who perceive and report detriments to patient care."[50] The majority opinion also noted that Wright's whistleblowing was internal, and held that internal whistleblowing " 'could not be the basis of a public policy exception to the at-will rule.' "[51]

[c]   Burdens of Proof

Both courts applying the common-law public policy tort and courts applying state whistleblowing statutes differ on the burden of proof an employee must meet. New York courts have interpreted that state's whistleblowing statute as requiring the employee to prove that the employee reported an employer's *actual violation* of a statute.[52] The Ohio whistleblowing statute, conversely, protects an employee who blows the whistle if the employee *reasonably believes* a statute has been violated.[53]

The Texas Court of Appeals case of *Johnston v. Del Mar Distributing Co.*[54] raises the issue of whether an employee is protected for inquiring as to whether or not conduct is illegal. Del Mar instructed employee Nancy Johnston to package a semi-automatic weapon for delivery by United Parcel Service, and to label the package "fishing gear." Johnston called the U.S. Treasury Bureau of Alcohol, Tobacco & Firearms to ask whether this was legal (it probably *was* legal, as Del Mar was not using the U.S. Postal Service and was not sending the package across state lines). A few days later, Johnston was fired. The Texas court held that she had a cause of action for wrongful discharge in violation of public policy. The court reasoned that the public policy tort protecting employees who refuse to perform illegal acts would be undermined if employees were not protected from inquiring whether a particular act is legal. Moreover, the court held that Johnston did not need to prove that sending the package would actually have been illegal; it would be sufficient for her to show that she had a reasonable, good-faith belief that sending the package would have been illegal.

[d]   The Sarbanes-Oxley Act of 2002

The Sarbanes-Oxley Act[55] prohibits publicly traded companies from retaliating against employees who provide information or assist in an investigation of fraud or a violation of federal securities law. The Act protects two types of activity. The first is providing information or assisting in an investigation regarding conduct which the employee reasonably believes constitutes a violation of several federal laws

---

[50] *Id.* at 1247 (Liacos, C.J., dissenting).

[51] *Id.* at 1245 (quoting Smith-Pfeffer v. Superintendent of the Walter E. Fernald State Sch., 533 N.E.2d 1368 (Mass. 1989)).

[52] Bordell v. Gen. Elec. Co., 667 N.E.2d 922, 923 (N.Y. 1996).

[53] O.R.C. § 4113.52(A)(3), (B).

[54] 776 S.W.2d 768 (Tex. App. 1989).

[55] 18 U.S.C. § 1514A(a); *see generally* Cherry, *supra* note 34, at 1064-67.

relating to fraud, such as securities fraud, wire fraud, mail fraud, and fraud against shareholders.[56] This type of whistleblowing activity, however, is protected only if the information or assistance is provided to a federal regulatory or law enforcement agency, to Congress, or internally to a supervisor or other management-level person; the whistleblowing is not protected if it is provided only to the press.[57] The second type of protected activity is filing, testifying, participating in, or otherwise assisting in a proceeding that relates to any rule or regulation of the Securities and Exchange Commission (SEC) or any other federal law that relates to fraud against shareholders.[58]

The whistleblowing part of the Sarbanes-Oxley Act is administered by the Department of Labor, which has delegated its authority to the Secretary of the Occupational Safety and Health Administration.[59] The Act initially adopted the procedures for beginning a whistleblowing action set forth in the Wendell H. Ford Aviation Investment and Reform Act, and parts were later amended in 2010 by the Dodd-Frank Act.[60]

To receive protection under the Sarbanes-Oxley Act, a whistleblowing employee must file a complaint within 180 days of the alleged retaliation. The complaint must make out a prima facie case of retaliation by establishing by a preponderance of evidence that (1) the whistleblower was engaged in activity protected by the Act, (2) the employer was aware of the protected activity, (3) the whistleblower suffered an adverse employment action, and (4) the whistleblower raised an inference that the protected activity was a contributing factor to the adverse employment action.[61] The employer, after receiving notice of the complaint, has twenty days to produce clear and convincing evidence of a non-retaliatory reason for the adverse employment action.[62] If the employer fails to do so, the Assistant Secretary of Labor will investigate the complaint and issue a reasonable cause finding within sixty days.[63] Either party may then request administrative hearings to review the Secretary's ruling, and may then appeal to a federal court of appeals.[64] If the Secretary fails to issue a ruling within 180 days after the initial filing of the complaint, the whistleblower may remove the complaint to federal district court.[65]

---

[56] 18 U.S.C. § 1514A(a).

[57] *Id.*

[58] *Id.*

[59] 29 C.F.R. § 1980.101; *see infra* § 15.02[F][1] (discussing adjudication procedures). Thus far, the Sarbanes-Oxley Act has failed to provide much protection for whistleblowers. *See* Richard Moberly, *Unfulfilled Expectations: An Empirical Analysis of Why Sarbanes-Oxley Whistleblowers Rarely Win*, 49 Wm. & Mary L. Rev. 65 (2007). However, recent changes in personnel and policy at OSHA and the panel that hears these cases, as well as amendments to the Act, may result in more protection for covered whistleblowers. *See* Richard Moberly, *Sarbanes-Oxley's Whistleblower Provisions — Ten Years Later*, 64 S.C. L. Rev. 1 (2012), *available at* http://papers.ssrn.com/sol3/papers.cfm?abstract_id=2064061.

[60] 49 U.S.C. § 42121(b); Pub. L. No. 111-203, 124 Stat. 1376 (2010).

[61] Welch v. Cardinal Bankshares Corp., 2003-SOX-15 (Dep't of Labor ALJ Jan. 28, 2004).

[62] 29 C.F.R. § 1980.104.

[63] *Id.* at § 1980.105.

[64] 18 U.S.C. § 1514A(a).

[65] *Id.*

The Act provides for "all relief necessary to make the employee whole" — including reinstatement, back pay, and attorneys fees — but does not include punitive damages.[66]

Under the Dodd-Frank Act, whistleblowers may also be able to receive a "bounty." If a whistleblower reports possible security fraud to the SEC and, after an investigation, the SEC imposes a fine or penalty of more than $1 million, then the whistleblower may be entitled to an amount equal to between 10 and 30% of the fine or penalty.[67]

[e]   Whistleblowing Lawyers

The Sarbanes-Oxley Act required the SEC to adopt rules of professional conduct for attorneys practicing before the Commission who might be aware of violations of securities law.[68] The SEC adopted rules *requiring* attorneys to report "evidence of a material violation" of securities law up the corporate ladder. Lawyers *may*, but are not required to, reveal confidential information to the SEC to the extent reasonably necessary to prevent a material violation "likely to cause substantial injury to the financial interest or property of the issuer [of corporate securities] or investors."[69]

However, outside the context of securities fraud, whistleblowing lawyers often receive considerably less protection. An example is *Balla v. Gambro, Inc.*[70] Roger Balla was an in-house counsel for Gambro, which distributed kidney dialysis equipment made by its parent company in Germany. On one shipment of equipment, the parent company sent Gambro a letter explaining, in "medical-ese," that the equipment did not work and would put patients at risk. Balla told Gambro to return the equipment to Germany because it did not comply with regulations of the United States Food & Drug Administration (FDA). Gambro decided to sell the equipment anyway. Balla protested to the company president and got fired. The next day, Balla called the FDA, which seized the equipment and later determined that it did not comply with FDA regulations.

Balla sued in Illinois state court for wrongful discharge in violation of public policy. Recall from § 6.02[A] above that Illinois defines public policy broadly as "what is right and just."[71] But for the fact that he was an attorney, Balla had a good case. He was in a jurisdiction that defined public policy broadly, he was complaining about a matter pertaining to public health and safety, he could arguably pigeonhole his claim as a refusal to commit an illegal act (i.e., to participate in the import and distribution of non-compliant medical equipment), and though he was an internal whistleblower when fired, he had threatened to go external and ultimately called the FDA the day after his termination.

---

[66] *Id.* § 1514A(c).

[67] *See* Moberly, *Ten Years Later, supra* note 59, at 45.

[68] 15 U.S.C. § 7245.

[69] 17 C.F.R. § 205.3.

[70] 584 N.E.2d 104 (Ill. 1991).

[71] Palmateer v. Int'l Harvester Co., 421 N.E.2d 876, 878 (Ill. 1981).

Nonetheless, the Illinois Supreme Court held that Balla had no claim. Allowing in-house attorneys to sue for wrongful discharge, the court reasoned, would discourage companies from revealing confidences to their attorneys in the course of obtaining legal advice, because companies would worry that those confidences would later be used against them in wrongful discharge suits. Besides, concluded the court, the public policy interest of protecting the health and safety of Illinoisans could be upheld without giving in-house attorneys a public policy tort, as attorneys have an ethical duty under the Illinois Code of Professional Responsibility to report a client's conduct that would result in death or serious bodily injury.

A dissent argued that the majority "ignore[d] reality"[72] when it concluded that ethical strictures alone would ensure that in-house attorneys always do the right thing by reporting client misconduct. In-house attorneys, noted the court, are dependent for their livelihood on their employer, and should be protected by the same public policy tort that protects other employees.

Courts in many states have rejected the rationale of *Balla* and have held that in-house attorneys can sue their employers for wrongful discharge in violation of public policy.[73] Many of these states, however, have rules of professional conduct permitting, but not requiring (as the Illinois Code did), an attorney to reveal client confidences that pose a danger to others.[74] These ethical rules presumably exert a weaker pressure on attorneys to report client misconduct, making the rationale for giving attorneys a tort for wrongful discharge that much stronger.

§ 5.03 INTENTIONAL INFLICTION OF EMOTIONAL DISTRESS

[A] Introduction

Another tort commonly brought in employment cases is the tort for intentional infliction of emotional distress (IIED), sometimes called the "tort of outrage." Many employment statutes and torts permit an employee to recover damages for emotional distress the employee suffers when the employer acts wrongfully, by, for example, firing the employee in violation of public policy or discriminating against the employee on the basis of race. Here, however, "emotional distress" is being used to describe a stand-alone tort that an employer may commit even if the employer's conduct otherwise is entirely lawful. In a discharge case of an at-will employee, for example, the employee might sue the employer for IIED not because the employer fired the employee for an impermissible reason, but because the employer fired the employee in an impermissible manner.

---

[72] *Balla*, 584 N.E.2d at 113 (Freeman, J., dissenting).

[73] *See, e.g.*, Crews v. Buckman Labs. Int'l, Inc., 78 S.W.3d 852 (Tenn. 2002); Burkhart v. Semitool, Inc., 5 P.3d 1031 (Mont. 2000); GTE Prods. Corp. v. Stewart, 653 N.E.2d 161 (Mass. 1995); Gen. Dynamics Corp. v. Rose, 876 P.2d 487 (Cal. 1994).

[74] *See, e.g.*, RESTATEMENT OF THE LAW GOVERNING LAWYERS §§ 66, 67 (2000); MODEL RULES OF PROFESSIONAL CONDUCT Rule 1.6(b)(1).

An example is *Agis v. Howard Johnson Co.*[75] In Agis, a hotel manager, suspecting employee theft in the hotel restaurant, called a meeting of the wait staff and threatened to fire them in alphabetical order until someone identified the thief. Not surprisingly, plaintiff Debra Agis was first in line to be fired under this procedure. After her firing, she sued for IIED. Though the trial court dismissed her IIED claim, the Massachusetts Supreme Court reversed.

The difficult part of the *Agis* case is identifying what, precisely, the employer did wrong. Agis was an at-will employee, so the employer had every legal right to fire her for no reason or even a nonsensical reason — and here the employer had an arguably legitimate reason (deterring theft). If the court gave Agis a tort claim based merely upon the *fact* of her discharge, that tort claim would be inconsistent with the doctrine of employment at will. Some courts have applied the tort of emotional distress to employers based on the *manner* in which the employer discharges an employee — parading a discharged employee out the door generally is not a good idea. Perhaps the *Agis* court concluded that the public and alphabetical manner of discharge was a calculated effort to induce employees to squeal or confess — and that was what put the hotel manager "over the line."

[B]   Elements

The *Agis* court cited the Restatement for the four elements of the emotional distress tort:

1. The defendant's conduct was *extreme and outrageous*, beyond all bounds of human decency,

2. The defendant *intended* to cause severe emotional distress to the plaintiff, or acted in disregard of a high probability that its conduct would inflict such harm,

3. The defendant proximately *caused* emotional distress to the plaintiff, and

4. The emotional distress was so *severe* that no reasonable person could be expected to endure it.[76]

A plaintiff's success on an emotional distress tort usually hinges on his or her ability to prove the first and fourth elements.

[1]   Extreme and Outrageous Conduct

The Restatement imposes an extremely high threshold for this element of the tort. The Restatement explains that conduct is considered extreme and outrageous "only where the conduct has been so outrageous in character, and so extreme in degree, so as to go beyond all possible bounds of decency, and to be regarded as atrocious, and utterly intolerable in a civilized community."[77] Courts, no doubt loath to encourage judicial resolution of every petty workplace dispute, have embraced

---

[75] 355 N.E.2d 315 (Mass. 1976).

[76] RESTATEMENT (SECOND) OF TORTS § 46.

[77] *Id.* cmt. d (1965).

this definition.[78] Many emotional distress torts are dismissed on summary judg-ment; as one court has put it, "it is extremely rare to find conduct in the employment context that will rise to the level of outrageousness necessary to provide a basis for the tort."[79] Part of the problem is that there are "no legal standards by which judges and juries can distinguish conduct which is extreme and outrageous from conduct which is not. [O]utrageousness is entirely in the eye of the beholder."[80]

Nonetheless, despite the high standards and definitional problems, some cases are easier than others. For instance, in *Bodewig v. K-Mart, Inc.*,[81] a customer accused a "shy, modest, young woman"[82] working as a cashier of theft. The male assistant manager strip-searched the cashier in the customer's presence. The cashier sued K-Mart, the assistant manager, and the customer for intentional infliction of emotional distress. Though the trial court dismissed the claims, the Oregon Court of Appeals reversed. Regarding K-Mart and the assistant manager, the court held that a jury could find it outrageous that the manager, "after concluding that [the cashier] did not take the customer's money, put her through the degrading and humiliating experience of submitting to a strip search in order to satisfy the customer, who was not only acting unreasonably, but was creating a commotion in the store."[83] Regarding the customer, the court held that a jury could find it outrageous that the customer's "entire course of conduct was intended to embarrass and humiliate [the cashier] in order to coerce her into giving [the customer the money], whether rightfully hers or not."[84]

An issue arising in many emotional distress cases is whether it should be easier, or harder, to state an emotional distress claim against an employer where there is a special relationship as opposed to against a stranger. The *Bodewig* court held that it should be easier.[85] One court has explained that, as opposed to most casual and temporary relationships, the workplace environment provides a captive victim and the opportunity for prolonged abuse.[86] Other courts, however, have suggested that the workplace is not a context deserving of enhanced tort protection, but rather a harsh environment in which employees should learn to tolerate abuse.[87]

---

[78] *See generally* David C. Yamada, *The Phenomenon of "Workplace Bullying" and the Need for Status-Blind Hostile Work Environment Protection*, 88 GEO. L.J. 475, 493-95 (2000).

[79] Hare v. H&R Indus., 67 Fed. Appx. 114, 2003 U.S. App. LEXIS 10304, *15 (3d Cir. 2003).

[80] Wornick Co. v. Casas, 856 S.W.2d 732, 736 (Tex. 1993) (Hecht, J., concurring).

[81] 635 P.2d 657 (Or. App. 1981).

[82] *Id.* at 662.

[83] *Id.* at 661.

[84] *Id.*

[85] The *Bodewig* court held that the cashier had to show that the customer *intended to cause emotional distress*, but that the cashier had to show only that the assistant manager (and, vicariously, K-Mart) *caused* the emotional distress. *Cf.* RESTATEMENT (SECOND) OF TORTS § 48 (1965) (lowering the threshold of outrageousness when the plaintiff is in a special relationship with the defendant).

[86] *See* Frank J. Cavico, *The Tort of Intentional Infliction of Emotional Distress in the Private Employment Sector*, 21 HOFSTRA LAB. & EMP. L.J. 109, 115-16 (2003) (citing GTE S.W., Inc. v. Bruce, 998 S.W.2d 605, 612 (Tex. 1999)).

[87] *See, e.g.*, Ky. Fried Chicken Nat'l Mgmt. Co. v. Weathersby, 607 A.2d 8 (Md. 1992).

[2]   Severe Emotional Distress

The other oft-disputed element of the emotional distress tort is the requirement that the plaintiff suffered severe emotional distress. Fright, embarrassment, frustration, humiliation, hurt feelings, worry, anxiety, vexation, anger, headaches, and insomnia are insufficient[88] — there must be more. Though physical manifestations of emotional injury are not required,[89] they certainly help. Similarly, though the *Bodewig* court found it sufficient that the cashier said she "had two or three sleepless nights, cried a lot and still gets nervous when she thinks about the incident,"[90] other courts have expressly required expert testimony to establish the requisite level of distress.[91]

---

[88] *See, e.g.*, Leavitt v. Wal-Mart Stores, Inc., 238 F. Supp. 2d 313 (D. Me. 2003); Jackson v. Creditwatch, Inc., 84 S.W.3d 397 (Tex. App. 2002).

[89] W. Page Keeton et al., Prosser and Keeton on the Law of Torts § 12, at 64 (5th ed. 1984).

[90] Bodewig v. K-Mart, Inc., 635 P.2d 657, 662 (Or. App. 1981).

[91] *See, e.g.*, Comstock v. Consumers Mkt., 953 F. Supp. 1096 (W.D. Mo. 1996).

Chapter 6

GOOD FAITH AND FAIR DEALING

SYNOPSIS

§ 6.01 Implied Covenant of Good Faith and Fair Dealing
    [A] Good Faith Not Applicable to At-Will Employment
    [B] Good Faith Protects Earned Benefits
    [C] Good Faith Requires General Fairness
    [D] The Restatement Approach

§ 6.01 IMPLIED COVENANT OF GOOD FAITH AND FAIR DEALING

The Uniform Commercial Code, Section 1-203, states: "Every contract or duty within this Act imposes an obligation of good faith in its performance or enforcement." Similarly, the Restatement (Second) of Contracts, Section 205, states: "Every contract imposes upon each party an obligation of good faith and fair dealing in its performance and its enforcement."

[A] Good Faith Not Applicable to At-Will Employment

Despite these seemingly universal statements, many courts have held that the implied covenant of good faith does not apply to at-will employment. An example is *Murphy v. American Home Products Corp.*,[1] in which accountant Joseph Murphy claimed that he was fired because he had told the board that company officers were engaging in accounting improprieties. Murphy argued that the covenant of good faith and fair dealing should be implied into his at-will employment contract, and that because it was part of his job to report accounting improprieties, his discharge violated the covenant. The New York Court of Appeals,[2] however, refused to recognize an implied covenant of good faith in the at-will relationship:

> In the context of [at-will] employment it would be incongruous to say that an inference may be drawn that the employer impliedly agreed to a provision which would be destructive of his right of termination. The parties may by express agreement limit or restrict the employer's right of discharge, but to imply such a limitation from the existence of an

---

[1] 448 N.E.2d 86 (N.Y. 1983).

[2] The New York Court of Appeals is the state court of highest authority, equivalent to the supreme court of most other states.

unrestricted right would be internally inconsistent.[3]

The court concluded that any such limitation on the employer's right to fire should come from the legislature, not the courts.[4] The dissent, however, pointed out that the at-will doctrine is itself a judicial creation, so there is no reason it cannot yield to the judicial doctrine (derived from the Uniform Commercial Code and the Restatement) implying the covenant of good faith into all contracts.

[B]   Good Faith Protects Earned Benefits

Other courts have implied the covenant of good faith into at-will employment, but have defined good faith narrowly to mean that employers cannot expropriate benefits already earned by employees. An example of this approach is *Fortune v. National Cash Register Co.*[5] Orville Fortune was a sixty-one-year-old salesperson for NCR. Fortune's employment contract specified that he was employed at-will, and that he would receive a fixed salary plus a commission on all sales made within his assigned territory. He would receive seventy-five percent of the commission if the territory was assigned to him on the date of the order, twenty-five percent if the territory was assigned to him on the date of delivery, and one hundred percent if the territory was assigned to him on both dates.

NCR made a five-million dollar sale within his assigned territory. This entitled him to seventy-five percent of the commission, which he received. However, the next business day after the sale, NCR fired Fortune. NCR later rescinded the discharge and re-assigned Fortune; this had the effect of removing from Fortune the territory in which he had made the big sale. Fortune never received the remaining twenty-five percent of the commission — NCR instead paid it to an installations person. Eighteen months later, NCR fired Fortune, and Fortune sued for the remaining twenty-five percent of the commission.

Because Fortune had not been assigned to the pertinent sales territory on the date of delivery, his contract did not entitle him to the twenty-five percent commission. He therefore could not recover under a straightforward breach of contract theory. However, the trial court submitted to the jury the issue of whether NCR had fired Fortune in bad faith to disqualify him from the twenty-five percent commission. The jury found that NCR had acted in bad faith, and awarded damages. The Massachusetts Supreme Court affirmed. The court held that "where, as here, commissions are to be paid for work performed by the employee, the employer's decision to terminate its at-will employee should be made in good faith."[6] Such good faith is lacking, the court found, where termination is motivated by the employer's desire to pay the employee as little of the commission as possible.[7]

---

[3] *Murphy*, 448 N.E.2d at 91.

[4] *Id.* at 92 n.2.

[5] 364 N.E.2d 1251 (Mass. 1977).

[6] *Id.* at 1256.

[7] The *Fortune* case is a bit unusual on this point, since NCR did pay the full commission amount — just not to Fortune.

Other courts have similarly applied the covenant of good faith and fair dealing to the at-will employment relationship in order to protect benefits previously earned by employees. Such accrued benefits have included not only commissions due, but also wages, profit sharing, pension benefits, sick pay, and severance benefits.[8]

[C]   Good Faith Requires General Fairness

A handful of courts have interpreted good faith in the at-will context much more broadly. For example, in *Monge v. Beebe Rubber Co.*,[9] an employer fired its employee because she refused to date her foreman. The New Hampshire Supreme Court held that a "termination by the employer of a contract of employment at will which is motivated by bad faith or malice or based on retaliation is not in the best interests of the economic system or the public good and constitutes a breach of the employment contract."[10]

Another example is *Metcalf v. Intermountain Gas Co.*[11] Armida Metcalf had health problems that required her to miss work for eight weeks. She took sick leave that she had accrued under the employer's policy, then sought to return to work. The employer, however, reduced her schedule to two hours a day, prompting her resignation. The Idaho Supreme Court held that Metcalf had a valid claim for breach of the implied covenant of good faith and fair dealing, reasoning that "[a]ny action by either party which violates, nullifies or significantly impairs any benefit of the employment contract is a violation of the implied-in-law covenant."[12] However, the court attempted to narrow its holding by rejecting "the 'amorphous concept of bad faith' as the standard for determining whether the covenant has been breached."

Whether the court effectively rejected this broader standard is open for question. Metcalf received the sick leave she had accrued; unlike Fortune, Metcalf received the benefit she had earned. Once she received that benefit, her employment was at will. Thus, the court's holding that she had a claim for bad-faith discharge necessarily imposed a limitation on the employer's ability to discharge at will. The court seems to have used good faith to imply into the employment relationship a promise that the employer would not retaliate against Metcalf for claiming the sick leave she had accrued.

Courts generally have rejected the application of tort remedies to employer violations of the implied duty of good faith and fair dealing. Instead, courts permit only contract damages.[13]

---

[8] *See* Susan Dana, *The Covenant of Good Faith and Fair Dealing: A Concentrated Effort to Clarify the Imprecision of its Applicability in Employment Law*, 5 Transactions: Tenn. J. Bus. L. 291, 300-02 nn.57-63 (2004) (collecting cases).

[9] 316 A.2d 549 (N.H. 1974).

[10] *Id.* at 551.

[11] 778 P.2d 744 (Idaho 1989).

[12] *Id.* at 749.

[13] *See, e.g.*, Foley v. Interactive Data Corp., 765 P.2d 373 (Cal. 1988).

[D] The Restatement Approach

The Restatement recognizes a duty of good faith. The RESTATEMENT (THIRD) OF EMPLOYMENT LAW § 2.06 (2009) provides: "Each party to an employment contract, including at-will employment, owes a nonwaivable duty of good faith and fair dealing to each other party, which includes an agreement by each not to hinder the other's performance under, or to deprive the other of the benefit of, the contract." Examples of bad faith include firing an employee to prevent the vesting or accruing of an employee right or benefit, and retaliating against an employee for acting in accordance with the employment contract or performing a legal obligation.

Chapter 7

THE FUTURE OF WRONGFUL DISCHARGE LAW

§ 7.01 A BRIEF REPRISE OF THE AT-WILL RULE

As described in Chapter 1,[1] the employment at-will rule reached its zenith in the early 1900s when the Supreme Court, in cases such as *Lochner v. New York*,[2] seemed to constitutionalize the rule. Since then, however, one exception after another has chipped away at the at-will rule.

This erosion of the at-will rule commenced during the Depression when Congress recognized that the right of employees to form labor unions would be meaningless if pro-union employees could be fired before they could organize a workplace. As a result, Congress in the National Labor Relations Act (NLRA)[3] prohibited employers from firing employees for engaging in concerted activity.[4] Some thirty years later, Congress passed Title VII of the Civil Rights Act of 1964 (Title VII),[5] prohibiting discrimination (including discharge) on the basis of race, color, religion, sex, and national origin. Since then, Congress had added age, disability, and pregnancy to the list.[6] In May 2008, President George W. Bush signed into law the Genetic Information Nondiscrimination Act ("GINA"), which prohibits employers from discriminating on the basis of an employee's genetic information.[7]

State legislatures by and large have kept pace with, or exceeded, their federal counterpart. All states, except three, have enacted general antidiscrimination laws

---

[1] *See supra* § 1.01[A].

[2] 198 U.S. 45 (1905).

[3] 29 U.S.C. §§ 151-163.

[4] 29 U.S.C. §§ 158(a)(1), (3).

[5] 42 U.S.C. § 2000e-2.

[6] 29 U.S.C. §§ 621-34. (age); 42 U.S.C. §§ 12101-12213 (disability). Pregnancy was added via an amendment to Title VII.

[7] Pub. L. No. 110-233, 122 Stat. 881 (2008) (codified in scattered sections of 26, 29, and 42 U.S.C.).

roughly parallel to the federal antidiscrimination laws. Many of these state laws forbid discrimination on grounds not covered by the federal laws, such as sexual orientation[8] and transgendered status.[9] Both federal and state legislatures also have enacted a panoply of statutes making it illegal to fire an employee for whistleblowing[10] or for engaging in lawful off-duty conduct.[11]

At the same time, state courts have further eroded the at-will rule by applying contract and tort principles to restrict employers' ability to fire employees. Courts, both federal and state, are far more likely today than they were forty years ago to enforce employer promises made orally[12] or in employee handbooks,[13] and to apply the covenant of good faith and fair dealing[14] to employee discharges. Courts also are more likely to apply tort doctrines like wrongful discharge in violation of public policy,[15] and intentional infliction of emotional distress,[16] to employee discharges and other adverse employment actions.

The resulting mélange of exceptions to the general rule of at-will employment is easy to critique, because it satisfies no one.[17] Employees live in perpetual fear that their lives will be turned upside down by an unexpected discharge or layoff. Employers, at perpetual risk of being sued by discharged or laid-off employees, must undertake expensive prophylactic measures such as meticulous documentation of every minor workplace transgression.

§ 7.02 DEFENDING THE AT-WILL RULE

Legal scholars such as Professor Richard Epstein[18] have defended the at-will rule on both libertarian and utilitarian[19] grounds. The libertarian defense centers on freedom of contract, and considers labor just another commodity subject to all the usual free-market rules of contract:

> So long as it is accepted that the employer is the full owner of his capital and the employee is the full owner of his labor, the two are free to exchange on whatever terms and conditions they see fit. . . . If the arrangement turns out to be disastrous to one side, that is his problem; and once

---

[8] *See, e.g.,* MINN. STAT. § 363A.08.

[9] N.J. STAT. ANN. § 10:5.

[10] *See supra* § 5.02[B][4].

[11] *See infra* § 9.03[A].

[12] *See supra* § 4.01[B].

[13] *See supra* § 4.04.

[14] *See supra* Chapter 6.

[15] *See supra* § 5.02.

[16] *See supra* § 5.03.

[17] Daniel J. Libenson, *Leasing Human Capital: Toward a New Foundation for Employment Termination Law*, 27 BERKELEY J. EMP. & LAB. L. 111, 112 (2006).

[18] Richard A. Epstein, *In Defense of the Contract At Will*, 51 U. CHI. L. REV. 947 (1984).

[19] Libertarians are concerned primarily with the maximization of personal liberties; utilitarians are concerned primarily with the aggregate maximization of wealth and happiness.

cautioned, he probably will not make that same mistake a second time.[20]

The libertarian defense also invokes the rights of private property and freedom of association: because the employer owns the workplace, the employer has the right to control who is in it; because the employer has a right to associate with whom it wants, the employer has the right to disassociate by discharge.[21] Professor Richard Power has analogized the employment relationship to a marriage: when one party wants out, the relationship cannot function effectively and the parties should be given a no-fault divorce.[22]

The utilitarian defense of the at-will rule emphasizes its efficiency advantages. Monitoring employees is difficult and expensive; fear of imminent discharge motivates employees to work as hard as they can.[23] The at-will rule is also cheap to administer, Epstein explains, whereas a just-cause rule would breed expensive litigation.[24] Moreover, the utilitarian defense sees little benefit to a just-cause rule, as good employees rarely get fired — the cost of hiring and training new employees, and the risk that other good employees will leave for a more even-handed employer, keep employers on their best behavior.[25] And even on the rare occasion that a good employee *does* get fired, that employee has nothing to worry about because he or she will have little difficulty finding a new job.[26] Epstein's is a very Panglossian world.[27]

§ 7.03   CRITIQUING THE AT-WILL RULE

There has been no shortage in recent years of academics willing to critique that at-will rule. From a libertarian perspective, Professor Lawrence Blades pointed out back in 1967,[28] followed by Professor Clyde Summers seven years later,[29] that employees' "freedom" of contract is cabined more than a little by their woefully insignificant bargaining power. Employees generally take whatever employers offer — including at-will employment — because employees have no meaningful alternative. Summers embraced the libertarian regard for property rights, but argued that employees should have a property right in their jobs.[30]

---

[20] Epstein, *supra* note 18, at 955.

[21] Libenson, *supra* note 17, at 119 (describing, but not defending, this argument).

[22] Richard W. Power, *A Defense of the Employment at Will Rule*, 27 ST. LOUIS U. L.J. 881, 888-89 (1983).

[23] Epstein, *supra* note 18, at 964-65.

[24] *Id.* at 970.

[25] *Id.*

[26] *Id.*

[27] In Voltaire's *Candide*, Dr. Pangloss's constant justification for the status quo is that he is living in the "best of all possible worlds." VOLTAIRE, CANDIDE 12 (Henry Morley & Lauren Walsh, transl., Barnes & Noble Classics 2003) (1759); *cf.* Pollyanna, Barney, etc.

[28] Lawrence Blades, *Employment at Will vs. Individual Freedom: On Limiting the Abusive Exercise of Employer Power*, 67 COLUM. L. REV. 1404 (1967).

[29] Clyde W. Summers, *Individual Protection Against Unjust Dismissal: Time for a Statute*, 62 VA. L. REV. 481 (1976).

[30] *Id.* at 506; *see also* Jack M. Beermann & Joseph William Singer, *Baseline Questions in Legal*

On the utilitarian side, Professor Theodore St. Antoine has argued that Epstein's calculus ignores the enormous costs to employees who lose their jobs, including "increases in cardiovascular deaths, suicides, mental breakdowns, alcoholism, ulcers, diabetes, spouse and child abuse, impaired social relationships, and various other diseases and abnormal conditions."[31] Professor Arthur Leonard similarly emphasized the central role that employment plays in people's lives.[32] Professor Daniel Libenson has written that defenders of the at-will rule "have little interest in the human dimension of the employment relationship or the capacity of its termination to harm the human dignity of employees."[33] Dean Stewart Schwab, who is hardly antagonistic to the law-and-economics movement, has argued that wrongful discharge law is needed to protect employees who are more heavily invested in their job than their employer is — particularly early-career employees who may have moved to take the job or quit a previous job in reliance on a job offer, and late-career employees who are about to retire.[34] Professor Pauline Kim's empirical work, demonstrating that most at-will employees mistakenly believe they can be fired only for cause,[35] calls into question Epstein's assumption that if employees *really* wanted for-cause employment they would contract with employers for it.

§ 7.04 ALTERNATIVES TO THE AT-WILL RULE

The list of viable alternatives to the at-will rule, unfortunately, is much shorter than the list of criticisms. Most have involved some variation on the theme of just-cause employment, perhaps after a limited probationary period (a temporary period during which the employee would be at-will).[36] The Model Employment Termination Act (META),[37] proposed in 1991, (1) creates a good-cause standard that applies to employees who have served longer than a year, (2) preempts most common law claims, and (3) establishes reinstatement as the preferred remedy. META, however, has been much-criticized by the legal academy,[38] and not a single state has adopted it. Similarly, although in 1987 Montana legislatively abandoned

---

Reasoning: The Example of Property in Jobs, 23 GA. L. REV. 911 (1989); Donald H.J. Hermann & Yvonne S. Sor, *Property Rights in One's Job: The Case for Limiting Employment-at-Will*, 24 ARIZ. L. REV. 763, 767-68 (1982). As discussed *supra* at § 4.03, some public employees have a property right in their jobs.

[31] Theodore J. St. Antoine, *A Seed Germinates: Unjust Discharge Reform Heads Toward Full Flower*, 67 NEB. L. REV. 56, 67 (1988).

[32] Arthur S. Leonard, *A New Common Law of Employment Termination*, 66 N.C. L. REV. 631, 675 (1988).

[33] Libenson, *supra* note 17, at 118.

[34] Stewart J. Schwab, *Life-Cycle Justice: Accommodating Just Cause and Employment at Will*, 92 MICH. L. REV. 8 (1993).

[35] Pauline Kim, *Bargaining with Imperfect Information: A Study of Worker Perceptions of Legal Protection in an At-Will World*, 83 CORNELL L. REV. 105 (1997).

[36] *See, e.g.*, Summers, *supra* note 29, at 524-25.

[37] 7 A.U.L.A. 421 (1991).

[38] *See, e.g.*, Kenneth A. Sprang, *Beware the Toothless Tiger: A Critique of the Model Employment Termination Act*, 43 AM. U. L. REV. 849 (1994).

the at-will rule in favor of a good-cause standard,[39] no other state has done so.

The failure of other states to replicate META or the Montana statute illustrates the political difficulty of replacing the at-will rule with just-cause employment. There are other issues as well. First, if employees value just-cause employment so highly, why don't they organize into a union, as nearly every collective bargaining agreement contains a just-cause employment provision? Second, is there a fair and efficient way to adjudicate the bevy of cases that would arise under a just-cause regime?

A few alternatives have been proposed. Professor Leonard has suggested "entitl[ing] all discharged employees to an explanation related to their work performance or economic needs of the employer."[40] Professor Libenson has suggested analogizing the employment relationship to that of a lessor and a lessee (in which the lessor owes a duty of good care to the lessee), and requiring employers to give "sufficient pretermination notice" to allow discharged employees to find comparable new jobs before losing the old ones.[41] Professor Robert Bird has proposed treating employment as a relational contract, which among other things would effectively expand the implied-contract doctrine. Professor Rachel Arnow-Richman has proposed the adoption of a universal "pay-or-play" system of employment termination under which, absent serious misconduct, employers would be required to provide advance notice of termination or offer wages and benefits for the duration of the notice period.[42] Finally, Professors Zev Eigen, Nicholas Menillo, and David Sherwyn have suggested a discharge standard in which employees may be discharged only for cause or upon the payment of severance, and a two-step grievance procedure that includes (1) meetings with the decision maker and the employer's director of human resources and (2) informal adjudication by administrative law judges.[43] [44] None of these proposals, however, have been adopted anywhere.

§ 7.05   DISMISSAL STANDARDS IN OTHER COUNTRIES

Although a detailed comparison of the American at-will rule with the dismissal standards in other countries is beyond the scope of this book,[45] suffice it to say that the United States is an international outlier. Most industrialized countries impose either a substantive standard akin to just-cause employment or elaborate procedural mechanisms, or both, as a prerequisite to discharge.

---

[39] Mont. Code Ann. § 39-2-901.

[40] Leonard, *supra* note 32, at 680.

[41] Libenson, *supra* note 17, at 114.

[42] Rachel Arnow-Richman, *Just Notice: Re-Reforming Employment at Will*, 58 UCLA L. Rev. 1 (2010).

[43] Zev J. Eigen, Nicholas F. Menillo, & David Sherwyn, *Shifting the Paradigm of the Debate: A Proposal to Eliminate At-Will Employment and Implement a "Mandatory Arbitration Act,"* 87 Ind. L.J. 271 (2012).

[44] Robert C. Bird, *Employment as a Relational Contract*, 8 U. Pa. J. Lab. & Emp. L. 149 (2005).

[45] *See generally* Roger Blanpain et al., The Global Workplace: International and Comparative Employment Law (2d ed. 2012) (describing workplace law in several countries).

In 1982, the International Labour Organization (ILO) adopted the Termination of Employment Convention.[46] This Convention provides that the "employment of a worker shall not be terminated unless there is a valid reason for such termination connected with the capacity or conduct of the worker or based on the operational requirements of the undertaking, establishment or service."[47] It also establishes procedural protections. An employer may not discharge an employee for conduct or performance reasons without first giving the employee the opportunity to defend himself.[48] An employee who believes she or he has been unjustifiably discharged is entitled to appeal to an impartial body such as a court, labor tribunal, or arbitrator.[49]

Thirty-six nations had signed this Convention as of summer 2012. The United States has not. Thus, it appears that the at-will rule will be the baseline legal rule in the United States for the foreseeable future, but that the rule will be subject to an ever-increasing array of exceptions.

---

[46] INTERNATIONAL LABOUR ORGANIZATION, TERMINATION OF EMPLOYMENT CONVENTION 158, art. 4.

[47] *Id.* at art. 4.

[48] *Id.* at art. 7.

[49] *Id.* at art. 8.

Chapter 8

EMPLOYEE FREE SPEECH AND POLITICAL PROTECTIONS

§ 8.01   INTRODUCTION

One of the most common misconceptions in employment law is that all workers enjoy federal constitutional protections for their speech and expression in the workplace. They do not. Similarly, by and large, American employees do not have constitutional protections based upon the Equal Protection Clause or how they choose to affiliate politically. In general, only where state action exists, as in the public employment context, do employees have Fourteenth and First Amendment protections.

Consequently, in discussing the equal protection, political affiliation, and speech rights of American workers, this Chapter is necessarily divided into the public workplace and the private workplace. As will be discussed below, private sector employees, unlike public employees, must rely upon non-constitutional, statutory, and tort-based theories for speech, conduct, and political protections. If they exist at all, such protections can be found in federal and state statutory schemes and common law doctrines.

§ 8.02   THE PUBLIC WORKPLACE

As a general matter, a public employer may not take adverse employment action against a public employee on a basis that infringes his or her constitutional rights.[1] Thus, although many public employees continue to be at-will employees,[2] they cannot be terminated, demoted, transferred, or subjected to other adverse employment actions, for exercising their constitutional rights. This underlying principle, sometimes referred to as the doctrine of unconstitutional conditions,[3] is developed below in the review of the equal protection case of *Engquist v. Oregon Department of Agriculture*,[4] the political affiliation case of *Rutan v. Republican Party*,[5] and the free speech case of *Garcetti v. Ceballos*.[6]

But before discussing those important constitutional cases, it is first necessary to note that public employees may also have a property interest in their jobs protected by the procedural component of the due process clause of the Fifth and Fourteen Amendments of the United States Constitution. Although a property interest in one's job does not guarantee continued employment, it does require the government employer to provide certain procedural protections before depriving the employee of the property interest associated with his or her employment.[7] So, in addition to the substantive protections provided for political, conduct-based, and expressive activity, the constitution provides public employees with important procedural rights that private sector employees, by and large, do not have.[8]

Moreover, public employees might enjoy more practically significant statutory employment rights under various civil service laws — a topic not covered in this

---

[1] Perry v. Sindermann, 408 U.S. 593, 597 (1972).

[2] However, a large number of public employees also have just cause protection under either a collective bargaining contract or civil service laws. For instance, in 2011, 37.0% of public sector employees were union members, more than five times higher the percentage than that of private-sector workers (6.9%) in the United States. *See* U.S. Department of Labor, Bureau of Labor Statistics, *Economics News Release: Union Member Summary* (Jan. 27, 2012), *available at* http://www.bls.gov/news.release/union2.nr0.htm.

[3] The doctrine of unconstitutional conditions in public employment law, and its current legal status, is discussed in some detail in Paul M. Secunda, *Neoformalism and the Reemergence of the Right-Privilege Distinction in Public Employment Law*, 48 SAN DIEGO L. REV. 907 (2011).

[4] 553 U.S. 591 (2008).

[5] 497 U.S. 62 (1990).

[6] 547 U.S. 410 (2006).

[7] *See* Cleveland Bd. of Educ. v. Loudermill, 470 U.S. 532, 541-42 (1985) (entitling public employee with property interest in his job to be notified of the charges against him and an opportunity to respond before being terminated). Generally, a property interest in public employment is found where one has a legitimate expectation of continued employment in his or her job based on a statute, ordinance, or an express or implied contract between the parties. *See Perry*, 408 U.S. at 601. Even without a property interest, under a stigma-plus claim, a public employee may not be deprived of a liberty interest by being stigmatized by his employer through publication of adverse employment information without first being provided with a name-clearing hearing. *See* Bd. of Regents of State Colls. v. Roth, 408 U.S. 564, 573 (1972); *see also* Paul v. Davis, 424 U.S. 693, 701 (1976); Wisconsin v. Constantineau, 400 U.S. 433, 437 (1971).

[8] If private sector employees have similar procedural protections, it would most likely be as a result of provisions in an individual employment agreement or employee handbook. *See supra* Chapter 6.

book in any detail.[9] At the same time, there are other statutory schemes, such as the Hatch Act and its state law analogues, which restrict, to varying degrees, public employees' political activities.[10]

[A] Public Employee Equal Protection Claims

Engquist v. Oregon Department of Agriculture involves a constitutional interpretation of equal protection doctrine in the public employment law context. In a closely divided Supreme Court case, the Court held that a "class-of-one" equal protection claim does not exist for public employees.[11] The facts of the case were fairly straightforward and common: a personality dispute existed between a worker and new supervisor, who replaced the agreeable previous supervisor, in a public-sector workplace. In addition to other constitutional and statutory claims, the employee sued her state employer under the Equal Protection Clause, arguing that her termination was for "arbitrary, vindictive, and malicious reasons." Put differently, even under constitutionally based rational basis review, the employee alleged that the State's adverse employment actions were without any rational basis and solely for arbitrary reasons and thus, violated her rights under the Equal Protection Clause. The jury agreed with the employee on this class-of-one equal protection claim and she was initially awarded $175,000 in compensatory damages and $250,000 in punitive damages.

The Supreme Court overturned the jury's verdict, finding that public employees cannot bring such class-of-one claims. It reasoned that the class-of-one theory was simply a "poor fit" for public employment and public employees only had equal protection claims if class-based discrimination existed (for instance, where a government employer refused to hire women, blacks, or Jews for certain jobs). The

---

[9] At the federal level, for instance, the Civil Service Reform Act of 1978, Pub. L. No. 95-454, 92 Stat. 1111 (1978) (codified in scattered sections of 5 U.S.C.), abolished the previous United States Civil Service Commission and in its place established the Office of Personnel Management (OPM) to deal with administrative and management issues, a Merit System Protection Board (MSPB) to review personnel decisions by individual federal agencies, and a Senior Executive Service (SES) to handle issues surrounding high-level, non-political appointments. A more thorough analysis of these federal civil service laws, and their relation to federal employees' constitutional rights under the First Amendment, can be found in Paul M. Secunda, *Whither the Pickering Rights of Federal Employees?*, 79 U. Colo. L. Rev. 1101 (2008).

[10] The Hatch Act, 5 U.S.C. §§ 1501-1508, 7321-7327, was passed in 1939 to fight political corruption among federal civil service workers by severely restricting their political activities. Many states passed similar laws. These prohibitions were loosened as a result of the Hatch Act Reform Amendments of 1993, Pub. L. No. 103-94, 107 Stat. 1001 (1993), and now federal employees can more actively participate in political campaigns, although not run for public office or engage in political activity during work. The Merit Systems Protection Board and its Office of Special Counsel are responsible for enforcement of the Hatch Act. A new Hatch Act reform bill, the Hatch Act Modernization Act of 2012 (S. 2170), would allow for a wider range of penalties when violations are found. As of the summer of 2012, it is still being considered by both houses of Congress.

[11] For those most familiar with reading about equal protection cases involving heightened judicial scrutiny because of a suspect classification or fundamental right, it might be surprising to learn that a whole field of equal protection jurisprudence — the so-called class-of-one cases — has existed for a long time outside of the public employment context. In such cases, the Court has historically recognized that the Equal Protection Clause protects against government action which "irrationally single[s] out . . . [a] 'class of one.' " *See* Village of Willowbrook v. Olech, 528 U.S. 562, 563 (2000).

majority opinion also based its holding on the need for greater latitude for the government in its employment role to maintain control and discipline in the workplace. Lastly, the Court argued that permitting rational basis review under a class-of-one equal protection theory would conflict with the general presumption of at-will employment in the United States (even though, as pointed out above, most public employees have just cause protections as union members or under civil service laws).

On the other hand, the dissenting opinion by Justice Stevens maintained that no compelling reasons existed for not applying the usual rational basis review to employment actions by the government and for "carv[ing out] a novel exception out of state employees' constitutional rights."[12] More specifically, he observed that, "[u]nless state action that intentionally singles out an individual, or a class of individuals, for adverse treatment is supported by some rational justification, it violates the Fourteenth Amendment's command that no State shall 'deny to any person within its jurisdiction the equal protection of the laws.' "[13] He therefore took issue with the majority's idea that public employment decisions are somehow special in being inherently discretionary and therefore, a poor fit for class-of-one treatment. Finally, Stevens also pointed out that although employment at will was the widespread practice in the United States in the 1890s, it has not been so widely followed in the public sector since the 1960s.[14]

Yet, consistent with the other public employee constitutional cases discussed in this Chapter, *Engquist* stands for the general proposition that government acting as employer has much more latitude to act against employees than the government as sovereign when it interacts with its citizens. For instance, Justice Marshall famously stated in *Pickering v. Board of Education*[15]: "[I]t cannot be gainsaid that the State has interests as an employer in regulating the speech of its employees that differ significantly from those it possesses in connection with regulation of the speech of the citizenry in general." On the other hand, prior to *Engquist*, the Court had never made the leap to hold that the Equal Protection Clause does not apply to individual public employees when government takes arbitrary administrative action against them. It might be that the Court in *Engquist* was concerned that federal courts would be overwhelmed if every government personnel decision could be challenged under the Equal Protection Clause (though statistics or other evidence do not exist that show that there has been a problem with these types of cases flooding the courts).

Thus, although public employees in the United States (who number over 20 million) potentially have constitutional rights because their government employers engage in state action, many such rights are restricted, or as in *Engquist*, completely discarded in the name of the government's managerial prerogative and

---

[12] *Engquist*, 553 U.S. at 610 (Stevens, J., dissenting).

[13] *Id.* (quoting U.S. Const. amend. XIV).

[14] *Id.* at 614 (quoting in part Keyishian v. Bd. of Regents of Univ. of State of N.Y., 385 U.S. 589, 605–06 (1967)) ("In the 1890's that doctrine applied broadly to government employment, but for many years now 'the theory that public employment which may be denied altogether may be subjected to any conditions, regardless of how unreasonable, has been uniformly rejected.' ").

[15] 391 U.S. 563, 568 (1968).

the "common-sense realization that government offices could not function if every employment decision became a constitutional matter."[16]

[B]   Public Employee Political Affiliation Protections

Political association cases in the public employment context, for their part, deal mostly with the so-called "spoils system" or political patronage, which rewards public employment based on loyalty to a given political party or candidate. In these cases, the Supreme Court has generally struck down laws which condition public employment on party affiliation. For instance, in *Elrod v. Burns*,[17] the plurality opinion written by Justice Brennan found that Illinois public employees, who performed non-confidential and non-policymaking work, could not be fired merely because of their partisan political affiliation. In this regard, Justice Brennan stated: "[P]atronage dismissals severely restrict political belief and association. Though there is a vital need for government efficiency and effectiveness, such dismissals are on balance not the least restrictive means for fostering that end."[18]

Four years later, a majority of the court upheld the major premises of *Elrod* in *Branti v. Finkel*.[19] There, Justice Stevens similarly found that assistant public defenders were non-confidential, non-policymaking officials whose employment could not be terminated solely based on their partisan political affiliation. The test articulated in *Branti* appears to be one of strict scrutiny: "[U]nless the government can demonstrate 'an overriding interest,' . . . 'of vital importance,' requiring that a person's private beliefs conform to those of the hiring authority, his beliefs cannot be the sole basis for depriving him of continued public employment."[20]

More recently, in *Rutan v. Republican Party of Illinois*,[21] the Supreme Court extended the holding of *Elrod* and *Branti* to other adverse employment decisions such as failures to hire, rehire, transfer, or promote.[22] Writing for the Court once again, Justice Brennan found that the Illinois Governor's practice of limiting state employment and beneficial employment-related decisions to those who supported the Republican Party unconstitutionally impinged on the rights to association and belief of employees who associated with the Democratic Party.[23] Nevertheless, the Court emphasized that its holding applied only to non-policymaking employees and that a government employer is still permitted to terminate policymaking workers for their political beliefs. At these higher levels, government decisionmakers are

---

[16] *Engquist*, 553 U.S. at 592 (quoting Connick v. Myers, 461 U.S. 138, 143 (1983)).

[17] 427 U.S. 347 (1976).

[18] *Id.* at 372.

[19] 445 U.S. 507 (1980).

[20] *See id.* at 515-16 (quoting *Elrod*, 427 U.S. at 362, 368).

[21] 497 U.S. 62 (1990).

[22] *See id.* at 74.

[23] The Court rejected the notion that these types of employment decisions should somehow be treated differently because they did not have the same impact on individuals' First Amendment rights as ultimate firing decisions. *See id.* at 73 (observing that "[e]mployees who find themselves in dead-end positions due to their political backgrounds *are* adversely affected") (emphasis in original).

allowed to politically discriminate to ensure loyalty to the governing party's political agenda.

[C]   Public Employee Free Speech: The *Connick*/*Pickering*/*Garcetti* Line of Cases

Whereas the *Rutan* line of cases protects government workers in their political affiliations, the speech and expression cases protect government workers from being terminated for privately or publicly criticizing their employers' policies on matters of public concern (at least as long as such employees are not speaking pursuant to their official duties).[24] The government employer in these cases, for its part, seeks to protect legitimate business interests in running an efficient workplace. Consequently, the strict scrutiny analysis applied to government employer actions in the political association cases is inappropriate. Instead, the question is one of government "reasonableness" under all the circumstances and courts engage in a balancing of the relevant employer and employee interests.

For public employees to make out First Amendment retaliation claims based on their speech:

> [They must] prove that the conduct at issue was constitutionally protected, and that it was a substantial or motivating factor in the termination. If the employee discharges that burden, the government can escape liability by showing that it would have taken the same action even in the absence of the protected conduct.[25]

Pickering v. Board of Education[26] was the first Supreme Court case to discuss what type of public employee speech deserves constitutional protection. In *Pickering*, a public school terminated a teacher for criticizing in a local newspaper editorial a school board proposal to increase taxes.[27] To determine whether the teacher's speech deserved constitutional protection, Justice Marshall stated that, "[t]he problem in any case is to arrive at a balance between the interests of the [public employee], as citizen, in commenting upon matters of public concern and the interest of the State, as an employer, in promoting the efficiency of the public services it performs through its employees."[28]

Important considerations in carrying out this balance include whether the statements in question impair the disciplinary authority of superiors, the harmony among co-workers, the close working relationships for which personal loyalty and confidence are necessary, the performance of the employee's duties, or the regular

---

[24] *See generally* Paul M. Secunda, *The (Neglected) Importance of Being* Lawrence: *The Constitutionalization of Public Employee Rights to Decisional Non-Interference in Private Affairs*, 40 U.C. Davis L. Rev. 85, 95-105 (2006).

[25] Board of Comm'rs, Wabaunsee Cty. v. Umbehr, 518 U.S. 668, 675 (1996) (citing Mt. Healthy City Bd. of Ed. v. Doyle, 429 U.S. 274, 287 (1977)).

[26] 391 U.S. 563 (1968).

[27] For the background story in *Pickering*, see Paul M. Secunda, Pickering v. Bd. of Education: Unconstitutional Conditions and Public Employment, *in* FIRST AMENDMENT LAW STORIES 265–291 (Richard Garnett & Andrew Koppelman eds., 2012).

[28] *Id.* at 568.

operation of the enterprise.[29] The role of the employee in the organization may also be a significant consideration, as employees who have confidential, policymaking, or public contact roles, may be more inhibited in what they can publicly say consistent with their employment. In *Pickering*, the balancing came out in favor of the public school teacher because the statement concerned a matter of public concern (i.e., whether the school system required additional funds) and there was no evidence that the statement interfered with the employee's job duties. Specifically, there was no showing that the employee's editorial comments interfered with the operation of the school in general or constituted a statement that could be confused as that of the school district itself.

The Supreme Court gave the *Pickering* balancing test an important additional gloss in the case of *Connick v. Myers*.[30] *Connick* involved a case in which an assistant district attorney in New Orleans circulated to coworkers a questionnaire concerning internal office affairs to discover whether a general job satisfaction problem existed. For her trouble, Connick was fired and the issue was: what counts as "speech on a matter of public concern" under the *Pickering* test? The *Connick* court ruled that even before a *Pickering* balance could occur, a court had to consider as a threshold matter whether the public employee was speaking on "a matter of public concern." Because the Court found that most of Connick's questionnaire concerned matters of private interest, it dismissed most of her First Amendment claims.

Although *Connick* establishes the centrality of the public concern test to the public employee free speech analysis, it provides little guidance as to how to draw the line between what is and what is not speech on a matter of public concern.[31] One must go case-by-case to get a sense of where that line might lie. *Rankin v. McPherson*[32] provides an example of the fact intensive nature of this analysis. In *Rankin*, a Texas constable fired an employee after overhearing her say after the Reagan assassination attempt that, "shoot, if they go for him again, I hope they get him."[33] The Court overturned the employee's termination, finding that the statement, when taken in context, was an indirect comment on Reagan's policies and was not literally a threat to kill the President. Consequently, the statement was protected as a statement concerning a matter of public concern and the court went

---

[29] *See* Rankin v. McPherson, 483 U.S. 378, 388 (1987). In other words, the public employer side of this constitutional balance focuses on whether the employee speech causes a substantial disruption to the public employer's enterprise. One commentator has pointed out that as a result the *Pickering* test constitutionalizes the heckler's veto and provides the least amount of free speech protection to those public employees who need it the most. *See* Randy J. Kozel, *Reconceptualizing Public Employee Speech*, 99 Nw. U. L. Rev. 1007, 1019 (2005).

[30] 461 U.S. 138 (1983).

[31] All *Connick* stated in this regard was that "[w]hether an employee's speech addresses a matter of public concern must be determined by the content, form, and context of a given statement, as revealed by the whole record." *Id.* at 147-48. One issue, however, that has been decided about the public concern test is that a statement made by a public employee in a private conversation criticizing a public official may be considered speech on a matter of public concern. *See Rankin v. McPherson*, 483 U.S. 378, 386 (1987); Givhan v. W. Consol. Sch. Dist., 439 U.S. 410, 415-16 (1979).

[32] 483 U.S. 378 (1987).

[33] *Id.* at 381.

on to find that under the *Pickering* balance, the First Amendment rights of the employee outweighed the efficiency interests of the employer.

In any event, *Connick* remains a substantial hurdle for public employees wishing to garner the protection of the First Amendment for his or her speech.[34] Nevertheless, the public employee free speech terrain became even rockier for employees after the Court's 5-4 decision in *Garcetti v. Ceballos*.[35] In *Garcetti*, the Supreme Court discussed what constitutional protections, if any, are available to a public employee when that employee speaks out publicly on matters pursuant to her job duties. In that case, a deputy district attorney for Los Angeles County claimed that his public employer retaliated against him by assigning him to less desirable work as a result of his writing a memo criticizing the issuance of a warrant in a criminal case. The Court found that because the deputy district attorney was not speaking *as a citizen* on a matter of public concern, but rather *as an employee* of the government, *Connick*'s public concern test and the constitutional balancing of interests under *Pickering* need not even be reached. The apparent consequence of this holding is that the newly minted "official-capacity speech" category of *Garcetti* will further erode the free speech protections of public employees and place a premium on public employers drafting comprehensive job descriptions. There is also the possibility that rather than seeking to resolve workplace issues internally as part of their jobs, future public employees will prefer to air dirty laundry publicly in order to be seen as not acting pursuant to their official job duties.[36]

§ 8.03   THE PRIVATE WORKPLACE

Because of the lack of state action in the private workplace, private employers do not generally have to concern themselves with constitutional issues.[37] Nevertheless, a number of courts have sought to use available statutory schemes and common law doctrines to protect private sector employee political association and free speech rights. As the next two subsections establish, however, private sector employees still only enjoy limited protection when engaging in these types of activities, as the employment-at-will doctrine remains largely intact in the private workplace.

---

[34] *See, e.g.*, City of San Diego v. Roe, 543 U.S. 77 (2004) (per curiam) (finding that police officer who sold explicit videos of himself on eBay was not engaged in expression on a matter of public concern); *see also Secunda, supra* note 24, at 87–88, 127–30 (discussing *City of San Diego* in context of public employee free speech and substantive due process rights).

[35] 547 U.S. 410 (2006).

[36] Another argument against the *Garcetti* holding is that by not allowing public employees to blow the whistle on inefficient or corrupt government services, those in the best position to hold the government to account will be less likely to do so. *See The Supreme Court — Leading Cases, Public Employee Speech*, 120 HARV. L. REV. 273, 276 (2006) (discussing Justice Souter's dissent in *Ceballos*).

[37] Constitutional issues can nevertheless arise in the private employment context if the government seeks to apply a statutory employment law to employees or employers in an unconstitutional manner.

[A]   *Novosel v. Nationwide Insurance Co.* and Using Public Policy Torts for Political Protection

The Third Circuit, interpreting Pennsylvania law, was among the first to utilize a tort theory to protect the political association rights of private sector employees.[38] In *Novosel v. Nationwide Insurance Co.*,[39] an employee was fired by his employer after he refused to lobby on a political issue on the employer's behalf. Based on the tort of wrongful discharge in violation of public policy,[40] the court found that the employer's termination was in violation of Pennsylvania's public policy because that policy encompassed rights of political expression and association derived from both the federal and Pennsylvania state constitutions.[41]

Although *Novosel* was not subjected to further appellate review, an important development in its subsequent history was the "Statement of Judge Becker sur the Denial of the Petition for Rehearing." In that Statement, Judge Becker wrote that:

> [T]he opinion ignores the state action requirement of first amendment jurisprudence, particularly by its repeated, and, in my view, inappropriate citation of public employee cases, and by its implicit assumption that a public policy against government interference with free speech may be readily extended to private actors in voluntary association with another.[42]

As it turns out, Becker's criticism of the *Novosel* approach has become the consensus view on political affiliation rights of private sector employees. Not only has not a single other court followed *Novosel's* novel approach for protecting private sector employee political associations,[43] but even the Third Circuit and the Pennsylvania state courts have since repudiated *Novosel's* holding.[44]

---

[38]   Other courts that have applied public policy tort analysis to private sector political affiliation cases include: Chavez v. Manville Prods. Corp., 777 P.2d 371 (N.M. 1989) (reinstating employee, on public policy grounds, after he was terminated for refusing to place his name on an employer-initiated telegram supporting federal legislation); Davis v. La. Computing Corp., 394 So. 2d 678 (La. Ct. App. 1981) (holding, based on public policy grounds, that state statute protected employee from being fired for deciding to run for political office).

[39]   721 F.2d 894 (3d Cir. 1983).

[40]   Public policy torts had been historically limited to cases involving the refusal to commit unlawful acts, the fulfillment of a public obligation (like jury duty), or the exercise of a statutory right, see *supra* § 6.02[B], although there have been other courts, like *Novosel*, which had taken a broader view of when an employer acts in violation of public policy. *See, e.g.*, Palmateer v. Int'l Harvester Co., 421 N.E. 2d 876, 878 (Ill. 1981) ("In general, it can be said that public policy concerns what is right and just and what affects the citizens of the State collectively").

[41]   *Novosel*, 721 F.2d at 899 ("[A] cognizable expression of public policy may be derived in this case from either the First Amendment of the United States Constitution or Article I, Section 7 of the Pennsylvania Constitution").

[42]   *Id.* at 903.

[43]   Edmondson v. Shearer Lumber Prods. 75 P.3d 733, 738-39 (Idaho 2003) (finding that *Novosel* has not been "endorsed by any other court").

[44]   Borse v. Piece Goods Shop, Inc., 963 F.2d 611 (3d Cir. 1992) (retreating from *Novosel's* interpretation of Pennsylvania's constitution); Paul v. Lankenau Hosp., 569 A.2d 346 (Pa. 1990) (disapproving of *Novosel's* interpretation of the Pennsylvania Constitution).

Consequently, the current state of the law is that unless private sector workers have statutory or contractual protections, such as under a state Hatch Act, individual employment contract, or company handbook, they remain without workplace protection for their political affiliations or beliefs.

[B]   Private Sector Employee Free Speech, the National Labor Relations Act, and Off-Duty Conduct Statutes

Not surprisingly, and for similar reasons as in the political expression cases, private sector employees have also not fared well in employment free speech cases. However, union and non-union workers have found some degree of speech protection under Section 7 of the National Labor Relations Act (NLRA).[45] Although Section 7 primarily protects union members and those in the process of organizing a union when engaging in concerted activities for mutual aid and protection, the Supreme Court has made clear that non-union employees have the same rights in appropriate circumstances.[46]

For instance, in *Timekeeping Services, Inc.*,[47] a data collection products company fired an employee for publicly and inappropriately disagreeing by company-wide email with a revision made to the vacation policy by the chief operating officer. The National Labor Relations Board (NLRB) found that the company's action violated the employee's right to engage in concerted activity for mutual aid and protection and ordered him reinstated with back pay. Specifically, the employee's action in sending the critical email to fellow employees was concerted in that he sought to enlist others in his cause, it was protected because the objective of the conduct legitimately sought to preserve the existing vacation policy for all employees, and the manner in which he protested the policy was not of such an intolerable character as to make the employee unfit for further employment.[48] In short, in circumstances where the conditions for protected activity under Section 7 are met, private sector employees (whether in a union or not) may be able to find some statutory protection for their speech.[49]

---

[45]   29 U.S.C. § 157.

[46]   NLRB v. Wash. Aluminum Co., 370 U.S. 9 (1962).

[47]   323 N.L.R.B. 244 (1997).

[48]   The NLRB's General Counsel has recently extended this analysis of what constitutes protected activity under the NLRA to the Facebook and social media context in three recent General Counsel Memoranda. *See* NLRB, Operations Memorandum 12-59 (May 30, 2012), *available at* http://www.nlrb.gov/publications/operations-management-memos; NLRB, Operations Memorandum 12-31 (January 24, 2012), *available at* http://mynlrb.nlrb.gov/link/document.aspx/09031d45807d6567; NLRB, Operations Memorandum 11-74, *available at* http://mynlrb.nlrb.gov/link/document.aspx/09031d458056e743. *See also* Christine Neylon O'Brien, *The First Facebook Firing Case Under Section 7 of the National Labor Relations Act: Exploring the Limits of Labor Law Protection for Concerted Communication on Social Media*, 45 SUFFOLK U. L. REV. 29 (2011).

[49]   *See, e.g.*, Parexel Int'l, LLC, 356 N.L.R.B. No. 82 (2011) (finding nurse protected under NLRA when she was fired for complaining to her supervisor that she was paid less than co-workers).

For an example of a court finding employee conduct to be indefensible and therefore not protected by Section 7, see Endicott Interconnect Techs., Inc. v. NLRB, 453 F.3d 532 (D.C. Cir. 2006). *See also* NLRB v. Local 1229, IBEW (Jefferson Standard Broadcasting Co.), 346 U.S. 464 (1953) (seminal case setting

In addition to this type of NLRA-based protection, private sector employees may have additional speech rights when they are away from their jobs. Some states have passed off-duty conduct statutes, which generally prohibit employers from terminating employees for engaging in lawful conduct outside of the workplace.[50] For instance, the Colorado lifestyle discrimination statute[51] protects employees engaging in certain lawful off-duty activities. However, such statutes generally have limitations like those of Colorado's statute which permit employers to base adverse employment action on lawful off-duty conduct if such conduct "[r]elates to a bona fide occupational requirement or is reasonably and rationally related to the employment activities and responsibilities of a particular employee," or would result in the employee having a conflict of interest.[52] There are also definitional limits that courts have applied to narrow these statutes' reach.[53]

---

out standards for finding employee disloyal conduct during labor dispute to be unprotected under Section 7).

[50] States with broad off-duty conduct statutes currently include California, Colorado, New York, and North Dakota. See CAL. LAB. CODE § 96(k); COLO. REV. STAT. § 24-34-402.5(1); N.Y. LAB. LAW § 201-d(2); N.D. CENT. CODE §§ 14-02.4-01 to -03. Additionally, a Connecticut statute protects employees, both on-duty and off-duty, from suffering adverse employment consequences for engaging in First Amendment-type activities. See CONN. GEN. STAT. ANN. § 31-51q. For additional discussion of off-duty conduct statutes in the privacy rights context, including smoker protection laws, see *infra* § 9.03[A][3].

[51] COLO. REV. STAT. § 24-34-402.5(1).

[52] *Id.*

[53] As an example, New York courts have limited their off-duty conduct statute by finding that personal relationships do not constitute "lawful recreational activities." See McCavitt v. Swiss Reins. Am. Corp., 237 F.3d 166, 167 (2d Cir. 2001).

Chapter 9

EMPLOYEE PRIVACY PROTECTIONS

SYNOPSIS

§ 9.01   INTRODUCTION

In contrast to the equal protection, political activity, and free speech issues discussed in the previous chapter which mostly concern government employees, there are more traditional invasions of privacy torts available to protect employees in the private sector both on- and off-the-job. These common law privacy rights are currently being examined in Chapter 7 of the Restatement of Employment Law.[1]

---

[1] Restatement (Third) of Employment Law 16 (Council Draft No. 6, Sept. 30, 2011), *at* http://extranet.ali.org/docs/Employment_Law_CD6_online.pdf (on file with author) ("[Chapter 7] concerns the

Private sector employees may also be able to use state off-duty conduct statutes for additional privacy protections.[2]

Public employees, on the other hand, may have greater workplace privacy protections under the Fourth Amendment when it comes to searches of their physical and electronic workplace locations and when it comes to being subject to drug testing.[3] Public employees may also have rights to sexual privacy, under the substantive component of the due process clause in light of the Supreme Court's decision in *Lawrence v. Texas*.[4]

Finally, many workers have both federal and state legal protections against testing of their genetic make-up and their honesty. As to the latter, employers use honesty testing to immunize themselves from charges by third parties that they have negligently hired or retained an employee with dangerous tendencies.

§ 9.02   PRIVACY CLAIMS ON-THE-JOB

[A]   Public Employment

Initially, the Supreme Court examined public employees' rights to privacy at work in *O'Connor v. Ortega*.[5] While Dr. Ortega, the chief of professional education for psychiatry residents at a California state hospital, was on administrative leave and being investigated for alleged improprieties, hospital officials thoroughly searched his office desk, cabinets, and papers, and subsequently seized personal items without his consent. On Dr. Ortega's claim that this invasion of his office was an unconstitutional search and seizure, the Court held that the Fourth Amendment prohibitions against unreasonable searches and seizures potentially could apply to the public workplace.

In deciding whether public employees have such protections, the Supreme Court directed lower courts to first decide whether the employee has a reasonable expectation of privacy in different parts of his or her office. If so, a court next should balance the privacy interests of the employee against the legitimate interests of the employer in running an efficient governmental workplace.[6] The

---

protections afforded through the common law to employee privacy and autonomy interests that supplement constitutional, statutory and regulatory protections accorded those interests.").

  [2] *See supra* § 8.03[B].

  [3] For a view that there is an increasing convergence of public employee and private employee workplace privacy rights in the American workplace, *see* Paul M. Secunda, *Privatizing Workplace Privacy*, 88 Notre Dame L. Rev. ___ (forthcoming 2013) (maintaining that recent Supreme Court case law has leveled down public employee workplace privacy protection to that of their private sector counterparts).

  [4] 539 U.S. 558 (2003).

  [5] 480 U.S. 709 (1987) (plurality opinion).

  [6] More specifically, the two-step plurality test requires consideration of whether under the operational realities of the workplace the employee had a reasonable expectation of privacy and if so, whether the employer's intrusion upon that expectation "for noninvestigatory, work-related purposes, as well as for investigations of work-related misconduct [was reasonable] under all the circumstances." *Id.* at 725–26.

"special needs" for legitimate work-related, non-investigatory intrusions and investigations for work-related misconduct mean that it is not necessary to obtain a warrant based on probable cause in this context. Such searches are instead judged by their overall reasonableness.

In *Ortega*, then, the Court held that the Fourth Amendment prohibitions against unreasonable searches and seizures apply to the public workplace.[7] However, the Justices diverged over what the applicable test should be and whether Ortega had a reasonable expectation of privacy in the office itself.[8] Although a majority of justices agreed that Dr. Ortega at least had a legitimate expectation of privacy in his desk and file cabinets, the Court remanded the case to determine, given the employer's interests, whether the scope of the intrusion was reasonable.[9]

According to the plurality decision written by Justice O'Connor, in deciding whether public employees have privacy protections at the workplace, a court should first decide whether the employee has a reasonable expectation of privacy in their office or personal effects based on the "operational realities of the workplace." Thus, "[p]ublic employees' expectations of privacy in their offices, desks, and file cabinets . . . may be reduced by virtue of actual office practices and procedures, or by legitimate regulation," and, therefore, "whether an employee has a reasonable expectation of privacy must be addressed on a case-by-case basis."[10] The upshot is that government employees have reduced expectations of privacy or no expectation of privacy at all, depending on whether the public employer has promulgated the necessary anti-privacy policies.

If a court finds that the employee has a reasonable expectation of privacy, the plurality next would have courts apply a "special needs" analysis for both legitimate work-related, non-investigatory intrusions and investigations for work-related misconduct. The plurality concluded that it was not necessary to obtain a warrant based on probable cause because it would be impracticable for the government employer to obtain a warrant in this context. Such searches are instead judged on "reasonableness under all the circumstances," which in turn balances "the invasion of the employees' legitimate expectations of privacy against the government's need for supervision, control and the efficient operation of the workplace." Finally, the reasonableness of the employer search is judged from the perspective of whether the search was reasonable in its inception and in its scope.

In his concurring opinion in *Ortega*, Justice Scalia stated that he would have generally presumed that governmental employees' offices and the personal items therein, are covered by the Fourth Amendment. But rather than employ an ad-hoc inquiry based on reasonableness as the plurality did, he would have held that searches to "retrieve work-related materials or to investigate violations of

---

[7] *Id.* at 717 ("[W]e reject the contention . . . that public employees can never have a reasonable expectation of privacy in their place of work. Individuals do not lose Fourth Amendment rights merely because they work for the government instead of a private employer.").

[8] *Id.* at 718–19.

[9] On remand, the Ninth Circuit found that the scope of the search of Ortega's office was unreasonable. *See* Ortega v. O'Connor, 146 F.3d 1149, 1159 (9th Cir. 1998).

[10] *Id.* at 718.

workplace rules — searches of the sort that are regarded as reasonable and normal in the private-employer context — do not violate the Fourth Amendment."[11] Justice Scalia's legal framework would therefore treat privacy rights in the public workplace the same as privacy rights in the private workplace.

More recently, the Supreme Court revisited public employee workplace privacy rights in the case of *City of Ontario v. Quon*.[12] In Quon, a SWAT officer for the City of Ontario in California alleged Fourth Amendment privacy violations in relation to a police department's audit of text messages sent to and from his work pager. The city discovered that the officer had been using the pager for non-work-related purposes and that some of the messages were sexually explicit. As a result of the investigation, the officer was found to have violated city work rules and discipline.

The Supreme Court reviewed Quon's claims that the City's handling of his text messages constituted an unreasonable search and seizure under the Fourth Amendment. Importantly, during trial, the jury determined that the purpose of the City's audit was non-investigatory and only undertaken to determine whether the usage limit for the pagers was sufficient. The audit was not done to investigate Quon for workplace misconduct.

All the Justices agreed that the Fourth Amendment applied to the audit of the text messages. Yet, the Court did not decide formally whether Quon had a reasonable expectation of privacy in the text messages and did not decide the appropriate test for determining the reasonableness of the search in light of those privacy expectations. Instead, writing for a unanimous court, Justice Kennedy maintained that even if the employee had a reasonable expectation of privacy in his employer-provided pager, the city's search of the pager was reasonable under both legal tests advanced by the plurality and concurring opinions in *Ortega*. First, under the plurality test, the employer's search was reasonable because it was motivated by a legitimate work-related purpose and was not excessive in scope. Second, under the test outlined by Justice Scalia in his concurring opinion, it was reasonable because it would be considered "reasonable and normal" in the private sector workplace.

Additionally, Justice Kennedy examined a number of factors that could potentially play a role in determining whether an employee has a reasonable expectation of privacy in future cases. For instance, Kennedy tantalizingly wondered whether the increased use of smart phones and other devices means that employees will have more or less privacy in such devices. Having noted the potential relevant issues, the Court punted, maintaining that it "would have difficultly predicting how employees' privacy expectations will be shaped by [evolving technology] or the degree to which society will be prepared to recognized those expectations as reasonable."[13]

---

[11] *Id.* at 732 (Scalia, J., concurring in the judgment).

[12] 130 S. Ct. 2619 (2010).

[13] *Id. See also* U.S. v. Jones, 132 S. Ct. 945, 962 (2012) (Alito, J., concurring in judgment) ("Dramatic technological change may lead to periods in which popular expectations are in flux and may ultimately produce significant changes in popular attitudes. New technology may provide increased convenience or security at the expense of privacy, and many people may find the tradeoff worthwhile. And even if the

In the end, however, the *Quon* majority did not pick a particular test because the City of Ontario prevails under either test. The problem with this current state of affairs in the workplace privacy context is that inevitably a case will come along that will require a determination of whether an employee has a reasonable expectation of privacy in electronic equipment provided by their government employer and it is unclear on what legal grounds those future cases will be decided.[14]

[B] The Tort of Invasion of Privacy

Employees in the private sector must generally rely on invasion of privacy torts for their workplace privacy claims. There are four different types of invasion of privacy torts, which were developed by Dean Prosser in the Restatement of Torts. They are:

- Intrusion upon an employee's seclusion

- Placing other before the public in a false light

- Appropriation of name or likeness

- Giving publicity to private facts[15]

The primary on-the-job privacy claim is intrusion upon seclusion. Like the Fourth Amendment claims discussed above, part of the focus of this claim is on an employee's reasonable expectation of privacy in the workplace. But the exact legal question posed by intrusion upon seclusion cases is somewhat different, asking whether intrusive employer conduct would be highly offensive to the reasonable person. The objective nature of this inquiry insures that employers do not become liable based on the subjective feelings of hypersensitive employees.

---

public does not welcome the diminution of privacy that new technology entails, they may eventually reconcile themselves to this development as inevitable.").

[14] The Court has taken this same unsatisfying approach in another recent employment privacy case, *NASA v. Nelson*, 131 S. Ct. 746, 751 (2011) ("We assume, without deciding, that the Constitution protects a privacy right of the sort mentioned in *Whalen* and *Nixon*."). That privacy right involves the privacy "interest in avoiding disclosure of personal matters" under the substantive component of the Due Process Clauses of the Fifth and Fourteenth Amendments. *See* Whalen v. Roe, 429 U.S. 589, 599–600 (1977); Nixon v. Administrator of General Services, 433 U.S. 425, 457 (1977). The Fourth Amendment did not apply to the informational privacy interests in Nelson because the background employment inquiries to third parties in that case "were not Fourth Amendment 'searches' under *United States v. Miller*, 425 U.S. 435 (1976), and . . . the Fourth Amendment does not prohibit the Government from asking questions about private information." *Id.* at 765. But see United States v. Jones, 132 S. Ct. 945, 957 (2012) (Sotomayor, J., concurring) ("[I]t may be necessary to reconsider the premise that an individual has no reasonable expectation of privacy in information voluntarily disclosed to third parties. This approach is ill suited to the digital age, in which people reveal a great deal of information about themselves to third parties in the course of carrying out mundane tasks.").

[15] RESTATEMENT (SECOND) OF TORTS § 652A. Of these four potential types of invasion of privacy claims, this book discusses three: intrusion upon seclusion, false light claims, and public disclosure of private facts. Intrusion upon seclusion will be discussed in this chapter, while the latter two are discussed in Chapter 10. The other type of privacy claim concerning appropriation of name or likeness rarely occurs in the workplace context and is not discussed further in this book. It should also be noted that Chapter 7 of the soon-to-be-released RESTATEMENT (THIRD) OF EMPLOYMENT LAW will also address the protections afforded through the common law to employee privacy and autonomy interests.

K-Mart Corp. Store No. 7441 v. Trotti,[16] from the Texas Court of Appeals, involves a classic on-the-job privacy claim involving the intrusion upon seclusion invasion of privacy tort. In *Trotti*, a female K-Mart employee had a locker at work with a personal lock on it. Nonetheless, she found one day that her locker had been opened and her purse inside had been disturbed. Although her manager initially denied going through her belongings, he later admitted to looking for stolen goods in her locker. The court remanded the case for a new trial because the trial judge gave a faulty instruction. Additionally, the court commented that the employee had a reasonable expectation of privacy in the locker because even though the locker belonged to K-Mart, it had permitted the employee to place her own lock on it. The question on remand was whether her employer's action in going through her locked locker without her permission would be highly offensive to a reasonable person, but the answer to that question would be dependent upon whether she had a reasonable expectation of privacy in her locker in the first instance.

If this were a case where the employer maintained control over the locker by having its own locks and knowing the combinations, or if the employee handbook had specifically stated that employee lockers could be searched at any time, the female employee would likely not have had the same expectation of privacy. In such a case, a court would probably not consider any subsequent invasion of her locker to be highly offensive to a reasonable person.

This intrusion upon seclusion analysis is not limited to lockers, but could also apply to other places and items in which private sector employee have privacy interests, such as their phone calls, computers, email, and internet communications. Responding to the potential of privacy liability, many employers have added policies to employee handbooks which make clear that employers control all of these electronic communications and can monitor them to insure that such communications are not being used for improper purposes (e.g., personal phone calls or internet pornography). Such policies also insure that employees do not develop reasonable expectations of privacy in these electronic communications while at work.

[C] Wiretap Act and Electronic Communication and Privacy Act (ECPA)

Congress entered the workplace privacy fray by passing the Wiretap Act,[17] which, among other things, deals with the ability of a person, including an employer, to listen in on others' phone calls. The general rule, although there are some important exceptions,[18] is that an employer either needs the consent of one or both of the parties to the communication.

---

[16] 677 S.W.2d 632 (Tex. App. 1984).

[17] Title III of the Omnibus Crime Control and Safe Streets Act of 1968, 18 U.S.C. §§ 2510-2520.

[18] There is an exception to the wiretapping statute consent provisions when an employer has a legitimate business reason for listening to employee communications in the ordinary course of business. *See, e.g.*, Arias v. Mut. Cent. Alarm Servs., Inc., 202 F.3d 553 (2d Cir. 2000). *But see* Watkins v. L.M. Berry & Co., 704 F.2d 577 (11th Cir. 1983) (finding ordinary course of business exception not limitless).

More recently, the Wiretap Act was amended by the Electronic Communications Privacy Act of 1986 (ECPA).[19] Title I of the ECPA bans the interception or disclosure of electronic communications, while Title II, the Stored Communication Act (SCA), regulates access to stored electronic communications. Like the wiretapping statute, the ECPA is subject to a fairly broad exception that allows employers to monitor computer use for work performance purposes.

Over the past decade, the ascendancy of the Internet has led to some difficult legal issues under the ECPA. For instance, in *Konop v. Hawaiian Airlines, Inc.*,[20] Konop was a pilot for Hawaiian Airlines who maintained a password-protected website that was critical of his employer and fellow employees, and encouraged alternative union representation. A Hawaiian Airlines official gained access to Konop's website without his permission by using the password of other pilots, who gave their passwords to the official. Konop sued under the EPCA, claiming that the unauthorized access amounted to an unlawful interception of an electronic communication. Although the court concluded that the website qualified as an "electronic communication," the court did not believe that accessing a website entailed an "interception" of the electronic communication under Title I of ECPA.[21] As far as Konop's claim under the SCA, the court concluded that there was indeed access without authorization of an electronic communication service in electronic storage. However, the court reversed summary judgment for the airline on the question of whether an exception to the SCA applied because the other pilots, who had access to Konop's website, had given the airline official permission to use their passwords to access the site. The question on remand was whether these other pilots were "users of the website" at the time they authorized the airline official to access it, because only "users" could lawfully permit a third-party's access to a private website under the SCA. *Konop* illustrates just some of the many complexities associated with applying the EPCA to Internet use in the workplace.

More recently, in *Pure Power Boot Camp v. Warrior Fitness Boot Camp*,[22] a district court considered a case concerning an employer that accessed the personal email accounts of former employees who left to form a competing fitness center business. The employer was able to access these email accounts because, among other reasons, one of the former employees had left his username and password information on the employer's computers "such that, when the Hotmail website was accessed, the username and password fields were automatically populated." The employer had an employee handbook policy which stressed that email users of the employer computer system had no expectation of privacy in any of their electronic communications on that system and that email should not be used for personal matters. The evidence from these personal emails suggested that the former employees were using their personal email accounts during business hours to set their competing business and to take clients from their former employer, all

---

[19] 18 U.S.C. §§ 2510-2522, 2701-2712.

[20] 302 F.3d 868 (9th Cir. 2002).

[21] The court would have required instead that there be an "acquisition of a communication contemporaneous with transmission." *Id.* at 876.

[22] 587 F. Supp. 2d 548 (S.D.N.Y. 2008).

in breach of their duties of loyalty to their employer.[23] The question presented, in the subsequent employer's breach of duty of loyalty lawsuit against the employees, was whether the former employees' emails were collected by their employer in violation of the ECPA and the SCA and thus, such emails should be deemed inadmissible into evidence.

In determining this legal question, the court emphasized that the case concerned emails that were "stored and accessed directly from accounts maintained by outside electronic communication service providers." Thus, the court found that the SCA should prevent the employer from using the emails in its case against the former employees because the employer accessed an electronic communication service and obtained an electronic communication while it was still in electronic storage without the permission of the former employees. The court rejected the employer's argument that authorization to access the former employees' personal accounts had been given either by operation of the employer's internet policy or because the employees had left username and password information on the employer's computer system. The court rejected the notion that carelessness of the former employees equaled consent. In contrast, the ECPA did not apply to this set of facts because accessing an electronic communication that has already been delivered does not constitute "interception" for purposes of that statute.

Pure Power Boot Camp thus stands for the proposition that although an employer can, through an appropriately written electronic communication policy, search its own computers for inappropriate employee email and Internet activity, it may not have the same ability, without employee authorization, to access employee personal email accounts set up with third-party providers. On the other hand, posts on social networking sites like Facebook may be deemed "public," regardless of privacy settings, and therefore, employees may not have the same reasonable expectation of privacy in such postings.[24] In response to employee and prospective employee privacy concerns in their Facebook postings, at least two states (Maryland and Illinois) have passed laws making it unlawful for employers to pressure applicants or employees to reveal their Facebook or other social media passwords.[25]

Interestingly, the former employees in *Pure Power Boot Camp* did not bring a claim against their employer under the SCA, but used the statute as grounds for asking the court to uses its inherent equitable authority to fashion appropriate sanctions against the employer. Under its discretionary power, and considering that the former employees may have had "unclean hands" themselves, the court prohibited the employer from using as evidence the former employees' personal emails in its own legal action against these employees (though the court kept open the possibility of allowing the emails to come in for impeachment purposes if the former employees "open[ed] the door.").

---

[23] Employee breaches of the duty of loyalty to their employer are discussed *infra* § 11.03[A].

[24] *See* Romano v. Steelcase Inc., 907 N.Y.S.2d 650 (2010).

[25] *See* Jason Keyser, *Illinois Facebook Law Makes It Illegal for Employers to Ask for Logins*, Associated Press (Aug. 1, 2012), *available at* http://www.huffingtonpost.com/2012/08/01/illinois-facebook-law_n_1730077.html.

§ 9.03 PRIVACY CLAIMS OFF-THE-JOB

Employee off-the-job privacy claims provide perhaps even more difficult legal questions, because it is not always clear why an employer should be able to control what the employee does while away from work. Although the common law does not provide much protection for employees, more recently states have passed off-duty conduct statutes which protect employees who engage in certain off-duty activities. Moreover, the Supreme Court has adopted a substantive due process approach to sexual privacy rights which may lead to protections for public employees in making important decisions in their personal and private lives, especially in matters pertaining to sex.

[A] Legal Off-Duty Conduct

[1] Common Law Protections

The lack of protection for legal off-duty conduct by employees under the common law is no better exemplified than in the case of *Brunner v. Al Attar*.[26] Brunner, an employee at Al Attar's paint and body shop, was fired for endangering other workers after refusing to give up her off-duty volunteer work to help victims of AIDS. The court found that Brunner could not make out a tort claim for wrongful discharge on the basis of public policy because none of the Texas public policy exceptions to the at-will doctrine applied to the facts of her case.[27] Because the court was unwilling to create another public policy exception for legal off-duty conduct, Brunner lost the case.

It would seem that the lack of protection for employee off-duty privacy would not only apply where the employer does not want the employee to engage in some activity outside of work (like smoking for health insurance cost reasons)[28], but also where the employer wants the employee to do something outside of the employee's job responsibilities and the employee refuses. Consider an employee at a civic-minded company like Ben & Jerry's who refuses to do community service work and is fired as a result. Based on the reasoning of *Brunner*, it would appear that the employee would not have a common law remedy for that type of situation either.[29]

Finally, *Brunner* was analyzed under the public policy tort rubric, but would she have had more luck if she brought an invasion of privacy claim? It is unclear, but at least with regard to an off-duty romantic relationship, there is a chance that the invasion of privacy tort would provide some protection. Although *Mercer v. City of Cedar Rapids*[30] did not protect the off-duty relationship between a police officer and her superior, the court indicated that, unlike more highly-regulated public sector

---

[26] 786 S.W.2d 784 (Tex. App. 1990).

[27] For instance, Brunner was not terminated after being asked to perform an illegal act by her employer. *See id.* at 785; *see also supra* § 6.02 (discussing public policy tort claims).

[28] Although, as discussed below, it should be pointed out that a number of states by statute protect smokers against such workplace discrimination. *See, e.g.*, N.J. Stat. Ann. § 34:6B-1.

[29] However, the employee might have a claim under the Fair Labor Standards Act (FLSA), 29 U.S.C. §§ 201-219, if the employer seeks to compel the employee to "work" off-the-clock. *See infra* § 12.02[D].

[30] 104 F. Supp. 2d 1130 (N.D. Iowa 2000).

police employment, the interests involved in private sector employment might be different. In such private sector cases, it may be possible for an employee to show that he or she had a legitimate expectation of privacy and an intrusion into that relationship would be highly offensive to a reasonable person.[31]

[2] The Union Context

The state of affairs is substantially better for union employees who have just cause protection under a collective bargaining contract. Under the nexus doctrine, labor arbitrators have permitted employers to discipline employees for off-duty conduct only if that conduct has a detrimental impact on the workplace.[32] In other words, there needs to be some "nexus" between an employee's off-duty conduct and the business of the employer. As early as 1957, arbitrators looked to three factors to determine if the requisite nexus existed to discipline employees for off-duty conduct: (1) whether the conduct harms the employer's product or reputation, (2) whether the conduct renders the employee unable to effectively perform his or her job, or (3) whether the conduct leads other employees to refuse to work with him or her.[33] Because there is the real potential of an employer abusing the nexus test to dispose of trouble-making or unwanted employees, arbitrators also have required that the connection between the injury caused to the employer's business and the employee's off-duty conduct be reasonable and discernible.[34]

[3] State Off-Duty Conduct Statutes

More recently, a significant number of states have passed statutes to protect the legal, off-duty conduct of employees.[35] These statutes generally can be broken down into two categories: lawful use of consumable products (such as tobacco) and other lawful off-duty conduct (such as recreational activities).[36] The most common form of the first type of off-duty conduct statute prevents discrimination against smokers. For example, under the North Carolina Smokers' Rights Law,[37] it is an:

> unlawful employment practice for an employer to fail or refuse to hire a prospective employee, or discharge or otherwise discriminate against any employee with respect to compensation, terms, conditions, or privileges of employment because the prospective employee or the employee engages in or has engaged in the lawful use of lawful products if the activity occurs off

---

[31] *Id.* at 1178.

[32] *See* Paul M. Secunda, *Getting to the Nexus of the Matter: A Sliding Scale Approach to Faculty-Student Consensual Relationship Policies in Higher Education*, 55 Syracuse L. Rev. 55, 66-73 (2004).

[33] W.E. Caldwell Co., 28 Lab. Arb. Rep. (BNA) 434, 436-37 (1957) (Kesselman, Arb.).

[34] Inland Container Corp., 28 Lab. Arb. Rep. (BNA) 312, 314 (1957) (Ferguson, Arb.).

[35] These statutes were also discussed in connection with free speech issues surrounding private sector employment. *See supra* § 8.03[B].

[36] *See* Marisa Anne Pagnattaro, *What Do You Do When You Are Not at Work?: Limiting the Use of Off-Duty Conduct as the Basis for Adverse Employment Decisions*, 6 U. Pa. J. Lab. & Emp. L. 625, 640 (2004).

[37] N.C. Gen. Stat. § 95-28.2.

the premises of the employer during nonworking hours.[38]

Yet, similar to nexus doctrine cases in the union context, employers are able to act against off-duty smokers if their smoking, "adversely affects the employee's job performance or the person's ability to properly fulfill the responsibilities of the position in question or the safety of other employees."[39] As far as the second category, and as discussed in the previous chapter, a smaller group of states have more comprehensive statutes protecting lawful off-duty conduct.[40] These statutes have been applied to areas as diverse as supervisors' relationships with subordinate employees outside of work[41] and to engagement in outside political activities.[42]

[B]   Romantic Relationships

State off-duty conduct statutes have been interpreted by some courts not to apply to off-duty romantic relationships.[43] Nonetheless, some courts have used a theory of wrongful discharge based on preexisting contract rights, the implied covenant of good faith and fair dealing,[44] and the tort of intentional infliction of emotional distress (IIED),[45] to protect the rights of private sector employees who have been fired for engaging in off-duty romantic relationships.[46] For example, in *Rulon-Miller v. IBM Corp.*,[47] a top-performing female employee was fired after her supervisor discovered she was having a romantic off-duty relationship with a competitor's employee. Based on a memo put out by IBM's founder, the Watson Memo, which set up a company policy not to unnecessarily interfere with the personal lives of employees, the court found that the firing violated the company's own policy and amounted to a wrongful discharge. The court also went on to find that the manner in which the employee was fired was extreme and outrageous and found in her favor on the IIED claim as well.[48]

---

[38] *Id.* § 95-28.2(b).

[39] *Id.*

[40] *See supra* § 8.03[B].

[41] *See* Tavani v. Levi Strauss & Co., 2002 Cal. App. Unpub. LEXIS 10794 (Cal. Ct. App. Nov. 21, 2002) (finding employee not protected by California off-duty conduct statute because employee's effectiveness was undermined by romantic relationship with subordinate).

[42] *See* Richardson v. City of Saratoga Springs, 667 N.Y.S.2d 995 (N.Y. App. Div. 1998) (holding that New York off-duty conduct law violated where employee was denied promotion and had job duties modified due to outside political activities).

[43] *See* McCavitt v. Swiss Reins. Am. Corp., 237 F.3d 166 (2d Cir. 2001) (finding "lawful recreational activities" under New York off-duty conduct statute does not encompass off-duty romantic relationships).

[44] *See supra* § 5.05.

[45] *See supra* § 6.03.

[46] The invasion of privacy tort might also be available to prevent intrusions into private employees' off-duty romantic relationships. *See supra* notes 15-16 and accompanying text.

[47] 208 Cal. Rptr. 524 (Cal. Ct. App. 1984).

[48] Although an IIED finding was made in *Rulon-Miller*, generally such findings are rare in the employment law context because such conduct must be "utterly intolerable in a civilized society." *See supra* § 6.03. Rulon-Miller's supervisor's conduct was highly inappropriate, but it is doubtful that many other courts would even allow this claim to reach a jury.

Although Rulon-Miller was able to recover on a theory of wrongful discharge, it appears that the reasoning of the court would not protect an employee who did not work at a company with a policy like that found in IBM's Watson Memo.[49] Indeed, the holding of *Rulon-Miller* seems to represent the exception rather than the rule.[50] Nevertheless, the *Rulon-Miller* court did suggest that an employee who is fired for romantic off-duty conduct might also have a cause of action in those states which recognize claims for breach of the implied covenant of good faith and fair dealing.[51]

[C] Public Employee Sexual Privacy Claims in Light of *Lawrence v. Texas*

Although some states allow private employers to interfere with the private lives of their employees under a broad understanding of the employment-at-will doctrine, an important development in constitutional law may increase the sexual privacy rights of at least public employees. In *Lawrence v. Texas*,[52] the Supreme Court examined a criminal case involving the application of that state's anti-sodomy statute to the sexual activities of two consenting adult homosexuals in the privacy of their own bedroom. *Lawrence* altered the substantive due process constitutional landscape by striking down this statute, finding that the law furthered no legitimate state interest which could justify the government's intrusion into the personal and private lives of two consenting adults.[53]

One plausible reading of *Lawrence* is that it attaches some form of heightened judicial review when the government seeks to interfere with the private and personal lives of individuals.[54] Thus, analogizing to the *Connick/Pickering/Garcetti* line of First Amendment free speech cases discussed in Chapter 8, there is an argument that a court should have to undertake a constitutional balancing between public employees' rights to make decisions about their private affairs without government interference and public employers' rights to run an efficient governmental service. Under this balancing, only when a public employer has a substantial and legitimate interest in interfering with the private and personal lives

---

[49] *See, e.g.*, Patton v. J.C. Penney Co., 719 P.2d 854 (Or. 1986) (rejecting wrongful discharge claim for firing based on off-duty romantic relationship where no company policy to the contrary and no other exception to employment at-will doctrine applied). Indeed, a court even upheld the firing of an employee who was unlucky enough to walk in on her boss having an affair with his secretary. *See* Hillenbrand v. City of Evansville, 457 N.E.2d 236 (Ind. Ct. App. 1983).

[50] Other cases where employees have been found without a remedy after being discharged for off-duty romantic relationships include: Karren v. Far W. Fed. Sav. 717 P.2d 1271 (Or. Ct. App.), *review denied*, 725 P.2d 1293 (Or. 1986) (becoming engaged to be married); Staats v. Ohio Nat'l Life. Ins. Co., 620 F. Supp. 118 (W.D. Pa. 1985) (attending a convention with employee who was not spouse); Rogers v. IBM, 500 F. Supp. 867 (W.D. Pa. 1980) (affair with subordinate).

[51] That being said, even such an implied covenant claim must be based on the company having rules and regulations respecting employee's privacy in instances where the behavior does not impact the interests of the company. *See Rulon-Miller*, 208 Cal. Rptr. at 247-48.

[52] 539 U.S. 558 (2003).

[53] *Id.* at 578.

[54] *See* Paul M. Secunda, Lawrence's *Quintessential Millian Moment and Its Impact on the Doctrine of Unconstitutional Conditions*, 50 VILL. L. REV. 117, 128-36 (2005).

of its employees may it do so without violating its employees' sexual privacy rights under the due process clause of the Fourteenth Amendment.[55]

Although this new right to sexual privacy for public employees has not yet been examined by many courts, a North Carolina state court has recently found an 1805 fornication state statute unconstitutional based on *Lawrence*'s holding. There, a female sheriff dispatcher, who lived with her boyfriend, claimed that she was forced to quit her job by the Sheriff when she would not either marry her boyfriend or move out of the house.[56] The North Carolina state court found that the fornication law was unconstitutional because, based on *Lawrence*, the law violated the employee's constitutional right to liberty.[57] Thus, post-*Lawrence*, a government employer may be prohibited from firing a government employee based on private decisions a public employee makes regarding his or her personal life, unless the employer has substantial and legitimate reasons relating to governmental efficiency for doing so. In this regard, this sexual privacy test is similar to the nexus test in the union context, the standards under some state off-duty conduct statutes, and the First Amendment free speech analysis under *Pickering* and its progeny.

§ 9.04 DRUG TESTING

As with other areas of employment law concerning workplace rights potentially covered by constitutional provisions, the law of workplace drug testing is divided into public employment, where the Fourth Amendment applies, and private employment, where employees must rely on either statutory schemes or common law theories like the tort of invasion of privacy.

[A] Public Employees and the Fourth Amendment

Because state action exists in the public employment sector, employers must abide by the search and seizure constraints of the Fourth Amendment of the United States Constitution when physically searching an employee. Because removal of blood, urine, or other bodily fluids from a person for purposes of drug testing is considered a constitutional search which invades legitimate privacy expectations,[58] public employers are subject to the Fourth Amendment, but must only satisfy a less stringent "reasonableness" standard in order to engage in drug testing.[59]

---

[55] Paul M. Secunda, *The (Neglected) Importance of Being* Lawrence: *The Constitutionalization of Public Employee Rights to Decisional Non-Interference in Private Affairs*, 40 U.C. Davis L. Rev. 85, 122-27 (2006).

[56] *See* Steve Hartsoe, *ACLU Challenges N.C. Cohabitation Law*, Wash. Post, May 10, 2005, at A06.

[57] *Judge Rules N.C. Anti-cohabitation Law Unconstitutional*, USA Today, July 21, 2006, *available at* www.usatoday.com/news/nation/2006-07-21-cohabitation_x.htm?csp=34.

[58] *See* Skinner v. Ry. Labor Executives' Ass'n, 489 U.S. 602, 617 (1989).

[59] However, the California Supreme Court has found that job applicants have less protection under the Fourth Amendment than incumbent employees because an employer has a greater need to conduct suspicionless drug testing of applicants whom the employer has not had the opportunity to observe over a period of time. *See* Loder v. City of Glendale, 927 P.2d 1200 (Cal. 1997).

For instance, in *National Treasury Employees Union v. Von Raab*,[60] the question presented was whether federal customs agents could be subjected to drug urinalysis testing as a condition of their being promoted or transferred, even though there was no history of a drug problem in the Customs Service.[61] Using a constitutional balancing test based on a reasonableness standard, the court noted that the immediacy of the government's concern and the minimal nature of the intrusion outweighed the individual's privacy interest and permitted the government to drug test customs agents.[62]

The Supreme Court has also permitted drug testing of non-law enforcement public employees where there is reason to suspect that the employee has been under the influence of drugs. For instance, in *Skinner v. Railway Labor Executives'Ass'n*,[63] the Court applied a balancing test to determine that Federal Railroad Administration's regulations mandating that private railroads test for drugs and alcohol in employees involved with major railroad accidents was constitutional under the Fourth Amendment.[64] In short, public employees are most likely to be successful in challenging drug testing regimes in situations where employees are not involved in dangerous, sensitive work or where there is no evidence to suggest that employees have been using drugs.

More recently, the Supreme Court struck down in *Chandler v. Miller*[65] a state statute in Georgia that required random drug testing of candidates for public office. At this time, it is unclear whether *Chandler* signals that all random drug testing would be struck down as too intrusive of public employee's Fourth Amendment privacy rights, or whether *Chandler* can be limited to the ability of individuals to run for office since it did not involve public safety issues like *Von Raab* or *Skinner*. Lower courts have generally disagreed over whether suspicionless random drug testing is consistent with the Fourth Amendment.[66]

Finally, public school teachers have been found to be more like the employees in *Von Raab* than the candidates for public office in *Chandler* in that they hold not only a safety-sensitive position, but also because they have a strong influence over impressionable children. For instance, in *Knox County Education Ass'n v. Knox*

---

[60] 489 U.S. 656 (1989).

[61] *See id.* at 659.

[62] *Id.* at 677. The importance of the government interest in ensuring that these federal employees, who carried guns and interdicted drugs, were drug-free led the Court to conclude that the constitutional balance favored the employer and that the drug testing was reasonable under the Fourth Amendment. In finding in the government employer's favor, the Court also noted the diminished expectation of individual privacy that comes with jobs involving the interdiction of drugs.

[63] 489 U.S. 602 (1989).

[64] *Id.* at 616-18. *Von Raab* and *Skinner* were decided on the same day. *Von Raab* was a 5-4 decision, while *Skinner* was 7-2. The difference in how the Justices voted is usually attributed to the fact there was more of a history of a problem of drug abuse, and more suspicion after the accident, in *Skinner.*

[65] 520 U.S. 305 (1997).

[66] *Compare* Romaguera v. Gegenheimer, 162 F.3d 893 (5th Cir. 1998) (disallowing drug testing of employee at Clerk's office), *with* Stigile v. Clinton (D.C. Cir. 1997) (permitting urinalysis of those with access to Old Executive Office Building).

County Board of Education,[67] the Sixth Circuit Court of Appeals considered whether the school district could drug test its teachers randomly or based on suspicion. The court answered both questions in the affirmative, finding on the more controversial random drug testing issue that "the suspicionless testing regime is justified by the unique role school teachers play in the lives of school children and the *in loco parentis* obligations imposed upon them."[68]

[B]　Private Employees and Invasion of Privacy

So what rights to be free from drug testing do private sector employees have, given that they cannot claim the protections of the Fourth Amendment? Such challenges usually maintain that the process of specimen collection invades employees' privacy[69] or that the test itself reveals sensitive private information.[70] In making these claims, private employees rely on legal arguments based on state constitutional provisions, statutory regimes, or common law doctrine, and are generally less successful than their public employee counterparts.

Luedtke v. Nabors Alaska Drilling, Inc.[71] provides an overview of the different legal theories that can be advanced by a private employee challenging an employer's drug testing scheme. In *Luedtke*, Paul and Clarence Luedtke worked on an oil rig for Nabors Alaska Drilling. During a twenty-eight-day leave of absence, Paul had a physical at which he gave a sample of urine. Unbeknownst to Paul, his urine was tested for drugs and a positive result for marijuana came back. Consequently, he was suspended. Thereafter, Nabors instituted a drug testing program for all employees, and Paul and Clarence refused to be tested. They were then both terminated.

The Alaska Supreme Court remanded the case on whether Paul's initial suspension violated the implied covenant of good faith and fair dealing, as the drug testing there was completed without a formal policy in place and without Paul's knowledge.[72] The court found, however, that the termination of Paul and Clarence for refusing to submit to the drug test did not violate their privacy rights under any legal theory. Specifically, the court held that the termination: (1) did not violate the Alaska's constitution right to privacy because those provisions did not apply to private actors,[73] (2) did not constitute a public policy tort[74] because the employer

---

[67]　158 F.3d 361 (6th Cir. 1998).

[68]　*Id.* at 365. It stands to reason, based on these very same principles, that public university professors who do not play the same role in college students lives and do not hold "safety sensitive" positions most likely may not be subject to random or any other type of drug testing.

[69]　*See, e.g.*, Kelley v. Schlumberger, 849 F.2d 41 (1st Cir. 1988) (direct observation by supervisor of urine specimen collection is overly intrusive).

[70]　*See, e.g.*, Capua v. City of Plainfield, 643 F. Supp. 1507 (D.N.J. 1986) (discussing dangers of overinclusive test results provided to employers as a result of drug testing).

[71]　768 P.2d 1123 (Alaska 1989).

[72]　On remand, the lower court disagreed that there was a good faith violation, but the Supreme Court of Alaska ordered damages as a matter of law when it heard the case again. *See* Luedtke v. Nabors Alaska Drilling, Inc., 834 P.2d 1220 (Alaska 1992).

[73]　Some states, like California, allow private-sector employees to bring claims based on state constitutional privacy protections. *See* Semore v. Pool, 266 Cal. Rptr. 280 (Cal. Ct. App. 1990).

had the right to make sure employees did not put themselves or others in danger,[75] (3) did not amount to an intrusion into privacy because the employees refused to be drug tested,[76] and (4) did not violate the implied covenant of good faith and fair dealing[77] because the test was proposed at a time reasonably contemporaneous to the employees' work time and notice of the adoption of the test was given to the employees. In all, private employees will likely have a difficult time mounting state constitutional or common law challenges to private work place drug testing programs as long as some basic procedural benchmarks, concerning notice and timeliness, are followed by the employer.[78]

Nevertheless, there are both federal and state statutory schemes that require consideration when deciding whether to test private sector employees for drug use.[79] About half of the states now have statutory schemes regulating drug testing. Some of these schemes are limited to procedural protections,[80] some are primarily concerned with employee privacy,[81] while still others seek to limit employer liability for instituting testing as long as certain minimal standards are followed.[82]

The Louisiana drug testing statute[83] is of the procedural variety and was at issue in *Sanchez v. Georgia Gulf Corp.*[84] In *Sanchez*, a twenty-six-year veteran employee of the company was fired after he tested positive for cocaine during a random drug screen urinalysis. The employee argued that the positive cocaine results attributed to him were invalid as a matter of law because he was not given the ability, consistent with the procedural protections of the statute, to discuss the medications that he was taking, and the effect they may have had on his sample,

---

[74] *See supra* § 6.02.

[75] At least one well-known case from California has pointed out that it is somewhat paradoxical to talk of a public policy of protecting privacy rights. *See* Luck v. S. Pac. Transp. Co., 267 Cal. Rptr. 618 (Cal. Ct. App. 1990). One possible way to argue for such a conception is to say that privacy is a public benefit. For additional background on the *Luck* case, see Pauline T. Kim, *The Story of* Luck v. Southern Pacific Transportation Co.: *The Struggle to Perfect Employee Privacy, in* EMPLOYMENT LAW STORIES (Samuel Estreicher & Gillian Lester eds., 2006).

[76] There appears to be a "dilemma of consent" or Catch-22 for employees who refuse to take a drug test. On the one hand, if they refuse to be tested, there has been no intrusion of which to complain, but on the other hand, if they had consented, there would have been diminished expectations of privacy and it would have been harder to say that the testing was highly offensive to them as a reasonable person.

[77] *See supra* § 5.05

[78] As a side note, drug testing is not considered a medical examination for purposes of the Americans with Disabilities Act of 1990 (ADA), 42 U.S.C. §§ 12101-12213, and thus, does not run afoul of that statutory regime either.

[79] For instance, because some states permit the use of "medical marijuana," courts have had to consider whether the legality of such marijuana use insulates some employees from discipline for violating drug testing rules. Courts in two states, Oregon and California, have both concluded that medical marijuana users are not immunized from employer discipline in such cases. *See* Emerald Steel Fabricators, Inc. v. Bureau of Labor & Indus., 230 P.3d 518 (Or. 2010); Ross v. RagingWire Telecomms., Inc., 174 P.3d 200 (Cal. 2008).

[80] *See, e.g.*, ME. REV. STAT. ANN. tit. 26, § 681.

[81] *See, e.g.*, VT. STAT. ANN. tit. 21, §§ 511-519.

[82] *See, e.g.*, UTAH CODE ANN. §§ 34-38-1 to -15.

[83] LA. REV. STAT. ANN. §§ 49:1001-49:1021.

[84] 853 So. 2d 697 (La. Ct. App. 2003).

with the Medical Review Officer (MRO) interpreting the results. The court found that it was mandatory that the MRO consult with the employee to verify that the positive cocaine result was not caused by prescription medication or other health conditions. The lack of consultation ran afoul of the employee protections contained in the statute and required the court to invalidate the drug test as a matter of law.[85]

In another case involving an employee suing his employer for violating the state drug testing statute, *Sims v. NCI Holding Corporation*,[86] the Iowa Supreme Court found that in drug testing its employee, the employer violated statutory notice requirements. In *Sims*, the employee was in a "safety sensitive position" because he oversaw the operation of the company's steel decoiling machines and operated a forklift to transport very heavy items. In accordance with company policies that the employee previously acknowledged, he was picked for a random drug testing and failed. Although the company complied with many of the procedural requirements of the Iowa drug testing statute, the court concluded that the company violated the statute by failing to substantially comply with provisions requiring written notice by certified mail (they only provided the necessary notices orally) of the positive drug test, the employee's right to obtain a confirmatory test, and the right to be reimbursed for taking such a second test. Although this "victory" for the employee did not lead to his reinstatement or damages for wrongful termination (perhaps because the test results were never shown to be falsely positive), it did provide a lesson for other employers about the importance of strictly following drug testing statute procedures and gave the employee in *Sims* the ability to recover the costs of bringing his lawsuit.

As far as federal statutory schemes, Congress passed the Drug Free Workplace Act of 1988,[87] which applies to all federal contractors and federal grantees. It requires that covered employers notify employees that all illegal drugs are prohibited from the workplace and requires employers to establish drug-free awareness programs. The Act, however, does not specifically refer to drug testing.

§ 9.05 POLYGRAPHS AND HONESTY TESTING

Because of the increasing use of polygraph and honesty testing by employers to screen employees and applicants for deception, there has been much litigation surrounding these tests involving claims of wrongful discharge, invasion of privacy, defamation, and intentional infliction of emotional distress. As a result, both the federal government and some states have responded with statutes and regulations which largely outlaw polygraphs for private employment purposes and restrict the use of honesty tests.

---

[85] The Louisiana Court of Appeals later vacated this opinion and found that the drug-testing statute did not prohibit the employer from discharging the at-will employee, even though the employer failed to comply with the statutory procedures for conducting a drug test in Louisiana. *See* Sanchez v. Ga. Gulf Corp., 860 So. 2d. 277 (La. Ct. App. 2003), *writ denied*, 869 So. 2d 877 (La. 2004).

[86] 759 N.W.2d 333 (Iowa 2009).

[87] 41 U.S.C. §§ 701-707. Executive Order 12,564 requires drug-free workplace programs to be instituted for federal employees, but unlike the Drug Free Workplace Act, requires drug testing for employees in sensitive positions and permits it for additional employees in other circumstances. 51 Fed. Reg. 32,889 (1986) (codified in 5 U.S.C. § 7301).

[A] Polygraph Testing

Congress passed the Employee Polygraph Protection Act of 1988[88] in response to growing evidence that employees were suffering adverse employment consequences as a result of "failing" polygraph exams that were generally not considered by experts to be scientifically valid. The Act makes it unlawful for an employer to require or request an employee or applicant to submit to a polygraph or use the results of such tests, except in limited circumstances.[89] For instance, the Act permits employers to request an employee to submit to a polygraph as part of an ongoing investigation involving economic loss or injury to the employer's business, as long as certain procedures are satisfied.[90] However, in such circumstances, employees may not be asked degrading or intrusive questions concerning religious, racial, political, sexual, or union beliefs. Violations of the Act subject employers to civil penalties and to private causes of action.

The Act does not apply to public employers, national defense and security contractors, security guard firms, and drug manufacturers and distributors.[91] Regarding the exemption for public employees, Congress concluded that polygraph abuses concerning public employees were less problematic because federal and state courts could use constitutional protections to protect such employees.[92] States are still permitted to have more restrictive polygraph laws than the federal statute.[93]

[B] Honesty Testing

Honesty tests (also referred to as paper-and-pencil tests, integrity tests, or psychological tests) use various types of questions to determine whether a job applicant will be dishonest or his or her hiring will lead to counterproductive outcomes. As with polygraph tests, there is still substantial disagreement over whether these tests can really predict dishonest behavior.[94]

Nevertheless, honesty testing is not considered a type of lie-detecting test generally prohibited by the Employee Polygraph Protection Act of 1988 or similar anti-polygraph state laws. Some states like Massachusetts and Rhode Island restrict the use of honesty testing as an employment screening device, but most

---

[88] 29 U.S.C. §§ 2001-2029.

[89] *Id.* § 2002.

[90] *Id.* §§ 2006(d), 2007.

[91] *Id.* § 2006.

[92] Indeed, California courts have found that public employees cannot be compelled to take a polygraph test under state constitutional privacy provisions when the questions posed are highly personal and not related to the job duties the employee must perform. *See* Long Beach City Employees Ass'n v. City of Long Beach, 41 Cal. 3d 937, 945 (1986).

[93] 29 U.S.C. § 2009.

[94] There is a further debate over whether employees can game the system by answering questions in a way that reflects their understanding of how the employer wants these questions answered. However, there is some counter-evidence to suggest that applicants generally do not engage in "fakery" when completing such tests. *See* Ann Marie Ryan & Paul R. Sackett, *Pre-Employment Honesty Testing: Fakability, Reactions of Test Takers, and Company Image*, 1 J. Bus. & Psych. 248 (1987).

states generally permit such tests. Many employers continue to use such testing, especially in the retail trade.

Although honesty testing generally is permitted by most states, employers can set up their testing in such a way to run afoul of state constitutional privacy provisions and federal and state antidiscrimination laws. A prime example is the California case of *Soroka v. Dayton Hudson Corp.*[95] In *Soroka*, a class of successful and unsuccessful job applicants for store security officer positions at Target Stores throughout California challenged an honesty test. The 704 true-false question test asked a number of sensitive religious and sexual orientation questions, such as, "I believe in the second coming of Christ," and "I am very strongly attracted by members of my own sex."[96] Although the employer sought to use the answers to determine traits such as dependability, reliability, emotional stability, and the tendency to follow directions, the court found that under state constitutional and statutory law the test violated the applicants' privacy rights without compelling justification and discriminated against applicants with regard to their religion and sexual orientation[97] without any job-related justification. Consequently, although honesty testing remains a viable option for employers seeking to root out dishonest employees, such tests must be fashioned so as not to violate individuals' constitutional and statutory rights.

One of the reasons that employers are increasingly using honesty and psychological testing is to avoid being sued over an employee who causes harm to a third party while engaged in work for the employer.[98] In such situations, vicarious or respondeat superior liability is generally not available against the employer because when the employee engages in criminal or intentionally tortious activity against another individual, he or she is not acting within the scope of employment. Instead, injured parties rely on the tort of negligent hiring or retention, maintaining that the mere hiring or retaining of the employee for the job was negligent given the employee's propensities to cause harm to others. The negligent hiring and retention tort is based on the proposition that employers have the duty to protect employees and customers from other employees who the employers know, or should reasonably know, pose a danger to third parties. Employers breach this special duty when they fail to exercise reasonable care in their hiring processes, or in their other employment decisions, by not taking action

---

[95] 1 Cal. Rptr. 2d 77 (Cal. Ct. App. 1991).

[96] *Id.* at 79-80.

[97] Discrimination on the basis of sexual orientation would only be at issue in states and localities like California which have prohibitions against this form of discrimination. Federal antidiscrimination law under Title VII does not cover sexual orientation discrimination.

[98] Employers also are increasingly conducting criminal background checks of employees and applicants for these same reasons. In doing so, employers must be aware that if they contract out the criminal background check to a third-party service provider, they will come under the provisions of the Fair Credit Reporting Act (FCRA), 15 U.S.C. §§ 1681-1681t, because such background check agencies are considered "consumer reporting agencies" for purposes of the law. The FCRA requires that the employer tell the employees/applicant about the preparation of the report, that the employer obtain a signed release from employees/applicants before collecting information, and that the employer provide a copy of the completed report to the employees/applicants if the background check leads to denial or loss of employment. For a case discussing the FCRA in the employment context, see Lewis v. Ohio Prof'l Elec. Network LLC, 190 F. Supp. 2d 1049 (D. Ohio 2002).

against employees based on information available to them that would suggest an employee represents a foreseeable risk. More succinctly, an employer is liable if:

- It failed to exercise reasonable care in its hiring or retention process,

- Such negligence was a cause of harm or injury to a third party, and

- A reasonable employer should have foreseen such injury or harm.

Employers avoid this type of liability by using pre-employment testing as a way to identify those employees with violent propensities who should not be hired in the first place. A classic case in this area is *Thatcher v. Brennan*.[99] In *Thatcher*, a medical supply salesperson (Brennan) became involved in a fight with another man (Thatcher) after completing some office work at the post office. Thatcher sued Brennan's employer under a theory of *respondeat superior* and negligent hiring. The court found that vicarious liability against the employer was not available because Brennan was not acting in the scope of his employment, but rather in a purely personal way, when he harmed Thatcher. On the negligent hiring theory, although an employer-administered psychological test had shown that Brennan had an "aggressive" personality, the court found this evidence was insufficient to put the employer on notice that Brennan had violent attributes and would likely attack another person while performing his job duties.[100] In short, in order to hold employers liable for negligent hiring or retention, employers must have known, or should have known, about past violence on the employee's part and hired him anyway.[101] It also seems that to the extent that an employer hires an employee for a job where that employee is likely to come into contact with identifiable third parties, such as with repair persons or service installers who go to customers' homes, the more closely the employer needs to check the employee for past instances of aggression or violence to avoid being found negligent under this tort theory.

§ 9.06   GENETIC TESTING

Along with drug testing, polygraphs, and honesty testing, genetic screening tests are increasingly being used by employers to determine which employees are predisposed to certain inheritable diseases and conditions. Employers desire this information to determine health insurance costs and to keep at-risk employees away from jobs which require handling of dangerous substances. Although such testing is far less pervasive than honesty testing because of the costs involved, as the technology becomes cheaper, genetic testing may become more prevalent.

---

[99] 657 F. Supp. 6 (S.D. Miss. 1986).

[100] On the other hand, the trucking company in *Malorney v. B&L Motor Freight, Inc.*, 496 N.E.2d 1086 (Ill. App. Ct. 1986), did not sufficiently check references or the background of a truck driver who had previous convictions for violent sex crimes, and thus a hitchhiker raped by that truck driver was permitted to proceed to trial on her claim of negligent hiring by the employer.

[101] Employees have been less successful in claiming negligent hiring liability in cases in which the employer has not administered psychological testing to an employee. *See* S. Bell Tel. & Tel. Co. v. Sharara, 302 S.E.2d 129 (Ga. Ct. App. 1983) (reversing trial court determination that telephone company was liable for negligent hiring where company did not psychologically test telephone repairman who attacked a woman after installing a phone in her home).

As discussed previously in Chapter 7, the Genetic Information Nondiscrimination Act ("GINA"),[102] which prohibits employers from discriminating on the basis of an employee's genetic information in employment or in the provision of health insurance, became law in 2009. GINA also limits employers' acquisition, use, storage, and disclosure of an employee's genetic information. Before enactment of the federal GINA law, 34 states had their own laws protecting against genetic discrimination in the workplace.[103] These laws are based on similar privacy and reliability concerns discussed above with regard to other types of employment testing.[104] Also, in the area of employee benefits, the Health Insurance Portability and Accountability Act of 1996 (HIPAA)[105] prohibits an employer-provided health plan from using health-related factors relating to an employee's genetics to deny or limit eligibility for coverage under such a plan or to charge an individual more for coverage.[106]

---

[102] Pub. L. No. 110-233 (2008).

[103] *See* CCH HEALTH CARE COMPLIANCE, *Genetic Nondiscrimination Bill Advances*, Feb. 15, 2007, *available at* health.cch.com/news/healthcare-compliance/031407a.asp. In addition, Executive Order 13145, issued by President Clinton in 2000, prohibits discrimination in federal employment based on genetic information. 65 Fed. Reg. 6,877 (2000).

[104] For instance, the American Medical Association's Council on Ethical and Judicial Affairs found that genetic screening alone does "not have sufficient predictive value to be relied on as a basis for excluding workers." *See* COUNCIL ON ETHICAL AND JUDICIAL AFFAIRS OF THE AMERICAN MEDICAL ASSOCIATION, *Use of Genetic Testing By Employers*, 266 J. AM. MED. ASS'N 1827, 1830 (1991).

[105] Pub. L. No. 104-191, 110 Stat. 1936 (1996). HIPAA is analyzed in greater detail *infra* § 14.04[F].

[106] ERISA §§ 701(b)(1)(B), 702(a)(1)(F) (codified at 29 U.S.C. §§ 1181-1182).

Chapter 10

DEFAMATION AND EMPLOYMENT REFERENCES

§ 10.01   INTRODUCTION

Whenever an employer publicizes the reasons for firing an employee, gives a negative reference to a subsequent employer, or discloses sensitive employee information to other employees, there is a risk that the employer will be subject to either a defamation or invasion of privacy claim. Defamation claims, as well as false light invasion of privacy claims, focus on reputational injuries to persons as a result of false statements being published to others about them. Invasion of privacy claims based on public disclosure of private facts, on the other hand, focus on the violation of employee informational privacy interests when true statements of facts are disclosed to the general public and the public has no legitimate concern in knowing those facts.

§ 10.02   THE TORT OF DEFAMATION

[A]   The Basic Framework

To state a claim for defamation, a plaintiff must show: (1) a false and defamatory statement concerning another, (2) an unprivileged publication to a third party, (3) fault amounting at least to negligence on the part of the publisher, and (4) the existence of special harm caused by the publication.[1]

[1] False and Defamatory Statement

Regarding the first element of the defamation claim, the requirement of a false and defamatory statement, even seemingly innocuous statements made by an employer can lead to a defamation action that survives summary judgment. For instance, in *Elbeshbeshy v. Franklin Institute*,[2] a personality dispute erupted between two co-workers. The employer decided to terminate one, but fabricated the actual reason for his termination, saying that the employee exhibited a lack of cooperation. The federal district court refused to grant summary judgment for the employer, finding that the terminated employee had a potential valid defamation claim on these facts.

As an initial matter, the statement was defamatory in that it lowered the employee's reputation in the relevant community.[3] In this regard, the court, somewhat controversially, concluded that the words "lack of cooperation" could be taken to mean that the employee was "irremediably insubordinate, obnoxious, and antagonistic" and this would deter others from associating or dealing with him.[4] Because the court also found that there was publication of the statement inside the company to at least one other person, and that there was a genuine issue of material fact of whether the employer abused its privilege to evaluate the performance of its employees (abuse of conditional privileges in this context will be discussed further below), the employee's defamation claim was allowed to proceed.

In light of *Elbeshbeshy* and similar cases in which relatively mild reasons for an employee's firing give rise to a finding that a statement was defamatory, many employers have concluded that it makes more sense to fire an employee without giving any explanation. Although this practice might make sense from a defamation standpoint (as discussed further in § 10.03), such termination procedures would likely be susceptible to employment discrimination challenges, especially when the employee in question is a member of a protected group and has been treated dissimilarly in comparison to similarly situated employees outside of their group.

[2] Publication and Self-Publication

Although *Elbeshbeshy* makes clear that the publication prong of the defamation claim is met as long as there is communication of the statement to at least one other person, even if the person is within the same company,[5] an additional difficult issue

---

[1] RESTATEMENT (SECOND) OF TORTS § 558. Many of these issues concerning defamation, employer references, and public disclosure of private facts, will be addressed in Chapter 6 of the RESTATEMENT (THIRD) OF EMPLOYMENT LAW.

[2] 618 F. Supp. 170 (E.D. Pa. 1985).

[3] RESTATEMENT (SECOND) OF TORTS § 559.

[4] *Elbeshbeshy*, 618 F. Supp. at 171.

[5] As far as publication, the majority rule followed in *Elbeshbeshy* is that the statement does not have to be published outside of the company to meet this element, as long as at least one other person hears the statement. Other courts have taken the view that intra-corporate publication is just the "corporation" talking to itself, and consequently, there has been no publication to support a defamation claim. *See, e.g.,*

arises in this area. Take for example the self-publication cases. In these cases, the employer tells only the employee the reasons for his or her termination; nevertheless, the employee reveals the reason in subsequent job interviews in response to questions about previous employment. In such self-publication situations, some courts have found that the publication element has been met for a defamation claim.[6] As a result of these cases, a number of state legislatures have responded by protecting employers from defamation in such instances.[7]

[3] Fault

Because defamation is a tort, the publisher of the defamatory statement is thought to have to make the statement with some degree of fault. There is some question about what level of fault a private plaintiff suing a defendant must show to establish a defamation claim. Although from a constitutional perspective, different levels of culpability apply in defamation cases involving public officials, public figures, or media defendants,[8] there has never been a definitive consensus on the fault question in private-sector employment defamation cases. Most courts follow the Restatement of Tort language and require fault at least of the negligence variety.[9]

[4] Special Harm

The damages element under the defamation tort generally requires a showing of special harm. Nevertheless, the establishment of special harm is usually not at issue in employment law cases. Historically, defamation was thought to consist of oral defamation (slander) and written defamation (libel). This distinction was important because only certain types of slander claims, so-called slander *per quod* claims, required the showing of special harm — in particular, that the defamatory statement actually caused monetary losses to the plaintiff based on the reactions to the statement by others.[10] So-called slander *per se* cases did not require such a showing because these statements were considered defamatory on their face without reference to other facts. Employees claiming defamation fall generally into this latter category, as the statement itself can be shown to have caused damages in the form of loss of job opportunities. In any event, oral statements damaging one's profession have traditionally been considered slander *per se* without further need of proof of special harm.[11]

Monahan v. Sims, 294 S.E.2d 548 (Ga. Ct. App. 1982).

  [6] *See* Theisen v. Covenant Med. Ctr., 636 N.W.2d 74 (Iowa 2001); Lewis v. Equitable Life Assurance Soc'y, 389 N.W.2d 876 (Minn. 1986). *But see* Olivieri v. Rodriguez, 122 F.3d 406 (7th Cir. 1997) (finding the doctrine of compelled self-defamation inconsistent with the fundamental principle of mitigation of damages).

  [7] *See, e.g.*, COLO. REV. STAT. ANN. § 13-25-125.5; MINN. STAT. ANN. § 181.933

  [8] Gertz v. Robert Welch, Inc., 418 U.S. 323 (1974); New York Times v. Sullivan, 376 U.S. 254 (1964).

  [9] RESTATEMENT (SECOND) OF TORTS § 580B.

  [10] Although special damages are not generally required to support a libel claim, some states do recognize different forms of libel. These states require that special damages be proven in libel *per quod* cases to show that the defamatory writing caused monetary harm to the plaintiff.

  [11] RESTATEMENT (SECOND) OF TORTS § 573.

[B]   Conditional Privileges and Abuse of Privilege

As a general matter, employers have a conditional privilege to publish the reasons for an employee's termination to other employees. Privileges in defamation law are recognized to take into account that certain conduct furthers interests of societal importance which should be protected even if it causes harm to the plaintiff. For instance, under the "common interest" privilege theory,[12] co-workers have an interest in knowing about the reasons for termination of others to quell rumors of unjustified firings and to give employees guidelines for future acceptable workplace conduct.

Nevertheless, this privilege is conditional and may be lost if abused.[13] Abuse of the privilege occurs most commonly where the defendant knows the matter to be false, or acts in reckless disregard as to its truth or falsity.[14] This is sometimes referred to as the "actual malice" or "common law malice" standard, and is the same fault standard used in First Amendment defamation claims involving public officials and public figures. Abuse of the privilege may also occur if the alleged defamer engages in excessive publication of the defamatory statement "by speaking defamatory words in the presence of persons whose knowledge of them is unnecessary to the protection of the interest in question."[15]

The case of *Zinda v. Louisiana Pacific Corp.*[16] provides a typical application of the common interest privilege, and a discussion of excessive publication, in a somewhat unusual employment defamation case. In *Zinda,* an employee filled out a job application form to work for an employer who, among other things, manufactured roofing material. The employee had stated on his application form that he did not suffer from any ongoing personal health issues. However, the employer was able to determine that the employee lied on his application with regard to his personal health history when the employee a year later filed a products liability action against this same employer! The products liability claims alleged that two years prior to his employment with the company, the employee suffered permanent injuries when his garage's roof, built with the employer's materials, collapsed under him. The employer, not surprisingly, fired the employee for falsification of his employment forms and then printed the reason for his termination in the company newsletter.

On the employee's claims for defamation, the court concluded that the employer had a conditional privilege to publish the reason for the employee's firing in the newsletter in order to satisfy other employees' legitimate interest in knowing the reasons why a fellow employee was discharged. The common interest privilege also existed to protect the employer's interest in maintaining morale and productivity which otherwise might suffer if rumors were allowed to fester. Finally, in the

---

[12] *Id.* § 596.

[13] In contrast to the conditional privileges in these employment law cases, absolute privileges from defamation liability exist for, among others, judicial officers performing judicial functions and attorneys, parties, and witnesses participating in judicial proceedings. *Id.* §§ 585-588.

[14] *Id.* § 600.

[15] *Id.* § 604 cmt. a.

[16] 440 N.W.2d 548 (Wis. 1989).

particular context of *Zinda*, the court concluded that the privilege should also be recognized because truthfulness and integrity in the employment application process is an important common interest.

Although evidence adduced indicated that information about the employee's termination for falsification of employment forms was discussed between two women at the hospital where the employee's wife worked, the court found that the privilege was not abused because this additional dissemination did not amount to excessive publication. The court concluded that the privilege should not be lost where the publication only involved an incidental communication to persons not within the scope of the privilege.[17]

[C] False Light Claims

Similar to defamation claims, and sometimes alleged at the same time in the same cases, are false light invasion of privacy claims. These claims involve giving publicity to a matter that places a person before the public in a false light. Like other privacy claims in the private-sector workplace discussed in Chapter 9, the issue in these cases is whether placing the individual in a false light would be highly offensive to a reasonable person. The Restatement of Torts provides that "the actor [must have] knowledge of or acted in reckless disregard as to the falsity of the publicized matter and the false light in which the other would be placed," but takes no stance on whether mere negligence is enough to establish a false light claim.[18]

Although false light and defamation are similar and sometimes are analyzed under the same legal framework, it is not necessary to allege a defamatory statement to prevail on a false light claim.[19]

§ 10.03 EMPLOYMENT REFERENCES

When an employer is asked to give an employee a reference, particular defamation concerns come to the fore. Specifically at issue is whether an employer has abused a conditional privilege to speak about the employee. In such cases, and consistent with the abuse of privilege analysis in § 10.02[B], the issue is whether the reference is given with actual malice or with reckless disregard of the truth. The employee generally must make this showing by clear and convincing evidence (as opposed to the normal preponderance of the evidence standard).

---

[17] On the other hand, in the more recent case of *Noonan v. Staples, Inc.*, 556 F.3d 20 (1st Cir. 2009), the company was found to have abused the conditional privilege when it sent a mass email informing some 1500 other employees that the plaintiffs had been fired for failing to comply with company travel and expense policies. Although the email was truthful, and truth is sometimes referred to as an absolute defense to malice, Massachusetts law allows an exception to the truth defense if actual malice can still be established. Summary judgment was reversed for the employer and the case was sent back for trial on this ground because the evidence established that this type of mass email had never been sent before to such a large group of co-employees and the possibility of excessive publication existed.

[18] RESTATEMENT (SECOND) OF TORTS § 652E. As a result of the ambivalence on the negligence issue, it actually may be more difficult to allege an invasion of privacy claim than a defamation claim in some jurisdictions.

[19] *See, e.g.*, Brennan v. Kadner, 814 N.E.2d 951, 959 (Ill. App. Ct. 2004).

Sigal Construction Corp. v. Stanbury[20] outlines the dangers that employers face in giving references without factual support. In *Stanbury*, the employer's project manager gave a former employee a less-than-glowing review to another employer, stating, among other things, that the employee was "detailed oriented to the point of losing sight of the big picture."[21] Based on this and other evidence, the court affirmed a $250,000 defamation verdict for the employee, finding that the common interest conditional privilege had been abused by the former employer. Specifically, the statements in question were made without the project manager having supervised, evaluated, or even worked with the employee, and the manager based his reference to the other employer on rumors and his "general sense" of the employee.[22] The project manager also led the prospective employer to believe he had worked on a project with the employee when he had not. Under these circumstances, the court found that the employer's reference was not only negligent, but rose to the level of actual malice in its reckless disregard of the truth, and thus permitted a finding that the privilege to give the reference had been abused.

Although the court in *Stanbury* sought to reassure employers that most employee references will not lead to defamation liability as long as the employer avoids gossip and speaks truthfully about the sources of the information conveyed, many employers have responded either by refusing to give references at all or by giving very limited information in response to a reference request (so-called, "name, rank, and serial number" information). Indeed, one study recently found that 53% of employers had blanket policies against providing any form of employment reference for current or former employees and of those who provided information, 25% limited the information to just verification of employment.[23] Such limited information may only include an affirmation that the employee worked for the employer, the dates of the employment, and the position that the employee held. In response to the lack of employee references in the current legal environment, a large number of states have passed legislation giving qualified immunity to employers who give references to prospective employers.[24] However, it appears that many of these state statutes do no more than codify the current common law standards and thus, employers may still be unwilling to provide employee references in these states.

---

[20] 586 A.2d 1204 (D.C. 1991).

[21] *Id.* at 1206.

[22] The court also noted that the Supreme Court's decision in *Milkovich v. Lorain Journal Co.*, 497 U.S. 1 (1990), stood for the proposition that there was not a "wholesale exemption" from defamation claims for statements of opinion and that, "expressions of 'opinion' may often imply an assertion of objective fact." *Stanbury*, 586 A.2d at 1209 (quoting *Milkovich*, 497 U.S. at 18). Because the court found, however, that the statements in the employment reference were expressions of fact, the court concluded that it need not consider the implications of *Milkovich* for mixed statements of fact and opinion.

[23] *See* STEVEN L. WILLBORN ET AL., EMPLOYMENT LAW: CASES & MATERIALS 326 (5th ed. 2012) (citing SOCIETY FOR HUMAN RESOURCES MANAGEMENT, 2004 REFERENCE AND BACKGROUND CHECKING SURVEY REPORT 16–18 (2005)). Such a state of affairs can hardly be considered surprising because although the legal liability standard is relatively high in this area (i.e., actual malice), most of the benefits of giving such a reference go directly to the prospective employer, while most of the detriment (in the form of liability) falls squarely on the employer giving the reference.

[24] *See, e.g.*, OKLA. STAT. tit. 40, § 61; TENN. CODE ANN. § 50-1-105.

Giving falsely positive references is not the solution to the employment reference problem. Consider the case of *Randi W. v. Muroc Joint Unified School District*,[25] in which a school district gave a positive reference to an employee who was discharged for sexual misconduct. The school district was sued in tort for fraud and negligent misrepresentation when that employee later sexually abused a thirteen-year-old student at the new school.

Some prospective employers, desiring to obtain candid information about employees, have asked employees for waivers, in which the employee promises he or she will not sue the employer giving the reference for defamation. Generally, such waivers provide referring employers immunity from defamation claims.[26] Employers and employees have also entered into "limited-reference agreements" which, as part of an employment separation agreement, require employers to give a neutral reference to other prospective employers. When such agreements have been breached by an employer giving a negative reference, most courts have held that employees have the right to pursue a breach of contract claim.[27]

§ 10.04 INVASION OF PRIVACY CLAIMS

Chapter 9 identified the various types of invasion of privacy torts.[28] In addition to intrusion upon seclusion claims discussed in Chapter 9 and the false light privacy claims discussed in § 10.02[C] in connection with defamation, public disclosure of private facts is another type of privacy claim that sometimes arises in the employment context.[29]

Public disclosure of private fact claims, like other invasion of privacy torts, require that the disclosure of the private facts be highly offensive to a reasonable person, but these claims additionally require that such facts not be a legitimate concern to the public.[30] Public disclosure of private facts claims are different from generic defamation claims in two ways: (1) they involve a true statement of facts, and (2) the focus, rather than on publication to a third party, is on unwanted publicity to the public at large. Like defamation claims, however, some states subject this type of claim to conditional privilege and abuse of privilege analyses.[31]

---

[25] 929 P.2d 582 (Cal. 1997).

[26] *See* Cox v. Nasche, 70 F.3d 1030 (9th Cir. 1995); RESTATEMENT (SECOND) OF TORTS § 583 (stating that consent to publication of defamatory matter concerning the person is a complete defense to a defamation claim).

[27] *See* Resnik v. Blue Cross & Blue Shield, 912 S.W.2d 567 (Mo. Ct. App. 1995). *But see* Picton v. Anderson Union High Sch. Dist., 57 Cal. Rptr. 2d 829 (Cal Ct. App. 1996) (refusing to enforce limited-reference agreement where school had obligation to report circumstances of employee's termination to state administrative agency).

[28] *See supra* § 9.02[B] & note 5.

[29] RESTATEMENT (SECOND) OF TORTS § 652D.

[30] *Id.* Consequently, disclosure of facts in the public record, such as those disclosed in legal pleadings, will not give rise to a claim of this type. Information about one's sexual relations, on the other hand, is normally a private matter and disclosure of such information to the general public could lead to a successful public disclosure of private facts claim.

[31] *See, e.g.*, Zinda v. La. Pac. Corp., 440 N.W.2d 548, 556 (Wis. 1989) (applying Wisconsin privacy statute).

Often, these claims arise when personnel files of one employee are shown to other employees without a sufficient business justification. For instance, in *Eddy v. Brown*,[32] the Oklahoma Supreme Court considered a public disclosure of private facts claim in the context of a supervisor disclosing to a limited number of other employees that the plaintiff had seen a psychiatrist. The court rejected a claim of unreasonable publicity because only a small group of co-workers were told, and this tort normally requires that the general public be informed.

In a more employee-friendly case, *Bratt v. IBM Corp.*,[33] an employee was referred by his supervisor to a psychiatrist under contract with IBM. Later, the psychiatrist discussed her findings, without the employee's consent, with a number of IBM officials. The court found for the plaintiff on the privacy claim after balancing the employer's legitimate need for the information against the substantiality of the intrusion into the employee's privacy. In this sense, the tort of public disclosure of private facts appears to borrow from Fourth Amendment privacy jurisprudence in the public employee context by balancing employer and employee interests in determining the reasonableness of the disclosure.

---

[32] 715 P.2d 74 (Okla. 1986).

[33] 785 F.2d 352 (1st Cir. 1986).

Chapter 11

THE DUTY OF LOYALTY, TRADE SECRETS, COVENANTS NOT TO COMPETE, AND EMPLOYEE INVENTIONS

§ 11.01   INTRODUCTION

Up until this Chapter, most of the employment law doctrine discussed in this book has focused on employee rights in the workplace, including rights derived from exceptions to the at-will employment doctrine and rights surrounding speech, political, privacy, and reputational interests. But employees also expressly and implicitly make promises, and undertake duties, for the benefit of their employers. For instance, employees may agree not to use their employer's confidential information for the benefit of a competitor employer, to take customers or co-employees with them to a new employer when leaving their old employment, or to claim for themselves inventions created using company equipment and materials.

This Chapter sets forth the various duties and promises that employees make to employers and that are protected to different degrees under common law and statutory law.[1] It discusses: (1) common law duties of loyalty; (2) common law and statutory torts of misappropriation of trade secrets; (3) noncompetition clauses (also referred to as covenants not to compete); and (4) invention agreements. Many of these employee commitments to safeguard employer's business interests are made in separate signed employment agreements at the beginning, middle, or end of the employment relationship.

Before reviewing the substantive law, however, this Chapter first considers some theoretical underpinnings to give the reader a broader understanding of the ways in which the law treats these assorted employee undertakings.

§ 11.02   THE THEORY: OF HUMAN CAPITAL AND HIGH VELOCITY MARKETS

One of the foundational questions in this area of the law is: when should it be permissible to require employees to sign restrictive agreements or to be subject to restrictions concerning the sharing of employment-related information? This is an important question because some of these restrictions, like covenants not to compete, greatly interfere with employees' ability to earn a living. Works by Paul Rubin and Peter Shedd on human capital theory and Alan Hyde on high-velocity markets provide some important insights.

[A]   Rubin and Shedd on Human Capital

In *Human Capital and Covenants Not to Compete*,[2] Paul Rubin and Peter Shedd built a framework for analyzing when courts should enforce trade secrets and non-competition clauses. The article applies economist Gary Becker's distinction between general and firm-specific training, or put somewhat differently, the distinction between general human capital and specific human capital.[3] Whereas general training may be utilized in many different firms, firm-specific training uniquely benefits the employer that provides it.

The article then further divides general human capital into training that an employee can afford (e.g., education) and training that an employee cannot afford (e.g., the specifics of a trade secret). Employers will pay costs associated with

---

[1] Even in the public sector, such employee duties and promises generally do not implicate federal or state constitutional law. Additionally, it should be noted that most of these topics are addressed in Chapter 8 of the RESTATEMENT (THIRD) OF EMPLOYMENT LAW.

[2] 10 J. LEG. STUDIES 93 (1981).

[3] *See generally* GARY S. BECKER, HUMAN CAPITAL (1964).

general human capital only when it is too expensive for the employee to do so. The function, then, of trade secrets and noncompetition clauses is to protect an employer's investment in general training in these situations. On the other hand, courts must hesitate to enforce all trade secrets because full enforcement would prevent an employee from using the general training for which the employee has paid.

The basic message of the article, then, is that courts should enforce trade secrets and noncompetition clauses only if those secrets or clauses involve special knowledge, which the employee could not pay for on their own. Trade secrets worth billions of dollars would be a prototypical example of special knowledge which an employee cannot afford and which a court should be willing to protect as a trade secret or by enforcing a noncompetition clause concerning its future use with a competitor employer.

Although Rubin and Shedd's model provides a useful starting point for considering when a court should enforce trade secrets and non-competition clauses, a number of subsequent works have illustrated how the model does not necessarily explain why employers still continue to provide general training that employees can afford, as in the law firm or temporary work context.[4]

[B] Hyde on High-Velocity Markets

Professor Alan Hyde provides another insight into trade secrets and noncompetition law in considering how two very different parts of the country legally regulate employee movement and information exchange between companies. In *Working in Silicon Valley: Economic and Legal Analysis of a High-Velocity Labor Markets,*[5] Hyde discusses the different approaches to trade secrets taken in California's Silicon Valley as opposed to in Boston's Route 128 technology corridor.

On the one hand, Silicon Valley is a high-velocity market in which workers move rapidly from job to job, taking their skills and knowledge with them. This is possible because California generally does not permit noncompetition clauses[6] and Silicon Valley employers rarely litigate trade secret disputes. It can be argued that this state of affairs has contributed to the spectacular rate of growth in Silicon Valley. On the other hand, the Route 128 corridor in Massachusetts is an example of a market in which restrictive trade secret and noncompetition laws prevent worker movement, and thus information, from firm to firm. The result is that Massachusetts has larger firms but smaller overall growth in the technology sector.

The point Hyde seeks to make is that when information is "non-rivalrous," in that the information can be used by as many firms as cheaply as it can be used by

---

[4] *See, e.g.*, Daron Acemoglu & Jorn-Steffen Pischke, *Beyond Becker: Training in Imperfect Labour Markets*, 109 Econ. J. 112 (1999); David H. Autor, *Why Do Temporary Help Firms Provide Free General Skills Training?*, 116 Q. J. Econ. 1409 (2001).

[5] Alan Hyde, Working in Silicon Valley: Economic and Legal Analysis of a High-Velocity Labor Market (2003).

[6] California permits non-competition clauses only in cases involving the sale of a business. *See infra* note 27.

one firm,[7] dissemination of information is more important to growth than is the creation of that same information. In other words, in such situations, it might actually make sense for high tech companies to share their trade secrets or other proprietary information with their competitors as the ensuing economic growth will be worth more to the company than if they had kept this type of information to themselves.

§ 11.03   THE DUTY OF LOYALTY AND THE MISAPPROPRIATION OF TRADE SECRETS

The common law protects an employer's proprietary information and customers through the common law duty of loyalty and through the tort of misappropriation of trade secrets. The trade secret tort has been codified to some degree in all states through the adoption of the Uniform Trade Secrets Act (UTSA).[8]

[A]   Common Law Duty of Loyalty

The common law duty of loyalty requires that an employee must be loyal and work in the employer's best interests as long as the employee is still employed by the employer.[9] Many issues concerning the duty of loyalty arise when an employee prepares to compete with his current employer in the future. It is important to emphasize that these duty-of loyalty-claims concern only *pre-termination* conduct by a disloyal employee. Disloyal post-termination conduct is instead dealt with under the tort of misappropriation of trade secrets or through various types of noncompetition and confidentiality clauses (which will be discussed in more detail below).

Jet Courier Services v. Mulei[10] provides a common set of circumstances in a duty of loyalty case. Mulei, a high-level employee with Jet Courier, decided to strike out on his own with a competitor company, ACT. While still working for Jet Courier, Mulei successfully solicited both customers and co-employees to come to ACT after he left Jet Courier. Relying upon the Restatement (Second) of Agency, the Colorado Supreme Court found that "an agent is subject to a duty to his principal to act solely for the benefit of the principal in all matters connected with his agency."[11] Although an employee is permitted to *prepare to make arrangements* to compete with his or her employer prior to leaving the company,

---

[7] Hyde borrows the rivalrous/non-rivalrous distinction from Paul Romer's New Growth Theory, which divides human capital into these further sub-categories of knowledge. *See* Paul M. Romer, *Endogenous Technological Change*, 98 J. Pol. Econ. S71 (1990). Examples of non-rivalrous knowledge include programs, instructions, protocols, designs, and other know-how. Rivalrous knowledge, on the other hand, concerns knowledge where the use by one person precludes the use by another.

[8] *See, e.g.*, Cal. Civ. Code §§ 3426-3426.10.

[9] A similar claim exists against high-level corporate fiduciaries in corporate law under the doctrine of usurpation of corporate opportunities. Under the corporate opportunities doctrine, a corporation's directors, officers, or controlling shareholder, cannot convert a business opportunity for the corporation into a personal benefit for themselves. *See generally* Robert C. Clark, Corporate Law § 7.2.1 (1986).

[10] 771 P.2d 486 (Colo. 1989) (en banc).

[11] Restatement (Second) of Agency § 387. *See also* Restatement (Third) of Employment § 8.01.

the employee *must not engage in active competition* with the employer while still employed. As the *Mulei* court aptly observes, the difficult question in these duty of loyalty cases is deciding where the line exists between mere preparation to compete and active competition.

With regard to solicitation of a company's existing customers, employees may advise current customers that they will be leaving their current employment, but any pre-termination solicitations of customers for a new competing business violates employees' duty of loyalty. The court remanded on the solicitation-of-customers question so that the lower court could determine whether Mulei's conversations with Jet Courier's customers crossed the line into impermissible solicitations.

The inquiry concerning solicitation of co-employees is a little more complex because the question becomes whether the solicitation caused the other employee to breach her contract with the employer. However, unlike intentional interference with contractual relations claims, which generally require that employees have more than an at-will contract, the *Mulei* court found that the nature of the employment relationship was just one factor to consider in deciding whether soliciting co-employees caused a duty of loyalty breach. Consequently, the court also remanded the co-employee solicitation part of the case so that the lower court could apply an ad-hoc balancing test to determine if impermissible solicitation of co-employees had taken place. Under this balancing test, the court directed the trial court to consider: (1) the nature of the employment relationship, (2) the impact or potential impact of the employee's actions on the employer's operations, and (3) the extent of any benefits promised or inducements made to co-workers to obtain their services for the new competing enterprise. In this balancing, no single factor is dispositive and the solicitation need not be successful for a breach of the duty of loyalty to be found.[12]

Moreover, the mere fact that a breaching employee keeps his current company profitable during the impermissible solicitations is irrelevant. The focus is rather on whether the employee acted solely for the benefit of her employer or whether she did more than merely make preparations to compete with the employer while still employed. Furthermore, even if the employer does not abide by all conditions in an employee's employment agreement, that does not give the employee the right to breach her duty of loyalty. If the employer breaches the employment terms, the employee's proper recourse is to quit and sue for damages, not to compete against the employer while still employed.

Finally, with regard to the measurement of damages when there is a breach of the duty of loyalty: "The general rule is that an employee is not entitled to any compensation for services performed during the period he engaged in activities constituting a breach of his duty of loyalty even though part of these services may have been properly performed."[13] On the other hand, if the employee can establish that she were due compensation for discrete periods when no impermissible solicitations took place, compensation for those periods would not be forfeited.

---

[12] *Mulei*, 771 P.2d at 497.

[13] *Id.* at 499-500.

Under this apportionment approach, for instance, Mulei's contract stated that his salary was to be paid on a monthly basis and his bonus on a quarterly basis. To the extent that any breaches of the duty of loyalty occurred during any part of a given month or a given quarter, Mulei would lose his entire salary for that month or bonus for that quarter.

Notice that the above analysis does not change even if one considers that Mulei signed a covenant not to compete some six months after starting work for Jet Courier. The duty of loyalty claim does not depend on the existence of a contract and focuses instead on pre-termination, not post-termination, activities.

Another interesting case involving the common law duty of loyalty can be found in *Food Lion, Inc. v. Capital Cities/ABC, Inc.*[14] In that case, undercover news reporters posing as Food Lion supermarket employees uncovered that the store was backdating expired fish products and engaging in other unhealthy food practices. When these news reporters broadcast their findings on national television, they and their television network were sued for breach of duty of loyalty, among other claims. The Fourth Circuit found that the reporters had breached their duty of loyalty to Food Lion, stating that although an employee does not breach that duty by merely holding two jobs at the same time, the reporters violated their duty when they acted with the intent of harm to the interests of Food Lion.[15]

[B]   The Tort of Misappropriation of Trade Secrets

The tort of misappropriation of trade secrets exists both under the common law and under state statutes adopting the Uniform Trade Secrets Act (UTSA). The UTSA largely mimics the legal analysis that occurs under the tort approach to misappropriation of trade secrets.[16] Some version of the UTSA has now been adopted by 44 states (interestingly, New York and Massachusetts have not adopted the statutory scheme). The practical effect of the statutory scheme, as opposed to the common law, is unclear since the same basic principles appear to apply to both. However, the UTSA, with its standardized definitions, will likely lead to more consistent outcomes in trade secrets cases.

To establish a misappropriation of trade secret claim under the UTSA, a plaintiff must establish that there exists a "trade secret" and that it has been "misappropriated." A trade secret, in turn, is defined as:

> [I]nformation, including a formula, pattern, compilation, program, device, method, technique, or process, that: (1) derives independent economic

---

[14] 194 F.3d 505 (4th Cir. 1999) (applying North Carolina law).

[15] Interestingly, at least one other court disapproved of the *Food Lion* Court's approach to the common law duty of loyalty. *See* Dalton v. Camp, 548 S.E.2d 704 (N.C. 2001) (finding such a duty of loyalty is not even recognized as an independent cause of action under North Carolina law).

[16] Congress has also passed the Economic Espionage Act of 1996, 18 U.S.C. §§ 1831-1839, which turned misappropriation of trade secrets into a criminal offense. The impact of the law is not yet clear, but some cases have started to percolate through the courts. *See, e.g.,* United States v. Martin, 228 F.3d 1 (1st Cir. 2000) (convicting chemist and prospective employer for violating Act for transmitting proprietary information of current employer to prospective employer).

value, actual or potential, from not being generally known to the public or other persons who can obtain economic value from its disclosure or use; and (2) is the subject of efforts that are reasonable under the circumstances to maintain its secrecy.[17]

In short, because trade secrets must be generally unknown to the public, a company must put into place reasonable measures to maintain their secrecy. Because of the importance of maintaining secrecy to gain trade secret protection, most companies use confidentiality provisions to establish that they have mechanisms in place to keep the information in question secret. Alternatively, in the digital age, companies can place such confidential information in encrypted form or by utilizing computer password protection.[18]

Consider what it means to maintain the secrecy of a trade secret in a misappropriation of trade secret case that occurred under the Vermont Trade Secrets Act (which is based on the UTSA), *Dicks v. Jensen*.[19] There, defendant former employees, who were hired to run a lodge and associated bus tours, left their employer's lodge and solicited their former employer's bus tour customers to start their own lodge and bus tours. In their previous job, the former employees had been responsible for advertising, soliciting, and organizing their former employer's bus tours and had utilized mass mailing lists and direct telephone solicitations to drum up business. Their employer claimed that the former employees had unlawfully misappropriated its customer list, which qualified as a trade secret. Although the Supreme Court of Vermont affirmed summary judgment for the former employees, they did not do so on the ground relied upon by the trial court (i.e., that the customer lists could not be a trade secret because the underlying information was readily ascertainable from underlying information and had not been developed through "extraordinary effort"). Instead, the court found that the customer lists did not qualify for trade secret protection because there was no evidence that the employer took any steps to maintain its secrecy.

"Misappropriation," on the other hand, has a rather convoluted definition under the UTSA. The UTSA defines misappropriation as:

(1)   Acquisition of a trade secret of another by a person who knows or has reason to know that the trade secret was acquired by improper means; or

(2)   Disclosure or use of the trade secret of another without express or implied consent by a person who:

    (A)   Used improper means to acquire knowledge of the trade secret; or

    (B)   At the time of disclosure or use, knew or had reason to know that his or her knowledge of the trade secret was:

---

[17] Unif. Trade Secrets Act § 1(4) (amended 1985), 14 U.L.A. 537 (2005).

[18] Because of the contractual nature of such confidentiality provisions, an employer not only could base a trade secrets misappropriation claim on such language, but would also have a separate action for breach of the confidentiality provision itself under the standard common law of contract.

[19] 768 A.2d 1279 (Vt. 2001).

     (i)   Derived from or through a person who had utilized improper means to acquire it;

     (ii)   Acquired under circumstances giving rise to a duty to maintain its secrecy or limit its use; or

     (iii)   Derived from or through a person who owed a duty to the person seeking relief to maintain its secrecy or limit its use; or

    (C)   Before a material change of his or her position knew or had reason to know that it was a trade secret and that knowledge of it had been acquired by accident or by mistake.[20]

The case of *MAI Systems Corp. v. Peak Computer Inc.*,[21] provides one example of a misappropriation of trade secret case involving further discussion of the terms "trade secret" and "misappropriation" under a version of the UTSA. Both Peak and MAI serviced MAI computers, operating systems, and software. An employee, Eric Francis, left MAI to work for Peak and, shortly thereafter, three other co-employees joined Francis at Peak. A number of MAI clients also switched over to Peak after learning of Francis's move. MAI sued Peak, its president, and Francis, claiming misappropriation of trade secrets contained in its customer lists, Field Information Bulletins (FIBs), and MAI software. The Ninth Circuit Court of Appeals ended up remanding MAI's claim regarding the FIBs to determine whether there was actual misappropriation of these trade secrets and overturned the lower court's holding that MAI had trade secrets in its computer software, as the trade secrets in question were not specifically identified.

The most interesting part of the court's discussion, however, concerned whether MAI had protectable trade secrets in its compiled customer database. The court applied the two-step analysis of determining whether the customer lists constituted a trade secret and if so, whether these trade secrets were misappropriated. Finding that the information in the MAI customer database was not generally known and was of economic value to others and that MAI sought to keep this information secret, the court determined this information was a trade secret. With regard to misappropriation, the question turned on whether Francis used the customer list information to improperly solicit MAI clients without MAI's expressed or implied consent. On this point, the court concluded that although misappropriation under the UTSA does not refer to merely announcing a new business affiliation to current clients, misappropriation does occur if an employee uses information from a customer database to solicit these same customers for a new employer. Significantly, misappropriation can occur even though the employee never physically took the customer lists and seemed to solicit former clients based on his memorization of the lists. Because the evidence in the case was clear that Francis had inappropriately solicited former MAI clients based on his knowledge of MAI's customer lists, amounting to impermissible misappropriation under the UTSA, the court found for MAI on its misappropriation of trade secret claim.

---

[20] Unif. Trade Secrets Act § 1(2) (amended 1985), 14 U.L.A. 537 (2005).

[21] 991 F.2d 511 (9th Cir. 1993).

Unlike *MAI*, many courts have allowed ex-employees to contact clients of their former employers without finding a violation of any trade secret laws, reasoning that an employee's recollection of particular information about a former client is not generally considered confidential.[22] However, trade secret violations are more likely to be found when an employer spends much money in developing a customer list and a similar list could not be replicated without great expense.[23] In other words, the greater the expense to develop a customer list, the more likely it will be protected as a trade secret.

Finally, although many features of the *MAI* case look a lot like the duty of loyalty case discussed in the previous section, the primary difference is that misappropriation of trade secret cases concern post-termination, as opposed to pre-termination, conduct. Indeed, because trade secret protection lasts beyond the employment relationship, it is considered to be a more powerful tool for employers than the common law duty of loyalty.

Although most misappropriation of trade secrets cases involve the *actual* misappropriation of a trade secret, the UTSA also covers *threatened* misappropriation of trade secrets under the inevitable disclosure doctrine. Under that doctrine, threatened misappropriation can be enjoined where there is a high probability of inevitable and immediate use of trade secrets.

For example, in *Pepsico, Inc. v. Redmond*,[24] the Seventh Circuit considered whether the hiring of the former California General Manager of Pepsico by its competitor, Quaker Oats, would inevitably lead to the employee disclosing Pepsi's trade secrets to Quaker Oats. The companies competed in both the "sports drink" and "new age drink" markets, with Pepsi producing the All Sport, Lipton Iced Tea, and Ocean Spray brands and Quaker Oats producing the Gatorade and Snapple brands. Although the defecting employee was bound by a confidentiality agreement not to disclose Pepsi proprietary information to competitors, Pepsi believed that the very nature of its former employee's new position with Quaker Oats would make disclosure of this information inevitable.

Based on these facts, the Seventh Circuit preliminarily enjoined Pepsi's former general manager from working for Quaker Oats for a period of time and permanently enjoined him from disclosing Pepsi's trade secrets.[25] The court based its reasoning on the fact that the employee held a high position at Pepsi which gave him access to inside information and trade secrets, including Pepsi's strategic plans concerning how it was going to compete with companies like Quaker Oats. The employee's intimate knowledge of Pepsi's strategic plans would inevitably and immediately lead him to disclose that information to Quaker Oats in his new position because he would substantially be in charge of pricing, costs, and marketing of similar products. Of course, the threatened misappropriation seemed all the more

---

[22] *See* Walter Karl, Inc. v. Wood, 528 N.Y.S.2d 94, 98 (App. Div. 1988).

[23] *See* Allen v. Johar, Inc., 823 S.W.2d 824 (Ark. 1992).

[24] 54 F.3d 1262 (7th Cir. 1995).

[25] Preliminary injunctions, even more than damages, are of particular importance in trade secret litigation, because it is essential that employers keep their confidential information from being used for the benefit of competitor employers in the first place.

likely because the employee had apparently lied when explaining his situation with Quaker Oats to Pepsi in the first instance.

However, the mere fact that a person assumes a similarly titled position at a competitor company does not, without more, make it inevitable that he or she will use or disclose the former's trade secret information. Instead, there must be some showing that the employee's new employment will inevitably lead him or her to rely on the former employer's trade secrets. For instance, in *EarthWeb, Inc. v. Schlak*,[26] Schlak was the head of Web content for EarthWeb, but ended up taking a new position at ITworld.com. EarthWeb sought to enjoin Schlak from working with ITworld.com under an inevitable trade secret disclosure theory. Unlike the *Pepsico* case, however, the court, applying New York law, found the inevitable disclosure doctrine did not apply because Schlak's position at his new employer was functionally completely different than the one he held at EarthWeb. Perhaps more importantly, Schlak did not have the same amount of high-level, vital information that the employee had in the *Pepsico* case.

Different states are more or less willing to apply the inevitable disclosure doctrine, and New York is one of those states that will only find trade secret misappropriation under this theory in rare and compelling circumstances, which were not present in *EarthWeb*.

§ 11.04   COVENANTS NOT TO COMPETE

When it comes to protecting confidential, proprietary information and relationships with customers and employees, many employers are not comfortable relying solely on the common law duty of loyalty or the common law/statutory prohibition against the misappropriation of trade secrets. Additionally, and especially in relation to workers who have vital and unique information about the company, companies require such employees to sign covenants not to compete (also called noncompetition clauses). Under the terms of these provisions, the employee agrees not to compete against the employer directly, usually during a specified time and in a specified geographical area. Because such contractual promises may place substantial obstacles in the way of employees' earning a livelihood, such agreements are strictly construed as potential restraints on trade and are not favored by the law. Indeed, one state, California, makes most such agreements statutorily unenforceable as a matter of public policy.[27] Also, attorneys as a group are prohibited from entering into noncompetition agreements under Model Rule of Professional Conduct 5.6, as such agreements are viewed as interfering with a client's fundamental right of being able to be represented by the attorney of her choice.

Nevertheless, most states do permit covenants not to compete under appropriate circumstances, and the touchstone of any court's analysis in this area is whether the agreement is reasonable.[28] Noncompetition law tends to be very much state-

---

[26]   71 F. Supp. 2d 299 (S.D.N.Y. 1999), *aff'd*, 2000 U.S. App. LEXIS 11446 (2d Cir. 2000).

[27]   *See* CAL. BUS. & PROF. CODE § 16600. As previously noted, *supra* note 6, this prohibition does not apply to covenants ancillary to the sale of a business.

[28]   A different, less stringent, standard applies if the covenant is ancillary to the sale of the business

oriented and attorneys are always required to consult their own state statutes and common law precedent for more specific guidance. And even then, each case is decided on its specific facts. However, there are factors that most courts consider before enforcing a covenant not to compete and those factors are discussed below.

[A]　Factors to Consider for Enforceability

In these cases, courts must balance an employer's right to protect itself against unfair competition with regard to its trade secrets and the employee's right to earn a living. In undertaking this balance, there are at least four factors that courts consider before enforcing a noncompetition agreement: (1) whether the employer is seeking to protect a legitimate interest through the employment restraint, (2) whether the employment restraint is reasonable in duration, (3) whether the employment restraint is reasonable in terms of geography, and (4) whether the employment restraint is supported by adequate consideration.[29]

[1]　Employer's Legitimate Interest and Employee Unique Skills

First and foremost, covenants not to compete are only enforced if an employer is seeking to protect a legitimate interest.[30] In order to have a protectable legitimate interest, the employer must establish that the employee has knowledge of a trade secret, has information which pertains particularly to an employer, or has other specialized knowledge sufficient to justify enforcement of the covenant. In other words, there generally has to be a showing that the employee's skills or knowledge is special, unique, or extraordinary (consistent with the *Rubin* and *Shedd* analyses discussed above).

Rem Metals Corp. v. Logan[31] represents a case in which the court found a lack of a protectable interest and consequently, did not enforce the covenant. In *Rem Metals*, Logan was a welder of precision titanium castings for Rem. Only two other companies did this type of sophisticated welding, and Logan had left Rem to work for one of these competitors. While at Rem, Logan had signed an employment agreement which included a noncompetition clause that stated that he could not work in the State of Oregon for a direct competitor of Rem for six months after terminating his employment. In deciding that this covenant not to compete was

---

rather than to an employment contract. *See, e.g.*, Hudgins v. Amerimax Fabricated Prods., 551 S.E.2d 393, 396 (Ga. App. Ct. 2001).

[29] As part of the general reasonableness inquiry, a few states also ask whether enforcing the non-competition clause would be against the public interest. *See, e.g.*, Harris v. Primus, 450 N.E.2d 80, 84 (Ind. App. Ct. 1983); All Stainless, Inc. v. Colby, 308 N.E.2d 481, 485 (Mass. 1974).

[30] This is the approach taken by the Restatement of Employment Law: "A covenant in an agreement between an employer and former employee restricting a former employee's working activities is enforceable if it is reasonably tailored in scope, geography, and time to further a protectable interest of the employer." *See* RESTATEMENT (THIRD) OF EMPLOYMENT LAW § 8.06 (T.D. No. 4, 2011). Further, the Restatement of Employment Law identifies employer legitimate interests as: confidential information, customer relationships, investments in employer's public investment in the market, and purchase of a business owned by the employee. *Id.* at § 8.07.

[31] 565 P.2d 1080 (Or. 1977).

unenforceable, the Oregon Supreme Court focused on whether Rem had a protectable interest and found Logan did not have a specialized skill as a result of working at Rem, but a skill that could have easily been learned elsewhere and was readily known throughout the industry. In short, general knowledge or skill acquired through training or experience at a given employer remains the employee's to exploit.

On the other hand, when the employee possesses specialized or unique knowledge about the employer's business, the employer has a sufficiently legitimate interest to support enforcement of a noncompetition clause. For instance, in *Outsource International, Inc. v. Barton & Barton Staffing Solutions*,[32] a former employee of a temporary staffing company, who had signed a covenant not to compete and confidentiality agreement, sought to strike out with a similar company of his own. The employee hired former co-workers and eventually acquired twelve Outsource clients. The court found that Outsource had invested much time and effort into developing qualified workers through an elaborate employee screening process and into maintaining customer relations through an extensive customer service system. Under Illinois law, a legitimate business interest, sufficient to enforce a noncompetition agreement, exists where the customer relationships are "near-permanent" and the former employee would not have had contact with those customers but for his previous employment. A legitimate business interest also may exist where the employee obtained trade secrets or other confidential information through his previous employment. Because the customer loyalty enjoyed by Outsource met the customer relationship test and the uniqueness of the product that it provided in the temporary staffing industry satisfied the trade secret test, the court enforced the restrictive covenant because it was necessary to protect a legitimate business interest.[33]

[2] Duration of Covenant

In deciding whether an overall covenant not to compete is reasonable, courts consider how long after employment has ended the covenant would prohibit the employee from working for other employers. As a general rule of thumb, two to three year post-employment covenants are considered reasonable, but longer covenants are generally found to be unreasonable and unenforceable.[34]

---

[32] 192 F.3d 662 (7th Cir. 1999).

[33] Judge Posner dissented, relying in part on the analyses of *Rubin* and *Shedd* discussed in § 11.02[A], maintaining that such covenants *should* be enforced: "If covenants not to compete are forbidden, the employer will pay a lower wage, in effect charging the employees for the training. There is no reason why the law should prefer this method of protecting the employer's investment to a covenant not to compete." *Id.* at 671 (Posner, J., dissenting). Nevertheless, Judge Posner concluded that Illinois courts would not enforce the covenant based on their traditional, and unreasonable, hostility to such agreements and the limited types of business interests that qualify for protection under Illinois noncompetition law.

[34] But, as discussed below, some fast-paced industries, especially those involving the Internet, may require shorter time periods for restrictive covenants to be enforced, in part because there tends to be no geographical limitations in such industries.

Nevertheless, there are some cases in which the lack of any durational limit on the covenant did not make it unreasonable. In *Karpinski v. Ingrasci*,[35] a prominent oral surgeon engaged another oral surgeon to start a new practice and had him sign a non-compete agreement that had no temporal limitation and which included a five-county area in upstate New York. The second oral surgeon ended up competing against the first in the proscribed area and the New York Court of Appeals enforced the agreement even though there was no durational limit. The court found that the lack of a durational element was not fatal as long as the geographical scope of the covenant was reasonable. Because the area covered by the agreement was relatively small, the court found the covenant enforceable.[36]

[3] Geographic Scope of Covenant

Not only must a covenant not to compete be of reasonable duration, but it also must be reasonable in the geographical area it covers. In the *Karpinski* case discussed in the previous subsection, the covenant was reasonable because it covered only a specific five-county area in upstate New York where the first dentist actually practiced oral surgery. On the other hand, courts will scrutinize the nature of the job to see whether geographical limitations are reasonable. For example, if a person has worked previously for an employer that only does business in the western part of the United States, it is not reasonable to hold that employee to a covenant which prohibits him or her from competing against that employer in the eastern part of the United States. Additionally, if the two dentists were the only two oral surgeons in the Ithaca area and thus enforcement of the covenant was tantamount to creating a monopoly for the one oral surgeon, there is reason to believe that the covenant may not have been enforced in such circumstances.[37]

Nevertheless, there are some jobs, especially those involving the Internet, where it is possible to be viewed as being everywhere in the world at once. In such cases, courts have been willing to enforce noncompetition agreements without any geographical scope.[38] But if there is a covenant without geographical scope, it is much more important that there be a fairly short durational aspect to the agreement. Thus, it is not uncommon to see Internet-based noncompetition agreements with durations ranging from six months to one year.

---

[35] 268 N.E.2d 751 (N.Y. 1971).

[36] Interestingly, as it turns out, the dentist in violation of the covenant in *Karpinski* ended up working in the restricted area anyway after reaching a financial agreement with the first dentist. The ultimate outcome of this case illustrates that although the law may provide the default rule, parties can contract around such rules if they so desire.

[37] *See* Iredell Digestive Disease Clinic, P.A. v. Petrozza, 373 S.E.2d 449 (N.C. Ct. App. 1988), *aff'd*, 377 S.E.2d 750 (N.C. 1989) (refusing to enforce covenant among gastroenterologists in rural area where result would be to leave the community with only one doctor).

[38] *See, e.g.*, Briggs v. R.R. Donnelley & Sons, 446 F. Supp. 153 (D. Mass. 1978) (enforcing non-compete clause with no geographical limitation where employee had worldwide customer contacts).

[4] Adequate Consideration

Because covenants not to compete are contractual in nature, they are governed by such contract principles and doctrines as consideration, the statute of frauds,[39] and parol evidence. Regarding consideration, the primary issue is whether an employer can force a current employee to sign a restrictive covenant mid-employment. Various courts have disagreed whether mere continuation of employment is adequate consideration to support a covenant not to compete[40] or whether some additional consideration must be given in the form of a bonus or other compensation to support the new undertaking.[41] Generally, when the covenant not to compete is entered into at the beginning of employment, most courts agree that adequate consideration exists in the form of the employee agreeing to commence employment in the first place.[42]

[B] Special Issues Under Covenants Not to Compete Law

Although most covenant-not-to-compete cases are decided based on some combination of the factors discussed in the previous section, there are some issues that repeatedly occur in this area and, therefore, merit additional attention.

[1] Employees Who Are Terminated

One recurring issue in the noncompetition area concerns whether non-compete agreements are enforceable in situations where the employee is fired rather than voluntarily quits. The argument against enforcing covenants under such circumstances is either that the employer should not be able both to fire an employee and then prevent her from obtaining subsequent employment or that the employee could not be so valuable to the organization and worthy of a non-compete clause if the employer is willing to voluntarily forgo employing him or her.[43] The counter-argument points out that regardless of how poorly performing an employee is, the employee may still have in his or her possession specialized or unique information which can be used by direct competitors to compete unfairly against the employee's former employer and therefore, the reasonableness of the covenant should not turn on how the employee came to leave his or her employment.[44] Additionally, making a distinction based on whether an employer leaves employment voluntarily or involuntarily might lead to employees seeking termination to avoid the application

---

[39] Here the issue is whether oral covenants not to compete should be enforceable. One court has found the statute of frauds inapplicable in such circumstances. *See* Metcalfe Invs., Inc. v. Garrison, 919 P.2d 1356 (Alaska 1996).

[40] *See, e.g.*, Curtis 1000, Inc. v. Suess, 24 F.3d 941 (7th Cir. 1994) (finding expectation of continued employment adequate consideration to support non-compete clause).

[41] *See, e.g.*, Poole v. Incentives Unlimited, Inc., 548 S.E.2d 207 (S.C. 2001) (requiring additional consideration to support mid-employment restrictive covenant).

[42] *Id.* (finding adequate consideration would have existed if covenant entered into at initial hiring).

[43] *See* Insulation Corp. v. Brobston, 667 A.2d 729 (Pa. Super. Ct. 1995); Ma & Pa, Inc. v. Kelly, 342 N.W.2d 500 (Iowa 1984).

[44] *See* Robert S. Weiss & Assoc. v. Wiederlight, 546 A.2d 216 (Conn. 1988).

of a noncompetition agreement.[45]

[2]   Blue-Penciling and Other Responses to Overbroad Covenants

If a court finds a covenant not to compete to be overbroad, the court generally takes one of three courses of action: (1) re-writes the offensive clause,[46] (2) "blue-pencils" the offending portion,[47] or (3) strikes the entire covenant.[48] With the blue-penciling approach, a court enforces only the reasonable parts of the covenant as long as the various clauses are capable of separation. If a court, on the other hand, decides to strike the entire covenant, it is so that employers will not have the incentive to write covenants that substantially and unreasonably interfere with an employee's ability to earn a living.

The Court of Appeals of New York (its highest court) considered whether an overly-restrictive clause in the accounting firm context should be invalidated completely or just partially. In *BDO Seidman v. Hirshberg*,[49] as part of a covenant not to compete, a former accountant for a large firm signed a "reimbursement clause" which required the accountant to compensate his former employer (to the tune of an amount equal to one-and-a-half times the fees the firm had charged that client over the last fiscal year) for serving any client of the firm's Buffalo office within 18 months after the termination of his employment. Although the lower court had held this clause to be an invalid and unenforceable covenant, the Court of Appeals of New York partially enforced it using blue-penciling techniques.

More specifically, the court found this covenant overbroad "in some respects" because former employees should be able to compete against their former firms as long as they do not use unfair means to compete. On the other hand, the court opined that protection of customer relationships the employee acquired in the course of his employment may be a legitimate employment interest subject to lawful restrictions since otherwise former employees could exploit the goodwill of a client which had been initially maintained at employer expense. Consequently, the court blue-penciled the reimbursement clause to the extent that it could be interpreted either (1) to restrict the employee in performing services for former firm clients with whom he never acquired a relationship during his former employment; or (2) to restrict the employee from performing services for former firm clients that he independently recruited to the firm by himself and through no firm expense.[50] *BDO Seidman* thus provides a ready example of how courts use their blue-penciling

---

[45] As discussed *infra* § 13.02[B][1], there are additional reasons, relating to eligibility for unemployment compensation, why an employee may prefer to be fired rather than to voluntarily quit.

[46] *See, e.g.*, Dean Van Horn Consulting Assocs. v. Wold, 395 N.W.2d 405 (Minn. Ct. App. 1986).

[47] *See, e.g.*, Timenterial, Inc. v. Dagata, 277 A.2d 512 (Conn. Super. Ct. 1971).

[48] *See, e.g.*, CAE Vanguard, Inc. v. Newman, 518 N.W.2d 652 (Neb. 1997); White v. Fletcher/Mayo/Assocs., 303 S.E.2d 746 (Ga. 1983).

[49] 712 N.E.2d 1220 (N.Y. 1999).

[50] As far as whether the accounting firm was entitled to liquidated damages for the enforceable parts of the noncompetition clause, the *BDO Seidman* Court remanded the case to more sufficiently develop the record as to whether the amount fixed in the agreement was excessive as far as actual damages sustained and, therefore, constituted an unenforceable penalty.

authority to balance the respective interests of employer and employee in these covenant not to compete cases.

[3] Confidentiality and Non-Solicitation Agreements

Provisions in employment contracts that prevent an employee from disclosing confidential materials of his or her previous employer at any time generally are not subject to the same reasonableness criteria that apply to noncompetition agreements. Such clauses are more likely to be upheld because, if they are entered into voluntarily, they do not place the same obstacles in the employee's way of earning a living. In scrutinizing confidentiality agreements, courts have applied lesser standards, such as whether "the information is of such a character as to be protectable under the common law of unfair competition."[51]

On the other hand, because non-solicitation agreements, which prohibit an employee from soliciting the services of former co-employees or customers for his or her new employer for a period of time in a given area, can interfere with a person's livelihood, these agreements tend to be analyzed under the same reasonableness test used for covenants not to compete.[52]

[4] Covenants in Employee Severance Agreements

Employers appear to be more frequently placing covenant not to compete clauses in employee severance agreements to keep valuable employees from competing directly against them for a period of time. The advantage for employers of putting such clauses directly into the severance agreement is that the employee will forfeit severance benefits if he or she later competes against his or her former employer. Nevertheless, such clauses in severance agreements will still be scrutinized under the reasonableness test that applies to all covenants.

[5] Employer Suits Against Subsequent Employers

Not only may an employer seek to enforce a reasonable covenant not to compete against the employee, but the employer may seek to sue the subsequent employer under theories of tortious interference with contractual relations or unfair trade practices. In *United Laboratories Inc. v. Kuykendall*,[53] for instance, a subsequent employer was successfully sued by a former employer under a theory of intentional interference with restrictive covenants and unfair trade practices. The subsequent employer had interfered with the employee's previous employment contract by promising to pay for any legal costs associated with the employee breaching his noncompetition clause.

---

[51] *See* Bell Fuel Corp. v. Cattolico, 544 A.2d 450, 458 (Pa. Super. 1988).

[52] *See, e.g.*, Sysco Food Services of Eastern Wis., LLC v. Ziccarelli, 445 F. Supp. 2d 1039, 1048-49 (E.D. Wis. 2006) (applying covenant not compete reasonableness standard to non-solicitation agreement).

[53] 403 S.E.2d 104 (N.C. Ct. App. 1991).

§ 11.05   EMPLOYEE INVENTIONS

Employee invention law asks: who has the right to an invention when an employee develops an invention while employed by a company, during company time, and with company funding and resources? This is an important question since it has been estimated that 80%-90% of all inventions in the United States are made by employed inventors.[54]

The answer to this question depends primarily on the source of law and the specific circumstances of each case. There are generally considered to be three sources of employee invention law: (1) the common law, (2) contractual agreements, and (3) statutory law.

[A]   The Common Law: The Duty to Assign and the Shop Right Rule

Generally, where an employer hires an employee to design a specific invention or to solve a specific problem, the employee has a duty to assign the resulting patent for the invention to the employer.[55] Where the employee is not hired specifically to design or invent, but nevertheless develops an invention during working hours with the use of the company's equipment and materials, the employer is granted an irrevocable, but non-exclusive, right to use of the invention under the "shop right rule." A shop right can be seen as an employer's royalty or fee and as a way of protecting an employer's investment in providing the facilities and materials to make the invention possible.[56]

Such a right is not only non-exclusive, but also non-transferable as the case of *Francklyn v. Guilford Packing Co.*[57] makes clear. The employee Francklyn, while employed as a clammer and while using his employer's resources, modified a clam harvester and received a patent for his new design. Based on the common law of employee inventions, because Francklyn was not hired to design and invent, but nevertheless utilized employer materials during his time at work to make the invention, his employer was granted a shop right in the new clam harvester invention. Francklyn had also agreed to allow his employer to use the invention without paying royalties. The court, however, forbade the employer from selling its

---

[54] Ingersoll-Rand Co. v. Ciavatta, 542 A.2d 879, 886 (N.J. 1988).

[55] Such a duty to assign would not apply if the individual was an independent contractor rather than an employee. *See* Community for Creative Non-Violence v. Reid, 490 U.S. 730 (1989). Independent contractors have greater rights in their inventions than employees based on the nature of their relationship with the employer. *See, e.g.,* New York Times Co. v. Tasini, 533 U.S. 483 (2001) (upholding ability of freelance writers for newspaper to retain copyrights).

This common law duty to assign finds a parallel in copyright law under the "works for hire" doctrine. Under that copyright doctrine, the employer is presumed to be the author of the work produced by the employee during his or her employment with the employer. *See* Twentieth Century Fox Film Corp. v. Entertainment Distributing, 429 F.3d 869, 877 (9th Cir. 2005).

[56] Additionally, by allowing employers and employees to split ownership of an invention in such instances, shop rights eliminate the possibilities of "hold outs," who seek to exploit the other party by holding out and demanding a higher price for their part of a multi-component invention. *See* Robert P. Mergens, *The Law and Economics of Employee Inventions*, 13 HARV. J.L. & TECH. 1, 12-13 (1999).

[57] 695 F.2d 1158 (9th Cir. 1983).

shop right to another concern, which wished to buy the license to the invention so that its product would not infringe Francklyn's patent. In short, a shop right holder is not free to assign his right to another person because it is a limited personal right that can be utilized only by the employer.

[B]   Contractual Agreements

Because the common law doctrine can be somewhat vague and ambiguous in defining the rights of employers and employees in employee inventions, many employers use written contracts to allocate invention rights. Such contracts generally require an employee to assign to the employer any invention that was designed or conceived during employment regardless of whether the employee was specifically hired to design the invention. These contractual agreements therefore provide greater rights for employers than the common law and courts generally consider such contractual undertakings valid.[58]

Although most contractual invention agreements entered into voluntarily by employers and employees are enforceable, a special class of these agreements, so-called holdover clauses, may not be. *Ingersoll-Rand Co. v. Ciavatta*[59] provides a classic example of an employer seeking to use a holdover clause to obtain rights to a former employee's invention that was not developed during the employee's employment with the employer. In *Ciavatta*, an Ingersoll-Rand employee who was not specifically hired to design or invent, patented a coal mine stabilization field. Although the employee had signed a standard invention agreement requiring him to assign any invention designed or conceived during his employment, he was terminated before coming up with this invention, which competed with Ingersoll-Rand's in the stabilizer field. The invention agreement had a holdover clause requiring an employee to assign inventions conceived or developed within one year after termination of his employment if such an invention was attributable to work done during his or her employment.

The court first found that there was no evidence that the employee conceived of the invention while still employed and, thus, the invention did not come under the literal terms of the holdover clause. The court further held that even if the clause applied by its terms, it was unreasonable and unenforceable. Although the court did not find that holdover clauses were void *per se*, the court applied a reasonableness test, similar to that found in covenant not to compete law, and balanced the employee's interest in using general skills and knowledge against the employer's interest in protecting investment in research and development. Because the employee used no trade secrets and relied upon only publicly known information in designing his invention, the court concluded the balance favored the employee and therefore, the holdover clause was unreasonable.

---

[58] If, on the other hand, the employer seeks to have the employee assign inventions that were developed entirely on the employee's own time and without employer resources, some states have statutory restrictions preventing the enforcement of such agreements. *See infra* § 11.05[C].

[59] 542 A.2d 879 (N.J. 1988).

[C]   Statutory Law: The Case of California

A number of states have adopted legislation that regulates the type of contractual invention agreements that may be entered into between employers and employees. These statutes restrict the instances in which employers may compel the assignment of employee inventions. California Labor Code § 2870 is a good example of such a statutory restriction of invention agreements. It states:

> (a) Any provision in an employment agreement which provides that an employee shall assign, or offer to assign, any of his or her rights in an invention to his or her employer shall not apply to an invention that the employee developed entirely on his or her own time without using the employer's equipment, supplies, facilities, or trade secret information except for those inventions that either:

> (1) Relate at the time of conception or reduction to practice of the invention to the employer's business, or actual or demonstrably anticipated research or development of the employer; or

> (2) Result from any work performed by the employee for the employer.

> (b) To the extent a provision in an employment agreement purports to require an employee to assign an invention otherwise excluded from being required to be assigned under subdivision (a), the provision is against the public policy of this state and is unenforceable.

In short, statutory restrictions like California's prevent employers from using their disparate bargaining power to require employees to assign inventions under circumstances that would be considered unfair or inequitable.

Chapter 12

REGULATION OF COMPENSATION AND LEAVE TIME

§ 12.01   INTRODUCTION

Laws governing employees' compensation and leave include some of the oldest employment legislation in the United States, as well as some of the most recent. The hallmark compensation statute is the Fair Labor Standards Act (FLSA),[1] a major part of the New Deal that still prompts significant political and legal battles. The Act's three pillars — the child labor, minimum wage, and overtime provisions — reflect the Depression-era concerns from which they arose. However, the minimum wage and overtime laws in particular continue to provide important protections for many workers and remain a vital concern for any employment lawyer.

States play a role in regulating employee compensation as well. Most states have statutes regulating the manner in which employers must pay wages. Frequently, these statutes also limit employers' ability to make deductions or garnishments from wages and require prompt payment of wages after the end of the employment relationship.

In contrast to the long history of compensation legislation, the primary leave statute in the United States — the Family and Medical Leave Act (FMLA) [2] — was enacted in 1993. This statute reflects, in part, the desire to alleviate some of the burdens that working women face because of their generally disproportionate role as caretakers.[3] Its protections still fall far short of most European countries, many of which require paid family leave.[4] However, the FMLA's guarantee that employees have the right to return to their job, or a substantially equivalent one, after the birth or adoption of a child or caring for themselves or a close family member who is seriously ill, can be an important factor in many employees' ability to remain in the workforce.

§ 12.02   FAIR LABOR STANDARDS ACT

The Fair Labor Standards Act[5] arose from the ashes of the Supreme Court's *Lochner* era, in which the Court repeatedly invalidated protective workplace legislation.[6] The FLSA was successfully enacted in 1938 with the purpose of

---

[1] 29 U.S.C. §§ 201-219.

[2] *Id.* §§ 2601, 2611-2619, 2651-2653.

[3] *See* Nev. Dep't. of Human Res. v. Hibbs, 538 U.S. 721, 729–36 (2003) (holding that equality policy allowed Congress to provide for private suits for damages against unconsenting states under the FMLA's family leave provisions). *But see* Coleman v. Court of Appeals of Md., 132 S. Ct. 1327 (2012) (holding that lack of equality policy in FMLA's self-care provision did not permit private suit for damages against states). The FMLA, however, gives both men and women leave rights for family and medical leave. *See infra* § 12.04.

[4] For example, every Western European country, unlike the United States, requires some form of paid maternity leave, which can extend from three months to a year. Those countries provide some form of paid paternity leave as well. *See* Gillian Lester, *A Defense of Paid Family Leave*, 28 Harv. J. L. & Gender 1, 2 (2005).

[5] 29 U.S.C. §§ 201-219.

[6] *See* Lochner v. New York, 198 U.S. 45 (1905) (striking down New York law limiting number of hours that bakers could work because the law unconstitutionally interfered with implicit right of freedom of contract under the Fourteenth Amendment's due process clause); *see also* Adair v. United States, 208

eliminating the harmful effect on the economy caused by "labor conditions detrimental to the maintenance of the minimum standard of living necessary for health, efficiency, and general well-being of workers."[7] The FLSA addresses these purposes through three major provisions: (1) prohibiting child labor in most instances, (2) requiring a minimum wage, and (3) requiring that employers pay a premium for "overtime" — hours worked beyond the typical 40-hour workweek. There are also recordkeeping requirements[8] and an anti-retaliation provision.[9]

[A] Coverage

The FLSA represented a significant transformation in the governance of the American workplace. Reflecting this important policy shift, the FLSA applies broadly to most workplace relationships. This coverage, however, is not absolute. Questions about a worker's status as an employee, the type of job that an employee performs, and whether express statutory exemptions apply are important considerations that may preclude application of the FLSA.

Classifying a worker as an "employee" under the FLSA involves a different analysis than the traditional common-law *Darden* test for distinguishing employees from independent contractors.[10] The statute itself is less than helpful; "employee" is defined merely as "any individual employed by an employer."[11] This circular definition is typical of employment statutes, yet a bit more clarity may be gleaned through the FLSA's definition of "employ," which states in full that " '[e]mploy' includes to suffer or permit to work."[12] Courts have placed a great deal of emphasis on the "suffer or permit to work" language because it is absent from most other statutory definitions of employee. This additional language has been held to evidence a congressional attempt to create a more expansive definition of employee.[13] Accordingly, a worker will be treated as an employee under the FLSA not if he or she meets the common-law *Darden* test, but rather if he or she meets a broader "economic realities" test.

As described in more detail in Chapter 2,[14] the economic realities test does not follow the *Darden* test's stress on a purported employer's "right to control" a

---

U.S. 161 (1908) (striking down federal law prohibiting yellow-dog contracts in railroad industry as an unconstitutional interference with freedom of contract under the Fourteenth Amendment's due process clause).

[7] 29 U.S.C. § 202(a) (stating that these labor conditions burden commerce, constitute unfair competition, and lead to labor disputes that burden and obstruct commerce); *see also* Nicholson v. World Bus. Network, Inc., 105 F.3d 1361 (11th Cir. 1997) (discussing FLSA policy).

[8] 29 U.S.C. § 211.

[9] *Id.* § 215(a)(3).

[10] *See supra* § 2.01[D] (discussing *Darden* test).

[11] 29 U.S.C. § 203(e)(1). Public employees generally are covered by the FLSA. *See id.* § 203(e)(2).

[12] *Id.* § 203(g).

[13] Sec'y of Labor v. Lauritzen, 835 F.2d 1529 (7th Cir. 1987).

[14] *See supra* § 2.01[C].

worker.[15] Rather, the primary focus of the economic realities test is whether a worker, as a matter of economic reality, is dependent upon the business for which he or she works.[16] The factors used in the economic realities test — which have some overlap with the *Darden* test — include: the alleged employer's control over the manner in which the work is performed, the alleged employee's opportunity for profit or loss based on his or her managerial skills, the alleged employee's investment in equipment or materials, the alleged employee's employment of workers, whether the alleged employee provides a service requiring special skills, the permanence and duration of the working relationship, the extent to which the service is an integral part of the alleged employer's business, and the degree to which the alleged employee economically depends on the alleged employer.[17] In practice, economic dependence is the determinative consideration, and it will exist if all the factors establish that the workers are so dependent upon the business that they should be considered employees, rather than independent contractors in business for themselves.[18]

Even if a worker is considered an employee under the economic realities test, FLSA coverage is not certain. The employee must be engaged in some activity related to interstate commerce, whether individually or via an employer.[19] This commerce nexus is important because it allows the statute to fall under Congress's constitutional authority to legislate. Yet, because the Supreme Court has long interpreted "interstate commerce" broadly, this limitation is often easy to satisfy.[20] Moreover, the Department of Labor (DOL) typically assumes that any employer doing at least $500,000 in business a year affects interstate commerce sufficiently to be covered by the FLSA.[21]

Finally, the FLSA expressly excludes certain classes of employees. In addition to the administrative, executive, and professional exemptions to overtime provisions discussed below,[22] several other types of employees are excluded from FLSA protections, including but not limited to the following:[23]

---

[15] The right to control is considered under the economic realities test, but it is not the most important factor.

[16] *Lauritzen*, 835 F.2d at 1534.

[17] *Id.* at 1535-38.

[18] *Id.* Judge Easterbrook's concurrence in *Lauritzen* provides an interesting analysis of "dependence." He would consider whether the workers are of the type that the FLSA was intended to protect. According to Judge Easterbrook, such workers are those with little human capital. *See id.* at 1539-40 (Easterbrook, J., concurring).

[19] *See* 29 U.S.C. § 203(r), (s); 29 C.F.R. §§ 776.0-776.30.

[20] Tony & Susan Alamo Found. v. Sec'y of Labor, 471 U.S. 290, 296 (1985).

[21] 29 U.S.C. § 203(s)(1)(A)(ii); 29 C.F.R. § 779.22.

[22] *See infra* § 12.02[D][2].

[23] For more examples of exemptions under the FLSA, see *supra* § 2.02[A]. Although each exemption may have a somewhat different rationale, much of the impetus for the FLSA exemptions was the concern that application of the Act would destroy certain industries. *See* Robert D. Lipman et al., *A Call for Bright-Lines to Fix the Fair Labor Standards Act*, 11 HOFSTRA LAB. L.J. 357, 363-64 (1994); *see also* Christine Jolls, *Fairness, Minimum Wage Law, and Employee Benefits*, 77 N.Y.U. L. REV. 47 (2002) (discussing justifications for certain exemptions); Deborah Malamud, *Engineering the Middle Classes: Class Line-Drawing in New Deal Hours Legislation*, 96 MICH. L. REV. 2212 (1998) (discussing reasoning

Exemptions from both minimum wage and maximum hour (overtime) requirements:

- employees of certain amusement or recreational establishments, or organized camps;[24]

- employees who catch, pack, or load seafood;[25]

- certain agricultural employees who work for small employers, who are immediate family members of the employer, or who work in range production of livestock;[26]

- employees of limited circulation newspapers;[27]

- casual babysitters;[28] and

- learners, apprentices, and disabled employees hired under a special certificate.[29]

Exemptions to only maximum hour (overtime) requirements:

- most railway and airline employees;[30]

- announcers, news editors, and chief engineers of the major radio or television stations in small cities;[31]

- various employees engaged in specialized agricultural work;[32] and

- fire and law enforcement employees of small public departments.[33]

The Supreme Court, in 2007, reviewed a specific FLSA exemption in *Long Island Home at Care, Ltd. v. Coke*.[34] In *Coke*, the Supreme Court reversed a decision of the Second Circuit striking down the DOL's interpretation of the exemption of employees providing domestic companionship services for individuals who cannot care for themselves.[35] The DOL rule at issue exempted not only workers who are paid by the family receiving companionship services, but also workers who are paid by a third-party employer or agency.[36] Much of the Supreme

---

behind administrative, executive, and professional exemptions).

[24] 29 U.S.C. § 213(a).

[25] *Id.* 213(a)(5).

[26] *Id.* § 213(a)(6) (describing also the exemption for certain piece-rate agricultural employees).

[27] *Id.* § 213(a)(8).

[28] *Id.* § 213(a)(15).

[29] *Id.* §§ 213(a)(7), 214.

[30] *Id.* § 213(b)(2), (b)(3).

[31] *Id.* § 213(b)(9).

[32] *Id.* § 213(b)(12)-(b)(16).

[33] *Id.* § 213(b)(20).

[34] 127 S. Ct. 2339 (2007).

[35] Coke v. Long Island Care At Home, Ltd., 376 F.3d 118 (2d Cir. 2004) (citing 29 U.S.C. § 213(a)(15)), *reversed*, 127 S. Ct. 2339 (2007).

[36] 29 C.F.R. § 552.109(a).

Court's decision involved administrative law issues beyond the scope of this book.[37] However, the Court also upheld the substance of the third-party rule, ruling that it was valid because Congress intended the DOL to determine whether the companionship service exemption should cover employees paid by third parties.[38]

Recently, the DOL issued a proposed rule that would maintain and further clarify the domestic service exemption, but eliminate the ability of third-party employers or agencies to take advantage of the exemption; the rule was still pending at time of publication of this book.[39]

[B] Child Labor

Although not a major source of litigation, the prohibition against child labor was one of the three primary tenets of the FLSA. As described by a court a few years after the FLSA's enactment, the purposes of the child labor protections are two-fold:

> At the outset it should be recalled that the child labor provisions of the law were enacted in the year 1938, and its purposes were both economical and sociological. The entire nation had been affected with a depression that was world-wide. It was desirable to protect adult employees against the competition of minors. Moreover, the Congress was afforded an opportunity by reason of prevailing conditions to enact a law long agitated [for] and exceedingly desirable to protect children against harmful labor.[40]

The FLSA's child labor prohibition is, at least superficially, straightforward. Under Section 12 of the FLSA, employers are prohibited from engaging in "oppressive child labor."[41] The Act directly prohibits employing oppressive child labor, or delivering or shipping of goods produced by a business employing such labor within the last thirty days.[42] An exception to this latter "hot cargo" prohibition exists, however, if the business delivering or shipping the goods acted in good faith and received written assurances from the producer or dealer that no oppressive child labor was used.[43]

The question then is what constitutes "oppressive child labor." Because the FLSA's definition expressly gives the DOL the authority to define this term, the

---

[37] These issues centered on the Court's holding that the DOL regulation was entitled to a heightened level of deference under Chevron U.S.A., Inc. v. Natural Res. Def. Council, Inc., 467 U.S. 837 (1984), despite the regulation being listed as being interpretative rather than legislative and despite a challenge to the sufficiency of the DOL's notice. *Coke*, 127 S. Ct. at 2349-52; *see also infra* note 295 (discussing *Chevron*).

[38] *Coke*, 127 S. Ct. 2346-47.

[39] *See* Application of the Fair Labor Standards Act to Domestic Service, 76 Fed. Reg. 81190-01 (proposed Dec. 27, 2011) (to be codified at 29 C.F.R. § 552).

[40] Lenroot v. Interstate Bakeries Corp., 55 F. Supp. 234, 236 (D. Mo. 1944), *aff'd in part and rev'd in part*, 146 F.2d 325 (8th Cir. 1945). The FLSA child labor restrictions, in combination with compulsory school attendance laws, attempt to keep children in school rather than at work.

[41] 29 U.S.C. § 212.

[42] *Id.* § 212(a), (c).

[43] *Id.* § 212(a).

agency's regulations take on special importance. Those regulations define oppressive child labor as any employment of a child who does not meet the minimum age standards — generally sixteen years old for nonagricultural jobs.[44] The DOL may allow children between fourteen and sixteen years old to work certain jobs under specific conditions.[45] Indeed, the regulations currently allow for fourteen to sixteen years olds to work in most jobs if the work does not interfere with their schooling or health; the work occurs outside of school hours; and the work does not exceed three hours a day or eighteen hours a week while school is in session, and eight hours a day or forty hours a week while school is not in session.[46] The DOL may also set an eighteen year old minimum for jobs it finds to be particularly hazardous.[47] The minimum age standards do not apply to children working for a parent or guardian except in certain hazardous jobs.[48] In addition, good faith will rarely be a defense to liability because an employer's responsibility for complying with the FLSA's child labor laws "approaches strict liability."[49]

The FLSA relaxes the rules significantly, however, for agricultural work.[50] For example, the minimum age for agricultural work during school hours is sixteen years old; outside of school hours, the standard is fourteen years old.[51] Moreover, a twelve or thirteen year old may perform agricultural work with the written consent of his or her parent or guardian.[52] Other industries have special rules as well; for instance, the prohibitions against child labor do not apply to child performers in movies, theater, radio, or television productions.[53]

Because of the specific exceptions and rules applicable to certain industries employing minors, it is crucial to confirm whether a special rule applies. It also is important to note that states may, and often do, provide additional protections.[54]

The penalties for violating the FLSA's child labor provisions involve civil penalties of no more than $11,000 for each unlawfully employed child.[55] Such fines

---

[44] 29 C.F.R. §§ 570.1(b), (c), 570.2; *see* Martin v. Funtime, Inc., 963 F.2d 110 (6th Cir. 1992).

[45] 29 C.F.R. § 570.2(a)(1)(i). The types of permissible jobs were expanded in a 2010 DOL amendment of this regulation. *See* 29 C.F.R. §§ 570.33, 570.34.

[46] *Id.* §§ 570.31, 570.33 (not permitting work in mining, with most power machinery, helping with motor vehicles, public messenger services, transportation, communications, public utilities, construction, and warehouse storage), 570.34, 570.35 (work-time maximums).

[47] *Id.* § 570.2(a)(1)(ii). Examples of such jobs include excavation, manufacturing explosives, mining, and operating many types of power-driven equipment.

[48] *Id.* § 570.2(a)(2).

[49] *Martin*, 963 F.2d at 115.

[50] *See* 29 U.S.C. § 213(c).

[51] 29 C.F.R. § 570.2(b)

[52] *Id.*

[53] 29 U.S.C. § 213(c)(3). The FLSA specifically addresses several other types of work, including paper loading, automobile driving, and wood product processing. *Id.* § 213(c).

[54] *See generally* Marie E. Failinger, *"Too Cheap To Work for Anybody But Us": Toward a Theory and Practice of Good Child Labor*, 35 Rutgers L.J. 1035 (2004).

[55] 29 U.S.C. § 216(e); *see Martin*, 963 F.2d 110. Much larger fines are available if death or serious injury results.

are paid to the federal government, not the child.[56] Indeed, the FLSA does not provide a private right of action for child labor violations; rather, the DOL investigates and prosecutes violations.[57]

[C] Minimum Wage

It is difficult to find a more politically sensitive workplace issue than the minimum wage. Supporters of the minimum wage argue that it aids the working poor; opponents, however, point to the minimum wage's potential negative effect on employment rates.[58] Increased unemployment could occur if the minimum wage is high enough to prompt employers to avoid paying more wages by shifting resources to less labor-intensive means of production. Yet, it is unclear at what level unemployment — a portion of which always includes individuals looking for better jobs — is a significant problem, as well as how much the minimum wage truly helps the poor.[59] In any event, the political heat generated by attempts to raise the minimum wage far exceed the actual effects, positive or negative, of the relatively low wage levels currently at issue.

Despite the political turmoil, the FLSA's minimum wage requirements produce few significant litigation issues. Indeed, the political controversy may have an important ancillary benefit. The juxtaposition of political controversy and relative legal clarity may not be a coincidence, as the attention given to minimum wage politics means that most people — both employers and employees — are likely aware that employers must pay a minimum wage. Moreover, it is usually easy to determine whether an adequate wage was paid, although determining an employee's wage can be a source of confusion in some instances.

From 1997 to 2007, the federal minimum wage was $5.15 per hour.[60] In May 2007, a new graduated minimum wage increase was enacted which increased the minimum wage to $5.85 an hour on July 24, 2007; $6.55 an hour on May 25, 2008; and $7.25 an hour on May 25, 2009.[61] States may also implement their own minimum wage legislation and many states have minimum wages that exceed the

---

[56] 29 U.S.C. § 216(e).

[57] *Id.*; *see infra* § 12.02[E] (discussing enforcement of FLSA).

[58] Much of the debate centers on the minimum wage provision's efficacy in improving welfare and its potential costs to the economy. *See generally* STEVEN L. WILLBORN ET AL., EMPLOYMENT LAW: CASES AND MATERIALS 594–600 (5th ed. 2012) (providing basic economic description of minimum wage).

[59] The academic literature debating the effects of the minimum wage is immense, although one could summarize many of the analyses by stating that, at current levels, the minimum wage's effect on both poverty and the unemployment rate is small. *See, e.g.*, John T. Addison & Barry T. Hirsch, *The Economic Effects of Employment Regulation: What Are the Limits?*, *in* GOVERNMENT REGULATION OF THE EMPLOYMENT RELATIONSHIP 145 (Bruce E. Kaufman ed., 1997); DAVID CARD & ALAN KRUEGER, MYTH AND MEASUREMENT: THE NEW ECONOMICS OF THE MINIMUM WAGE (1995); Daniel Shaviro, *The Minimum Wage, Earned Income Tax Credit, and Optimal Subsidy Policy*, 64 U. CHI. L. REV. 405 (1997).

[60] 29 U.S.C. § 206(a)(1).

[61] U.S. Troop Readiness, Veterans' Care, Katrina Recovery, and Iraq Accountability Appropriations Act of 2007, Pub. L. No. 110-28 § 8102, 121 Stat. 112, 188 110th Cong. (May 2007). House Democrats introduced legislation in the summer of 2012 that would increase the minimum wage to $10.00 an hour and would require an annual increase tied to inflation.

federal level.[62] A state cannot, however, prevent an employee covered by the FLSA from being paid less than the federal minimum wage rate.

Special minimum wage rules apply to several different categories of employees. FLSA-covered agricultural employees were traditionally treated differently, but they have been entitled to the same minimum wage as nonagricultural employees since 1977.[63] Domestic workers must also be paid the minimum wage unless their compensation is not considered a wage under the Social Security Act; domestic workers who do not earn a wage under that statute will still be entitled to the minimum wage if they work for at least eight hours a week, even if those hours consist of work for multiple households.[64] However, employees classified as working in a "bona fide executive, administrative, or professional capacity" are not covered at all by the FLSA's minimum wage protection.[65]

One of the most common special minimum wage rules deals with employees, such as waiters, who regularly and customarily receive at least $30 a month in tips as part of their compensation.[66] These employees are entitled to wages of only $2.13 per hour if, in combination with their tips, they earn the federal minimum wage rate.[67] Employers must make up the difference if the combined wage and tips for any given hour are below the minimum wage rate.[68]

Newly hired young employees may also be paid a lower wage rate; an employer can pay an employee who is under twenty years old $4.25 per hour for the first ninety calendar days of employment.[69] The reason for this youth subminimum wage is to prevent young workers, who generally have fewer skills and experience, from being disproportionately rejected for new jobs following an increase in the minimum wage.[70] Employers, however, are prohibited from replacing older or more experienced workers to take advantage of this exception.[71] Finally, employers can seek a waiver from the DOL to pay full-time students a lower wage rate if the student employees have limited hours or are enrolled in a high school vocational course.[72]

---

[62] The federal Department of Labor maintains a useful website that provides information on every state's minimum wage laws. *See* U.S. DEP'T OF LAB., MINIMUM WAGE LAWS IN THE STATES — JANUARY 1, 2012, *available at* www.dol.gov/esa/minwage/america.htm.

[63] 29 U.S.C. § 206(a)(5).

[64] *Id.* § 206(f); *see supra* notes 34–38 and accompanying text.

[65] *Id.* § 213(a)(1). The exclusion from the minimum wage is significantly tempered by these exemption rules, as they require a salary of at least $455 per week. These rules, which have far more impact with regard to overtime premiums, will be explored in more detail below. *See infra* § 12.02[D].

[66] 29 U.S.C. § 203(t).

[67] *Id.* § 203(m); *see* 29 C.F.R. §§ 531.50 to 531.60. In other words, if an employee receives the minimum $2.13 per hour, he or she must make at least $5.12 in tips per hour.

[68] 29 U.S.C. § 203(m). See *infra* § 12.03[E], for a discussion of state laws that prohibit employers from taking employee tips.

[69] *Id.* § 206(g)(1).

[70] WILLBORN ET AL., *supra* note 58, at 597 (describing possible effects of youth subminimum wage).

[71] *Id.* § 206(g)(2).

[72] 29 C.F.R. § 519.

When issues do arise under the FLSA's minimum wage provision typically they involve attempts to calculate an employee's actual wage. Although a traditional hourly wage poses few problems, unusual or irregular forms of compensation — such as bonuses — can be difficult to classify on an hourly basis. Similarly, determining an employee's work hours can be complicated. On-call time or an irregular schedule are just a couple of the work conditions that make it hard to establish how many hours in a week an employee actually works. Because hourly compensation is the fundamental concern of the minimum wage provision, answers to such questions are crucial for establishing a violation in a given case. These wage determination issues are also relevant to overtime premium claims, and they will be discussed in detail in Part E of this Section.

[D]   Overtime

The primary goal of the FLSA's overtime provision is to increase employment. This occurs by encouraging employers to hire more workers rather than paying overtime premiums to their current workforce. The overtime provision also acts to compensate employees who must work an excessive number of hours and to reduce employers' incentive to subject employees to such a high level of work.[73]

The FLSA's maximum hour (overtime) rules are relevant to far more workers than any other substantive rule in the statute. A large number of workers are eligible for overtime and many of them derive a significant portion of their income from the extra compensation they earn due to the FLSA's overtime premium. Moreover, overtime litigation significantly increased after the U.S. Supreme Court held that state and local government employers must comply with the FLSA's overtime provisions;[74] state employees such as police officers frequently work well over forty hours a week and can earn substantial amounts of overtime compensation.

As is often the case, applying the overtime rules appears simple at first blush, yet can involve many complicated issues. The basic overtime protection under Section 7 of the FLSA prohibits employment of over 40 hours in any given workweek — unless the employee receives no less than one-and-one-half times his or her "regular rate" of pay for each hour over 40 worked in any given "workweek."[75] Thus, the FLSA mandates a "time-and-a-half" wage floor for all overtime hours worked. Cash or other negotiable instruments are acceptable forms of payments, and the DOL's regulations state that the "reasonable cost" of certain in-kind payments may also be sufficient.[76] A public employer may require an employee to use compensatory time — leave time equivalent to one-and-one-half

---

[73] *See generally* WILLBORN ET AL., *supra* note 58, at 600–02.

[74] Pursuant to a 1974 amendment, the FLSA expressly applies to state and local employees. In 1976, the Supreme Court invalidated this extension on Tenth Amendment grounds, but the Court reversed course in 1985 and permitted FLSA coverage of state and local employees. Garcia v. San Antonio Metro. Trans. Auth., 469 U.S. 528 (1985) (overruling National League of Cities v. Usery, 426 U.S. 833 (1976)).

[75] 29 U.S.C. § 207(a)(1).

[76] 29 C.F.R. § 531.27; *see infra* § 12.02[E].

hours for each hour of overtime worked — as compensation for overtime, but private employers may not.[77]

These basic rules are only the starting point. The bulk of litigation revolves around whether the law entitles an employee to an overtime wage premium. The FLSA expressly excludes certain classes of employees; yet determining whether a given employee is part of an exempted class has proven to be difficult. Parties have struggled for years with the DOL's regulations, which are often complex and time-consuming to apply. In 2004, the DOL revised its overtime regulations, with at least the stated purpose of simplifying them.[78] The political uproar resulting from the DOL's initial proposals caused the agency to pull back from some of the changes; however, the new rules are substantively different in certain areas.[79] Moreover, despite the DOL's attempt to simplify matters, it is likely that at least for a while, litigation over the meaning of these exemptions will not decrease substantially.

The FLSA expressly exempts employees who work in a "bona fide executive, administrative, or professional capacity" from overtime protections.[80] Because the statute fails to describe these classifications, the DOL's regulations have become the paramount authority in this area. Under the current regulations, determining whether an employee is exempt from the FLSA's overtime rules — that is, determining whether the worker is not entitled to an overtime premium — falls under a two-part test. First, the employee must be paid a salary. Second, if the employee is salaried, she must perform a specified list of duties associated with a given classification. These two prongs are commonly referred to as the "salary basis test" and the "duties test." Failure to satisfy either prong means that an employee is not exempt and is entitled to a time-and-a-half overtime premium for every hour above forty worked in a given workweek.

[1] Salary Basis Test

To be classified as exempt under the FLSA, most employees must be paid a salary that is equivalent to no less than $455 per week.[81] A few types of workers, such as teachers, lawyers, and doctors, may be classified as exempt without satisfying the salary basis test.[82] For all other workers, however, a salary of at least $455 per week (amounting to about $23,600 a year) is a threshold requirement for exempt status. This threshold is low, as it barely exceeds the current federal poverty

---

[77] 29 U.S.C. § 207(o); Christensen v. Harris County, 529 U.S. 576 (2000) (holding that public employers could require the use of compensatory time).

[78] *See* Defining and Delimiting the Exemptions for Executive, Administrative, Professional, Outside Sales and Computer Employees, 69 Fed. Reg. 22,122 (April 23, 2004).

[79] Note also that the new regulations no longer use the "short" and "long" duties tests. The different applications of these two tests had attempted to ensure that more lower-salaried workers were eligible for overtime compensation.

[80] 29 U.S.C. § 213(a)(1) (exempting such employees from minimum wage rules).

[81] 29 C.F.R. § 541.600(a).

[82] *Id.* § 541.600(e).

level for a family of four.[83]

"Salary" is defined as regular compensation paid "on a weekly, or less frequent basis" and in a predetermined amount that "is not subject to reduction because of variations in the quality or quantity of the work performed."[84] In essence, a salaried employee is one who is paid whether or not there is work available at a given time. Moreover, an employer's practice of making certain deductions from an employee's compensation may prevent what otherwise appears to be a salary from being classified as such under the FLSA's overtime rules.

The deduction issue can be complicated. Its purpose is to prevent employers from using a salary structure to classify workers as exempt when, in reality, they are treated like hourly workers. Accordingly, to be considered salaried, an employee must not be subject to financial deductions based on quality or availability of work issues.[85] A true salaried employee typically is not penalized financially (that is, does not have his or her pay docked) for routine disciplinary matters and other similar quality issues, so evidence that an employer makes such deductions from an employee's wages may preclude a finding that the employee is exempt from the FLSA's overtime protections.[86]

Some deductions are allowed, however. An employee may satisfy the salary basis test if deductions were made, among other reasons, because the employee was absent for at least a full day; pursuant to a bona fide sick leave or disability plan; or to offset compensation received by the employee for jury fees, witness fees, or military pay while on active duty.[87] Moreover, a mere theoretical possibility or unused authority to make improper deductions will not violate the salary basis test; an employer's policies must create at least a "significant likelihood that actual [improper] deductions will occur."[88]

If, however, the employer has an actual practice of making improper deductions, the employees subject to those deductions generally will not be exempt.[89] Factors used to determine whether an "actual practice" exists include: the number of improper deductions (especially in comparison to the number of employee infractions that warrant some form of discipline), the time period of the improper deductions, the number and geographic location of employees subjected to improper deductions, the number and geographic location of managers who made the improper deductions, and whether the employer clearly communicated a policy allowing improper deductions.[90] A finding that improper deductions occurred

---

[83] The 2012 federal poverty level for a family of four is $23,050 annually. *See* Annual Update of the HHS Poverty Guidelines, 77 Fed. Reg. 4034, 4035 (Jan. 26, 2012).

[84] 29 C.F.R. § 541.602(a) (noting that an employee need not be paid for any week in which he or she did not work).

[85] Martin v. Malcolm Pirnie, Inc., 949 F.2d 611 (2d Cir. 1991); Abshire v. County of Kern, 908 F.2d 483, 486 (9th Cir. 1990).

[86] Auer v. Robbins, 519 U.S. 452, 456 (1997).

[87] 29 C.F.R. § 541.602(b)(5).

[88] *Auer*, 519 U.S. at 461; *see also* Ahern v. County of Nassau, 118 F.3d 118 (2d Cir. 1997).

[89] 29 C.F.R. § 541.603(a).

[90] *Id.*

means that every employee in the same classification who worked for the same manager making the deductions typically will not be considered salaried during the time period in which the improper deduction was made.[91]

Yet, the existence of an improper deduction is not the end of the analysis, for many employers still retain a valuable opportunity to maintain their employees' exempt status under the salary basis test. Even where an employer has made an improper deduction, the employees subjected to the deduction may still be considered exempt under the "window of correction." This window allows an employer to reimburse employees for deductions made inadvertently or for reasons other than a lack of work without losing employees' exempt status.[92] The reimbursement need not be made immediately after discovery of the improper deduction; indeed, an employer can take advantage of the window of correction even after litigation has begun.[93]

[2] Duties Test

If an employee's compensation arrangement satisfies the salary basis test, the analysis proceeds to the duties test. Under this test, the focus is not the form of an employee's compensation; rather, as the name implies, the actual job duties of the employee are the central issue. As explained in more detail below, each of the three exempt job classifications — executive, administrative, and professional — has a basic set of factors that will determine whether a salaried employee will be exempt. The DOL has expanded on these basic duties tests with many regulations and opinion letters that specifically address a wide variety of job situations. The basic factor test, therefore, should only be a starting point.

The DOL's regulations also make clear that certain classes of workers will never be considered exempt, even if they may otherwise appear to satisfy the duties test. These workers include manual laborers, most law enforcement officers, paramedics and emergency medical technicians, firefighters, and hazardous materials workers.[94]

Moreover, a new regulation alters the duties test if a worker is classified as a "highly compensated employee" — that is, if the employee's total annual compensation is at least $100,000.[95] Because that level of pay is considered a strong indication that the employee should be exempt, highly compensated employees need only perform *one* duty associated with a given classification, rather than all of the listed duties required for non-highly compensated employees.[96]

---

[91] *Id.* § 541.603(b).

[92] *Id.* § 541.603(c); *Auer*, 519 U.S. at 463; Martin v. Malcolm Pirnie, Inc., 949 F.2d 611 (2d Cir. 1991).

[93] *Auer*, 519 U.S. at 463.

[94] 29 C.F.R. § 541.3(a), (b)(1) (stating, in essence, that there is an irrebuttable presumption that all such employees, no matter their level of pay, lack the specialized intellectual instruction, managerial responsibility, or administrative work required under the duties test for any of the three exemptions).

[95] *Id.* § 541.601(a).

[96] *Id.* § 541.601(b)(4)(c).

Another of the recent regulatory changes affects an important term in all of the exemption categories. Most job duties listed require that they be a "primary duty" of the employee. Traditionally, the DOL had relied upon a "fifty percent rule of thumb," which presumed that a duty was primary if it took at least fifty percent of the employee's work time.[97] Exceptions always existed, however, and the DOL's new regulations explicitly eliminated the fifty percent rule (although the amount of time spent on a duty will always be relevant).[98] Instead, under current regulations, a duty will be primary if it is the "principal, main, major or most important duty that the employee performs."[99]

Finally, there exists a "combination exemption." This exemption applies where an employee performs certain duties from more than one exempt classification, but not enough duties to satisfy any single individual classification. For example, an employee who does not satisfy either all of the executive duties or all of the administrative duties may still be considered exempt if her primary duty consists of work listed under both the executive and administrative tests.[100] In other words, although no single classification is satisfied, exempt work from various classifications may make up an employee's primary duty for purposes of the exemption.[101]

[a]   Executive Exemption

The FLSA's executive exemption covers those employees normally thought of as managers. The general rule of the executive exemption states:

(a)   The term "employee employed in a bona fide executive capacity" . . . shall mean any employee:

[*Salary Basis Test:*]

　　(1)   Compensated on a salary basis at a rate of not less than $455 per week . . . exclusive of board, lodging or other facilities;

[*Duties Test:*]

　　(2)   Whose primary duty is management of the enterprise in which the employee is employed or of a customarily recognized department or subdivision thereof;

　　(3)   Who customarily and regularly directs the work of two or more other employees; and

　　(4)   Who has the authority to hire or fire other employees or whose suggestions   and   recommendations   as   to   the   hiring,   firing,

---

[97] *See generally* Donovan v. Burger King Corp., 672 F.2d 221, 226 (1st Cir. 1982).

[98] 29 C.F.R. § 541.700. The regulations do note that time will be a "useful guide" and that employees who spend more than 50% of their time on exempt work "will generally satisfy the primary duty requirement." *Id.* § 541.700(b).

[99] *Id.*

[100] *Id.* § 541.708.

[101] *See, e.g.,* Dalheim v. KDFW-TV, 918 F.2d 1220, 1232 (5th Cir. 1990).

advancement, promotion or any other change of status of other employees are given particular weight.[102]

In short, an employee satisfies the executive duties test if she has the primary duty of managing; normally directs the work of two or more employees; *and* has the authority or power to recommend the hiring, firing, or other major status changes of employees. An employee earning a salary of at least $100,000 — that is, a "highly compensated" employee — need only have one of those duty factors to satisfy the exemption.

The first factor, "management of the enterprise," refers to supervisory tasks that an employee can perform as long as those tasks are not directed by higher management to such a significant degree that it negates the employee's actual authority.[103] Tasks commonly associated with management includes training employees, managing production or sales records, evaluating employees' performance, disciplining employees, planning work to be done, providing for plant safety, planning the budget, controlling supply flow, and monitoring or implementing legal compliance measures.[104]

The "customarily and regularly directs" the work of two or more employees factor is relatively clear. "Two employees" requires direction of the equivalent of two full-time employees — for example, directing one full-time employee and two half-time employees would suffice.[105] Moreover, employees can be directed by more than one exempt executive, as long as each exempt executive individually directs two or more employees.[106] An assistant who directs employees' work only in the absence of a manager does not satisfy this factor.[107]

The DOL's new regulations added the third prong — the authority to hire, fire, or make other status changes, or to have particular weight given to status change recommendations. Because this factor was a recent addition, case law on this issue is sparse. The determination of an employee's authority to make status changes, which is common to other statutes' definition of managerial authority,[108] will likely come down to a factual finding whether the employee actually possesses the alleged authority. Whether "particular weight" is given to recommendations, however, opens the door for further ambiguity. The DOL's regulations list several factors that may be relevant to this question, including whether the employee's job duties include making suggestions and recommendations, the frequency with which such suggestions and recommendations are made, and the frequency with which the

---

[102] 29 C.F.R. § 541.100.

[103] Company direction that allows for discretion does not, by itself, preclude the executive exemption because ensuring that specified policy goals are carried out is an executive function. Donovan v. Burger King Corp., 672 F.2d 221, 226 (1st Cir. 1982).

[104] 29 C.F.R. § 541.102.

[105] *Id.* § 541.104(a).

[106] *Id.* § 541.104(b).

[107] *Id.* § 541.104(c).

[108] The National Labor Relations Act's definition of "supervisor," for instance, includes the authority to "hire, transfer, suspend, lay off, recall, promote, discharge, . . . or discipline other employees, . . . or effectively to recommend such action." 29 U.S.C. § 152(11).

employer relied upon those suggestions and recommendations.[109] An executive employee's recommendations may still be given particular weight under the test even if higher management can overrule the employee, but the employee must make recommendations more than occasionally and the employer must seriously consider them.[110]

One issue that frequently arises in these cases involves employees who have managerial duties but perform a significant amount of non-managerial work, such as the manager of a fast-food restaurant. A recent example of such a case is *Morgan v. Family Dollar Stores, Inc.*,[111] in which the Eleventh Circuit upheld a jury's finding that Family Dollar store managers were not exempt executive employees. According to the court, the managers spent 80 to 90% of their time performing non-managerial duties. The court noted that this fell well below the DOL's general 50% guideline,[112] but recognized that this is not a firm rule. However, the court stressed that other factors supported the jury's finding, including the employer's description of these non-managerial duties as "essential," the heavy use of policy manuals and corporate directives that resulted in store managers rarely exercising discretion, the significant direct supervision that district managers had over the store managers, and the relatively small difference in the store managers' salaries over non-exempt assistant managers.

[b]   Administrative Exemption

Employees excluded from the FLSA as administrative employees are typically those who assist management in the general business operations of the company. The general rule of the administrative exemption states:

(a)   The term "employee employed in a bona fide administrative capacity" . . . shall mean any employee:

[*Salary Basis Test:*]

(1)   Compensated on a salary or fee basis at a rate of not less than $455 per week . . . exclusive of board, lodging or other facilities;

[*Duties Test:*]

(2)   Whose primary duty is the performance of office or non-manual work directly related to the management or general business operations of the employer or the employer's customers; and

(3)   Whose primary duty includes the exercise of discretion and independent judgment with respect to matters of significance.[113]

In sum, the administrative duties test requires an employee to have the primary duty of office or non-manual work related to general business operations *and* that

---

[109]   29 C.F.R. § 541.105.

[110]   *Id.*; Davis v. Mountaire Farms, 453 F.3d 554 (3d Cir. 2006).

[111]   551 F.3d 1233 (11th Cir. 2008).

[112]   *See supra* note 98.

[113]   29 C.F.R. § 541.200.

primary duty must involve discretion and independent judgment regarding significant matters.

Whether an employee's primary duty is "directly related to the management or general business operations" is a frequently litigated issue. The DOL has traditionally applied a production-versus-administrative test to address this issue — not, as some parties have argued, a white collar/blue collar distinction.[114] The regulations define this duty as "work directly related to assisting with the running or servicing of the business, as distinguished, for example, from working on a manufacturing production line or selling a product in a retail or service establishment."[115] A rule of thumb for analyzing this duty test is to ask whether the employee is directly involved with making or producing the actual product of the company or, instead, whether the employee is involved with the general operations of the business entity itself. If the former is true, the employee is not an administrative employee and may be entitled to overtime; if the latter is true, the employee may be an exempt administrator.

An example of this production/administrative distinction is a local television news producer who is directly involved with the creation of aired news segments. Because the business's product is the news broadcast itself, the news producer's direct involvement with the development of that product means that the administrative exemption will generally not apply.[116] Other types of jobs that the DOL's regulations specifically mention as typically not being directly related to business operations are inspectors, comparison shoppers, and product graders.[117]

In contrast, jobs that will generally be considered as a direct part of business operations include work in tax, accounting, budgeting, insurance, advertising, human resources, computer networks, executive assistance, and purchasing.[118] Moreover, one of the controversial new regulations was the inclusion of "team leaders" as a presumptive administrative employee. Such an employee — one "who leads a team of other employees assigned to complete major projects for the employer (such as purchasing, selling, or closing all or part of the business; negotiating a real estate transaction or a collective bargaining agreement; or designing and implementing productivity improvements)" — will generally meet the administrative duties test under the DOL's current regulations.[119]

Determining whether an employee "exercise[s] . . . discretion and independent judgment with respect to matters of significance" is fact-specific.[120] This factor generally implies that an employee has the authority to make independent choices

---

[114] Bothell v. Phase Metrics, Inc., 299 F.3d 1120, 1125-26 (9th Cir. 2002); Dalheim v. KDFW-TV, 918 F.2d 1220 (5th Cir. 1990).

[115] 29 C.F.R. § 541.201(a).

[116] *Dalheim*, 918 F.2d at 1229-31.

[117] 29 C.F.R. §§ 541.203(g), (h), (i), (j).

[118] *Id.* §§ 541.201(b), 541.203; Reich v. John Alden Life Ins. Co., 126 F.3d 1 (1st Cir. 1997) (discussing production/administrative distinction as applied to insurance marketing representatives).

[119] 29 C.F.R. § 541.203(c).

[120] *Id.* § 541.200; *see generally* O'Bryant v. City of Reading, 197 Fed. App'x 134 (3d Cir. 2006).

without direct supervision.[121] Yet, even if more senior managers review an employee's actions and recommendations, it is possible to find that he or she exercises discretion and independent judgment — as long as the employee can freely evaluate and compare different options.[122] Moreover, "matters of significance" refers to the "level of importance or consequence of the work performed."[123]

Courts use a totality of the circumstances test to determine whether an employee exercises discretion and independent judgment with respect to matters of significance. Factors to consider when analyzing this duty include, but are not limited to, whether the employee has authority: to formulate management policies or operating practices, to carry out major assignments in conducting the operations of the business, to perform work that affects business operations to a substantial degree, to commit the employer in matters that have significant financial impact, to waive or deviate from established policies and procedures without prior approval, and to take part in planning long- or short-term business objectives.[124] However, just because an employee's actions may have a significant impact on the employer's business does not necessarily satisfy this prong; rather, the nature, not the consequences, of the employee's work is the central issue.[125]

[c]   Professional Exemption

The FLSA's professional exemption covers those employees normally thought of as either learned or creative professionals. The general rule of the professional exemption states:

(a)   The term "employee employed in a bona fide professional capacity" . . . shall mean any employee:

[*Salary Basis Test:*]

   (1)   Compensated on a salary basis at a rate of not less than $455 per week . . . exclusive of board, lodging or other facilities;

[*Duties Test:*]

   (2)   Whose primary duty is the performance of work:

      (i)   Requiring knowledge of an advanced type in a field of science or learning customarily acquired by a prolonged course of specialized intellectual instruction; or

      (ii)   Requiring invention, imagination, originality or talent in a recognized field of artistic or creative endeavor.[126]

---

[121] 29 C.F.R. § 541.202(c).

[122] *Id.* §§ 541.202(a), (c).

[123] *Id.* § 541.202(a).

[124] *Id.* § 541.202(b).

[125] *Id.* § 541.202(f); *Dalheim*, 918 F.2d at 1231.

[126] 29 C.F.R. § 541.300.

The highly compensated employee rule has no real impact under the professional exemption because salaried employees will be exempt if their primary duty is that of either a learned or creative professional.

The learned professional test requires work in an advanced field of knowledge that usually requires specialized schooling. This refers to intellectual work that involves the regular exercise of discretion and judgment, not work that is routine, manual, or physical.[127] Advanced knowledge must be obtained at a level beyond high school and typically involves specialized academic instruction, frequently accompanied by a degree, that is a prerequisite to enter the profession.[128] A degree, however, is not necessary, as work experience and intellectual instruction may suffice.[129] The knowledge must be in a field that is similar to law,[130] medicine,[131] accounting, theology, teaching,[132] engineering, and other sciences. In contrast, fields such as the mechanical arts or skilled trades, are not considered fields of "science or learning."[133] The DOL's regulations also specifically address several jobs that may be considered a learned profession, including nurses, chefs, accountants, paralegals, dental hygienists, physician assistants, and funeral directors.[134]

The creative professional exemption applies to employees who use invention, imagination, originality, or talent in recognized fields of arts or creativity — as distinguished from work that may be produced with general manual or intellectual ability.[135] Artistic or creative fields are those such as music, writing, acting, and art.[136] Being part of such a field, however, is not sufficient. Rather, an employee's work must involve some sort of creativity, as opposed to work using only "intelligence, diligence, and accuracy."[137] This means that an employee who merely copies work or by rote completes someone else's creative work, such as certain types of animators, will not be a creative professional.[138] Jobs that will typically be classified as a creative professional include actors, musicians, composers, writers, cartoonists, and painters with significant discretion.[139]

---

[127] *Id.* § 541.301(b).

[128] *Id.* §§ 541.301(a), (d).

[129] *Id.* § 541.301(d).

[130] *Id.* § 541.304; Kavanagh v. City of Phoenix, 87 F. Supp. 2d 958 (D. Ariz. 2000).

[131] 29 C.F.R. § 541.304.

[132] *Id.* § 541.303.

[133] *Id.* § 541.301(c). The regulations give as an example those lawyers who are allowed to practice despite not having attended law school. *Id.*

[134] *Id.* § 541.301(e).

[135] *Id.* § 541.302(a).

[136] *Id.* § 541.302(b).

[137] *Id.* § 541.302(c).

[138] *Id.*

[139] *Id.* Journalists may be creative professionals as well if they use originality, imagination, or talent (such as on-air journalists), as opposed to work that relies more on intelligence, diligence, and accuracy (such as collecting public information). *Id.*; Dalheim v. KDFW-TV, 918 F.2d 1220, 1229 (5th Cir. 1990).

[E]   Determining Wage Rates

Determining whether and how much an employer owes under the FLSA's minimum wage and overtime provisions depends on the calculation of an employee's wages and hours, or so-called "regular rate." Take, for example, an employee who earns $10 per hour and normally works 8 hours a day for 5 days a week, totaling 40 hours per week. The employee's base wage rate is $10 per hour. Because the wage exceeds $7.25 per hour, the minimum wage provisions are not at issue.[140] If the employee works more than 40 hours in a week and is entitled to an overtime premium, each hour above 40 worked in that week must be paid at one-and-one-half times the base wage — in this case, the overtime wage would be $15 per hour (1.5 x $10 = $15).

The calculation becomes more complicated, however, as the facts diverge from this basic scenario. Two main variances may occur. The first involves unusual or variable compensation arrangements that make it difficult to determine the wage used to calculate the employee's hourly base wage rate. The second involves work schedules that complicate the calculation of the amount of hours an employee works in a given week, which, in turn, directly affect the base wage rate calculation.

Unusual or variable forms of compensation may include bonuses, board and lodging, in-kind payments, and a panoply of other arrangements. For minimum wage purposes, the starting point for analyzing such compensation is Section 3(m) of the FLSA, which expressly contemplates nontraditional forms of payment by defining "wage" as including the "reasonable cost . . . to the employer of furnishing . . . board, lodging, or other facilities, if [they] are customarily furnished by such employer to his employees."[141] "Other facilities" can include a wide range of in-kind benefits including, but not limited to, certain types of meals, tuition, general merchandise from a company store, fuel, and transportation.[142]

The value of these in-kind benefits is generally determined based on the actual, reasonable cost to employers as determined by "good accounting practices."[143] Yet, the DOL has the regulatory authority to determine the "fair value" of in-kind payments for a class of employees based on average costs to a group of employers, rather than looking to a specific individual employer's actual cost.[144]

Providing "facilities" primarily for the benefit of the employer will not count toward an employee's wage.[145] Examples of such facilities include tools of the trade and other materials incidental to business operations, construction costs for the employer, and purchasing and laundering uniforms required by the employer.[146] In

---

[140]   If the employee's wage was $7.00 per hour, she would be entitled to an additional $0.25 for every hour that she received that wage because that is the difference between the minimum wage and the employee's actual wage. *See supra* note 61.

[141]   29 U.S.C. § 203(m).

[142]   29 C.F.R. § 531.32.

[143]   *Id.* §§ 531.3(a), (c).

[144]   29 U.S.C. § 203(m).

[145]   29 C.F.R. §§ 531.3(d)(1), 531.32.

[146]   *Id.* § 531.3(d)(2).

Marshall v. Sam Dell's Dodge Corp.,[147] the district court held that the value of an automobile provided to a salesperson for his personal and business use may be included as wages, but only if its provision was not primarily for the benefit of the employer.[148] Even though the employee used the company car mainly for personal use, the court held that it could not be counted as a wage because it was provided "primarily for the benefit or convenience of the employer."[149]

A related and unresolved issue is whether an employer can require an employee to accept in-kind compensation. The DOL promulgated a regulation stating that, to be counted as wages, an employee must accept in-kind payments voluntarily and without coercion; however, several circuit courts have invalidated that regulation as contrary to the FLSA's language.[150]

For overtime purposes, the classification of unusual or irregular compensation falls under Section 7(e) the FLSA, which refers to the wage rate used to determine the base for overtime premiums as the "regular rate."[151] This is the rate that is multiplied by one-and-one-half to determine the overtime premium for each week that it is owed.[152] Section 7(e)'s baseline counts "all remuneration for employment" as part of the regular rate, which may include many of the in-kind payments counted in the minimum wage calculations.[153] Many payments, however, are expressly excluded by the FLSA's overtime provisions.[154]

These exclusions include gifts, such as holiday bonuses not tied to performance; vacation, holiday, or sick leave payments; travel expenses; premiums for retirement, life, or health insurance; extra payments made for working holidays or overtime hours; and income derived from most stock options and stock purchase plans.[155] Bonuses, in particular, frequently cause confusion in this area. The most significant factor in determining whether bonuses will be treated as part of the regular rate is whether they were at the employer's sole discretion and not part of an employee's expected compensation.[156] If the employer retains such discretion, the bonus is treated as a gift not tied to performance and is not counted as part of the regular rate.[157] For instance, in *Dunlop v. Gray-Goto, Inc.*,[158] the employer and its employees had an understanding that the employees would receive fringe benefits, including bonuses that were not tied to the employees' performance, in

---

[147] 451 F. Supp. 294 (N.D.N.Y. 1978).

[148] *Id.* at 304.

[149] *Id.* (citing 29 C.F.R. § 531.32(c)).

[150] 29 C.F.R. § 531.30. *But see* Herman v. Collis Foods, Inc., 176 F.3d 912 (6th Cir. 1999) (invalidating voluntary requirement); Donovan v. Miller Props., Inc., 711 F.2d 49 (5th Cir. 1983) (same); Davis Bros., Inc. v. Donovan, 700 F.2d 1368 (11th Cir. 1983) (same).

[151] 29 U.S.C. § 207(e).

[152] *Id.* § 207(a).

[153] 29 C.F.R. § 531.27.

[154] 29 U.S.C. § 207(e).

[155] *Id.*

[156] 29 U.S.C. § 207(e); Dunlop v. Gray-Goto, Inc., 528 F.2d 792 (10th Cir. 1976).

[157] 29 C.F.R. § 778.211; O'Brien v. Town of Agawam, 350 F.3d 279, 295 (1st Cir. 2003).

[158] 528 F.2d 792 (10th Cir. 1976).

lieu of overtime premiums for work in excess of 40 hours. The Tenth Circuit held that parties could not circumvent by agreement the FLSA's approach to classifying bonuses and other fringe benefits. In contrast, a bonus that is tied to performance, or one that is paid regularly enough to have become part of the employee's expected compensation, will be included in the regular rate.

When a bonus is included for overtime purposes, its value generally will be apportioned over the period of time for which is was earned.[159] For example, if an employee earned a $5,000 annual bonus based on her performance in the preceding year, the bonus will be apportioned over that entire year — in this case, $100 per week (assuming 50 work weeks for that year).

Marshall v. Sam Dell's Dodge Corp.[160] provides an example of how the treatment of bonuses may differ under the FLSA's overtime and minimum wage provisions. The employees in *Marshall* were salespersons who alleged that for certain periods during the year, their compensation was below the minimum wage. One of the issues was how to count weekly, monthly, and annual bonuses that the employees earned for selling a certain number of automobiles during the relevant time period. The court held that for minimum wage purposes, bonuses — including the monthly and annual ones at issue in that case — were to be counted as part of the employees' wages during the week in which they were *paid*.[161] This contrasts with the DOL's overtime rules, which would have apportioned the monthly and annual bonuses over the weeks in which they were *earned*.[162]

The second major issue in determining wage rates is the computation of hours. The FLSA strictly applies on a work-week basis, which means that generally each week is analyzed independently of any other week.[163] There have been several legislative attempts to change this rule — for example, by computing overtime based on an 80-hour biweekly period, rather than a 40-hour weekly period[164] — but none has been successful thus far. Accordingly, compensation in any given week must result in an hourly wage of at least $7.25 an hour[165] and that wage will be used as the base for any overtime premium owed.

Although determining the wage rate is often simple for more traditional hourly wage jobs, many work schedules do not fit this mold.[166] Employees required to be

---

[159] 29 C.F.R. § 778.209.

[160] 451 F. Supp. 294 (N.D.N.Y. 1978).

[161] *Id.*

[162] 29 C.F.R. § 778.209(a).

[163] 29 U.S.C. §§ 206(b), 207(a); 29 C.F.R. § 778.104; *Marshall*, 451 F. Supp. at 302.

[164] This is commonly referred to as a "Flex-Time" Bill, which would also allow compensatory time to be provided in lieu of overtime premium pay. *See* Family Time and Workplace Flexibility Act, S.317, 108th Cong. (2003). Note that public employees may have compensatory time off counted as overtime pay. 29 U.S.C. § 207(o).

[165] *See supra* note 61.

[166] A further example is how to calculate the regular rate for fluctuating workweeks. The rate of pay for a fluctuating workweek schedule is determined for each week individually; thus, an employee may be entitled to minimum wage compensation or overtime premiums in one week, but not another. 29 C.F.R. § 778.114

"on call," for example, raise the question of whether on-call time should be included as part of the wage rate. The central issue for on-call time is whether the employee may use her time "effectively for [her] own purposes." If so, on-call time is not compensable; if not, an employer must pay the employee for that time.[167] For instance, in *Bright v. Houston Northwest Medical Center Survivor, Inc.*,[168] the employee was a biomedical equipment repair technician who, when not at work, was always on call. During the on-call time, he could not be intoxicated, he always had to be reachable by a beeper, and he always had to be within approximately twenty minutes of work. He was not paid for on-call time unless he had to come in to work. The Fifth Circuit held that the employee was not entitled to compensation for his on-call time because he could "use his on-call time effectively for his own personal purposes," despite the restrictions he faced during those time periods.[169] Limited flexibility is not enough to trigger entitlement to wages; rather, an employee must face very strict restrictions, such as being required to stay at a fixed location.

Another issue that has prompted significant litigation recently is whether time spent "donning and doffing" clothing or equipment is compensable. Under the Portal-to-Portal Act,[170] travel to and from work is not typically compensable for either minimum wage or overtime purposes. Moreover, the compensable "workday" period starts when the employee's first principal activity begins and ends when the last principal activity is completed.[171] This workday concept is important, for any activity during the workday that is an "integral and indispensable part of the principal activities" of the employee's job is compensable.[172] In many workforces, employees must "don and doff" protective gear, which is not directly a "principal activity" and the issue in the lower courts has been whether employers must pay for that time. In *IBP, Inc. v. Alvarez*,[173] the Supreme Court held that "any activity that is 'integral and indispensable' to a 'principal activity' is itself a 'principal activity'" that is compensable.[174] This compensable type of activity includes the donning and doffing of protective gear, as well as the time walking to and from the changing area and waiting to begin work.

---

[167] 29 C.F.R. § 785.17; Armour & Co. v. Wantock, 323 U.S. 126 (1944); Skidmore v. Swift & Co., 323 U.S. 134 (1944).

[168] 934 F.2d 671 (5th Cir. 1991) (en banc).

[169] *Id.* at 677-78.

[170] 29 U.S.C. § 254(a) (amending FLSA).

[171] 29 C.F.R. § 790.6(b).

[172] IBP, Inc. v. Alvarez, 126 S. Ct. 514, 521 (2005) (quoting Steiner v. Mitchell, 350 U.S. 247, 256 (1956)).

[173] 126 S. Ct. 514 (2005).

[174] *Id.* at 525 (citing Department of Labor regulations).

[F]   Enforcement

The Secretary of Labor has the primary authority to enforce the FLSA. The Secretary (through the Wage and Hour Division) may investigate and gather information about employers' compliance with the FLSA.[175] To assist this investigative function, employers are required to maintain relevant records on their employment practices, including the wages of and hours worked by their employees.[176]

If the Secretary determines that an employer has violated the FLSA, the Wage and Hour Division can pursue an action in any court of competent jurisdiction.[177] The FLSA provides employees with a private right of action as well, which may be brought in a competent state or federal court.[178] Unlike employment discrimination actions, plaintiffs do not need to notify the Secretary or comply with any other administrative exhaustion requirements. The statute of limitations for suits brought by either the Secretary or an individual is two years, except for willful violations, which have a three-year statute of limitations.[179] Remedies available for FLSA violations include unpaid minimum wages and overtime compensation, liquated damages, reinstatement, and injunctive relief.[180] Certain willful violations may also subject an employer to a criminal conviction, with fines up to $10,000 and imprisonment of no more than six months.[181] Moreover, violations of the child labor protections may result in civil fines of no more than $11,000 for each employee at issue.[182]

The potential damages involved in FLSA cases, particularly for overtime premiums, have resulted in an increasing number of collective action suits against large employers.[183] Wal-Mart, for example, has faced several actions alleging overtime violations against a sizeable number of workers.[184] Indeed, in a recent case brought by the DOL, Wal-Mart agreed to a settlement providing over 86,000

---

[175]   29 U.S.C. §§ 211, 212.

[176]   *Id.* § 211(c).

[177]   *Id.* § 216(c). An individual may be held liable for violations of the FLSA under limited circumstances, such as when an individual high in the corporate structure is considered part of the employer's "enterprise." *See, e.g.*, Martin v. W.E. Monks & Co., 805 F. Supp. 500, 501-02 (S.D. Ohio 1992) (holding that president and majority shareholder were individually liable).

[178]   *Id.* § 216(b). Note that state sovereign immunity may limit an employee's ability to obtain monetary damages against a state employer in both state and federal court. Alden v. Maine, 527 U.S. 706 (1999).

[179]   29 U.S.C. § 255(a).

[180]   29 U.S.C. § 216(b). The amount of a liquidated damage award is equal to the unpaid minimum wages or overtime compensation. *Id.* In other words, such an award doubles the damages.

[181]   *Id.* § 216(a).

[182]   *Id.* § 216(e); *see supra* § 12.02[B].

[183]   The normal class action rules of Federal Rule of Civil Procedure 23 do not apply to FLSA claims; group claims under that statute fall under 29 U.S.C. § 216(b), which requires plaintiffs to opt-in rather than opt-out under Rule 23. For a more thorough discussion of FLSA collective actions, see Scott Moss & Nantiya Ruan, *The Second-Class Class Action: How Courts Thwart Wage Rights by Misapplying Class Action Rules*, 61 Am. U. L. Rev. 523 (2012).

[184]   *See, e.g., Big Class of Wal-Mart Workers Can Proceed in Washington Overtime Case, Court*

employees with a total of $33 million to compensate them for unpaid overtime premiums.[185]

§ 12.03　WAGE PAYMENT LAWS

[A]　Overview

In contrast to the protections under the FLSA and FMLA,[186] wage payment laws for the most part originate from state law. Not surprisingly, there is a wide variety of these laws, but the common theme generally is to protect against employers withholding part of employees' earned wages. These protections normally guarantee the form of wage payments, ensure that recently separated employees receive all wages owed to them, restrict employers' ability to withhold or garnish wages, and prevent employers from taking employees' tips.

As is always the case with state law issues, the particulars of any given jurisdiction could differ significantly from one to the next. What follows are examples of various types of wage payment laws, but readers should consult the relevant laws in their jurisdictions.

[B]　Form of Wage Payment

The most common type of "form-of-wage" laws requires that wages be paid in cash or by check.[187] Scrip, coupons, or other things that must be redeemed later are generally prohibited.[188] These laws seek to end the older practice of employers paying employees in coupons that could be redeemed only at an employer-owned business, often at inflated prices. A more modern problem that could be addressed under these laws is the practice of requiring immigrant employees to spend their wages on employer-provided room and board.[189]

Form-of-wage laws also frequently impose a minimum period of time that an employer can wait before paying wages.[190] This prevents, for instance, employers

---

Affirms, Daily Lab. Rep. (BNA) No. 138, at A-2 (Jul. 16, 2006) (describing class of approximately 53,000 employees).

[185] *See Wal-Mart to Pay More Than $33 Million In Settlement with DOL Involving Overtime*, Daily Lab. Rep. (BNA) No. 17, at AA-1 (Jan. 26, 2007) (describing Chao v. Wal-Mart Stores, Inc., No 07-2007 (W.D. Ark. settled Jan. 25, 2007)).

[186] *See infra* § 12.04 (discussing FMLA).

[187] *See, e.g.*, C.R.S. § 8-4-102(1) (requiring, in Colorado, payment of wages with any "order, check, draft, note, memorandum, or other acknowledgment of indebtedness" if "payable upon demand without discount in cash at a bank").

[188] *See, e.g., id.* § 8-4-102(3) (prohibiting, in Colorado, payment of wages with "any scrip, coupons, cards, or other things redeemable in merchandise unless such scrip, coupons, cards, or other things may be redeemed in cash when due").

[189] *Cf.* Bureerong v. Uvawas, 922 F. Supp. 1450, 1478 (C.D. Cal. 1996) (holding that involuntary wage deductions violated California law prohibiting employer from coercing employees to make purchase (citing Cal. Lab. Code § 450)).

[190] *See, e.g.*, C.R.S. § 8-4-103(1) (requiring, in Colorado, payment of wages on regular paydays of no more than one month or 30 days, whichever is longer); 26 M.R.S.A. § 621-A(1), (2) (requiring, in Maine,

from paying an employee for a year's work at the end of the year. Moreover, a number of state wage laws emulate New York's, which requires different payment schedules depending on the employer or type of work performed, including taking special care to require weekly payments for manual laborers.[191]

[C] Wage Payment After Separation

Other wage payment laws attempt to ensure that employees receive all earned wages after the employment relationship has ended. These laws frequently require that employers pay all wages within a certain period of time after the employee quits or is terminated. The purpose of these laws is to prevent employers from delaying, or failing to pay altogether, wages earned by employees who no longer have the promise of continued work to entice prompt wage payments from their employers.[192] A typical statute requires payment within a few days of separation, thereby ensuring prompt payment of a final paycheck.[193] Some laws also require payment for accrued vacation leave.[194]

Colorado, for example, has a statute requiring wage payments to occur immediately if the employer terminates an employee. If, on the other hand, an employee quits, payment is due on the next scheduled payday.[195] Moreover, an employer is subject to a penalty of fifty percent of the wages owed if it fails to make a timely payment in response to an employee's demand for his or her wages.[196] Finally, since 2003, employers in Colorado no longer have a good faith defense for failing to make wage payments.[197]

[D] Restrictions on Assignment and Garnishment

Many states prevent or limit employers' ability to assign or garnish employees' wages. One reason is that some garnishments can be so significant that it may appear that the employee is an indentured servant. Maine's wage garnishment statute addresses this concern by stating that:

---

payment of wages at regular intervals of no more than 16 days and no later than eight days after wage was earned).

[191] N.Y. McKinney's Lab. Law §§ 190, 191.

[192] See, e.g., Stoll v. Goodnight Corp., 469 So. 2d 1072, 1075 (La. Ct. App. 1985).

[193] See, e.g., La. Rev. Stat. Ann. § 23:631 (requiring, in Louisiana, payment of last paycheck by next paydate or within 15 days after a discharge or resignation, whichever date occurs first); 26 Me. Rev. Stat. Ann. § 626 (requiring, in Maine, that employer pay wage of separated employee in "reasonable time" after employee demands payment).

[194] La. Rev. Stat. Ann. § 23:631(D).

[195] C.R.S. § 8-4-109(1); see also N.Y. McKinney's Lab. Law § 190(1)(d)(3) (requiring payment to terminated employee no later than next regular payday).

[196] C.R.S. § 8-4-109(3) (specifying that penalty applies if the employee demands payment within 60 days after separation and the employer fails to comply within 10 days of the demand).

[197] Co. Legis. 286 (2003) (deleting "good faith legal justification for such refusal" from current C.R.S. § 8-4-109(3)). This good faith defense had been possible in various situations, such as where an employee violated his or her duty of loyalty to the employer. See Jet Courier Serv., Inc. v. Mulei, 771 P.2d 486, 501 (Colo. 1989) (remanding on this issue).

No person, firm or corporation shall require or permit any person as a condition of securing or retaining employment to work without monetary compensation or when having an agreement, verbal, written or implied that a part of such compensation should be returned to the person, firm or corporation for any reason other than for the payment of a loan, debt or advance made to the person. . . . [T]he word "debt" means a benefit to the employee. Debt does not include items incurred by the employee in the course of the employee's work . . . , such as cash shortages, inventory shortages . . . , damages to the employer's property in any form or any merchandise purchased by a customer.[198]

In *Beckwith v. United Parcel Service*,[199] the First Circuit held that a statute in Maine prohibited an employment agreement under which an employee would pay United Parcel Service (UPS) for losses caused by the employee in return for UPS giving the employee his job back. The employee had violated UPS's policies by improperly releasing packages, which resulted in significant losses of merchandise. As a result, UPS fired the employee, who then offered to pay for the losses if he got his job back. UPS and the employee subsequently entered into an agreement to withhold a portion of the employee's wages every week until all the losses were reimbursed.[200] Later, the employee sued to invalidate the agreement under the Maine statute and his claim was eventually upheld by the First Circuit.

The court held that the parties could have entered into an agreement to ensure that the employee compensated UPS for the losses; however, the *manner* in which they had done so in this case violated state law. Maine's law sought to protect employees from the risk of unfair agreements that can arise from tying payments to work performed. In particular, the agreement was "harmful and unfair because it deprives the worker of wages earned before he has had a chance to decide on a given payday how best to allocate his available resources."[201] Moreover, the automatic deduction deprived the employee of any flexibility to react to an unexpected financial crisis. Thus, the court noted, the parties could have entered into an agreement under which the employee would pay back the cost of damages as a condition of reinstatement — as long as the payments did not come directly out of the employee's wages.[202] Another option for an employer in UPS's position would have been to sue the employee for damages.[203]

---

[198] 26 M.R.S.A. § 629; *see also* C.R.S. § 8-4-105 (Colorado wage deduction provision); Truelove v. N.E. Capital & Advisory, Inc., 95 N.Y.2d 220 (2000) (citing N.Y. McKinney's Lab. Law § 193).

[199] 889 F.2d 344 (1st Cir. 1989).

[200] *Id.* The employee was to have $50 deducted each week until the total $7,814 was paid. *Id.*

[201] *Id.* at 349.

[202] *Id.* at 348 n.6. An employer also could not try to circumvent this limitation by, for example, conditioning a paycheck on the employee's payment of a certain amount to offset damages caused by the employee. Male v. Acme Mkts., Inc., 264 A.2d 245 (N.J. Super. Ct. App. Div. 1970). *But see* Stoll v. Goodnight Corp., 469 So. 2d 1072 (La. Ct. App. 1985) (holding that Louisiana statute permitted an employer to require an employee to give back a portion of wages).

[203] *Male*, 264 A.2d at 246; Restatement (Second) of Agency § 401.

A further example of an anti-wage deduction law was discussed in the New York case of *Truelove v. Northeast Capital & Advisory, Inc.*,[204] which also illustrates a common problem in applying such laws — how to define "wage." *Truelove* addressed the common issue of whether an employee was due a bonus after resigning. The employee sued to obtain a bonus that was awarded for the previous year, but was to be paid in quarterly installments the following year. He had resigned after the first payment and the employer refused to pay any further installments. New York law prohibits most reductions from wages, which the employee claimed entitled him to the remaining bonus payments.

The New York Court of Appeals (the highest court in the state) rejected his claim, holding that the bonus was not a "wage," which New York defined as "the earnings of an employee for labor or services rendered."[205] The bonus failed under this definition because it was tied more to the employer's financial success than the employee's individual performance. This test is similar to that in the FLSA[206] and is a good reminder that, before a wage deduction law applies, the compensation at issue must constitute a wage.[207]

Finally, unlike most other wage protections laws, federal legislation plays a role with regard to garnishments. In the Consumer Credit Protection Act,[208] Congress limited the amount of wages that can be subject to garnishment and prohibited an employer from terminating an employee because garnishment had been required for one debt. States may also have similar garnishment restrictions.[209]

[E]   Tips

Many states prohibit employer interference with employees' tips. This protection is particularly important given that tips often constitute a substantial portion of many employees' compensation.[210] Further, because employers may initially collect all tips, which are often difficult to track, the potential for abuse is high.

A typical tip protection statute prohibits an employer from interfering with the tips of an employee who works in a business where the payment of tips is customary.[211] Some states have more limited protections — for example,

---

[204] 95 N.Y.2d 220 (2000).

[205] *Id.* at 223-24 (citing N.Y. McKinney's Lab. Law § 190(1)).

[206] *See supra* note 157.

[207] This issue may also arise for stock options. *See* IBM v. Bajorek, 191 F.3d 1033 (9th Cir. 1999) (holding, in anti-deduction case, that stock option was not a wage under California law) (citing Cal. Lab. Code § 221).

[208] 15 U.S.C. §§ 1673-1674.

[209] *See, e.g., In re* Robinson, 240 B.R. 70 (Bankr. N.D. Ala. 1999) (discussing Ala. Code § 6-10-7). The Consumer Credit Protect Act permits state garnishment laws if the Secretary of Labor finds that they provide equivalent protection. 15 U.S.C. § 1675.

[210] *See supra* notes 66–68 and accompanying text.

[211] *See, e.g.*, C.R.S. § 8-4-103(2)(6) (prohibiting, in Colorado, employer from taking control of tips unless the public is notified that tips are the property of the owner).

protecting only tips that are automatically deducted from a bill.[212] Tips may also be expressly protected from deductions or garnishments.[213]

§ 12.04 FAMILY AND MEDICAL LEAVE ACT

One of the more recently enacted federal employment statutes[214] is the Family and Medical Leave Act of 1993 (FMLA).[215] Because the FMLA requires only unpaid family and medical leave,[216] it is best to think of the statute as a job-security law. Although the FMLA's protections are still far less than those of most European countries,[217] the Act has quickly become an important entitlement for many workers. Female employees, in particular, can face significant hurdles to employment because of their disproportionate burden of caretaking duties. The FMLA seeks to lessen that imbalance by granting employees leave to fulfill these familial duties.[218] Disabled employees face employment challenges as well, and the FMLA assists these workers by requiring leave during periods in which they are unable to work because of a serious health condition.[219] As the following material illustrates,

---

[212] *See, e.g.*, Owens v. Univ. Club of Memphis, Appeal No. 02A01-9705-CV-00103, 1998 Tenn. App. LEXIS 688 (Tenn. Ct. App. Oct 15, 1998) (describing T.C.A. § 50-2-107(a)(1) and requiring that automatically deducted tips be given to employee by the same day or the next regularly scheduled payday).

[213] *See, e.g.*, T.C.A. § 50-2-107(a)(2) (stating that tips "payment shall not be reduced, docked or otherwise diminished to penalize an employee for any actions in connection with the employee's employment, if it is derived from a mandatory service charge or tip collected from customers, members or patrons").

[214] A much older form of leave is currently embodied in the Uniform Services Employment and Reemployment Rights Act ("USERRA"), which has existed in some form since World War II. In addition to prohibiting employment discrimination based on military status, USERRA provides leave rights to any "person whose absence from a position of employment is necessitated by reason of service in the uniformed services." 38 U.S.C. § 4312(a). This situation arises most with National Guard or Reserve members who must take time off to train or are called up for active duty. These employees are entitled not just to return to their jobs and continued health benefits — which is largely the extent of protection under the FMLA — but also a period of just cause protection, and uninterrupted seniority credit for retirement benefits. *Id.* at §§ 4311–18. Beyond these protections, USERRA simply requires that an employer treats military leave the same as other types of leave. For example, in *Rogers v. City of San Antonio*, 392 F.3d 758 (5th Cir. 2004), an employer did not have to provide employees returning from USERRA-protected leave missed opportunities for overtime and training because it did not give those opportunities to other employees on non-military leave. However, depending on the evidence presented on remand, the employer in *Rogers* may have unlawfully refused to provide extra days off for good attendance and other conditions that the military employees missed but that the employer allegedly provided to employees on other forms of involuntary leave, such as jury duty. For a more thorough description of USERRA's protections, as well as state laws that provide similar protection, see Jeffrey M. Hirsch, *Can Congress Use Its War Powers to Protect Military Employees from State Sovereign Immunity?*, 34 SETON HALL L. REV. 999, 1013–16, 1037–42 (2004).

[215] 29 U.S.C. §§ 2601-2654.

[216] The FMLA requires unpaid leave for an employee following the birth or adoption of a child, for an employee to care for a close family member with a serious medical condition, or when the employee cannot work because of a serious health condition. *See infra* § 12.04[B][1], [2].

[217] *See supra* note 4.

[218] Nev. Dep't of Human Res. v. Hibbs, 538 U.S. 721 (2003).

[219] WILLBORN ET AL., *supra* note 57, at 697.

the extent to which the FMLA fulfills these goals depends largely on the interpretation given to its provisions.

[A] Coverage

The FMLA applies to fewer employers and employees than most other federal employment statutes. An "employer" is defined as any person engaged in commerce, or any activity affecting commerce, "who employs fifty or more employees for each working day during each of twenty or more calendar workweeks in the current or preceding calendar year."[220] The FMLA expressly includes as an employer anyone acting on the employer's behalf in dealing with employees, any successor of an employer, and any public agency, as defined by the FLSA.[221]

An "eligible employee" is defined as a worker who has been employed by a covered employer for at least twelve months and for at least 1,250 hours during the previous twelve-month period.[222] However, a worker who would otherwise be classified as an employee is excluded if she is employed at a worksite with less than fifty employees, if the employer has less than a total of fifty employees within seventy-five miles of that worksite.[223]

[B] FMLA Rights

The FMLA was enacted to help, in particular, working women by alleviating some of the disproportionate burdens they face in caring for family members.[224] Accordingly, the FMLA enables employees to take unpaid leave for the birth or adoption of a child, or to care for themselves or a close family member who is seriously ill.[225] Moreover, under a 2008 amendment, the FMLA requires unpaid leave for family members of soldiers called for active duty to take care of matters related to the active duty, such as attending military-sponsored functions, making financial and legal arrangements, and arranging for alternative childcare.[226] During FMLA leave, an employee cannot lose any accrued benefits, including life insurance, health insurance, sick leave, annual leave, and pensions.[227] Moreover, the FMLA acts as a floor, not a ceiling; thus, an employer may not provide any

---

[220] 29 U.S.C. § 2611(4)(A)(i).

[221] *Id.* § 2611(4)(A)(ii)-(iii). The Government Accountability Office and the Library of Congress are also expressly considered "employers." *Id.* § 2611(4)(A)(iv).

[222] *Id.* § 2611(2)(A).

[223] *Id.* § 2611(2)(B) (also excluding certain federal officers).

[224] *See id.* § 2601; Nev. Dep't. of Human Res. v. Hibbs, 538 U.S. 721 (2003).

[225] *See infra* § 12.04[B][1]. By granting leave rights to all employees, the FMLA also intended to encourage men to shoulder more caretaking duties.

[226] National Defense Authorization Act for FY 2008, Pub. L. No. 110-181, § 585, Public Law (2008). The amendment also gives employees additional leave — beyond their normal FMLA leave — for up to 26 weeks during a 12-month period to care for a soldier with a serious illness or injury incurred during active duty.

[227] 29 U.S.C. § 2611(5).

fewer benefits or leave than the FMLA requires, but is free to provide more.[228]

[1] Leave and Restoration

The FMLA's central provision is the requirement to provide employees leave under certain circumstances. Any eligible employee is entitled to a total of twelve workweeks of FMLA-eligible leave during any twelve-month period.[229] The twelve weeks may consist of a continuous period of leave, or leave taken on an intermittent or reduced schedule.[230] "Intermittent leave" refers to leave for a single reason taken in separate periods of time,[231] and "reduced leave" consists of a schedule in which the employee works fewer than her normal hours.[232] An employee is entitled to intermittent or reduced leave only if the schedule is medically necessary; however, an employer and employee may agree to an intermittent or reduced FMLA leave schedule for the birth, adoption, or placement of a child.[233]

The major question in a large number of FMLA cases is whether the reason for an employee's leave request is covered by the statute. An employee will be entitled to FMLA leave if the reason for the request falls under any one of four triggering events:

(1) the employee is caring for a newly born child, as long as the leave is completed within twelve months of the child's birth;

(2) the employee is adopting a child or taking in a child for foster care, as long as the leave is completed within twelve months of the child's placement for adoption or foster care;

(3) the employee is caring for a spouse, child, or parent with a "serious health condition"; or

(4) a "serious health condition" makes the employee unable to perform his or her work functions.[234]

Despite common misperceptions, these leave requirements do little more than guarantee that an employee may return to her job, or a substantially equivalent position, after taking approved leave. Unlike most European countries (and the City of San Francisco[235]), the FMLA requires only *unpaid* leave; although an employer can provide paid leave that satisfies the FLMA's leave requirements, it need not do

---

[228] 29 C.F.R. § 825.700. Individual states may, and often do, provide greater family and medical leave benefits. *See* U.S. DEP'T OF LAB., FEDERAL VS. STATE FAMILY AND MEDICAL LEAVE LAWS, *available at* www.dol.gov/esa/programs/whd/state/fmla/index.htm.

[229] 29 U.S.C. § 2612(a)(1).

[230] *Id.* § 2617(d).

[231] 29 C.F.R. § 825.800 (including appointments for medical evaluations or treatments related to a serious health condition).

[232] 29 U.S.C. § 2611(9); 29 C.F.R. § 825.203(c)(1) (including part-time work while recovering from a serious health condition).

[233] 29 U.S.C. § 2612(b)(1).

[234] *Id.* § 2612(a)(1)(A)–(D), (a)(2).

[235] PAID SICK LEAVE ORDINANCE, S.F., CAL., ADMIN. CODE § 12W.17.

so.[236] Moreover, an employer that provides paid vacation, personal, family, or sick leave may require an employee to use any accrued paid leave as part of her twelve-week FMLA leave.[237] An employee may also elect to use paid leave for FMLA leave purposes.[238] Yet, if an employee's accrued leave totals less than twelve weeks, any additional FMLA leave may be unpaid.[239]

Upon completion of FMLA leave, an employee is entitled to return to the same or equivalent position.[240] However, if it is medically necessary for an employee to take intermittent or reduced leave — or the employer voluntarily agrees to such leave for the birth, adoption, or placement of a child — the employer may temporarily transfer the employee to an alternate position that better accommodates the leave schedule and has equivalent pay and benefits.[241] Also, after the employee's return from FMLA leave, he or she must keep any employment benefits accrued before the leave began, although the employee does not have an FMLA right to accrue employment benefits or seniority while on leave.[242]

If spouses both work for the same employer, they must share the twelve weeks of leave taken for the birth, adoption, or placement of a child, or for the care of a sick parent.[243] Thus, the FMLA may permit both paternity and maternity leave, but the parents can only take a total of twelve weeks of leave if they work for the same employer.

[2] Health Benefits

Given the statute's emphasis on medical leave, it is no surprise that the FMLA takes special care to protect employees' health benefits while on covered leave. The protection is straightforward: while on FMLA leave, the employer must maintain the employee's coverage under any group health plan at the same level and conditions that would exist if the employee were not on leave.[244]

Health coverage becomes less certain, however, if the employee ultimately fails to return to work from FMLA leave for reasons that were not out of his or her control or not because of another period of FMLA leave prompted by a serious

---

[236] 29 U.S.C. § 2612(c).

[237] *Id.* § 2612(d)(2)(A) (stating that employer may require employee to use paid vacation, personal, or family leave for any FMLA purpose except for a serious health condition that makes the employee unable to perform her work functions), (d)(2)(B) (stating that paid vacation, personal, family, or sick leave may be used for any "serious health condition" purpose, whether affecting the employee or a covered family member).

[238] *Id.* § 2612(d)(2)(A).

[239] *Id.* § 2612(d)(1).

[240] *Id.* § 2614(a)(1) (stating that "equivalent" includes "equivalent benefits, pay, and other terms and conditions of employment"). Note that an employee of a "local educational agency" or private elementary or secondary school faces special limitations on his or her ability to take intermittent or reduced schedule leave, or to take leave with less than five weeks left in a term. *See id.* § 2618.

[241] *Id.* § 2612(b).

[242] *Id.* §§ 2614(a)(2), (a)(3).

[243] *Id.* § 2612(f). Spouses do not have to share leave for their individual serious health conditions.

[244] *Id.* § 2614(c)(1).

health condition.[245] When an employee fails to return without one of these two justifications, the employer is entitled to recover all company-paid premiums for the entire period that the employee was on FMLA leave.[246]

[3] Interference and Retaliation Prohibitions

To ensure employees' access to FMLA leave and benefit rights, the statute prohibits employers from restraining, denying, or interfering with an employee's exercise those rights.[247] In other words, if an employee is entitled to leave under the FMLA, this provision makes it unlawful for an employer to refuse to provide such leave. The FMLA also contains an anti-retaliation provision that contains both "participation" and "opposition" clauses. The participation clause prohibits any discharge or discrimination in retaliation against "any individual" who started a cause of action; gave, or is about to give, information in connection with an inquiry or proceeding; or testified, or is about to testify, in any inquiry or proceeding.[248] The FMLA's opposition clause prohibits employer retaliation against an employee who opposed any action that is unlawful under the statute.[249] For instance, if an employee complained that the employer had unlawfully refused to give other employees their FMLA leave, the employer is not allowed to retaliate against the employee. Moreover, employers are required to post a notice informing employees about their rights under the FMLA.[250]

The analysis for determining whether an employer unlawfully refused to grant an employee leave, reinstatement, or benefits guaranteed under the FMLA is, at least superficially, uncomplicated. In such cases, the employee need only show by a preponderance of the evidence that she was entitled to the FMLA substantive right.[251] The employer's intent is not relevant in such cases.[252] In contrast, retaliation cases depend in part on the employer's intent and, therefore, use an analysis that is familiar in the employment context, albeit more complicated than the FMLA's basic interference approach.

Almost all federal circuit courts analyze claims that an employer made an adverse employment action against an employee's exercise of FMLA rights under the *McDonnell Douglas*[253] framework created for actions under Title VII of the Civil Rights Act of 1964.[254] For example, in *King v. Preferred Technical Group*,[255]

---

[245] *Id.* § 2614(c)(1)(B).

[246] *Id.* § 2614(c)(2).

[247] *Id.* § 2615(a)(1).

[248] *Id.* § 2615(b).

[249] *Id.* § 2615(a)(2).

[250] *Id.* § 2619(a).

[251] *See* Rice v. Sunrise Express, Inc., 209 F.3d 1008, 1016-17 (7th Cir. 2000).

[252] *See* Bachelder v. Am. W. Airlines, Inc., 259 F.3d 1112, 1123 (9th Cir. 2001) (comparing FMLA interference claims to Section 8(a)(1) claims under the National Labor Relations Act, 29 U.S.C. § 158(a)(1)).

[253] 42 U.S.C. §§ 2000e to 2000e-17.

[254] McDonnell Douglas v. Green, 411 U.S. 792 (1973). For cases applying this framework, *see, e.g.,* Metzler v. Fed. Home Loan Bank of Topeka, 464 F.3d 1164 (10th Cir. 2006); King v. Preferred Technical

the Seventh Circuit explained its analysis of FMLA retaliation claims. In so doing, the court explicitly adopted the *McDonnell Douglas* framework.[256]

As the Seventh Circuit noted in *King*, under the first prong of *McDonnell Douglas* the plaintiff has the burden of persuasion to make out her prima facie case. Establishing the prima facie case requires proof that: (1) the employee engaged in protected activity, (2) the employer engaged in adverse employment action against the employee, and (3) the "employer would not have taken the adverse employment action but for the employee's protected activity."[257] If the employee establishes the prima facie case, the employer must then articulate a legitimate, non-discriminatory reason for the adverse action. Although this may be referred to a shifting burden, the employer carries only the burden of *production*, not persuasion; the employee retains the burden of persuasion throughout the case. Thus, if the employer produces a legitimate, non-discriminatory reason, the employee has the burden to show that the employer's reason was not the true motivation — that is, that it is "pretext" — and that the employee's protected conduct was the actual reason for the employer's action.

[C] Serious Health Condition

The statutory definition of "serious health condition" is relatively brief, stating only that the term "means an illness, injury, impairment, or physical or mental condition that involves (A) inpatient care in a hospital, hospice, or residential medical care facility; or (B) continuing treatment by a health care provider."[258] The Department of Labor's regulations provide far more explanation for this term.

To meet the definition of "inpatient care," an employee or an employee's covered family member must have an impairment that involved an overnight stay "in a hospital, hospice, or residential medical care facility."[259] "Inpatient care" also includes "any period of incapacity" (e.g., an inability to work, attend school, or perform other regular daily activities due to the serious health condition; treatment for the condition; or recovery from the condition), or "any subsequent treatment" related to the inpatient care.[260]

Alternatively, an employee may show that a condition involved "continuing treatment by a health care provider." This prong includes any one of five different scenarios, which are summarized as follows:

(1) A period of incapacity of more than three consecutive days and any subsequent treatment or period of incapacity relating to the same

---

Group, 166 F.3d 887 (7th Cir. 1999); Hodgens v. Gen. Dynamics Corp., 144 F.3d 151 (1st Cir. 1998). The Ninth Circuit has left open whether it will use *McDonnell Douglas* in such cases. *See Bachelder*, 259 F.3d at 1125 n.11.

[255] 166 F.3d 887 (7th Cir. 1999).

[256] *Id.* at 892.

[257] *Id.*

[258] 29 U.S.C. § 2611(11).

[259] 29 C.F.R. § 825.114.

[260] *Id.*

condition, that also involves:

    (A)   Treatment two or more times by a health care provider,[261] or

    (B)   At least one treatment by a health care provider that results in a regimen of continuing treatment.[262]

(2)   Any period of incapacity due to pregnancy or prenatal care.[263]

(3)   Any period of incapacity, or treatment for such a period, that resulted from a "chronic serious health condition," which is defined as a condition that:

    (A)   Requires periodic visits for treatment;

    (B)   Continues over an extended period of time; and

    (C)   May cause episodic, rather than a continuing, periods of incapacity (such as asthma, diabetes, and epilepsy).[264]

(4)   A permanent or long-term period of incapacity caused by a condition may be untreatable. A health care provider must provide continuing supervision, but need not be actively treating the condition. Examples include Alzheimer's, a severe stroke, or a terminal illness.[265]

(5)   Any period of absence to receive or recover from multiple treatments by a health care provider if the treatments were for restorative surgery after an injury, or for a condition that would likely cause a three-day or more period of incapacity without treatment, such as chemotherapy or radiation for cancer, physical therapy for severe arthritis, or dialysis for kidney disease.[266]

An employee is entitled to leave for a serious health condition only where that condition "makes the employee unable to perform the functions of the position."[267] Similar to the Americans With Disabilities Act (ADA),[268] treatment for substance abuse may be covered; however, leave resulting from an employee's use of an illegal substance does not constitute a serious health condition.[269]

---

[261] *Id.* § 825.114(a)(2)(i). "Treatment . . . by a health care provider" under this regulation includes "treatment by a nurse or physician's assistant under direct supervision of a health care provider, or by a provider of health care services (e.g., physical therapist) under orders of, or on referral by, a health care provider." *Id.* § 825.114(a)(2)(i)(A). "Treatment" also includes any non-routine examination to determine if a serious health condition exists or to evaluate such a condition. *Id.* § 825.114(b).

[262] *Id.* § 825.114(a)(2)(i)(B).

[263] *Id.* § 825.114(a)(2)(ii).

[264] *Id.* § 825.114(a)(2)(iii).

[265] *Id.* § 825.114(a)(2)(iv).

[266] *Id.* § 825.114(a)(2)(v).

[267] 29 U.S.C. 2612(a)(1)(D); *see* Whitaker v. Bosch Braking Sys. Div., 180 F. Supp. 2d 922, 933 (W.D. Mich. 2001).

[268] 42 U.S.C. §§ 12101-12213.

[269] 29 C.F.R. § 825.114(d).

One example of how courts typically analyze the serious health condition requirement is *Whitaker v. Bosch Braking Systems Division*.[270] *Whitaker* involved a pregnant factory worker with severe morning sickness and complications that posed significant risks to her pregnancy if she continued working on her feet. The employee claimed that she had a serious health condition under the "[a]ny period of incapacity due to pregnancy" prong.[271] The district court held that pregnancy, per se, is not a serious health condition; rather, a period of incapacity as a result of the pregnancy is a necessary element of the claim. The employee in *Whitaker* was able to meet this standard by showing that her doctor told her that she could not work because of her pregnancy complications. Moreover, she established that she was unable to perform the functions of the position because her doctor said she was unable to work overtime, which was an essential requirement for her job.[272]

[D]   Notice and Certification Requirements

An employee's duty to notify the employer of his or her intent to take FMLA leave depends in large measure on whether the leave was foreseeable or not. When an employee intends to take FMLA leave for the birth, adoption, or foster care placement of a child, he or she must give the employer at least thirty days' notice before the date that the leave is to begin.[273] However, if the birth, adoption, or placement is to take place in less than thirty days, the employee need only "provide such notice as is practicable."[274] Similarly, if FMLA leave is required due to the treatment of a serious health condition,[275] the employee must give the employer at least thirty days notice or, if that is not possible, as early as practicable.[276] When such leave is foreseeable, the employee must also make reasonable efforts to schedule the treatment to avoid disrupting the employer's business.[277] If leave is not foreseeable, such as when a medical emergency occurs, an employee is generally expected to notify his or her employer within one to two days of learning that leave is necessary.[278]

Notice may not be feasible, and the lack of notice therefore excusable, when a serious health condition makes the employee unable to provide notice.[279] For example, in *Byrne v. Avon Products, Inc.*,[280] a model employee suddenly began hiding out in a break room and was ultimately hospitalized with severe depression.

---

[270]   180 F. Supp. 2d 922 (W.D. Mich. 2001).

[271]   *Id.* at 926 (citing 29 C.F.R. § 825.114(a)(2)(ii)).

[272]   *Id.* at 933. The employee in *Whitaker* was asking merely to work regular, non-overtime, hours because of her pregnancy complications; this type of scheduling request may be protected by the FMLA's intermittent leave provision. *Id.*; 29 C.F.R. §§ 825.205, 825.800.

[273]   29 U.S.C. § 2612(e)(1).

[274]   *Id.*

[275]   *See supra* § 12.04[C].

[276]   29 U.S.C. § 2612(e)(2)(B); Manuel v. Westlake Polymers Corp., 66 F.3d 758, 764 (5th Cir. 1995).

[277]   29 U.S.C. § 2612(e)(2)(A) (scheduling must be subject to health care provider's approval).

[278]   29 C.F.R. § 825.303.

[279]   *Id.*

[280]   328 F.3d 379 (7th Cir. 2003).

The district court held that the notice provided by the employee's sister after the hospitalization was not sufficient, because ten days had elapsed during which the employee spent much of his work day sleeping in the break room. The Seventh Circuit reversed and remanded, holding that a reasonable trier of fact could believe that a person with major depression "could not have told his employer about the problem and requested leave," in which case "notice was not 'feasible' and was unnecessary even if the change in behavior was not enough to alert [the employer] to a need for medical leave."[281]

Because the FMLA is silent as to what constitutes "notice," employers frequently argue that whatever information the employee provided was insufficient. These claims are not often successful, however, as the DOL's regulations take a very broad view of what constitutes notice.[282] The regulations make clear that the form of notice need not even mention the FMLA; rather, the employee must only request leave and provide a reason that qualifies under the FMLA.[283] In other words, when asking for leave, the employee must give the employer enough information to reasonably apprise the employer that FMLA leave is requested.[284] If the employer wants further information, it must ask.[285] Yet, employees cannot be too cavalier about the information they provide, for the burden to notify their employers still has some teeth.

The district court's finding in *Reich v. Midwest Plastic Engineering, Inc.*,[286] provides an example of how employees can fail to meet their burden to provide sufficient notice. The employee in *Reich* was a pregnant woman who was ultimately hospitalized with a serious case of chicken pox. The district court found that she failed to provide proper notice because when telling her employer that she had chicken pox, she failed to give enough information to make the employer realize that she was under continuing treatment and eventually hospitalized because of her condition.[287] In other words, she failed her burden to inform her employer "with sufficient detail to make it evident that the requested leave was protected as FMLA-qualifying leave."[288]

An employer need not take an employee's word that the requested leave is covered by the FMLA. Instead, an employer can require the employee to obtain certification from a health care provider that states, in part: (1) the date that the serious health condition began, (2) the probable duration of the serious health condition, and (3) the health care provider's knowledge of the appropriate medical

---

[281] *Id.* at 382.

[282] *See, e.g., Manuel*, 66 F.3d at 763.

[283] 29 C.F.R. §§ 825.208(a)(2), 825.303.

[284] *See* Cruz v. Publix Super Mkts., Inc., 428 F.3d 1379, 1383-86 (11th Cir. 2005) (comparing cases); *Manuel*, 66 F.3d at 764.

[285] 29 C.F.R. § 825.303.

[286] No. 1:94-CV-525, 1995 U.S. Dist. LEXIS 12130 (W.D. Mich. July 26, 1995).

[287] The employee had earlier given notice to her employer before she missed work to care for her children when they had chicken pox.

[288] *Id.* at *3.

facts.[289] Where appropriate, an employer may also ask that a certification state that the employee is needed to care for a covered family member, that the employee cannot perform her work functions, and the dates and duration of treatments that require an intermittent or reduced leave schedule.[290] A general requirement that all requests for leave be accompanied by certification is not sufficient, however; an employer must inform each employee seeking FMLA leave that certification is required.[291] Even after an employee obtains certification, the employer may still require — at its expense — a second opinion from an outside health care provider.[292] An employer may also require the employee to provide recertifications "on a reasonable basis."[293] Finally, an employer may require an employee who has taken leave because of his or her own serious health condition to obtain certification that he or she is fit to return, if the requirement is pursuant to a uniformly applied policy.[294]

Under DOL regulations, employers are required to provide employees with written notice if the employer intends to classify leave under the FMLA.[295] In *Ragsdale v. Wolverine World Wide, Inc.*,[296] however, the Supreme Court struck down the regulatory penalty for violating this notice requirement — a penalty that would have prevented any leave, paid or unpaid, that the employer failed to properly designate from counting against the employee's twelve weeks of FMLA leave.[297] The Court held that this penalty was not connected to any harm caused by the improper notice and was therefore "incompatible with the FMLA's comprehensive remedial mechanism."[298] The problem, according to the Court, was that the penalty allowed employees to bring an FMLA suit without showing any impairment of their rights that resulted in statutory harm. For example, the employer in *Ragsdale* had provided the employee thirty weeks of unpaid sick leave,

---

[289] *Id.* § 2613(a), (b); *see* Whitaker v. Bosch Braking Sys. Div., 180 F. Supp. 2d 922, 931-32 (W.D. Mich. 2001).

[290] 29 U.S.C. § 2613(b).

[291] *See* Perry v. Jaguar of Troy, 353 F.3d 510, 514 (6th Cir. 2003). However, if an employee is already aware that certification is required, an employer may not have a duty to specifically request certification for each subsequent FMLA request. *See* Allender v. Raytheon Aircraft Co. 339 F. Supp. 2d. 1196, 1205 (D. Kan. 2004).

[292] 29 U.S.C. § 2613(c). If the second opinion differs from the first, the employer may obtain at its own expense a third opinion, approved by the employer and employee, to finally resolve the difference in opinions. *Id* § 2613(d).

[293] *Id.* § 2613(e).

[294] *Id.* § 2614(a)(4). Also, an employer can require an employee to periodically provide the employer the employee's status and intent to return to work. *Id.* § 2614(a)(5).

[295] 29 C.F.R. § 825.208(a), 301(c). The Department of Labor's FMLA regulations (like its FLSA regulations) are reviewed under the Supreme Court's *Chevron* analysis, which defers to an agency's formal interpretation of an ambiguous statutory provision as long as the regulation is not arbitrary, capricious, or manifestly contrary to the statute. *See* Ragsdale v. Wolverine World Wide, Inc., 535 U.S. 81, 86 (2002); Chevron U.S.A., Inc. v. Natural Res. Def. Council, Inc., 467 U.S. 837, 844 (1984).

[296] 535 U.S. 81 (2002).

[297] 29 C.F.R. § 825.700(a), *overruled by Ragsdale*, 535 U.S. 81.

[298] 535 U.S. at 89. The dissent argued that the regulation fell within the DOL's authority to promulgate regulations that are "necessary to carry out" the FMLA. *Id.* at 100 (citing 29 U.S.C. § 2654) (O'Connor, J., dissenting).

albeit without the proper notice of designation. Thus, the Court held that the penalty would grant some employees more than the "careful balance" of twelve weeks of leave per year that Congress intended.[299] The Court also stated that the regulation, contrary to the FMLA's express admonition,[300] would discourage employers from granting more generous leave policies.[301]

Ragsdale is important not just because it struck down the particular regulation, but also because it indicates that the Court will strictly enforce the statutory limitation that employer liability extends "only to compensation and benefits lost 'by reason of the violation,' for other monetary losses sustained as a direct result of the violation, and for 'appropriate' equitable relief."[302] Accordingly, employers and courts have increasingly used *Ragsdale* to call into question other DOL rules related to the requirement that an employer notify employees that it will classify leave under the FMLA.[303]

[E] Enforcement

Enforcement of the FMLA is modeled on the FLSA. Accordingly, enforcement authority is granted both to the Secretary of Labor and to private individuals to pursue a federal or state action. The Secretary has the power to review records that employers are required to maintain[304] and to investigate claims under authority provided it by the FLSA.[305]

Either an employee or the Secretary may bring a civil action against an employer in any state or federal court of competent jurisdiction, as long as it meets the two-year statute of limitations (the statute of limitations is three years for willful violations).[306] However, if the Secretary pursues a claim, the private right of

---

[299] *Id.* at 94. The Court stated that this penalty was disproportionate and inconsistent with the FMLA, as evidenced by the maximum $100 fine for willful violations of the general FMLA notice posting requirement. *Id.* at 95 (citing 29 U.S.C. § 2619(b)).

[300] 29 U.S.C. § 2653 ("Nothing in this Act . . . shall be construed to discourage employers from adopting or retaining leave policies more generous than any policies that comply with the requirements under this Act.").

[301] 535 U.S. at 95.

[302] *Id.* at 89 (citing, respectively, 29 U.S.C § 2617(a)(1)(A)(i)(I), (a)(1)(A)(i)(II), (a)(1)(B)).

[303] *See, e.g.*, McGregor v. Autozone, Inc., 180 F.3d 1305 (11th Cir. 1999). Indeed, in part of the opinion not reviewed by the Supreme Court, the Eighth Circuit's *Ragsdale* decision struck down the general regulatory requirement that employers provide proper notice of designation. *See* Ragsdale v. Wolverine Worldwide, Inc. 218 F.3d 933, 937 (8th Cir. 2000) (striking down 29 C.F.R. § 825.208(a), which required employer to notify employee of designation of FMLA leave); *accord McGregor*, 180 F.3d at 1308. The Eight Circuit's *Ragsdale* decision focused on the problem caused by the regulatory penalty for not providing proper notice; however, at least one court has suggested that, although the Supreme Court specifically refused to address the broader issue, *Ragsdale*, 535 U.S. at 88, the Court's *Ragsdale* decision suggests that Section 825.208(a) is unenforceable and invalid. *See* Roberson v. Cendant Travel Servs., Inc., 252 F. Supp. 2d 573, 577 (M.D. Tenn. 2002) (noting that Sixth Circuit precedent is unclear on this point). *But see* Downey v. Strain, 510 F.3d 534 (5th Cir. 2007) (declining to follow *McGregor*).

[304] 29 U.S.C. § 2616(b).

[305] *Id.* § 2616(a). This authority includes the power to issue subpoenas. *Id.* § 2616(c).

[306] *Id.* §§ 2617(a)(2), (b), (c).

action is terminated until the Secretary dismisses the claim without prejudice.[307] Possible damages for violations of the FMLA include back pay, compensatory damages up to twelve weeks of the employee's wages, and if the violation was in bad faith, liquidated damages.[308] A successful plaintiff is also entitled to attorney's fees and may receive equitable relief.[309]

Unlike most other employment statutes, individuals acting on the behalf of a private employer may be held liable for FMLA violations.[310] An individual may be considered an employer under the FMLA, and therefore personally liable, when, for example, the individual controlled the employee's ability to take FMLA leave and participated in the violation,[311] or the individual possessed authority to hire and fire the employee.[312] Individual liability may result from other situations involving a similar degree of control.[313] Thus, individuals who occupy a high position in a business must be particularly wary of FMLA issues, as they could be personally liable for violations of the Act.

A worker's ability to bring an FMLA claim may depend on his or her employment status. It appears that prospective employees may sue under the FMLA, although there is a question whether they are considered "employees" under the statute.[314] The only two circuits to have addressed this issue have deferred to a DOL regulation which states that prospective employees are considered "employees" and can therefore bring an FMLA cause of action against an employer.[315] These holdings rely in part on the Supreme Court's same conclusion under the FLSA,[316] upon which Congress expressly based the FMLA definition of "employee."[317] Moreover, former employees may sue for money damages based on a claim of retaliation under the FMLA, but may not seek leave

---

[307] *Id.* § 2617(4).

[308] *Id.* § 2617(a)(1). Liquidated damage awards provide "double damages," as they are equal to the employer's liability for an employee's compensation and benefits. *Id.* § 2617(a)(1)(A)(iii). A court may reduce the liquidated damage amount if the employer acted in good faith and reasonably believed it was acting lawfully. *Id.*

[309] *Id.* §§ 2617(a)(1)(B), (a)(3). The Secretary also may seek injunctive relief. *Id.* § 2617(d).

[310] The FLSA allows individual liability under limited circumstances. *See supra* note 177.

[311] Freemon v. Foley, 911 F. Supp. 326, 330-31 (N.D. Ill. 1995).

[312] Cantley v. Simmons, 179 F. Supp. 2d 654, 658 (S.D. W. Va. 2002).

[313] *See* Sandra F. Sperino, *Under Construction: Questioning Whether Statutory Construction Principles Justify Individual Liability Under the Family and Medical Leave Act*, 71 Mo. L. Rev. 71 (2006) (discussing scenarios that may result in individual liability and arguing that the FMLA did not intend to permit individual liability).

[314] The issue hinges on whether former employees are included in the FMLA's statement that "any one or more employees" may bring a suit for an FMLA violation. *See* 29 U.S.C. § 2617(a)(2).

[315] 29 C.F.R. § 825.220(c); *accord* Smith v. BellSouth Telecomms., Inc., 273 F.3d 1303, 1307-13 (11th Cir. 2001) (holding that former employee challenging employer's failure to rehire was considered an "employee" under the FMLA); Duckworth v. Pratt & Whitney, Inc., 152 F.3d 1 (1st Cir. 1998) (same).

[316] *See* Robinson v. Shell Oil Co., 519 U.S. 337, 341 (1997) (stating also that former employees are considered "employees" under the FLSA).

[317] The FMLA, 29 U.S.C. § 2611(3), defines "employee" explicitly by reference to the FLSA, 29 U.S.C. § 203(e), which provides that "the term 'employee' means any individual employed by an employer."

or reinstatement under the Act's substantive rights provisions.[318]

Finally, another DOL regulation prohibits an employee from waiving his or her rights to FMLA leave and reinstatement.[319] Under the previous version of Section 825.220(d), a circuit split developed over whether the prohibition extends beyond the waiver of an employee's prospective substantive FMLA rights.[320] In 2009, the DOL amended the regulation to prohibit waivers of prospective FMLA rights, but to explicitly allow "the settlement or release of FMLA claims by employees based on past employer conduct."[321]

---

[318] *See, e.g.*, Faris v. Williams WPC-I, Inc., 332 F.3d 316, 320 (5th Cir. 2003) (citing 29 C.F.R. § 825.220(d)).

[319] 29 C.F.R. § 825.220(d).

[320] *Compare* Taylor v. Progress Energy, Inc., 493 F.3d 454 (4th Cir. 2007) (holding that the previous version of Section 825.220(d) prohibited both prospective and retrospective waivers of all FMLA rights), *with Faris*, 332 F.3d at 320 (holding that the previous version of Section 825.220(d) permitted an employee to waive or settle a FMLA cause of action after the alleged violation had occurred).

[321] 29 C.F.R. § 825.220(d).

Chapter 13

UNEMPLOYMENT AND WARN

§ 13.01 INTRODUCTION

In the United States, protections for employees who have lost, or will soon lose, their jobs make up a diverse patchwork of federal and state regulations. These protections reflect the concerns of the times in which they were enacted and, therefore, often provide a narrow set of rights.

The unemployment insurance system, for example, is not intended to be an anti-poverty measure. Rather, reflecting the widespread unemployment of the Great Depression-era from which it arose, the system attempts to guarantee all newly unemployed workers — not just low-income workers — a financial cushion that allows them time to find appropriate new jobs. This system is quite large. Indeed, in the poor economy of 2009, unemployment insurance programs around the country paid over $116 billion to almost 14.1 million workers.[1]

---

[1] *See* STEVEN L. WILLBORN ET AL., EMPLOYMENT LAW: CASES AND MATERIALS 641 (5th ed. 2012) (noting that this amount included state regular benefits of $75 billion, state extended benefits of $4 billion, and federal

The concern for workers' ability to find new employment is also reflected in the Worker Adjustment and Retraining Notification Act (WARN), which provides notice rights to workers facing the loss of jobs as part of a plant closing or mass layoff. Recognizing the significant impact of plant closings and mass layoffs on local communities, Congress provided workers and their representatives, as well as state and local officials, the right to be notified of, and therefore prepare for, large-scale job losses.

§ 13.02   UNEMPLOYMENT INSURANCE

[A]   History and Overview of Unemployment Insurance in the United States

The current unemployment insurance (UI) system was originally enacted in 1935 as part of the New Deal. The extremely high level of unemployment that existed at that time, in addition to the competitive disadvantages that paying for such a system would place on the economy of a state acting on its own, prompted Congress to enact legislation encouraging states to create their own UI programs.[2] Part of the UI system's aim was to permit laid-off workers to maintain an acceptable standard of living and to search for a job that fully utilized their skills and experience.[3] Thus, the UI system provides temporary, partial wage replacement for experienced workers who are unemployed through no fault of their own.

The UI system was enacted pursuant to the Social Security Act of 1935.[4] The Act created a joint federal-state scheme that would encourage states to form their own UI programs. Under this scheme, the federal government does not directly provide UI benefits; instead, it provides funding to states with their own UI programs. The source of federal funding is an employer-paid tax, currently set at 6.2% of the first $7,000 in wages, on every covered employee in the United States.[5] Under the Federal Unemployment Tax Act (FUTA), an employer may offset this federal tax with any state UI taxes it pays, up to 5.4% of the $7,000 base wage (the remaining 0.8% goes, in part, to federal administrative costs). Most states, however, have implemented a base rate higher than the $7,000 federal base.

This offset structure gives states an incentive to create their own UI program because employers in a state without such a program will have to pay the federal UI tax, yet their employees will not receive any UI benefits. In short, employers in a state without a UI program would essentially fund programs in other states. Not

---

emergency benefits of $37 billion). Under a much better economy in 2005, there were only around $31.1 billion in benefits provided to almost eight million workers. STEVEN L. WILLBORN ET AL., EMPLOYMENT LAW: CASES AND MATERIALS 617 (4th ed. 2007).

   [2] *See* WILLBORN ET AL. (5th ed.), *supra* note 1, at 641 (noting that Wisconsin was the sole state with an unemployment system prior to 1935).

   [3] *See* Gillian Lester, *Unemployment Insurance and Wealth Redistribution*, 49 UCLA L. REV. 335, 340-45 (2001).

   [4] 42 U.S.C. §§ 501-504, 1101-1108.

   [5] *See* Lester, *supra* note 3, at 344 & n.30 (citing 26 U.S.C. § 3306(b)(1)).

surprisingly, this incentive has proved effective, as every state currently has its own UI program.

States receive significant funding via the FUTA system, but only if they comply with federal standards.[6] For instance, states must impose an "experience-rating" tax, which ties employers' payments in part to their history of layoffs. Although states use different approaches, the most prevalent technique to calculate the experience-rating tax ties an employer's state UI tax rate to an individual account consisting of the employer's UI contributions minus any UI benefits paid to its employees.[7] One result of the experience-rating tax is that many employers — those who have laid off few workers — pay far less than the 5.4% state tax rate, yet still get to credit the full 5.4% for purposes of offsetting the federal tax.

Federal standards impose several other mandates on states. For example, states must distribute weekly UI benefits to workers from a government office, rather than via the mail.[8] Moreover, states are prohibited from denying benefits because of a pregnancy, or termination of pregnancy, and from providing benefits to undocumented workers not authorized to work.[9] Accordingly, UI programs across the country share many core elements, although states still retain significant flexibility in shaping the specifics of their programs within the federal parameters.

One area in which states may vary is determining which workers are eligible for UI benefits. Generally, states base eligibility on a worker's length of time in the workforce, how the separation occurred, and the extent to which the worker is looking for a new job.[10] Thus, individuals who are new to the workforce, are part-time workers, voluntarily leave their jobs, and are not actively looking for new jobs will often not be eligible for UI benefits.[11] Workers who are eligible for UI benefits frequently must wait a week before receiving funds, and their eligibility usually lasts for up to twenty-six weeks. However, during economic recessions, Congress generally has extended benefit eligibility by at least thirteen weeks, but possibly much more. Finally, UI benefits in most states consist of payments of up to fifty percent of the worker's previous weekly wage, capped by a statutory maximum.[12]

---

[6] 26 U.S.C. §§ 3302, 3304. The federal government has issued guidelines for states to obtain eligibility for the tax offset.

[7] See WILLBORN ET AL. (5th ed.), *supra* note 1, at 642–43, 649; Lester, *supra* note 3, at 344-45 (describing different state techniques for imposing experience-rating taxes).

[8] 26 U.S.C. § 3304(a).

[9] *Id.*; see *infra* § 13.02[B][1] (discussing Supreme Court's interpretation of pregnancy discrimination provision).

[10] Most workers not classified as an independent contractor are covered by a UI program. *See* Lester, *supra* note 3, at 345 n.36. State and local government employees currently are also covered, although local schools are not subject to the federal UI tax.

[11] *See* EMPLOYMENT & TRAINING ADMIN., U.S. DEP'T OF LABOR, COMPARISON OF STATE UNEMPLOYMENT LAWS, ch. 5 [hereinafter COMPARISON OF STATE UNEMPLOYMENT LAWS], *available at* http://workforcesecurity.doleta.gov/unemploy/pdf/uilawcompar/2011/nonmonetary.pdf. These restrictions mean that less than forty percent of unemployed workers actually receive unemployment benefits. Moreover, individuals who are out of work but not actively seeking a new job are not included in the DOL's monthly unemployment data.

[12] A typical maximum cap is one-half to one-third of the state's average weekly wage. Because of the maximum benefit caps, the effective rate of wage replacement for employees receiving UI benefits is

Disputes regarding a worker's entitlement to UI benefits frequently center on eligibility, whether it is for a specific week of unemployment or the worker's entitlement to benefits in general. The most significant criteria for determining UI eligibility are the worker's compliance with the voluntary separation requirement, the willful misconduct prohibition, and the work search requirement.

[B]   Disqualifications from Benefits

Two of the major criteria for disqualifying workers from receiving UI benefits, voluntary separation and willful misconduct, both reflect worker actions that occur either during, or at the end of, employment and that bar a worker from receiving any UI benefits. In particular, a worker who voluntarily leaves his or her job without good cause, or engages in misconduct serious enough to warrant dismissal, is not among the group of workers that the UI system was intended to assist.

Depending on the state, however, disqualification can mean different things. The Department of Labor (DOL) has urged states to disqualify workers for only the average time needed to find suitable work in a given market, usually about six weeks. The DOL's reasoning is that any period of unemployment beyond that time is not because of the worker's disqualifying act, but because of market forces that the UI system is supposed to protect against. Although several states have followed the DOL's advice, many others disqualify workers for the entire span of a given period of unemployment.[13]

[1]   Voluntary Separation

All states deny UI benefits to workers who leave their jobs voluntarily and without good cause. Although some states categorically deny benefits in cases in which an employee voluntarily quits, most recognize a limited number of reasons that constitute good cause and that do not require the employee to forgo eligibility. Examples of good cause include an employee leaving due to sexual harassment, domestic violence threats, compulsory retirement, a new job that unexpectedly fails to materialize, school attendance, illness, and military service.[14]

Particularly difficult is how to classify employees who leave a job for family reasons, as they can be treated quite differently depending on the jurisdiction and the factual circumstances of a given case. For instance, some states classify an employee's resignation from a job to move with a family member as good cause,

---

about one-third of their former salary. In 2010, 11.2 million recipients received a weekly average of $304 for an average 19.4 weeks. WILLBORN ET AL. (5th ed.), *supra* note 1, at 643. During the recent recession, the federal government implemented several emergency UI measures that extended eligibility for benefits by up to 73 weeks — for a total of up to 99 weeks. *Id.* at 644. Once that maximum amount of time is reached, individuals are no longer eligible for any unemployment benefits.

[13] *See* WILLBORN ET AL. (5th ed.), *supra* note 1, at 658–60. There is a wide variety of approaches among the states. For example, if the worker has engaged in misconduct, he or she could be disqualified for as little as three weeks following the misconduct or for as long as his or her entire period of unemployment (plus the time it takes to earn a specified amount of wages). *See* COMPARISON OF STATE UNEMPLOYMENT LAWS, *supra* note 11, at 5-13.

[14] *See* COMPARISON OF STATE UNEMPLOYMENT LAWS, *supra* note 11, at 5-2; Lester, *supra* note 3, at 350.

while others do not.[15] Indeed, some states, like California, take into account nontraditional family relationships. In *MacGregor v. Unemployment Insurance Appeals Board*,[16] the California Supreme Court held that a worker was entitled to UI benefits after voluntarily leaving her job to move with her non-marital partner and their child. California has a relatively broad definition of good cause, which does not need to be tied to employment and can be solely personal in nature, although it must still be "imperative and compelling."[17] Despite the lack of a marital relationship, the worker in *MacGregor* was able to show a compelling reason for her resignation because she, her partner, and their child lived as a family unit and were moving so that her partner could care for his ill father. Other states, however, take a more limited view of the type of familial relationships necessary to establish good cause.[18]

Another common issue concerns employees who leave their jobs because of childcare responsibilities. For example, in *Jones v. Review Board of Indiana Employment Security Division*,[19] an Indiana court upheld the denial of benefits to an employee who was forced to leave work because childcare responsibilities prevented her from following a new schedule. The employee originally began working for the employer under an arrangement that fit with her childcare needs and the court noted that had she left because of the employer's change to that schedule, she may have been entitled to UI benefits.[20] However, because she initially agreed to the new work schedule, the court held that she abandoned the prior arrangement and could not rely on it to establish benefit eligibility. The court also held that the employer's threat to fire her if she did not work the new schedule did not make her resignation involuntary. According to the court, the employer did not force her to resign; rather, she chose not to continue working under the agreed-upon new schedule.[21] *Jones* illustrates the special problems that working women often face under the UI system. Because women are empirically the primary caregivers, cases that withhold benefits because of work-family conflicts affect

---

[15] *Compare* Yamauchi v. Dep't of Employment Sec., 638 P.2d 1253 (Wash. 1982) (en banc) (holding that quitting to move and get married was good cause), *with* Austin v. Berryman, 878 F.2d 786 (4th Cir. 1989) (upholding Virginia statute that stated that quitting to move with spouse was not good cause); Davis v. Employment Sec. Dep't, 737 P.2d 1262 (Wash. 1987) (holding that leaving job to move with longtime companion was not good cause). In part because of incentives provided by the federal government via its 2009 stimulus measures, more states — now approximately half — currently provide UI benefits to employees who quit because their spouse relocated, especially military spouses. *See* WILLBORN ET AL. (5th ed.), *supra* note 1, at 670–71.

[16] 689 P.2d 453 (Cal. 1984).

[17] *Id.* at 456.

[18] *See, e.g., Davis*, 737 P.2d 1262 (requiring move to be with "immediate family" to constitute good cause).

[19] 399 N.E.2d 844 (Ind. App. 1980).

[20] *Id.* at 845; *see also* Indianapolis Osteopathic Hosp. v. Jones, 669 N.E.2d 431 (Ind. Ct. App. 1996). However, the court also noted that in Indiana leaving work because of family responsibilities does not, by itself, constitute good cause in connection with work. *Jones*, 399 N.E.2d at 845 (citing Gray v. Dobbs House, Inc., 357 N.E.2d 900 (Ind. Ct. App. 1976)); *see also* Brown v. Indiana Dept. of Workforce Development, 919 N.E.2d 1147 (Ind. Ct. App. 2009).

[21] 357 N.E.2d at 846 (noting also that her motivation to resign was not the threat of discharge, but her childcare obligations).

women more. As described in more detail in Chapter 12, the Family and Medical Leave Act alleviates some, but certainly not all, of this disparity.[22]

The U.S. Supreme Court addressed another instance of a family related voluntary quit in *Wimberly v. Labor & Industrial Relations Commission*.[23] The employee in *Wimberly* took a leave of absence because of her pregnancy. Under the employer's policy, employees taking such leave were not given guarantees that they could return. When the employee asked to return to work, she was told that no positions were available. The Missouri Supreme Court denied the employee UI benefits under state law because she had left "work voluntarily without good cause attributable to [her] work or to [her] employer."[24] At issue before the Court was whether this law violated FUTA's mandate that "no person shall be denied compensation under such State law solely on the basis of pregnancy or termination of pregnancy."[25]

As the Court noted, states' treatment of pregnancy as "good cause" varies significantly. Missouri's definition of "good cause" was on the narrow end of the spectrum because it was defined as a reason for quitting that was directly linked to work or to the employer (e.g., workplace sexual harassment caused by a supervisor). This narrow definition of good cause was key, as the Court upheld Missouri's denial of benefits because the statute's work nexus applied to all employees, not just to employees who were pregnant. Under this interpretation of FUTA, states are prohibited from singling out pregnancy for worse treatment but, like Missouri, states can adopt a neutral rule that has the effect of disqualifying workers who quit because of pregnancy.[26]

[2] Willful Misconduct

In addition to voluntary separation, the other major disqualifying action by a worker is willful misconduct. Even when an employee is terminated, he or she may not be entitled to UI benefits because of actions that may include insubordination, violation of company rules, absences, or drug use.[27] Willful misconduct is distinct from mere incompetence, however, as a worker's inability to perform a job is generally not a reason to disqualify him or her from receiving UI benefits.[28]

At times, determining whether a worker's transgression is sufficiently serious to constitute willful misconduct is difficult. For example, absenteeism or refusals to

---

[22] *See supra* § 12.04.

[23] 479 U.S. 511 (1987).

[24] *Id.* at 513 (citing Mo. Rev. Stat. § 288.050.1(1)).

[25] *Id.* (quoting 26 U.S.C. § 3304(a)(12)).

[26] *Id.* at 517. Note that the Family Medical Leave Act currently gives employees who leave work for childbirth the right to return to their job within 12 weeks of the commencement of the leave. *See supra* § 12.04.

[27] *See* COMPARISON OF STATE UNEMPLOYMENT LAWS, *supra* note 11, at 5-11 to -12; Lester, *supra* note 3, at 350; *see also* 42 U.S.C. § 503(l)(1) (permitting states to require drug testing if, among other things, the employee is terminated because of illegal drug use).

[28] *See, e.g.*, Primecare Med., Inc. v. Unemployment Comp. Bd. of Review, 760 A.2d 483 (Pa. 2000) (holding that nurse terminated for failing licensing exam did not commit willful misconduct).

follow an employer's directive because of a conflict with family obligations may not be treated as willful if the family interest is particularly strong.[29] In *McCourtney v. Imprimis Technology, Inc.*,[30] the employee was denied UI benefits following her discharge for excessive absenteeism, which was the result of her need to care for her ill child. Minnesota defined "misconduct" in part as " 'conduct evincing such [willful] or wanton disregard of an employer's interests . . . or to show an intentional and substantial disregard of the employer's interests.' "[31] The state appellate court in *McCourtney* held that the employee's absenteeism was not misconduct because her absences were excused and caused by circumstances out of her control. In other words, because she had made good faith, albeit unsuccessful, efforts to resolve her work-childcare conflict, her absences did not constitute misconduct. The court, however, stressed that excessive absenteeism could be considered willful misconduct based on factors such as whether the employee's absences were deliberate, willful, or equally culpable, as well as the employee's work history, conduct, and underlying attitude. In contrast, the dissenting judge in *McCourtney* argued that the employee's excessive absenteeism was sufficient to find willful misconduct and that the majority's opinion would force employers into a catch-22 of having either to accept the costs associated with an employee's childcare-related absences or to pay more UI taxes to cover the employee's unemployment.[32]

[3] Work Search Requirement

Even when a worker is initially eligible for UI benefits, he or she must be not only willing and able to work, but also actively seeking a new job, to continue to receive benefits.[33] This requirement reflects one of the policy aims of the UI system, which is to provide benefits to workers during times when they are unable to get a job — not to compensate them for the initial job loss itself.[34] Thus, workers must look for work, and accept suitable employment when found, to be entitled to UI compensation.

States vary in their approaches to the work search requirement. Most assist workers in their search and often make contacts with employers on the workers' behalf. Moreover, workers frequently are required to certify their job search attempts at a local job center, or on-line through a state-sponsored unemployment benefits website, before receiving their benefits. States also sometime assign a

---

[29] *See* Martin H. Malin, *Unemployment Compensation in a Time of Increasing Work-Family Conflicts*, 29 U. Mich. J.L. Reform 131, 138 & n.30 (1996) (citing numerous cases).

[30] 465 N.W.2d 721 (Minn. Ct. App. 1991), *superseded by statute on other grounds*, Minn. Stat. § 268.095, subd. 6(a), (e) (2008) (providing exclusive definition of misconduct).

[31] *Id.* at 724 (quoting *In re* Claim of Tilseth, 204 N.W.2d 644, 646 (Minn. 1973) (distinguishing misconduct from "mere inefficiency, unsatisfactory conduct, failure in good performance as the result of inability or incapacity, inadvertencies or ordinary negligence in isolated instances, or good-faith errors in judgment or discretion are not to be deemed misconduct").

[32] *Id.* (Popovich, J., dissenting).

[33] 26 U.S.C. § 3304; 42 U.S.C. § 503(a)(12); Comparison of State Unemployment Laws, *supra* note 11, at 5-26.

[34] Fly v. Indus. Comm'n, 359 S.W.2d 481 (Mo. Ct. App. 1962).

certain number of employer contacts that a worker must make in a week. Failure to meet work search requirements generally will disqualify a worker from receiving benefits for any week in which the worker is not in compliance.[35]

Despite the work search requirement, workers need not accept any job offer. For example, FUTA specifically provides that benefits cannot be denied because a worker refuses to accept a position that is vacant because of a strike, lockout, or other labor dispute; that has wages, hours, or other conditions of the work substantially less favorable than the locality's prevailing wage; or that, as a condition of being employed, would require the worker to join a company union or prohibit the worker from joining any bona fide labor organization.[36]

States also consider whether a rejected job opportunity was suitable for the worker.[37] If not, the worker's refusal of that job will not forfeit eligibility for benefits, as the UI system was intended, in part, to gives workers the freedom to find a job that utilizes their particular skills and experience. Factors that states consider in determining the suitability of a job may include: the degree of risk to a worker's health, safety, and morals; the worker's physical fitness, prior training, experience, and earnings; the worker's length of unemployment and prospects for securing local work in a customary occupation; the effect on the worker's personal and family relations; and the distance of the available work from the worker's residence.[38] A worker's refusal to accept full-time work — because of child care issues, for example — has prompted varied approaches among states. Over half of the states allow for certain workers to accept only part-time work, but the other states require that all eligible workers be available for full-time employment.[39]

Other issues may also impact an employee's ability to work, which will in turn affect his or her eligibility for UI benefits. For example, some states have concluded that a temporary inability to seek work because of an illness does not bar an employee's eligibility.[40] Similarly, under certain circumstances, a worker may retain eligibility after declining a job that conflicts with his or her medical needs.[41] Yet, a more severe medical condition may make a worker unavailable for any suitable work and, thus, ineligible for UI benefits.[42]

---

[35] *See, e.g., In re* Claim of Paula Williams, 574 N.Y.S.2d 416 (N.Y. App. Div. 1991) (holding that worker did not satisfy work search requirement, and was ineligible for benefits, because of problems caused by a lack of child care).

[36] 26 U.S.C. § 3304(a)(5).

[37] COMPARISON OF STATE UNEMPLOYMENT LAWS, *supra* note 11, at 5-26.

[38] *Id.*; Imperial Foods, Inc. v. McQuaid, 874 S.W.2d 54 (Tenn. Ct. App. 1993).

[39] COMPARISON OF STATE UNEMPLOYMENT LAWS, *supra* note 11, at 5-23 to -24 (noting, for example, that California allows part-time work if it is part of the same employment conditions that the worker had when employed).

[40] *See, e.g.*, Mo. Div. of Employment Sec. v. Hankins, 700 S.W.2d 161 (Mo. Ct. App. 1985) (holding that three-day inability to seek work due to illness did not deprive worker of benefits for that week). *But see* Peglow v. Ross, 62 A.D.2d 257 (N.Y. App. Div. 1978) (holding that failure to seek work during week in which worker was hospitalized for two days disqualified him for benefits during that week).

[41] *See, e.g.*, Sem-Pak Corp. v. Com. Unemployment Compensation Bd. of Review, 501 A.2d 694 (Pa. Commw. Ct. 1985); COMPARISON OF STATE UNEMPLOYMENT LAWS, *supra* note 11, at 5-26.

[42] *See, e.g.*, Katz v. Levine, 51 A.D.2d 613 (N.Y. App. Div. 1976).

Finally, workers' desire to return to their former jobs may present difficult questions under the work search requirement. For instance, in *Knox v. Unemployment Compensation Board of Review*,[43] an employer laid off, because of a plant closure, an employee with seventeen years of seniority. The worker received UI benefits until he was referred to another employer for an open position that was similar to his previous job. During the interview, the worker told the employer that he could be recalled by his former employer and, if that happened, he would return to his previous job. Not surprisingly, the worker did not get the new position. The Pennsylvania court held that, by attaching conditions on his acceptance of a new position, the worker had failed to look for work in good faith. The court's reasoning was that the worker had effectively made himself unavailable for work by attaching conditions to his employment that a prospective employer would find unacceptable.[44] As *Knox* illustrates, workers must not only be diligent in seeking work, but must also be wary of any conditions they place on their hiring that may interfere with their availability.[45]

§ 13.03 WORKER ADJUSTMENT AND RETRAINING NOTIFICATION ACT OF 1988 (WARN)

Plant closings and mass layoffs can cause significant hardships for workers. Individual layoffs can be hard for any worker, of course, but widespread job losses can lead to greater problems. Most obviously, a worker who is part of a plant closing or mass layoff must compete with other laid-off workers for any available jobs. Moreover, the impact of these lost jobs often extends beyond the workers themselves. Particularly in smaller towns or anywhere else where the employer is a significant part of the local economy, the effects of a plant closing or mass layoff can ripple throughout the community.[46]

For these reasons, Congress enacted the Worker Adjustment and Retraining Notification Act of 1988 (WARN).[47] WARN attempts to mitigate some — but certainly not all — of the negative consequences of plant closings and mass layoffs by requiring employers in many instances to provide advanced notice to employees, unions, and state and local officials. With notice, workers and communities can better prepare for impending job losses and hopefully soften the blow associated with a plant closing or mass layoff through, for example, state job retraining programs or attempts to attract a new employer.

---

[43] 315 A.2d 915 (Pa. Commw. Ct. 1974).

[44] *Id.* at 915.

[45] Cases such as *Knox* also encourage employees to disguise or say nothing about their future plans.

[46] *See* WILLBORN ET AL. (5th ed.), *supra* note 1, at 654–55.

[47] 29 U.S.C. §§ 2101-2109; Watson v. Mich. Indus. Holdings, Inc., 311 F.3d 760, 765 (6th Cir. 2002) (noting that significant worker dislocation in the 1970s and 1980s prompted WARN's enactment).

[A] Coverage and Notice Requirement

The coverage of WARN is more limited than most employment statutes. The Act applies only to employers with 100 or more full-time employees[48] or employers with 100 or more employees who work, exclusive of overtime, at least 4,000 hours per week in the aggregate.[49] Whether "employee" is defined under the common law *Darden* test[50] or the FLSA's economic realities test[51] is unclear. One court has held that, because WARN's definition of employee does not have a broader definition like the one found under the FLSA, WARN uses the common law test.[52] Moreover, workers on leave or on temporary layoff who reasonably expect to be recalled may be classified as employees.[53]

WARN's core protection is its requirement that a covered employer notify employees, unions, and government officials about plant closings and mass layoffs.[54] The Act prohibits an employer from ordering a plant closing or mass layoff unless, at least 60 days prior, the employer gave notice of the action to each employee or the employees' representative,[55] as well as to designated state and local officials.[56]

The definitions of both a plant closing and a mass layoff under WARN require that an "employment loss" occur. Employment loss is defined as any one of three circumstances: a termination, unless it was for cause, was a voluntary departure, or was a retirement; a layoff of more than six months; or a reduction in work hours of more than fifty percent during each month of a six-month period.[57] Even if one of these three conditions is met, an employment loss will not have occurred if the plant closing or mass layoff is the result of a relocation or consolidation of the business and, prior to the closing or layoff, the employer offered to transfer employees to a different site within a reasonable commuting distance with no more

---

[48] 29 U.S.C. § 2101(a)(1) (excluding "part-time" employees from first prong of "employer" definition). "Full-time employee" is used in this discussion to differentiate a worker from a "part-time employee," which WARN defines as an employee who works on average fewer than twenty hours per week or who has worked for fewer than six of the twelve months preceding the date that notice is required. *Id.* § 2101(a)(8). Government employers — whether federal, state, or local — are not covered by WARN. 20 C.F.R. § 639.3(a).

[49] 29 U.S.C. § 2101(a)(2).

[50] *See supra* § 2.01[D].

[51] *See supra* § 2.01[C].

[52] Corbo v. Tompkins Rubber Co., Civil Action No. 00-4665, 2002 U.S. Dist. LEXIS 11830 (E.D. Pa. Jan. 23, 2002).

[53] 20 C.F.R. § 639.3(a) (defining "reasonable expectation of recall" as occurring when an employee understands, "through notification or through industry practice, that [his or her] employment with the employer has been temporarily interrupted and that [he or she] will be recalled to the same or to a similar job"); *see* Kildea v. Electro Wire Prods., Inc., 792 F. Supp. 1046 (E.D. Mich. 1992) (holding that temporarily laid-off workers are covered by WARN).

[54] 29 U.S.C. § 2102(a).

[55] An employee representative typically refers to a union. 20 C.F.R. § 639.3(d).

[56] 29 U.S.C. § 2102(a). The state and local officials include a state dislocated worker unit and the chief elected local official. *Id.* § 2102(a)(2).

[57] *Id.* § 2101(a)(6).

than a six-month break in service.[58] The "reasonable commuting distance" requirement may be waived if an employee accepts the employer's transfer offer within thirty days of the offer, plant closing, or mass layoff, whichever occurs later.[59]

If an employment loss exists, WARN's notice requirement still will not be triggered unless the employment loss occurs as part of a plant closing or mass layoff.

"Plant closing" is defined as a permanent or temporary shutdown of a worksite, or a facility or operating unit within a worksite, if the shutdown causes an employment loss for fifty or more full-time employees during any thirty-day period.[60] A "mass layoff," on the other hand, occurs when a reduction in employment not caused by a plant closing results in an employment loss during any thirty-day period for either 500 full-time employees or one-third of full-time employees, if one-third is the equivalent of fifty or more full-time employees.[61]

WARN attempts to protect against an employer spreading out employment losses to avoid meeting the minimum levels required under the definitions of a plant closing or mass layoff. Under WARN's aggregation rule, if various employees at a single worksite suffer employment losses at different times over a ninety-day period, the employment losses can be aggregated for the purposes of the notice requirement.[62] Employers can avoid application of the aggregation rule if they can show that the closings or layoffs were separate and distinct actions and were not attempts to avoid WARN's notice requirement.

Barring certain exceptions described below, if a plant closing or mass layoff occurs, notice of that action is required. Notice must be in writing and contain specific information about the action.[63] This information includes whether the plant closing or mass layoff is expected to be permanent or temporary, the expected date of the action, and the contact information of a company official who can provide further information. If the employees do not have a union representative, the employer must also write the notice in a way that is understandable to employees.[64] Finally, notice may be conditional. For example, the employer could satisfy WARN by informing employees that a plant closing or mass layoff will occur if a major contract is not renewed.[65]

---

[58] *Id.* § 2101(b)(2)(A).

[59] *Id.* § 2101(b)(2)(B).

[60] *Id.* § 2101(a)(2).

[61] *Id.* § 2101(a)(3).

[62] *Id.* § 2102(d).

[63] *Id.* § 2102(a); 20 C.F.R. § 639.7(a), (c)-(f).

[64] 20 C.F.R. § 639.7(d).

[65] *Id.* § 639.7(a)(3).

[B] Exceptions

WARN provides several exceptions to the requirement that an employer give sixty days advanced notice, or severance payments in lieu of notice,[66] before a plant closing or mass layoff. For instance, closings of temporary facilities will not trigger the WARN notice requirement, nor will layoffs caused by the end of a specified project, if the employees understood when they were hired that their term of employment would be limited.[67] Similarly, a closing or layoff caused by a strike or lockout generally will not trigger an employer's WARN duties.[68]

In addition to those more specific circumstances, WARN contains three general exceptions to its sixty-day notice requirement: faltering companies, unforeseen business circumstances, and natural disasters.[69] An employer seeking to take advantage of any of these three exceptions must still provide "as much notice as is practicable" and briefly state the reason for the reduction in the notification period.[70]

[1] Faltering Company

The first exception to the sixty-day notice requirement is the "faltering company" exception.[71] Under this exception, which applies only to plant closings, an employer can order a closing with less than sixty days notice if it reasonably and in good faith believes that giving the normal amount of notice would prevent the attainment of capital or business that would have enabled the employer to avoid or delay the shutdown.[72] In short, if the employer reasonably believes that notice would interfere with a deal that may keep the business afloat, the faltering company exception may apply.

For this exception to apply, an employer must have been actively seeking the new capital or business, and there must have been a realistic opportunity to obtain the capital or business. Moreover, the employer must objectively show that it reasonably believed that the potential customer or source of funding would not have completed the deal if notice of the plant closing occurred earlier.[73] Such a showing could include, for example, evidence that a source of funding would avoid doing business with a troubled company.

---

[66] WARN permits employers to substitute severance payments for notice, as long as the total time period still adds up to sixty days. For instance, an employer could give a combination of thirty days notice and thrity days severance instead of sixty days notice. *See infra* note 90.

[67] 29 U.S.C. § 2103(1).

[68] *Id.* § 2103(2) (noting also that a lockout will be exempt only if not ordered with the purpose of evading WARN).

[69] *Id.* § 2102.

[70] *Id.* § 2102(b)(3).

[71] 20 C.F.R. § 639.9(a).

[72] 29 U.S.C. § 2102(b)(1); 20 C.F.R. § 639.9.

[73] 20 C.F.R. § 639.9(a)(4); Childress v. Darby Lumber, Inc., 357 F.3d 1000 (9th Cir. 2004).

[2]   Unforeseen Business Circumstances

WARN's second exception to the sixty-day advanced notice requirement is an "unforeseen business circumstance," which applies to both plant closings and mass layoffs. This exception allows fewer than sixty days notice if the closing or layoff is the result of business circumstances that the employer could not reasonably foresee at the time that notice normally would have been required.[74]

The unforeseeable business circumstances exception requires an objective analysis that looks to whether a similarly situated employer, using reasonable business judgment, would have predicted the market circumstances that led to the plant closing or mass layoff at issue.[75] Under this analysis, a reasonably unforeseeable business circumstance typically involves "some sudden, dramatic, and unexpected action or condition outside the employer's control."[76] Examples include a sudden and unexpected termination of a major contract, a strike or other disruption at a major supplier, an unanticipated and dramatic economic downturn, and an unexpected government-ordered closing of a worksite.

One illustration of the unforeseen business circumstance exception came out of the Enron scandal. In *Roquet v. Arthur Andersen LLP*,[77] the Seventh Circuit examined Arthur Andersen's attempt to use this exception after it went out of business without the required sixty-days notice. The Department of Justice (DOJ) had been investigating Arthur Andersen's participation in the financial misconduct of one of its major clients, Enron. Before the DOJ issued a subpoena to Arthur Anderson, its employees destroyed thousands of Enron-related documents. This act prompted further investigation and rumors of possible indictments against individuals and the company itself. Ultimately, the DOJ indicted the company, triggering a massive client defection and, shortly thereafter, equally dramatic layoffs. Before the indictments, Arthur Andersen had told employees that it hoped to resolve its issues with the DOJ; thus, the company never gave employees sixty-days notice of the subsequent layoffs.[78]

At issue in *Roquet* was whether the indictment was an unforeseeable business circumstance — in particular, whether the indictment was foreseeable. The court held that it was not foreseeable because indictments against companies, rather than individuals, were rare and the company's negotiations with the DOJ had not indicated that such an indictment was likely. The court stressed that the *possibility* of an occurrence is not enough. Rather, the business circumstance must be *probable* to be considered foreseeable.[79]

According to the court, the rationale for this distinction was that:

---

[74]   29 U.S.C. § 2102(b)(2)(A).

[75]   20 C.F.R. § 639.9(b)(2) (noting also that an "employer is not required . . . to accurately predict general economic conditions that also may affect demand for its products or services"); Loehrer v. McDonnell Douglas Corp., 98 F.3d 1056 (8th Cir. 1996).

[76]   20 C.F.R. § 639.9(b)(1).

[77]   398 F.3d 585 (7th Cir. 2005).

[78]   *Id.* at 587-88.

[79]   *Id.* at 589.

WARN was not intended to force financially fragile, yet economically viable, employers to provide WARN notice and close its doors when there is a *possibility* that the business may fail at some undetermined time in the future. Such a reading of the Act would force many employers to lay off their employees prematurely, harming precisely those individuals WARN attempts to protect. A company that is struggling to survive financially may be able to continue on for years and it was not Congress's intent to force such a company to close its doors to comply with WARN's notice requirement.[80]

This explanation aptly shows the need to balance the interests of requiring notice against the desire to provide companies the chance to maintain operations and to avoid ever having to order a closing or layoff.

[3] Natural Disaster

The final exception to the sixty-day notice rule is a "natural disaster." WARN permits a plant closing or mass layoff with no notice — not merely fewer than sixty days, like the other two general exceptions — if "any form of natural disaster" makes advanced notice of the action impossible.[81] However, notice is still required to the extent it is practicable, even if after the fact.[82]

This exception is applicable only where the employer can demonstrate that the natural disaster directly caused the plant closing or mass layoff. If the employer cannot make that showing, it must attempt to rely on the unforeseen business circumstance exception. Examples of natural disasters that may excuse an employer's failure to provide notice include hurricanes, floods, earthquakes, droughts, tidal waves, tsunamis, and other similar acts of nature.[83]

[C] Enforcement

WARN's enforcement relies on private rights of action by aggrieved employees, unions, and local governments,[84] although the effectiveness of this method of enforcement has been questioned because it may not impose a sufficient probability that employers who violate the Act will be sued successfully.[85] The Department of Labor has authority to promulgate regulations under WARN, but it has no standing to bring suit to enforce the Act.[86]

Employees' remedies for employer violations of WARN include back pay; employee benefits, including medical costs that would have been covered by health

---

[80] *Id.* at 589-90 (quoting Watson v. Mich. Indus. Holdings, Inc., 311 F.3d 760, 765 (6th Cir. 2002)).

[81] 29 U.S.C. § 2102 (b)(2)(B).

[82] 20 C.F.R. § 639.9(c)(4).

[83] 29 U.S.C. § 2102(b)(2)(B); 20 C.F.R. § 639.9(c).

[84] 29 U.S.C. § 2104(a)(1), (a)(5), (a)(7); 20 C.F.R. § 639.1(d).

[85] *See* WILLBORN ET AL. (5th ed.), *supra* note 1, at 663 (citing 1993 report by the General Accounting Office).

[86] 20 C.F.R. § 639.1(d).

insurance if the employee still worked for the company; and attorney's fees.[87] Punitive damages do not appear to be available under WARN.[88] The amount of time over which such remedies will accrue is capped at sixty days, the period that the employee would have worked had the employer given proper notice.[89] However, the employer's liability can be reduced by any wages it pays to employees during the period of a violation or any voluntary and unconditional payments that are not required by any legal obligations.[90] An employer that unlawfully fails to notify government officials may also be civilly liable to the appropriate government unit for up to $500 a day.[91]

Finally, WARN makes clear that it is intended to be a floor, not a ceiling. The Act expressly states that its rights are in addition to, not a replacement for, any other rights contained in a contract or other statute.[92] Similarly, the DOL regulations stress that it is "civically desirable and it would appear to be good business practice" for employers to give workers, unions, and state and local governments advanced notice of large-scale terminations.[93]

---

[87] 29 U.S.C. § 2104(a)(1)(b), (a)(6).

[88] *See* Lewis v. Textron Auto. Co., 935 F. Supp. 68 (D.N.H. 1996); Finnan v. L.F. Rothschild & Co., Inc., 726 F. Supp. 460 (S.D.N.Y. 1989).

[89] 29 U.S.C. § 2104(a)(1) (stating also that liability will last for no longer than one-half the number of days that the employee worked for the employer).

[90] *Id.* § 2104(a)(2).

[91] *Id.* § 2104(a)(3) (eliminating liability to local government if the employer pays its liability to employees within three weeks after it ordered the plant closing or mass layoff).

[92] *Id.* § 2105; 20 C.F.R. § 639.1(g). For instance, many states and localities have their own WARN-like statutes. *See, e.g.*, Illinois Worker Adjustment and Retraining Notification Act, 820 Ill. Comp. Stat. Ann. 65/1-65/99 (applying to employers with seventy-five or more full-time employees and triggering notice when 250 full-time employees are laid off, or twenty-five or more employees are laid off if they constitute one-third of workforce).

[93] 20 C.F.R. § 639.1(e).

Chapter 14

EMPLOYEE BENEFIT PLANS UNDER ERISA

§ 14.01   INTRODUCTION

Employees receive many different types of compensation for their work. An increasingly large portion of this compensation, more than 30% in some cases, is in the form of non-wage employee benefits.[1] Employee benefits come in two generic flavors: deferred compensation and in-kind benefits. The primary example of deferred compensation plans are pensions or retirement plans. This type of compensation is earned in the present, but is not available to the employee until later (generally after reaching normal retirement age). On the other hand, compensation that is usable in the short-term (e.g., health, disability, or life insurance benefits) constitutes in-kind payments.

Although the provision of an employer-provided employee benefit plan is a voluntarily undertaking, such benefit plans have become increasingly popular as a form of employee compensation. These plans provide tax advantages to both employers and employees,[2] facilitate the retention of good employees, provide incentives for older workers to retire, and permit employees to receive more favorable terms for such benefits because of their employer's size.

---

[1] *See* STEVEN L. WILLBORN ET AL., EMPLOYMENT LAW: CASES AND MATERIALS 689 (5th ed. 2012).

[2] Tax advantages to employers for having ERISA pension plans were estimated to cost $142 billion dollars in lost tax revenue for fiscal year 2011, while health-benefit plans were estimated to cost $177 billion dollars. *See* WILLBORN ET AL., *supra* note 1, at 692.

Three federal laws, the Employee Retiree Income Security Act of 1974 (ERISA),[3] the Internal Revenue Code (IRC),[4] and now the recently Supreme Court-approved Patient Protection and Affordable Care Act (PPACA),[5] work in tandem to define employer legal obligations, and concomitant employee rights, with regard to the provisions of employer-provided benefits.[6] The three statutes serve different, but complementary, statutory purposes. Whereas ERISA seeks to protect assets of the plan and benefits promised to employees, the IRC provisions seek to provide tax incentives so that employers voluntarily adopt these employee benefit plans and do so in a way that does not discriminatorily advantage highly compensated employees. PPACA provides a mechanism to incentivize employers to offer one specific type of benefit to their workers: health insurance.

Because the topic of employee benefits concerns tax and employment issues, different parts of ERISA come under the purview of different federal agencies. The labor provisions are administered by the Department of Labor's (DOL) Employee Benefit Security Administration (EBSA), while the tax provisions are administered by the Department of Treasury. PPACA provisions are administered by both Health and Human Services (HHS) and EBSA.

The IRC contains tax provisions concerning "plan qualification," which apply especially to pension plans. Qualification of the plan permits employers and employees to qualify for important tax advantages.[7] Nonetheless, a more thorough consideration of the IRC tax provisions and the accompanying Department of Treasury regulations is beyond the scope of this book and will not be discussed further in this chapter.[8]

---

[3] 29 U.S.C. §§ 1001-1461. Following the practice of other ERISA books and scholars, this chapter refers to the original section numbers as enacted by ERISA in the "ERISA § " format, rather than to the United State Code section numbers. Additionally, Department of Labor Regulations found in 29 C.F.R. are referred to as "DOL Reg."

[4] All references to the "Code" or "Internal Revenue Code" are to the Internal Revenue Code of 1986 (IRC), as amended, codified as Title 26 of the United States Code. IRC §§ 1-9833.

[5] Pub. L. No. 111-148, 124 Stat. 119 (2010), as amended by the Health Care and Education Reconciliation Act of 2010, Pub. L. No. 111-152, 124 Stat. 1029 (2010). For the most part, PPACA was held to be constitutional by the U.S. Supreme Court in *National Federation of Independent Businesses v. Sebelius*, 132 S. Ct. 2566 (2012).

[6] This chapter discusses only employer-provided employee benefit plans that are subject to ERISA. Other federal programs also exist that provide retirement income and health care benefits. Social Security provides retirement income to elderly and disabled Americans, while Medicare and Medicaid provide health care benefits for the elderly, the disabled, and the poor.

[7] IRC § 401(a). Plan qualification issues are not covered here, but important issues include nondiscrimination requirements involving minimum coverage rules, nondiscrimination in benefits and contributions, and top heavy rules. *Id.* §§ 401(a)(4), 410(b), 416. Other significant IRC provisions include individual limits on the amount of benefits or contributions employees may receive and employer limits on the amount an employer may deduct for contributions to qualified plans. *Id.* §§ 401(a)(17), 402(g), 404, 414(v), 415. For additional readings on these topics, see generally LAWRENCE A. FROLIK & KATHRYN L. MOORE, LAW OF EMPLOYEE PENSION AND WELFARE BENEFITS 521-600 (3d ed. 2012).

[8] It is important to understand, however, that a number of ERISA provisions are duplicated in parallel IRC provisions, and some courts will utilize the IRC section number to refer to these sections. This chapter only utilizes the ERISA section number in such cases.

§ 14.02   EMPLOYEE RETIREE INCOME SECURITY ACT OF 1974 (ERISA)

ERISA is a comprehensive federal law that regulates the provision of employer-provided pension and welfare benefit plans.[9] Prior to its enactment, these plans were governed by a patchwork of federal and state laws that were generally ineffective in securing plan assets and protecting employees' ability to receive their promised employee benefits.

Although employers are not required to offer employee benefit plans to their employees, once such plans are adopted, ERISA provides the applicable legal framework. And once ERISA applies, its overarching importance in the realm of employee benefits law stems directly from the fact that it contains broad preemption provisions that significantly occupy the field of employee benefits law and supersede most contrary state laws.

[A]   Statutory Structure

ERISA is divided into four Titles, with Title I containing the lion's share of applicable employee benefit provisions and Title IV providing for an important system of plan termination insurance for certain forms of pension plans.[10] Title I, in turn, is divided into two subtitles. Subtitle A concerns general provisions regarding statutory findings and purpose (§ 2), definitions (§ 3), and exemptions from coverage (§ 4). Subtitle B contains the regulatory provisions and is divided into seven parts.

Part 1 of Subtitle B concerns reporting and disclosure requirements including the requirement of a summary plan description (SPD). Part 2 covers participation, vesting, benefit accrual standards, and how benefits have to be calculated and paid. Part 3 contains minimum funding standards. Part 4 involves provisions regarding the establishment of employment benefit plans, as well fiduciary standards and prohibited transaction rules. Part 5 concerns civil and criminal enforcement of the law, claim procedures, and preemption. Part 6 deals with group health plan issues involving continuation of health care coverage under COBRA. Part 7 covers group health plan requirements regarding portability and nondiscrimination rules under Health Insurance Portability and Accountability Act (HIPAA).

Different provisions of Title I pertain to different types of ERISA plans. Whereas Parts 1, 4, and 5 concern both pension and welfare benefit plans, Parts 2 and 3 only apply to pension plans, and Parts 6 and 7 only impact welfare benefit plans.

---

[9] ERISA involves many complex issues discussed in depth in ERISA-specific literature. *See, e.g.,* FROLIK & MOORE, *supra* note 5. Consequently, benefit accrual rules, optional forms of benefit, minimum funding standards, and multiemployer and multiple employer plans, including issues revolving around withdrawal liability under the Multiemployer Pension Plan Amendments Act (MPPAA) and the special preemption rules for multiple employer welfare benefit arrangements (MEWAs), are all beyond the scope of this book.

[10] Title II of ERISA amended the IRC to make it consistent with the new ERISA provisions, and Title III establishes the authority of the Departments of Labor and Treasury to enforce various provisions of Title I and Title II.

[B]   ERISA Plans

ERISA applies only to covered employee benefit "plans." Courts apply the *Dillingham* factors and the *Fort. Halifax* test to determine whether a "plan, fund, or program" is "established or maintained" by an employer and thus, qualifies for coverage under ERISA.[11] Under *Donovan v. Dillingham*,[12] there are four elements that must be present for a "plan" to exist under ERISA: (1) intended benefits; (2) intended beneficiaries; (3) a source of financing; and (4) a procedure to apply for and collect benefits. Additionally, in *Fort Halifax Packing Co. v. Coyne*,[13] the Supreme Court supplied a fifth factor when it required that there also be "ongoing plan administration." Consequently, a severance plan that provides for a one-time payment does not meet this ongoing administration scheme requirement and is not a plan under ERISA.

[1]   Types of ERISA Plans

Rather than relying on the distinction between deferred compensation and in-kind benefits, ERISA divides the universe of covered employee benefit plans into employee pension benefit plans and employee welfare benefit plans. Employee pension benefit plans are established and maintained by employers for the purpose of providing retirement income to employees through deferral of employee income until at least termination of employment.[14] Employee welfare benefit plans, on the other hand, are established and maintained by employers to provide benefit programs that include health, disability, and life insurance; training programs; reimbursement for day care centers; scholarship funds; and prepaid legal services.[15] With regard to welfare plans, this chapter focuses on health insurance plans because of their prevalence and importance in the workplace.

Although ERISA plans can also be categorized by the type and number of employers providing covered benefits, this chapter focuses solely on single employer plans run by individual employers.[16]

---

[11] The definitions of both employee pension benefit plans and employee welfare benefit plans require that a "plan, fund, or program" be "established or maintained" by an employer or union for the purposes of providing participants and beneficiaries either retirement income or certain in-kind benefits. *See* ERISA § 3(1), (2). As a participant generally must be an employee or former employee, *see* ERISA § 3(7), ERISA does not apply to independent contractors; courts use traditional agency concepts to determine whether a worker is a statutory employee under ERISA. *See* Nationwide Mutual Insurance Co. v. Darden, 503 U.S. 318 (1992) (setting forth common law "control" test for employee/independent contractor determinations under ERISA); *see also supra* § 2.01.

[12] 688 F.2d 1367 (11th Cir. 1988).

[13] 482 U.S. 1 (1987).

[14] ERISA § 3(2)(A).

[15] *Id.* § 3(1).

[16] Multiemployer plans are sponsored by more than one employer under provisions of a collective bargaining agreement for the benefit of union members, while multiple employer plans are sponsored by unrelated employers outside of a collective bargaining agreement. Different provisions apply to these benefit plan arrangements under ERISA. *See generally* JOHN H. LANGBEIN ET AL., PENSION AND EMPLOYEE BENEFIT LAW 64-71 (4th ed. 2006); COLLEEN A. MEDILL, INTRODUCTION TO EMPLOYEE BENEFITS LAW: POLICY AND PRACTICE 32, 236-37 (2004).

[2]   Plans Exempt from ERISA

Section 4 of ERISA establishes that certain types of employee benefits plans are exempt from coverage under the Act. Chief among them are government plans (federal, state, and local); church plans; and plans adopted to comply with workers' compensation, unemployment compensation, and disability insurance laws. State public pension plans, for instance, are subject to state statutory law, and not to ERISA.[17] The Department of Labor by regulation also excludes from ERISA coverage payroll practices related to employers using general assets to pay for sick leave, vacation, jury duty, and active military service.[18]

[C]   Plan Documents, Trust Requirements, and Plan Amendments

ERISA specifically prescribes how employee benefit plans must be established and what basic provisions they must contain. For instance, an ERISA plan must be contained in a written instrument that provides for one or more named plan fiduciaries who are responsible for the administration and management of the plan (fiduciary duties are discussed in greater detail in § 14.05[A]).[19] Additionally, plans *must* have four additional features: (1) a procedure for establishing and carrying out funding policy, (2) a procedure for allocating and delegating fiduciary responsibilities, (3) a procedure for amending the plan, and (4) a basis on which payments are made to and from the plan.[20] Employee benefit plans *may* also contain: (1) a provision authorizing a person to serve in more than one fiduciary capacity, (2) a provision authorizing the plan to hire advisors, and (3) a provision authorizing the appointment of investment managers.[21]

The requirement that there be a procedure for amending the plan includes the need to identify persons who have authority to amend the plan, which the Supreme Court has held to be satisfied with the mere statement that: "The Company reserves the right at any time to amend the plan."[22] Also, under ERISA's anti-cutback provisions, amendments of one type of pension plan, a defined benefit plan, cannot reduce a participant's accrued (or already earned) benefits in the plan.[23] Finally, under the settlor function doctrine, employers are generally able to establish, modify, or terminate pension or welfare benefit plans without being subject to fiduciary obligations.[24]

---

[17]   ERISA § 4(b).

[18]   DOL Reg. § 2510.3-1.

[19]   ERISA § 402(a).

[20]   *Id.* § 402(b).

[21]   *Id.* § 402(c).

[22]   *See* Curtiss-Wright Corp. v. Schoonejongen, 514 U.S. 73 (1995).

[23]   ERISA § 204(g). This anti-cutback rule does not apply to welfare benefit plans or to employer matching contributions in the defined contribution pension plan context. A plan amendment may reduce the future rate of benefit accrual as long as participants are properly notified in accordance with ERISA § 204(h).

[24]   *Curtiss-Wright Corp.*, 514 U.S. 73 (welfare plan context); Lockheed v. Spink, 517 U.S. 882 (1996) (retirement plan context). A settlor in trust law is one who creates a trust and is traditionally not also

ERISA plans must hold their assets in trust by one or more trustees. Such trustees come in two flavors: discretionary trustees and directed trustees.[25] Discretionary trustees have exclusive authority to manage and administer the plan, while directed trustees are subject to the directions of discretionary trustees. This distinction becomes important when considering issues of fiduciary liability. Both types of trustees are generally considered fiduciaries to some degree, but directed trustees' fiduciary duties are limited to the specific role they carry out for the plan.

[D] Summary Plan Description (SPD) and Reporting and Disclosure Requirements

ERISA contains several reporting and disclosure requirements. These documents and filings are mandated to keep employees informed about their benefits so that they can monitor plan administrators' performance. Fulfillment of these requirements also provides information to the government about whether plans are being operated in compliance with the law. ERISA requires plans to provide many different types of disclosures and notices, including: (1) a summary plan description (SPD), (2) summary annual report (SAR), (3) summary of material modifications (SMM), and (4) an annual report (Form 5500).[26]

Of these, the SPD is the disclosure requirement that is most frequently discussed in employment litigation. The SPD conveys information about the plan and must be written in a manner that can be understood by an average lay person. The SPD is required by statute to contain specific information such as eligibility requirements for participation, a description of the plan benefits, procedures for filing a claim, and the names and addresses of plan fiduciaries.[27] The SPD plays such an important role in plan administration that if there is a conflict between the plan document and the SPD, some courts will award the more generous benefits found in the SPD to plaintiffs under an estoppel theory because plaintiffs are entitled to rely on the statements made in the SPD. However, the U.S. Supreme Court has also made clear in *Cigna Corp. v. Amara*[28] that disclosures set forth in a SPD cannot be enforced as terms of the plan itself under Section 502(a)(1)(B), even though they provide communication with beneficiaries *about* the plan and may subject plan administrators to breach of fiduciary duty claims under Section 502(a)(3).[29] [30]

---

the fiduciary who administers and manages the trust. *See* RESTATEMENT (SECOND) OF TRUSTS § 3(1) (1959).

[25] ERISA § 403(a).

[26] *Id.* §§ 101, 103-104.

[27] *Id.* § 102.

[28] 131 S. Ct. 1866 (2011).

[29] Remedies under ERISA Sections 502(a)(1)(B) and (a)(3) are discussed *infra* § 14.05[C].

[30] *See, e.g.*, Burstein v. Ret. Account Plan for Employees of AHERF, 334 F.3d 365, 377-78 (3d Cir. 2003). Because of this, most employers now include "reservation of rights" language in their SPDs which allow them to modify or terminate the plan at will without facing liability from an estoppel or breach of fiduciary duty claim.

§ 14.03   RETIREMENT PLANS

As discussed above, employee benefit plans under ERISA are either employee pension benefit plans or employee welfare benefit plans. This section concerns employee pension benefit plans that are established and maintained for the purpose of providing retirement income for employees.

[A]   Types of Retirement Plans

Employee pension benefit plans come in two distinct types: defined benefit plans (DBPs) and defined contribution plans (DCPs). Because employers are responsible for providing a defined benefit amount to employees at retirement under DBP arrangements, there is more regulation of these plans so that the promised benefits are available upon retirement and plans do not default on their pension promises. For instance, ERISA provides minimum vesting, benefit accrual, and funding standards for DBPs and sets up an insurance scheme, operated by the Pension Benefit Guaranty Corporation (PBGC), in case of employer defaults. On the other hand, employers are only responsible to contribute money to employees' individual plan accounts under the DCP model and that is where their responsibility ends.

Although DBPs historically were the retirement plan of choice, there has been a significant shift to DCPs in recent years because DCPs generally cost less to operate, place fewer obligations on the employer, and provide portability for employees who move from one employer to the next.[31] For instance, from 1979 to 2001, the number of DBPs went from 139,489 to 51,000, while the number of DCPs went from 331,432 to 707,000.[32] Much of the decline in DBPs can also be attributed to economic difficulties in certain industries, such as the airline and automobile industries which have traditionally operated these types of plans, and the fact, as discussed in more detail in § 14.03[C], that the PBGC only provides for a fraction of the benefit owed when such plans default.

[1]   Defined Benefit Plans

In a defined benefit plan, an employer promises employees a defined amount of benefit upon retirement. The employee may elect to receive this benefit in different forms as noted later in this subsection, but the burden is placed on the employer to contribute funds to the pension plan on an actuarially sound basis so that sufficient funds exist to pay the worker their full pension. The total payment due to an employee is generally calculated by applying a formula based on years of service and an average final salary of the employee over a specified period of time (like three years).

Under these arrangements, the risk is placed on the employer to invest sufficiently to fund the on-going pension expenses. The required minimum funding of DBP plans is calculated based on a complex actuarial analysis revolving around

---

[31] *See* MEDILL, *supra* note 16, at 113–16.

[32] *See* MEDILL, *supra* note 16, at 114 (citing Colleen E. Medill, *Enron and the Pension System*, *in* ENRON: CORPORATE FIASCOS AND THEIR IMPLICATIONS (2004)).

factors such as age, length of service, projected future salary increases, and rate of return on plan investments.[33]

Benefits from a defined benefit plan are primarily paid in the form of an annuity, which comes in many forms, but generally provide a stream of payments to the employee for the rest of their lives. As a result of the annuity form of payment, not only is the risk of investment return on the employer, but so is the risk of employee longevity. ERISA also requires that DBPs contain payment features which permit a spouse to continue to receive some benefit from the plan after the death of the employee.[34]

[2] Defined Contribution Plans

Whereas the employer is responsible for providing the pension benefit to the employee upon retirement under defined benefit plans, defined contribution plans (sometimes referred to as individual account plans) only require the employer to a pay a defined amount into an employee's individual account. At that point, it is up to the employee to invest the pension funds in various financial instruments so that he or she will have sufficient funds available to last through retirement. In other words, DCPs place the risk of longevity and risk of investment loss on employees and there is no guarantee that a participant will received any specified amount of benefit at retirement.[35]

The 401(k) salary deferral plan, which may include an employer matching contribution component, is perhaps the most popular form of defined contribution plan. In a 401(k) plan, the employee directs the employer to divert a specified percentage of his or her salary into his or her retirement account rather than receiving it as cash compensation. The employer matching contribution provides incentive for employees to contribute greater amounts to these individual accounts.[36] Such contributions, like other retirement plan contributions, provide the advantage of tax deferral for the employee, and tax is not paid on this income until such funds are distributed from the account. Other types of DCPs, which are

---

[33] ERISA §§ 301-305.

[34] The qualified joint survivor annuity (QJSA) and qualified preretirement survivor annuity (QPSA) for surviving spouses are the default forms of distribution under defined benefit plans. See ERISA § 205. For a tragic case concerning the annuity options for surviving spouses and the gender equity issues implicated thereby, see *Lorenzen v. Employee Ret. Plan of the Sperry & Hutchinson Co.*, 896 F.2d 228 (7th Cir. 1990) (describing case where spouse lost significant survivor pension income under a QJSA and had to settle for much less money under a QPSA when her participant husband deferred retirement for six months and then died when his wife allowed life support to be withdrawn before his new retirement date).

[35] Professor Secunda has highlighted the problems surrounding 401(k) plans in: *401 K Follies: A Proposal to Reinvigorate the United States Annuity Market*, ABA Section on Taxation Newsquarterly 13–15 (Fall 2010).

[36] The Pension Protection Act of 2006 provides an additional mechanism for encouraging employees to save for retirement by permitting qualified automatic enrollment features, under which "each employee eligible to participate in the arrangement is treated as having elected to have the employer make elective contributions in an amount equal to a qualified percentage of compensation." Under such arrangements, employees are required to be given notice of their ability to opt-out before salary deferrals begin. *See* Pension Protection Act of 2006 (PPA), Pub. L. No. 109-280, 120 Stat. 780, § 902 (2006) [hereinafter PPA §].

categorized by the type of contribution the employer makes, include profit sharing plans and money purchase pension plans.[37]

One of the chief advantages of the DCP is that it is portable. If an employee moves to another employer, the employee can choose to directly roll-over his or her individual accounts either into his or her new employer's retirement plan or into an Individual Retirement Account (IRA), where the retirement monies will continue to grow tax-free. Employees tend to receive lump sums from their 401(k) plans upon retirement, and such funds may also be rolled-over into an IRA. Another advantage to these plans is that they may be set up to permit participants to receive plan loans from individual accounts in certain specified circumstances, including for hardship or for purposes of buying a primary residence.[38]

[3] Cash Balance Plans

For a time, much employment litigation revolved around hybrid pension plans referred to as cash balance plans. Cash balance plans are actually defined benefit plans to the extent that the employer is responsible for paying employees a benefit at retirement. Nonetheless, such plans are set up with hypothetical individual account balances that look like defined contribution plans and allow employees to follow the accumulation of their retirement monies within these plans. These hypothetical accounts are credited each year with a specified payment and interest amount and, in this sense, what is being promised is a rate of growth on the contributions rather than a given benefit level.[39]

Cash balance plans are popular among some employees because they are easier to understand and monitor, more portable, insured by the PBGC, and tend to provide lump sum payments to their participants. Employers like them because they permit more flexibility in administration.[40] However, the interest amount credited to these accounts had led older workers to claim that conversions to cash balance plans discriminate based on age. These workers claimed that their accounts had less time to accumulate interest earnings before retirement than similarly

---

[37] "Profit sharing" plans do not actually require that the company make a profit before it can contribute to an employee's retirement account. Such profit sharing plans give employers discretion from year to year to decide how much they wish to contribute to individual retirement accounts. On the other hand, "money purchase pension" plans require employers to pay a mandatory amount into individual accounts on a year-to-year basis. Another type of defined contribution plan, the complexities of which are beyond the scope of this chapter, is the employee stock ownership plan (ESOP) that invests primarily in qualifying employer securities. Employers may provide employees with more than one type of defined contribution plan and may even provide both DBPs and DCPs options to their employees at the same time.

[38] "In-service distributions" from an individual account plan are an exception to the normal anti-alienation rules against assigning or alienating plan benefits. See ERISA § 206(d). Qualified domestic relations orders (QDROs), which permit a plan administrator to pay a former spouse or other dependent from a participant's pension benefits, represent another exception to the anti-alienation provisions. ERISA § 206(d)(3).

[39] The individual accounts are "hypothetical" in the sense that such accounts are credited the same interest amounts regardless of the plan's actual investment experience.

[40] The argument is that it is easier to manage paying a predictable, fixed amount to each employee rather than having to chase the equity markets.

situated younger workers. The recently enacted Pension Protection Act of 2006 (PPA),[41] however, contains provisions which state that prospective conversions from traditional defined benefit plans to cash balance plans will not be deemed age discriminatory.[42]

[B] Participation and Vesting Standards

Part 2 of Title I of ERISA applies only to pension plans. There are two main requirements in these provisions relating to minimum participation standards and minimum vesting standards, which seek to protect eligible employees' ability to benefit from an employer's voluntarily established pension plan and to gain a vested interest in such benefits after working for the employer for a defined number of years.[43]

[1] Minimum Participation Standards

Employees are not necessarily able to immediately enroll in an employer's pension plan once they commence employment. That being said, ERISA's minimum participation standards require that eligible employees be able to enroll in a pension plan once they have attained the age of twenty-one and have completed one year of service for the employer.[44] One year of service for eligibility purposes means a twelve-month period during which the employee has worked at least 1000 hours. The twelve-month period begins for new employees when they commence employment. Once an employee becomes eligible to participate, he or she must be given the opportunity to participate within six months of the date of his or her eligibility.[45] Employers generally meet these enrollment requirements by setting up two open enrollment dates per year.

Minimum participation standards do not guarantee that all employees will be eligible to participate in an employer's pension plans. In making eligibility determinations, employers are permitted to distinguish among employees based on neutral business considerations, as long as eligibility standards do not impose an additional hidden service requirement.[46] Consequently, the age and service requirements discussed in these provisions only guarantee participation to those employees an employer has otherwise deemed eligible to participate in the plan.[47]

---

[41] Pub. L. No. 109-280, 120 Stat. 780 (2006).

[42] *Id.* at § 701(a)(1).

[43] ERISA §§ 202, 203. Other provisions under this Part include complicated benefit accrual requirements for pension plans and strong anti-alienation provisions protecting a plan participant's benefits from being assigned or alienated. *See id.* §§ 204, 206(d).

[44] *Id.* § 202(a)(1)(A). An employer also cannot condition participation in a pension plan based on the employee being too old. *See id.* § 202(a)(2).

[45] *Id.* § 202(a)(4).

[46] This situation could arise if an employer seeks to exclude a group of employees solely because they are part-time or temporary workers. Such workers can be excluded for other neutral business reasons, but not based entirely on the number of hours they work, as this would be equivalent to making certain groups of otherwise eligible employees work more than 1000 hours before being able to participate in the retirement plan.

[47] There are, however, minimum coverage provisions under the Internal Revenue Code's plan

[2] Minimum Vesting Standards

As already discussed, one of the primary purposes behind the enactment of ERISA was to protect employees from losing their pension benefits after devoting a substantial amount of their career to their employer.[48] To prevent such forfeiture of benefits, ERISA provides vesting schedules after which a pension benefit becomes non-forfeitable.[49] The impact of these vesting rules is that they help employers retain valuable employees for longer periods of time as employees may not be fully vested in their benefits until up to after seven years of employment. The vesting schedule primarily applies to defined benefit plans because participants are immediately vested in their own contributions to an individual account plan under a 401(k) or other defined contribution arrangements. Nevertheless, vesting schedules do apply to employer contributions under defined contribution plans, including to matching contributions under 401(k) arrangements.[50]

In the defined benefit context, ERISA responds to these potential forfeiture issues by requiring one of two different types of minimum vesting schedules: cliff vesting or graduated vesting. Under cliff vesting, an employee becomes fully vested in all earned retirement once he or she works for the employer for five years.[51] However, prior to completion of the fifth year, the employee has no right to such benefits. Under graduated vesting, an employee become incrementally vested in his or her retirement benefits so that after three years, the employee is twenty percent vested; after four years, forty percent vested; all the way up to seven years when he or she is full vested in his or her benefits.[52] In short, under ERISA's vesting schedules for defined benefit plans, an employer must at minimum fully vest its employees in their accrued benefits after seven years of employment.[53]

As far as determining whether an employee has a year of service for purposes of vesting, a plan must count all years of service for vesting.[54] In other words, an

---

qualification provisions which limit the ability of the employer to exclude certain employees from participating in the pension plan. *See* IRC § 410(b).

[48] Indeed, protection against the arbitrary forfeiture of employee benefits may have been "the" primary purpose behind ERISA's enactment. *McNevin v. Solvay Process Co.*, 60 N.E. 1115 (N.Y. 1901), is a classic example from a bygone era of how courts traditionally viewed employee benefits as mere gratuities that could be taken away at the employer's whim.

[49] ERISA § 203.

[50] As of 2007, following the enactment of the Pension Protection Act of 2006, the general vesting rule for contributions to *any* defined contribution plan is either full vesting after a three-year cliff or a six-year graduated period. *See* PPA § 904(b).

[51] ERISA § 203(a)(2)(A).

[52] *Id.* § 203(a)(2)(B).

[53] Employers cannot establish other vesting schedules for special circumstances outside of these minimum vesting standards. However, employers may provide for the forfeiture of benefits which are in excess of the benefits that must be vested after a certain amount of time under the minimum vesting rules. *See* Hummell v. S.E. Rykoff & Co., 634 F.2d 446 (9th Cir. 1980) (allowing for limited forfeitures of excess benefits, but striking down nonconforming, "bad boy" vesting schedule imposed on employees who had worked for the company less than seven years and then competed against employer within two years of terminating employment).

[54] There are statutory exceptions to this general rule of counting every year of service for vesting purposes. The most well-known is the "rule of parity," which permits employers not to count previous

employee can start counting years of service for vesting even before he or she has become eligible to enroll in the pension plan.[55]

[C] Plan Termination Issues and the PBGC

Because of the risks associated with employers maintaining defined benefit plans, ERISA establishes a scheme of plan termination insurance. Congress created the Pension Benefit Guaranty Corporation (PBGC) to administer this insurance program and provide some level of retirement income for employees under DBPs if the employer should default on pension promises. There is no need for termination insurance for defined contribution plans because the employer is only responsible for contributing to the employee's individual account, not for promising a defined amount upon retirement.[56]

PBGC payments for DBP terminations provide a percentage of the normal retirement benefit up to a limit set by statute. The cost of the PBGC is borne primarily by employers that maintain pension plans. Employers' contribution amounts are calculated both per participant and based on the amount of unfunded vested benefits the plan maintains.[57]

Terminations of defined benefit plans can be divided into two categories: standard terminations or distress terminations.[58] The primary difference is that in the former the employer has sufficient funds to pay all outstanding benefit liabilities, while there are insufficient funds in the latter instance. Distress terminations are further broken down into voluntary and involuntary terminations. The PBGC also has the ability to undo a termination and to restore plans to employer control under specific circumstances.[59]

[1] Distress Terminations with Insufficient Assets

Distress terminations with insufficient assets occur when an employer terminates a defined benefit pension plan without the ability to meet its outstanding pension promises. In such circumstances, employers are responsible in the first instance for such obligations,[60] but the PBGC then becomes a trustee of the plan,

---

years of employment for rehired employees under limited circumstances. *See* ERISA § 203(b).

[55] *Id.* § 202(b)(1).

[56] When an employer terminates a defined contribution plan, the primary effect is that participants become immediately and fully vested in their accrued benefits in the plan. IRC § 411(d)(3).

[57] The Pension Protection Act of 2006 and other similar recent legislation has continued to increase the annual premium amount that employers must contribute to the PBGC, while at the same time increasing minimum funding requirements for such plans. *See* PPA §§ 101-116, 401-412.

[58] There are also so-called "partial terminations," but these are not literally plan terminations at all. Such partial terminations occur when employers engage in mass layoffs or plan amendments that adversely affect the rights of a significant proportion of participants in a plan. In such scenarios, if the percentage reduction of plan participants as a result of involuntary terminations or plan amendment is generally more than fifty percent, then a partial termination has occurred and the accrued benefits of the terminated employees become fully and immediately vested (similar to what happens when a defined contribution plan is terminated).

[59] ERISA § 4047.

[60] *See* In re Defoe Shipbuilding Co., 639 F.2d 311 (6th Cir. 1981) (clarifying that company terminating

taking over the plan's assets and liabilities. So, the PBGC first uses whatever funds the employer has to satisfy pension obligations and then adds its own funds to ensure payment of a percentage of remaining "nonforfeitable" benefits up to a statutory limit.[61]

In some circumstances, it is the employer that initiates the distress termination. In such voluntary situations, the employer must give advance notice to the plan participants of the plan termination and must file appropriate documents with the PBGC. To qualify for a voluntary distress termination, the employer must show one of the following events has occurred: (1) insolvency or bankruptcy, (2) inability to pay debts when due and still continue in business, or (3) pension costs have become unreasonably burdensome as a result of the decline in the employer's workforce.[62]

Even if the employer does not wish to engage in a voluntary distress termination, such plans may be involuntarily terminated by the PBGC if additional long-terms losses may be incurred by the PBGC without such a termination.[63] The Supreme Court case of *PBGC v. LTV Corp.*,[64] demonstrates an initial involuntary termination, followed by a decision by the PBGC to restore the plan to its pre-termination status. In *LTV*, the company and its union had agreed to make up the difference between what the PBGC was covering as a result of an involuntary termination of the plan and what employees were owed under the plan. The PBGC has a policy against such "follow-on" plans because it considers these plans to be abusing the insurance program, resulting in the PBGC subsidizing an employer's on-going pension program. In these circumstances, the Court permitted the PBGC to restore the plan to its pre-termination status because the PBGC had determined that financial factors had changed significantly enough such that the restoration of the plan to the employer's control was appropriate.

[2] Standard Terminations with Sufficient Assets

An employer can also voluntarily terminate a pension if it has sufficient assets to pay off all outstanding pension liabilities. Under such a scenario, similar notices must be given to both plan participants and to the PBGC, but the PBGC need not provide any insurance coverage. Nevertheless, the question remains: who should receive the surplus plan assets once pension obligations have been satisfied? Once benefit liabilities are met, any such surplus may revert back to the employer if the

---

with insufficient assets is responsible in first instance for paying pension obligations and may not limit its liability through plan provisions to current amount of funds in plan).

[61] For example, for a plan terminating in 2008, the maximum benefit guarantee is $4,312.50 per month, or $51,750 per year, for a straight-life annuity that PBGC begins paying at age 65. *See PBGC's Guarantee Limits — An Update*, Pension Benefit Guaranty Corporation (Sept. 2008), *available at* http://www.pbgc.gov/docs/guaranteelimits.pdf.

"Nonforfeitable" benefits in this context means those benefits to which participants have earned entitlement under the plan as of the date of plan termination.

[62] ERISA § 4041(c).

[63] *Id.* § 4042 (providing PBGC authority to involuntarily terminate a plan if the "possible long-run loss of the [PBGC] with respect to the plan may reasonably be expected to increase unreasonably if the plan is not terminated.").

[64] 496 U.S. 633 (1990).

plan document provides for such a reversion.[65] But in order not to give employers incentive to cash in on their employee pension plans, the IRS places a fifty percent excise tax on such surplus plan asset reversions.

§ 14.04 HEALTH AND WELFARE PLANS

[A] Introduction

The second half of the ERISA universe consists of employee welfare benefit plans, with health plans (providing medical, surgical, or hospital benefits) being the most frequently litigated and discussed type of welfare plan.[66] As originally enacted, Title I of ERISA did not contain a single substantive provision relating to welfare plans. Only the reporting and disclosure rules, fiduciary obligations, enforcement, and preemption provisions applied to such plans.[67] Only later were substantive group health plan provisions added to ERISA in the form of COBRA, HIPAA, and most recently, PPACA. Among other things, these provisions afford employees protection against health insurance coverage loss when they move between jobs and provide many employees minimum essential health benefits under employer-provided health insurance plans. Because there is relatively little regulation of employee welfare plans, employers still have great discretion in determining eligibility criteria and what benefits to offer under such plans.

Health care plans are structured in a number of different ways and there are many different varieties. The primary characteristic that differentiates them is the number of managed care elements. Managed care elements include both employer financial control over the plan, as well as the degree of control over patient choices for doctors and services. Fee-for-service indemnity plans have no managed care elements, preferred-provider organizations (PPOs) have a moderate amount of these elements, and health maintenance organizations (HMOs) have the greatest amount of managed care elements.[68]

[B] Insured vs. Self-Insured Health Plans

In addition to how health plans are structured from a cost control or patient choice perspective, employer-provided health care plans are divided into two categories based on how the employer funds the health plan. Insured health plans

---

[65] ERISA § 4044(d). In such instances, there is no breach of fiduciary duty because the employer is free to terminate a plan under the settlor-function doctrine. *See* Dist. 65, UAW v. Harper & Row, Publishers, Inc., 576 F. Supp. 1468 (S.D.N.Y. 1983).

[66] Other types of welfare plans under ERISA § 3(1) include: accidental death plans, disability income plans (short-term and long-term), qualified long term care plans, group life insurance plans, educational assistance plans, dependent care assistance plans, severance pay plans (part of an on-going administrative scheme), and sick leave and vacation plans (not paid out of the general assets of the employer as a payroll practice).

[67] These provisions, which apply to both pension and welfare benefit plans, are discussed *infra* § 14.05.

[68] Health care plans come in a tremendous variety of types even within a given category, such as HMOs. A further discussion of different type of health plan models is beyond the scope of this chapter.

operate through insurance policies purchased from insurance companies by employers. Self-insured health plans, on the other hand, do not purchase insurance policies and self-fund to satisfy obligations to health plan participants.

The distinction between insured and self-insured plans becomes very important in the preemption context when deciding whether state health insurance laws apply to certain health plans. Although preemption, and the savings and deemer clauses, will be discussed in greater detail below,[69] the general point is that insured plans are subject to state insurance laws, such as mandated benefit laws, which regulate how the plan must be structured. Self-insured plans, on the other hand, are not subject to state insurance laws, and employer sponsors therefore have much more discretion in determining how to set up such health plans.

Because of the momentous significance of being characterized as self-insured for ERISA preemption purposes, there has been a dramatic increase in the number of self-insured plans in the United States. Although larger companies, with their greater revenue streams, are able to manage the risk of catastrophic health care claims, small employers are still able to set up self-insured plans by purchasing stop-loss insurance to protect against such risks. Stop-loss insurance policies provide that the insurer will step in and pay claims once such claims exceed a specified dollar amount. The point at which stop-loss insurance kicks in is called the attachment point. The lower the attachment point, the more that these self-insured plans start to resemble insured health plans. Nevertheless, the courts have made clear that employers who employ such stop-loss insurance, even with very low attachment points, are still considered to be self-insured and not subject to state insurance regulation.[70]

[C] Health Savings Accounts and High-Deductible Health Plans

Since 2004, employees have been permitted to set up individual, tax-exempt accounts, called health savings accounts (HSAs), to help pay off qualified health care expenses.[71] These HSAs have also been referred to as defined contribution health care plans because plan funds may be invested in various financial instruments tax-free. To take advantage of the tax advantages of paying for qualified medical expenses for beneficiaries using HSA funds, however, an employee must subscribe to a high-deductible health plan (HDHP), under which employees must pay a larger amount of out-of-pocket expenses before insurance coverage kicks in. Although HSAs themselves are not employee benefit plans subject to ERISA regulation (even when employers choose to contribute to these accounts), HDHPs are ERISA plans.[72]

---

[69] *See infra* § 14.05[B].

[70] *See* Am. Med. Sec., Inc. v. Bartlett, 111 F.3d 358 (4th Cir. 1997) (holding that ERISA preempts Maryland state law setting minimum attachment points because such plans are still self-insured plans subject to the deemer clause).

[71] *See* Medicare Prescription Drug Improvement and Modernization Act of 2003, Pub. L. No. 108-173, § 1201, 117 Stat. 2066 (2003).

[72] *See* Dep't of Labor, Field Assistance Bull. No. 2004-1 (2004).

Supporters of the HSA/HDHP model hope that consumers will become more aware of what health care costs and will not engage in wasteful health care spending for unnecessary medical procedures and services. Critics of these consumer-driven models believe that employees will just respond by putting off health care until conditions require more expensive treatment. They also worry about adverse selection: that healthy employees will flock to HSA/HDHP plans, leaving the traditional plans with sicker employees and much higher premium payments. In any event, such arrangements appear to becoming a permanent part of the employee health care landscape.

[D] Retiree Health Care Issues

Another controversial area in the health plan context involves the provision of retiree health benefits. Many employers over the years had promised to completely or partially subsidize their employees' health care throughout retirement. These promises have ended up costing companies a lot more money than originally contemplated and companies have been seeking to back out of these arrangements for quite some time now.

With regard to modifying or terminating health plan benefits, the general rule, under the settlor-function doctrine, is that employers are free to make changes to these plans as long as they did not use vesting or promissory language in plan documents when referencing such benefits.[73] Many employers, however, did use vesting language, promising retirees health care benefits "for life." Under such circumstances, courts may hold that employers have vested their retirees in their health benefits, meaning the employees cannot change the plans for retirees without incurring legal liability.

The issue becomes more complicated when employers have some documents that contain promissory language with regard to retiree health benefits, but also have documents which contain reservation of rights clauses that permit them to modify or terminate such plans at will. For instance, in *Sprague v. General Motors Corp.*,[74] General Motors had many different plan documents for early retirees and general retirees explaining retiree health benefits. Some of these documents offered lifetime benefits and some contained language giving General Motors the ability to amend the plans at any time. The court first determined that it was appropriate to focus on the language of the summary plan description (SPD) when there was a conflict between the SPD and actual plan document. Although the SPD had both lifetime benefit language and right-to-amend language, the court concluded that such language should be understood to mean that retirees have lifetime benefits only if the company decided not to change the plan.[75]

---

[73] The presumption is different in the union context where such retiree health benefit promises are part of collective bargaining agreements. In such cases, some courts consider retiree health benefits to be status benefits that survive the expiration of the collective bargaining agreement, unless there is contrary evidence to suggest that the parties agreed to different terms with regard to these benefits. *See* UAW v. Yard-Man, 716 F.2d 1476 (6th Cir. 1983).

[74] 133 F.3d 388 (6th Cir. 1998) (en banc).

[75] Of course, this is not the only way to interpret such conflicting plan language. The dissent vehemently argued that where there is such ambiguity in the SPD, other extrinsic evidence should be

Consequently, the retirees were not considered vested in these retiree health benefits and General Motors could modify the terms of the plan without violating the retiree's rights under any theory of law.[76]

[E]   COBRA and Continuation of Health Coverage

As stated previously, ERISA historically did not supply the same amount of substantive regulation for welfare plans as it did for pension plans (this dynamic can be seen to be shifting with the enactment of PPACA). More recently, however, substantive rights have been provided for group health care plan participants in the continuation of health care coverage context under the Consolidated Omnibus Reconciliation Act of 1985 (COBRA), now codified in Part 6 of Title I of ERISA. These additional protections were added to help employees bridge the gap in health insurance coverage when moving between jobs or when they or their dependents otherwise became ineligible for coverage under an employer's health plan.

Under COBRA, employers with twenty or more employees who maintain group health plans, whether insured or self-insured, must provide qualified beneficiaries the option to continue their health care coverage under the employer's plan for a specified period time after a qualifying event. The length of continuation coverage, and the identity of the qualified beneficiaries, depends on the type of qualifying event. For instance, if the qualifying event is any form of termination from employment, and that termination is not for engaging in "gross misconduct," the employee, spouse, and dependent children are entitled to purchase continuation coverage for up to 18 months.[77] Other qualifying events occur when there is a death of the employee, divorce or legal separation of employee, the covered employee becomes eligible for Medicare, or a dependent child ceases to be eligible for coverage under the terms of the plan. In these instances, the spouse and/or dependent child can receive COBRA continuation coverage for up to thirty-six months.

The employee must pay for the cost of health insurance, up to one-hundred percent of the applicable premium, plus up to a two-percent administrative fee. COBRA can therefore be expensive for former employees because they no longer are able to take advantage of the subsidized amount of the premium paid by the employer (which in some cases can be the entire premium) when they were still

---

consulted to determine if the retirees vested in their retiree health benefits. *See id.* at 408 (Boyce, J., dissenting).

[76] The court found that the retirees could not proceed on an equitable estoppel theory or breach of fiduciary claim because it was not reasonable to rely to their detriment on the lifetime benefit language when reservation of rights language existed in the same document. *See id.* at 404-06. *But see* James v. Pirelli Armstrong Tire Corp., 305 F.3d 439 (6th Cir. 2002) (finding employer breached its fiduciary duty to former employees in retiree health context by providing inaccurate information about future benefits under the plan).

[77] More complicated continuation coverage issues arise under COBRA when a worker is also covered by a spouse's health insurance plan. However, in *Geissal v. Moore Medical Corp.*, 524 U.S. 74 (1998), the Supreme Court held that an employer may not deny continuation coverage to a qualified beneficiary because he or she is covered under another health plan at the time he or she seeks coverage under COBRA.

employees. However, COBRA coverage usually is much less expensive than insurance the employee would be able to purchase on his or her own.

COBRA provides specific timetables regarding when plan participants must be notified about their COBRA rights and by what date they must elect COBRA coverage. For instance, a qualified beneficiary must elect continuation coverage within sixty days of the qualifying event or notice of the qualifying event, whichever is later.[78] Violations of COBRA subject employers to an excise tax penalty, currently set at $110 per day per qualified beneficiary. COBRA may be also enforced by plan participants under either a Section 502(a)(1)(A) action for a civil penalty or a Section 502(a)(3) action for appropriate equitable relief. Equitable relief for a typical COBRA claim would require an employer to cover an employee's medical expenses that were not covered by the health insurance plan because the former employee did not receive timely notice of his or her COBRA rights from the employer.

[F]　Health Insurance Portability and Accountability Act (HIPAA)

Congress enacted additional substantive rights for health plan participants in the form of the Health Insurance Portability and Accountability Act of 1996 ("HIPAA")[79] to further combat health care job-lock and address the need for nationwide portability of health care coverage.[80] Rather than placing the burden on the former employer to provide health insurance for employees in transition periods between jobs as COBRA does, HIPAA is primarily directed at the new employer. In this regard, HIPAA addresses concerns relating to the portability of health insurance coverage and pre-existing conditions exclusions, non-discrimination in the provision of health insurance, and the confidentiality of individuals' health information.[81] HIPAA preempts any inconsistent state law standards involving these issues, but does permit states to provide more generous benefits to employees.

---

[78]　ERISA § 606(a).

[79]　Pub. L. No. 104-191, 110 Stat. 1936 (1996).

[80]　In addition to COBRA and HIPAA protections, qualified medical child support orders (QMCSOs), created under the Omnibus Reconciliation Act of 1993 (OBRA), provide protection for dependent children in the health plan context, requiring employers to enroll dependent children in their parents' health care plans when presented with a valid order.

[81]　The HIPAA privacy regulations regulate how covered entities may use and disclose individual protected health information. See General Administrative Requirements, General Provisions, 45 C.F.R. §§ 160.101-160.104; Security and Privacy, Privacy of Individually Identifiable Health Information, 45 C.F.R. §§ 164.501-164.534. A more detailed discussion of the HIPAA Privacy Regulations does not directly involve employee benefits law under ERISA and, therefore, are beyond the scope of this chapter. For an in depth discussion of these topics, see generally Diane Kutzko et al., *HIPAA in Real Time: Practical Implications of the Federal Privacy Rule*, 51 DRAKE L. REV. 403 (2003); Peter A. Winn, *Confidentiality in Cyberspace: The HIPAA Privacy Rules and the Common Law*, 33 RUTGERS L.J. 617 (2002).

The portability provisions of HIPAA address access to plan benefits when moving between employers.[82] Under these provisions, it used to be that as long as an employee had prior health care coverage of 12 months, without a significant break in coverage, and enrolled in the new employer's health plan as soon as possible, the employer could not subject the employee to a preexisting condition coverage exclusion. Effective January 1, 2014, PPACA eliminates all preexisting condition coverage exclusions,[83] and so this part of HIPAA will soon become obsolete.

Under the non-discrimination provisions, a health plan may not charge a plan participant a higher premium or limit his or her eligibility for health benefits under the plan because of health-status related factors.[84] As discussed previously in Chapters 7 and 9, the Genetic Information Nondiscrimination Act ("GINA"),[85] which protects against genetic-based discrimination in employment and in the provisions of health insurance, now also adds to these types of employee protections. Such health-status related factors include medical conditions, claims experience, medical history, genetic information, and evidence of insurability. Nevertheless, these non-discrimination provisions do not prohibit employers from providing different benefits and plan features to different groups of employees and they do not regulate the premium amount employers may charge to employees, as long as such plan features apply equally to all similarly situated plan participants.

Like COBRA, HIPAA may be enforced through an excise tax penalty by the IRS or through private civil actions for appropriate equitable relief under Section 502(a)(3).

[G] Patient Protection and Affordable Care Act of 2010 (PPACA)

The enactment of the Patient Protection and Affordable Care Act of 2010 (PPACA)[86], and the recent finding by the U.S. Supreme Court that it is largely constitutional,[87] means that ERISA health plans must now also consider the impact of many PPACA provisions, including those concerning "grandfathered plans," "minimum essential benefits," and "health benefit exchanges." Effective January 1, 2014, PPACA will operate on a "play-or-pay system," meaning that many employers must either provide their employees a qualified health benefit plan or face a penalty to help their employees receive health benefits on soon-to-be-established health benefit exchanges (the penalty will be $2,000 per employee on employers with more than 50 employees who do not offer health insurance to their full-time workers).[88] Moreover, large employers, those with more than 200

---

[82] ERISA § 701.

[83] 42 U.S.C. § 300gg-2 (prohibiting preexisting condition exclusions).

[84] *Id.* § 702.

[85] Pub. L. No. 110-233 (2008).

[86] Pub. L. No. 111-148, 124 Stat. 119 (2010), as amended by the Health Care and Education Reconciliation Act of 2010, Pub. L. No. 111-152, 124 Stat. 1029 (2010).

[87] *See* National Federation of Independent Businesses v. Sebelius, 132 S. Ct. 2566 (2012).

[88] PPACA also requires that all individuals not covered by an employer-sponsored health plan or

employees, will be required to automatically enroll employees into health insurance plans offered by the employer (though employees may opt out of coverage).

As an initial matter, whether an employer-provided health plan is subject to all, or only some, of the new health insurance reforms under PPACA depends on whether the plan is considered to be a "grandfathered plan." A grandfathered plan is a group health plan that was in effect upon enactment of PPACA in March 2010.[89] These "grandfathered" plans are exempt from many, but not all, of the individual and group healthcare market reforms that are scheduled to be implemented in 2014. For instance, grandfathered plans must still comply with provisions relating to pre-existing health condition exclusions and the extension of dependent coverage to age 26. This issue and others like it highlight the need for employer-provided health plans to be vigilant about plan changes that could potentially jeopardize their grandfathered status.

As far as minimum coverage, the essential health benefits package offered by qualified health benefit plans under PPACA must include specific categories of benefits, meet certain cost-sharing standards, and provide certain levels of coverage. Beginning in 2014, minimum items and services include: (1) ambulatory patient services, (2) emergency services, (3) hospitalization, (4) maternity and newborn care, (5) mental health and substance abuse disorder services, (6) prescription drugs, (7) rehabilitative services and devices, (8) laboratory services, (9) preventive and wellness services, and (10) pediatric services (including oral and vision care).[90] Additionally, health insurance plans may no longer establish annual spending caps.

Significantly, self-insured health plans are not considered covered "health plans," and thus do not appear to have to comply with the requirements of the essential health benefits package.[91] As a result, additional incentives now seem to exist for companies to self-insure their health plans rather than purchasing health insurance coverage from a third party.

Finally, effective in 2014, state-based American Health Benefit Exchanges and Small Business Health Options Program (SHOP) Exchanges will be established.[92] Through these programs, individuals and small businesses with up to 100 employees can purchase qualified health coverage.[93] These exchanges will be administered by a governmental agency or a non-profit organization.[94] Although health benefit exchanges do not directly impact employer-provided health benefit

---

other health insurance program (like Medicare or Medicaid), have health insurance or pay a penalty.

[89] Patient Protection and Affordable Care Act (PPACA), § 1251(a)(1), Pub. L. No. 111-148, 124 Stat. 119 (2010).

[90] PPACA § 1302(a), (b)(1). These benefits are supposed to be consistent with the scope of benefits provided under a "typical" employer-sponsored plan. *Id.* § 1302(b)(2). Plans may, of course, provide more than the minimum essential benefit. *Id.* § 1302(b)(5).

[91] PPACA § 1301(b)(1)(B), § 2707. The essential health benefit requirements of section 1302 specifically do not apply to self-insured plans under Section 2707.

[92] PPACA § 1311(b).

[93] *Id.* § 1311(b)(1)(C).

[94] PPACA § 1311(d).

plans, their presence might cause smaller employers to forgo providing health coverage to their employees, suffer a penalty, and let their employees get their health coverage through these exchanges.

In all, PPACA will likely have many divergent effects upon employer-provided health benefit plans, both predictable and unpredictable. Significant issues these plans must consider include: how to maintain grandfathered plan status; whether to become self-funded to retain more discretion over health benefits offered to members; and whether to eliminate health coverage altogether, pay a penalty, and have employees instead join health benefit exchanges.

§ 14.05 COMMON ISSUES TO RETIREMENT AND WELFARE PLANS

Although a number of ERISA provisions apply only to either pension benefit plans or welfare benefit plans, there are three significant areas of the law that apply to all covered ERISA plans: fiduciary duties, preemption, and civil enforcement.

[A] Fiduciary Duties Under ERISA

ERISA places fiduciary duties on those who use their discretion to administer and manage employee benefit plans. The purpose of the fiduciary provisions is to ensure that persons with control over plan assets work in the sole interest of plan participants and beneficiaries and do not permit other considerations to sway their judgment concerning the operation of the employee benefit plan.

While ERISA fiduciaries are subject to strict fiduciary and co-fiduciary duties and must avoid certain prohibited transactions involving plan assets, non-fiduciaries are subject to little regulation under ERISA. It is therefore essential to determine who is an ERISA fiduciary.

[1] The Definition of an ERISA Fiduciary

ERISA sets out the fiduciary definition under Section 3(21)(A). Under this section, there are three main categories of ERISA fiduciaries: (1) persons who have discretionary authority over administration and management of the plan; (2) persons who have any authority over the assets of the plan (in other words, they somehow "touch the money"); and (3) persons who render investment advice to the plan for compensation.[95] Fiduciary status is based on functions actually performed, not on the title held by the person, so a person can be a fiduciary even if he or she did not know he or she was a fiduciary or intended to be a fiduciary. Additionally, an individual is only a fiduciary "to the extent" he or she performs fiduciary functions, meaning that there are both limited fiduciaries and all-purpose fiduciaries.

---

[95] With regard to investment advice provided in the 401(k) context, the Pension Protection Act of 2006 provides new safe harbors, which permit investment advice to be given, under limited circumstances, without causing the service provider to violate the prohibited transaction rules. This new safe harbor will also prevent turning employers into fiduciaries for hiring investment advisers who give potentially bad investment advice to individual participants. *See* PPA § 601.

There are four well-recognized exceptions to fiduciary status: (1) the ministerial functions exception applies to those who only assist in plan management and administration but do not engage in discretionary activities; (2) the professional services exception applies to any individual who provides professional services to the plan (e.g., accountants, lawyers, financial service companies); (3) the investment education exception applies to make clear that fiduciary status only applies when an individual provides investment advice for compensation, not just investment education; and (4) the settlor function exemption, mentioned previously, provides that employers are not fiduciaries when they merely establish, modify, or terminate an employee benefit plan. With regard to the professional services exception, attorneys for an employee benefit plan are not considered fiduciaries unless they engage in discretionary activities beyond their normal professional services. Finally, through case law, the Supreme Court in *Pegram v. Herdrich*[96] has also made clear that health maintenance organizations (HMOs) are not fiduciaries under ERISA when they engage in mixed eligibility/treatment decisions through their physicians.[97]

As discussed in the previous section, under the settlor function doctrine, employers are not fiduciaries unless they exercise some discretionary authority over the administration or management of employee benefit plans. Some employers purposefully decide to undertake discretionary activities with regard to their benefit plans by appointing their own officers or employees to act as plan administrators with day-to-day operational duties.[98] Such dual-role fiduciary situations, though prohibited under the common law of trusts, are expressly permitted under Section 408(c)(3) of ERISA. In dual-role fiduciary situations, an employer wears both a settlor and fiduciary hat, and the trick is to determine in which role the employer is acting when making decisions with regard to an employee benefit plan. Given the significant consequences of finding an employer to be a fiduciary, much litigation has revolved around this issue.[99]

---

[96] 530 U.S. 211 (2000).

[97] The distinction between eligibility decisions and treatment decisions made by HMOs is also an important one for purposes of ERISA preemption, as challenges characterized as eligibility decisions are completely preempted by ERISA § 502(a)(1)(B), whereas treatment decisions are not. For further discussion of these preemption and civil enforcement issues, see *infra* §§ 14.05[B], 14.05[C].

[98] The chief reasons why employers choose to adopt dual-role fiduciary models is to make plan administration less costly through use of their own personnel rather than having to hire a third party administrator. However, these dual-role fiduciary situations also raise complex ethical issues for attorneys who may purposefully or inadvertently represent these fiduciaries in both their corporate and employee benefit plan capacities. *See generally* Paul M. Secunda, *Inherent Attorney Conflicts of Interest Under ERISA: Using the Model Rules of Professional Conduct to Discourage Joint Representation of Dual Role Fiduciaries*, 39 J. Marshall L. Rev. 721 (2006).

[99] The classic case in the dual-role fiduciary context is *Varity Corp. v. Howe*, 516 U.S. 489 (1996), in which the dual-role employer was found to have acted in a fiduciary capacity when its officials gave misleading and inaccurate plan advice to a group of employees.

[2] Responsibilities of ERISA Fiduciaries

[a] Basic Fiduciary Duties

Section 404 of ERISA sets out four basic fiduciary duties for ERISA fiduciaries: (1) the duty of loyalty (also known as the exclusive benefit rule), (2) the duty of care or prudence, (3) the duty of prudent diversification of plan assets, and (4) the duty to follow plan terms unless contrary to ERISA.

The duty of loyalty requires that the fiduciary act in the sole interest of plan participants and for the exclusive purpose of providing benefits and defraying reasonable costs of administration.[100] The duty of care requires that a fiduciary act with the same care that a prudent fiduciary would under similar circumstances.[101] The prudent diversification standard, which applies mainly to defined benefit plans, requires plans to diversify their plan investments consistent with modern portfolio theory.[102] Finally, the duty to follow plan terms mostly comes into play when a limited fiduciary or directed trustee believes it cannot follow directions given to it without violating ERISA.[103]

The seminal case of *Donovan v. Bierwirth*[104] provides a good discussion of both the duty of loyalty and the duty of care. Regarding the duty of loyalty, the court described this standard as requiring the fiduciary to act with an "eye single" to the best interests of the plan participants. Regarding the duty of care, the court examined the steps a prudent fiduciary should take before committing plan funds for corporate purposes. More specifically, *Donovan* involved a hostile takeover bid in a situation where the target company officers were dual-role fiduciaries in that they served as both corporate officers and ERISA fiduciaries of the company's retirement plan. The corporate officers, in their ERISA fiduciary capacity, had the plan buy company stock at inflated prices to help fight off the takeover bid. Because the court concluded that the officers had placed the interests of the company over the interests of the participants in the retirement plan, it found a breach of fiduciary duty under ERISA.

Donovan points out the difficult circumstances that company officers place themselves in when they undertake to act as dual-role fiduciaries. In such situations, there are inherent conflicts of interest between their fiduciary duties to shareholders as corporate officers and their fiduciary duties to their employee

---

[100] ERISA § 404(a)(1)(A).

[101] *Id.* § 404(a)(1)(B). The duty of care is very much like the reasonable person standard under tort law. It focuses not on results, but on the process the fiduciary uses in making his or her decision.

[102] *Id.* § 404(a)(1)(C). Special rules apply to defined contribution plans. These rules provide that the holding of qualified employer securities is exempt from the diversification requirement, *see id.* § 404(a)(2), and that plan fiduciaries are not liable for individual investment decisions made by participants with regard to their individual accounts. *Id.* § 404(c)(1). Nevertheless, even in the defined contribution context, plan fiduciaries must exercise discretion is selecting and monitoring plan investment options, and ensure that such plan options do not charge unreasonable investment fees.

[103] *Id.* § 404(a)(1)(D). In these directed trustee situations, the trustee's fiduciary obligations are limited to determining whether the directions are proper and not contrary to the terms of the plan. *Id.* § 403(a)(1).

[104] 680 F.2d 263 (2d Cir. 1982).

benefit plan participants as ERISA fiduciaries.[105] Possible ways to proceed when these inherent conflicts arise include soliciting the advice of independent counsel or having the corporate officers resign as ERISA fiduciaries.

[b]   Co-Fiduciary Liability and Prohibited Transactions

Apart from the general fiduciary duties in Section 404, ERISA provides for additional fiduciary responsibilities under the co-fiduciary and prohibited transaction provisions. Section 405 provides for co-fiduciary liability for fiduciaries in three scenarios: (1) when the fiduciary knowingly conceals another fiduciary's breach, (2) when the fiduciary enables another fiduciary to commit a breach, and (3) when the fiduciary has knowledge of another fiduciary's breach and fails to take reasonable remedial action.[106] When a co-fiduciary breach occurs, the breaching co-fiduciaries are jointly and severally liable.

Prohibited transactions, on the other hand, prohibit fiduciaries and others closely affiliated with the plan, so-called "parties in interest," from engaging in transactions involving plan assets. Unlike the breach of fiduciary provisions, which must be applied to the circumstances of a given case, prohibited transaction rules "make illegal *per se* the types of transactions that experience ha[s] shown to entail a high potential for abuse."[107] Although this subsection does not go into great detail regarding these complex rules, Section 406 broadly restricts two types of prohibited transactions: (1) transactions that involve parties in interest under Section 406(a), and (2) transactions that involve plan fiduciaries under Section 406(b).[108] Each section creates categories of transactions involving plan assets that are illegal per se based on the identities of the parties alone, though the fiduciary restrictions are more strictly construed and prevent any form of self-dealing, conflict of interest, or kickback between the fiduciary and the plan.[109] Breaches of the prohibited transaction rules subject the breaching fiduciary to a tax penalty or to breach of fiduciary duty claims under Sections 502(a)(2) or 502(a)(3).

[3]   Duty to Inform Cases

The Supreme Court in *Varity Corp. v. Howe*[110] interpreted the duty of care and the duty of loyalty as requiring a fiduciary to inform plan participants of relevant information beyond the statutory reporting and disclosure requirements. Breaches

---

[105] Such conflicts also arise when ERISA fiduciaries seek to engage in "social investing" and invest in companies that promote certain social goals. This type of investment strategy may not always be in the best financial interest of plan participants and beneficiaries and therefore, run directly counter to the fiduciary provisions of ERISA.

[106] ERISA § 405(a). An exception to co-fiduciary liability applies if specific fiduciary duties have been previously allocated to different fiduciaries in a plan document. *Id.* § 405(c).

[107] Donovan v. Cunningham, 716 F.2d 1455, 1464-65 (5th Cir. 1983).

[108] Because fiduciaries are also parties in interest under ERISA, both ERISA Sections 406(a) and 406(b) apply to them.

[109] Additionally, under Section 408, there are both statutory and administrative exemptions to the prohibited transaction rules. However, the statutory exemptions do not apply to fiduciary prohibited transactions. *See* DOL Reg. §§ 2550.408b-2(a), (e).

[110] 516 U.S. 489 (1996).

of the duty to inform tend to arise in two contexts: early retirement cases and participant communication cases. Plaintiffs in these cases are able to bring claims for individual relief under Section 502(a)(3) because "appropriate" relief is not available under other sections of ERISA.[111]

[a]   Early Retirement Plan Cases

In the early retirement plan context, a company usually is reducing its workforce and wishes to induce workers to terminate their employment voluntarily through early retirement incentive packages. An employee wishing to participate in an enhanced retirement plan must indicate his or her willingness to do so within a defined window of time. If not enough employees voluntarily terminate during the first window of opportunity, employers often open additional windows with enhanced benefits. Employers run into fiduciary issues in these cases when employees who retired with less generous benefits claim that the company should have disclosed to them, consistent with acting in the employees' best interests, that more favorable benefits were under consideration.

In determining whether the employer in these scenarios has an obligation to inform employees about this potential second round of enhanced benefits, most courts base their decision on whether the more generous benefits were under "serious consideration" when the employee accepted the less-generous early retirement package.[112] The serious-consideration condition is satisfied when there is a: "(1) a specific proposal (2) [ ] being discussed for the purposes of implementation (3) by senior management with the authority to implement the change."[113] In *Beach v. Commonwealth Edison Co.*,[114] however, the Seventh Circuit held that the company did not breach its fiduciary obligations to an employee who retired early because the early retirement plan was not an amendment to the existing pension plan and did not come into existence until after the employee's retirement. Consequently, the court held the employer did not owe the employee any fiduciary duty concerning the early retirement benefits under this new plan.[115]

---

[111] *Id.* at 514. There is no liability under ERISA, however, if non-fiduciaries mislead the plaintiff. *See* Mertens v. Hewitt Assocs., 508 U.S. 248 (1993).

[112] Hockett v. Sun Co., 109 F.3d 1515 (10th Cir. 1997). Nevertheless, other courts have analyzed these cases under a more flexible materiality test under which serious consideration is but one factor. Under this materiality test, the issue is whether the misrepresentations or misleading information would induce a reasonable person to rely on those representations in making an informed decision about when to retire. *See* Ballone v. Eastman Kodak Co., 109 F.3d 118 (2d Cir. 1997).

[113] Fischer v. Philadelphia Elec. Co., 96 F.3d 1533, 1539 (3d Cir. 1996).

[114] 382 F.3d 656 (7th Cir. 2004).

[115] The dissent vehemently disagreed with this distinction between plan amendments and new plans, and would have found the employer to have a fiduciary duty because there was a nexus between the new benefits offered and the already-existing pension and welfare plans. *See id.* at 661 (Ripple, J., dissenting).

[b] Participant Communication Cases

Unlike early retirement cases, participant communication cases concern the daily, mundane exchange of information that occurs between plan fiduciaries and plan participants in matters such as clarifying ambiguous SPD language or helping participants comply with plan claim procedures. In these cases, plan participants claim that they relied on inaccurate, incomplete, misleading, or false information detrimentally provided to them by the plan fiduciary. Courts rule in favor of plaintiffs in participant communication cases by finding that plan fiduciaries either affirmatively misled plan participants in their communications with them,[116] or failed to communicate with participants when silence itself might be misleading.[117]

A classic and egregious participation communication case is the Supreme Court case of *Varity Corp. v. Howe*.[118] In *Varity*, the employer induced a large number of employees to shift from their current division to a new subsidiary, all the while providing misleading information about the future of their health benefits with the newly formed subsidiary. In fact, the newly formed subsidiary was doomed to failure from the first moment of its existence, and when the subsidiary did inevitably sink into receivership, the employees of the subsidiary not only lost their jobs, but also their health benefits. The Court concluded that company officials, acting in their fiduciary capacity, purposefully misled these employees through inaccurate statements about their health benefits with the new subsidiary. These Varity officials were under an obligation to inform the employees of the true state of affairs and by not doing so, they breached their fiduciaries duties to act with loyalty and care toward the plan participants.

[B] ERISA Preemption

Section 514 is ERISA's broadly-worded preemption provision that permits ERISA to supersede most state law which "relates to" employee benefit plans.[119] However, a state law may nevertheless be saved from ERISA preemption if it regulates insurance under the savings clause.[120] Finally, even if the state law regulates insurance, it may still be preempted under the deemer clause if it is being applied to a self-insured health plan.[121]

Prior to applying ERISA preemption principles, however, the question must be first asked if the employee benefit arrangement being impacted by the state law is a "plan" for purposes of ERISA. In this regard, plans must meet the *Dillingham/Fort Halifax* factors discussed in § 14.02[B] and must not be excluded from coverage under ERISA under Section 4(b) (e.g., government plans, church

---

[116] *See, e.g.*, Krohn v. Huron Mem. Hosp., 173 F.3d 542, 547-48 (6th Cir. 1999); Eddy v. Colonial Life Ins. Co., 919 F.2d 747, 750-51 (D.C. Cir. 1990).

[117] *See, e.g.*, Harte v. Bethlehem Steel Corp., 214 F.3d 446, 452 (3d Cir. 2000).

[118] 516 U.S. 489 (1996).

[119] ERISA § 514(a). State laws are defined expansively to include "all laws, decisions, rules, regulations or other State action having the effect of law, of any State." *Id.* § 514(c)(1).

[120] *Id.* § 514(b)(2)(A). This clause also saves laws regulating banking and securities, but these other types of law do not as frequently arise in employment law cases as insurance laws.

[121] *Id.* § 514(b)(2)(B).

plans, etc.). Finally, if the law in question relating to an employee benefit plan is either a state criminal law or another federal law, ERISA preemption does not apply.[122]

[1] Section 514 "Relates To" Language

Because the "relate to" language of Section 514 potentially has no meaningful limit, the Supreme Court has struggled mightily to bring some coherence to this provision. The Court's attempts can be broadly broken down into the early preemption cases and the modern preemption cases.

The early preemption cases applied a field preemption approach under which ERISA was thought to completely occupy the field of employee benefits law. For instance, in *Shaw v. Delta Air Lines, Inc.*,[123] the Court interpreted the "related to" language to mean that a state law is preempted if it makes "reference to" or has a "connection with" an ERISA plan. Later cases explicated these two additional sub-categories of preempted state laws. In *Pilot Life Insurance Co. v. Dedeaux*,[124] the Court held that state tort and contracts claims alleging improper processing of a benefits claim were preempted by ERISA because the state law claims were "connected with" the administration of an ERISA plan.[125] In *Ingersoll-Rand Co. v. McClendon*,[126] the Court examined a state wrongful discharge action based on a claim that the employee had been fired to prevent him from attaining pension benefits. The Court this time relied on the other prong of the "relates to" test and found the state law claim preempted due to the claim making "reference to" an ERISA plan because the existence of, and participation in, the plan was an essential element of the action.[127]

Modern preemption cases appear to abandon the broader field preemption approach in favor of a conflict preemption approach under which a state law is preempted only to the extent that it is impossible to comply with both ERISA and state law or where the state law interferes with the purposes and objectives of ERISA. The seminal preemption case in the modern era is *New York State*

---

[122] *Id.* §§ 514(b)(4), 514(d). Because contrary federal laws are not preempted by ERISA, it is necessary to consider the interaction of employee benefit plans with such federal laws as Title VII of the Civil Rights Act of 1964, as amended by the Pregnancy Discrimination Act, 42 U.S.C. §§ 2000e-2000e-17, the Age Discrimination in Employment Act, 29 U.S.C. §§ 621-634, the Americans with Disabilities Act, 42 U.S.C. §§ 12101-12213, and the Family and Medical Leave Act, 29 U.S.C. §§ 2601-2654. A comprehensive discussion of these issues, however, is beyond the scope of this chapter.

[123] 463 U.S. 85 (1983).

[124] 481 U.S. 41 (1987). *Pilot Life* now stands for the broader proposition that state common law claims having a connection with an employee benefit plan are preempted. This is the principle that the court applied to deny the mother's wrongful death claim in *Corcoran v. United Health Care, Inc.*, 965 F.2d 1321 (5th Cir. 1992). *See infra* note 158 and accompanying text.

[125] The Court also found that the Mississippi common law bad faith insurance claim was not saved under the savings clause from preemption as a law that regulates insurance.

[126] 498 U.S. 133 (1990).

[127] The later Supreme Court case of *California Division of Labor Standards Enforcement v. Dillingham Construction*, 519 U.S. 316, 325 (1997), makes clear that the "reference to" preemption test may also be satisfied by establishing that the state law purports to regulate ERISA plans exclusively.

Conference of Blue Cross & Blue Shield Plans v. Travelers Insurance Co.[128] *Travelers* creates a rebuttable presumption against ERISA preemption if traditional areas of state law are involved, such as family or insurance law. To determine whether preemption should apply, *Travelers* directs that two questions should be addressed: (1) whether there are compelling policy reasons under ERISA to preempt state law; and (2) if there is, does the state law undermine these policy objectives? Such compelling policy reasons are undermined by state law in instances where the law mandates the type of benefits a plan must provide[129] and where the law interferes "too much" with the policy of national uniformity of plan administration.[130]

Although the scope of ERISA preemption would appear not to be as expansive in the modern era under the *Traveler*'s test, there are still many state laws that do not survive ERISA preemption. For instance, in the context of state regulation of health care plans and providers, there has been much activity recently as state legislatures try to force especially larger employers to pay for a greater percentage of their employees' health care costs as a way to limit the number of employees on Medicaid. Such "Fair Share Health Care" legislation was passed in Maryland as the so-called Wal-Mart Bill,[131] which would have required Wal-Mart to spend eight percent of its payroll on health insurance costs for its employees.[132] In *Retail Industry Leaders Association v. Fielder*,[133] a trade association representing Wal-Mart challenged the Maryland law on ERISA preemption grounds. The Fourth Circuit held that the Fair Share law interferes "too much" with the uniform administration and management of Wal-Mart's health plan and, therefore, is preempted as having a connection with an ERISA plan. On the other hand, the Ninth Circuit upheld a similar state law against an ERISA preemption challenge in *Golden Gate Restaurant Association v. City & County of San Francisco*,[134] distinguishing a San Francisco ordinance from the Maryland scheme in *Fielder* by

---

[128]   514 U.S. 645 (1995).

[129]   *See* Metro. Life Ins. Co. v. Massachusetts, 471 U.S. 724 (1985). *Metropolitan Life* is discussed in more detail *infra* § 14.05[B][2].

[130]   Egelhoff v. Egelhoff, 530 U.S. 1242 (2000). Examples of state laws that interfere too much with the policy of national uniformity of plan administration and, therefore, relate to an employee benefit plan, include Rush Prudential HMO, Inc. v. Moran, 536 U.S. 355 (2002) (state law providing independent review procedures for denied benefit claims); UNUM Life Ins. Co. of Am. v. Ward, 526 U.S. 358 (1999) (state law making employer agent of insurance company); and *Egelhoff*, 530 U.S. 1242 (state law regulating plan participant's beneficiary designation). On the other hand, state laws that only indirectly interfere with ERISA policy objectives, and are not preempted, include *Travelers*, 514 U.S. 645 (state law imposing surcharge on health care plan insurer or plan assets), *Dillingham Construction*, 519 U.S. 316 (state law regulating wages paid at public construction work projects); and DeBuono v. NYSA-ILA Med. & Clinical Servs. Fund, 520 U.S. 806 (1997) (state law imposing a tax on hospitals, most of which do not operate ERISA plans). It is important to note that even if there is too much interference with ERISA policy objectives, the law can still be saved from ERISA preemption under the savings clause.

[131]   Maryland Fair Share Health Care Fund Act, Mᴅ. Cᴏᴅᴇ Aɴɴ., Lᴀʙ. & Eᴍᴘʟ. §§ 8.5-101 to -107.

[132]   The bill applies to all employers with over ten-thousand Maryland employees, but the other three employers in Maryland who fall into that category already spend at least eight percent of payroll on health insurance costs.

[133]   475 F.3d 180 (4th Cir. 2007).

[134]   546 F.3d 639 (9th Cir. 2008).

holding that the ordinance provided meaningful alternatives that allows employers to preserve the structure of their existing ERISA plans. In any event, ERISA preemption remains an on-going challenge for states and municipalities that are seeking to experiment with different ways of providing efficient and affordable health care to their citizens.

[2] The Savings Clause

Just because a state law is initially preempted under the "relates to" test does not mean the law will not survive preemption as a result of the operation of ERISA's savings clause.[135] For example, in *Metropolitan Life Insurance Co. v. Massachusetts*,[136] Massachusetts required health insurers (that is, companies that provided insured health plans to employers) to provide certain mental health benefits in their insurance policies under a state-mandated benefit law. These insurers argued that such laws should be preempted by ERISA because they were related to an employee benefit law. Although the Court agreed that ERISA preemption initially applied to these state-mandated benefit laws, it noted that such state laws could be subsequently saved from preemption under the savings clause if these laws regulate insurance. The Court applied a three-factor test (now superseded by the *Miller* decision as discussed below) and determined that the Massachusetts mandated benefit law was one that regulated insurance for purposes of ERISA. As a result, the law was saved from preemption and the state was permitted to require health insurers to provide the minimum specified mental health benefits.[137]

The Supreme Court in 2003 replaced the prior three-part test from *Metropolitan Life* with the two-prong *Miller* test for determining whether a state law regulates insurance.[138] Under *Miller*, a state law regulates insurance if it is "specifically directed toward entities engaged in insurance" and "substantially affect[s] the risk pooling arrangement between the insurer and the insured."[139] This change would probably have made no difference in *Metropolitan Life*, but it might lead to different outcomes in future cases where a court applies the savings clause.

There is one last point to make in the savings clause area. The Supreme Court has recently held that even if a state law is saved from preemption in the insured health plan context, it may still be preempted based on conflict preemption principles. Under *Aetna Health, Inc. v. Davila*,[140] such a conflict preemption override would occur if the state law duplicates a claim under ERISA § 502(a) *and* the state law claims expands the remedies otherwise available under this section. Under this theory, the *Davila* court held that an alternative tort claim and remedy

---

[135] ERISA § 514(b)(2)(A).

[136] 471 U.S. 724 (1985).

[137] Similarly, the Court found more recently that an otherwise-preempted state-based notice prejudice rule, which acts to permit late filing of claims by participants, was saved as a state law regulating insurance. *See* UNUM Life Ins. Co. of Am. v. Ward, 526 U.S. 358 (1999).

[138] Ky. Assoc. of Health Plans, Inc. v. Miller, 538 U.S. 329 (2003) (finding that Kentucky "any willing provider" law was saved from preemption as a law that regulates insurance).

[139] *Id.* at 342. For purposes of the *Miller* test, an HMO is an entity engaged in insurance. *See* Rush Prudential HMO, Inc. v. Moran, 536 U.S. 355, 367 (2002).

[140] 542 U.S. 200 (2004).

against HMOs under Texas law was preempted. On the other hand, a state law providing for independent review of benefit denials in *Rush Prudential HMO, Inc. v. Moran* did not provide additional remedies outside ERISA and, therefore, was not preempted.[141]

[3]   The Deemer Clause

Even after the savings clause operates to permit the state law regulating insurance, the deemer clause[142] must be considered if the health plan in question is self-insured. In those circumstances, the self-insured company is not deemed to be an insurance company subject to state insurance law and the savings clause no longer applies. The end result is that the state law is again preempted.

For instance, in *FMC Corp. v. Holliday*,[143] the question presented was whether a self-insured health insurance plan was subject to a Pennsylvania anti-subrogation law.[144] The preemption analysis was similar to that in *Metropolitan Life* in that the Pennsylvania law was initially considered preempted because it was related to an employee benefit plan and subsequently saved as a law that regulated insurance. However, applying the deemer clause, all self-insured employer plans are deemed not to be an insurance company for purposes of a state law regulating insurance companies. The upshot is that FMC Corp. and all other self-insured employers are exempted from state laws that regulate insurance like the Pennsylvania anti-subrogation law. Not surprisingly, because of this dichotomy between insured and self-insured plans, more and more employers are setting up self-funded health plans to avoid state insurance regulation. Moreover, as mentioned above, the fact that self-insured plans are exempted from the essential benefits package under PPACA may further accelerate the shift to self-insured funding arrangements by many employers.[145]

[C]   ERISA Civil Enforcement Actions

ERISA provides a "comprehensive and reticulated" scheme of civil enforcement under Section 502(a).[146] Because of the breadth of ERISA preemption, employee benefit claims must generally be brought under the ERISA enforcement provisions.[147] Many criticize the combination of broad preemption with an

---

[141] 536 U.S. 355 (2002).

[142] ERISA § 514(b)(2)(B).

[143] 498 U.S. 52 (1990).

[144] A subrogation clause requires a plan participant to reimburse the plan for any benefits paid if the participant also recovers on a claim in a tort action against a third party. Pennsylvania had a law, the Motor Vehicle Financial Responsibility Law, which prohibited plans from enforcing such subrogation provisions.

[145] *See supra* § 14.04[G].

[146] *See* Nachman Corp. v. PBGC, 446 U.S. 359, 361 (1980).

[147] Even without being a "prevailing party," parties, but especially ERISA plaintiffs, who have had "some degree of success on the merits" in the underlying lawsuit are entitled to their attorneys' fees under Section 502(g)(1). *See* Hardt v. Reliance Insurance Co., 130 S. Ct. 2149 (2010).

unsatisfactory remedial scheme as leading to an inequitable state of affairs for employee benefit plan participants.[148]

[1] Overview and Jurisdictional Issues

There are three major types of ERISA civil actions.[149] Section 502(a)(1)(B) claims are instituted to recover benefits, to enforce rights under the plan, or to clarify rights to future benefits. Section 502(a)(2), read together with Section 409, provides for breach of fiduciary duty claims and permits personal liability against individual fiduciaries to make the plan whole. Section 502(a)(3), the so-called "catch-all" provision, enjoins any act or practice which violates ERISA, but is limited to claims for "appropriate equitable relief."

Federal and state courts have concurrent jurisdiction over denial of benefit claims under Section 502(a)(1)(B), but federal courts have exclusive jurisdiction over Section 502(a)(2) and (a)(3) claims.[150] However, if a claim for benefits is filed in state court, a federal question is presented on the face of the complaint under the well-pleaded complaint rule and the claim may be removed by the defendant to federal court.[151] If, on the other hand, a plaintiff does not mention ERISA in his or her complaint for denied benefits and instead attempts to proceed on state law grounds, the doctrine of complete preemption allows the court to treat the complaint as if the appropriate ERISA claim was alleged and permits the claim to be removed to federal court.[152] If the plaintiff then does not amend the complaint to allege an ERISA violation, the claim may be dismissed for failure to state a claim.[153]

As far as other litigation and procedural issues, ERISA only provides a statute of limitations for breach of fiduciary claims.[154] For other claims, courts look to the most analogous state law statute of limitations where the court sits. Jury trials are not available under ERISA, as there is no right to monetary damages under the Act

---

[148] *See, e.g.*, Paul M. Secunda, *Sorry, No Remedy: Intersectionality and the Grand Irony of ERISA*, 61 HASTINGS L.J. 131 (2009).

[149] There are other civil actions, including under Section 502(a)(1)(A) for refusal to supply requested plan information, but this section focuses on the three most frequently utilized civil enforcement sections. ERISA also provides for potential criminal penalties for willful violations of the Act. ERISA § 501.

[150] *Id.* § 502(e)(1), (f). ERISA also contains provisions permitting nationwide service of process. *Id.* § 502(e)(2).

[151] 28 U.S.C. § 1441(a).

[152] *See* Metro. Life Ins. Co. v. Taylor, 481 U.S. 58 (1987). *Taylor* explains that Congress has so completely preempted employee benefits law through enactment of ERISA that any civil complaint raising an employee benefit claim is necessarily federal in character. Complete preemption is therefore an exception to the well-pleaded complaint rule. Lower courts are divided, however, over whether complete preemption applies to state law claims related to the relief provided for in ERISA Section 502(a)(2) and (a)(3).

[153] Another potential scenario is that the plaintiff adds the ERISA claim in addition to the already-existing state law claims. In such cases, courts will normally exercise supplemental jurisdiction over such state claims, only to then dismiss them as preempted by ERISA.

[154] ERISA § 413 (providing that breach of fiduciary claim must be brought within the earlier of three years of actual knowledge of the breach or within six years of either the last action that was part of an ongoing breach or the latest date the fiduciary could have cured the breach).

and its remedies are equitable in nature. Lastly, reasonable attorney's fees and costs may be recovered by either party,[155] but, unlike other employment-oriented civil rights statutes, the awarding of such fees to prevailing plaintiffs is not automatic, and courts generally apply a five-factor test instead.[156]

[2]   Claims For Benefits

Claims for benefits are by far the most common types of claims under ERISA. Such suits may be brought by a plan participant or beneficiary[157] against the plan for the value of denied benefits or rights. For instance, if a plan participant wishes to receive a particular heart procedure under the health plan and the plan administrator denies the claim, the participant may file a claim against the plan for recovery of the value of that heart procedure. However, other forms of relief, including compensatory and punitive damages, are not available under Section 502(a)(1)(B).

For example, in *Corcoran v. United Health Care, Inc.*,[158] a health plan denied a female plan participant extended hospital stay services for a high risk pregnancy. The participant ended up losing her baby and sued the plan for wrongful death. The court held, however, that she could only bring a Section 502(a)(1)(B) claim under ERISA because the health plan's decision to deny the requested benefit was an employee benefit-related eligibility determination, not a medial decision which could be subject to a medical malpractice claim.[159] Hence, ERISA preemption prevented her from bringing a state tort claim for compensatory and punitive damages for the loss of her child. Her relief was therefore limited to the value of the hospital services denied. *Corcoran* provides an example of how ERISA civil enforcement and preemption provisions work in tandem to deny employee benefit plan participants meaningful relief for their losses.

Before bringing a Section 502(a)(1)(B) claim in state or federal court, a plan participant must exhaust his or her internal claims procedures as described in Section 503 and its regulations.[160] These provisions require that plans contain reasonable procedures for filing claims for benefits, review procedures for such claims which require that the plan provide specific reasons for denying a claim, and appeal procedures to review adverse claim determinations.[161] This means that once a claim has been denied by a plan administrator, the plan participant must file an

---

[155] ERISA § 502(g)(1).

[156] *See* Eaves v. Penn, 587 F.2d 453, 465 (10th Cir. 1978) (outlining five-factor test for determining attorney's fees under ERISA).

[157] That being said, participants or beneficiaries may assign their rights to allow a health care provider to bring a claim against the plan for payment for services. *See, e.g.*, Dallas Cty. Hosp. Distr. v. Assocs. Heath & Welfare Plan, 293 F.3d 282, 285-86 (5th Cir. 2002).

[158] 965 F.2d 1321 (5th Cir. 1992).

[159] Decisions concerning the availability of benefits under the plan "relate to" an employee benefit plan. Courts therefore generally conclude that state tort law claims for wrongful death related to these decisions are preempted by ERISA. *See* Pilot Life Ins. Co. v Dedeaux, 481 U.S. 41 (1987).

[160] Courts recognize limited exceptions to the exhaustion requirement based on futility, abolishment of appeal procedure, or an immediate danger of irreparable harm.

[161] ERISA § 503; DOL Reg. § 2560.503-1.

appeal with the administrator and wait for a further adverse determination before bringing his or her benefit claim in state or federal court. Section 503 regulations set up various time limits by which a claim appeal must be filed and decided.[162] For instance, the regulations require that plans give participants at least sixty days to appeal any adverse benefit determination.

Once the internal claims procedures have been exhausted, and the claim has been filed by the participant in state or federal court, the next issue is what standard of review courts should use to review benefit determinations. The Supreme Court in *Firestone Tire & Rubber Co. v. Bruch*[163] directed that the benefit decision be reviewed *de novo* by the court, unless the plan contains language vesting the plan administrator with discretionary authority. If such discretionary language exists in the plan, the benefit determination decision is reviewed under a deferential arbitrary and capricious standard. Even if it is determined that the plan administrator is operating under a structural conflict of interest[164] in making the determination, the Supreme Court determined in a subsequent case, *Metropolitan Life Insurance Co. v. Glenn*,[165] that the same Firestone analysis should still apply. Writing for the majority, Justice Breyer stated: "We here decide that this dual role [of the plan insurer] creates a conflict of interest; that a reviewing court should consider that conflict as a factor in determining whether the plan administrator has abused its discretion in denying benefits; and that the significance of the factor will depend upon the circumstances of the particular case."[166] So, even though the *Glenn* Court recognized that a structural conflict is a type of a conflict that should be taken into account in determining whether a plan administrator acted arbitrarily and capriciously in its plan interpretation, it specifically declined to adopt special procedural rules for these types of cases. Unsurprisingly, the combination of the *Firestone* and *Glenn* decisions has led most employers to design plans with language investing its plan administrators with the necessary discretionary authority in order to take advantage of the more favorable review standard. Moreover, even when a plan administrator has engaged in an interpretation of the plan which is "arbitrary and capricious" under *Firestone* and *Glenn*, the Supreme Court in the recent case of *Conkright v. Frommert*[167] held that "one single honest mistake" does not eliminate continued *Firestone* deference to subsequent interpretations of the plan by the same plan administrator.

---

[162] Initially all claim decisions were treated uniformly, but the 2000 regulations set various time periods for different types of health and disability plans. *See* 42 Fed. Reg. 70,246 (Nov. 21, 2000).

[163] 489 U.S. 101 (1989).

[164] Structural conflicts exist both when the employer funds and administers the plan itself, but also where the employer pays an independent insurance company to fund, interpret, and administer a plan. In each of these situations, the insurance company or the employer has the economic incentive to deny plan claims and increase it own profits or reduce plan expenses.

[165] 554 U.S. 105 (2008).

[166] *Id.* at 108.

[167] 130 S. Ct. 1640 (2010).

[3]   Claims For Fiduciary Breaches Under Section 502(a)(2)

Plan participants and beneficiaries, the Secretary of Labor, and other fiduciaries may all bring a Section 502(a)(2) claim against a fiduciary for breach of his or her fiduciary duties under ERISA.[168] Section 502(a)(2) directly incorporates Section 409, which provides that breaching fiduciaries are personally liable to the plan to make good on any losses to the plan as a result of their breaching conduct.[169] Breaching fiduciaries must also disgorge any profits they obtain through inappropriate use of plan assets.

Based on the "loss to the plan" language in Section 409, an issue that arises in this context is whether a plan has actually suffered a loss as result of a fiduciary breach. For instance, in *Donovan v. Bierwirth*,[170] the court considered whether there had been an investment loss to the plan because it later turned out that the breaching fiduciary conduct had led to an investment gain of $13 million. The court held that "loss to the plan" for purposes of Section 409 should be measured by comparing what the plan actually earned versus what the plan would have earned if the there had not been a breach of fiduciary duty. In making this comparison, a court is to assume that the funds would have been used in the most profitable, plausible way among investment alternatives.

Finally, this type of claim does not provide plan participants or beneficiaries individual relief in any form. All potential remedies go to the plan. Specifically, the Supreme Court case of *Massachusetts Mutual Life Insurance Co. v. Russell*[171] stands for the proposition that plaintiffs may not recover compensatory or punitive damages under Section 502(a)(2). Consequently, a plaintiff seeking to recover individual relief for a breach of fiduciary duty must look to Section 502(a)(3)'s catch-all provision.[172]

Because remedies under Section 502(a)(2) are limited to the plan, a difficult issue arises in the 401(k) plan context: Can a breach of fiduciary duty claim related to an investment loss in a 401(k) plan be brought under Section 502(a)(2) when less than all participants have suffered investment losses in their accounts as a result of the breach? A clear answer emerged in *LaRue v. DeWolff, Boberg & Associates, Inc.*[173] In *LaRue*, the plan participant claimed that he lost money in his 401(k) pension account because the plan administrator breached its fiduciary duties by failing to timely institute the participant's investment instructions. Although lower courts had previously held that Section 502(a)(2) breach of fiduciary claims provide remedies only for the plan, the Court held "that although § 502(a)(2) does not provide a remedy for individual injuries distinct from plan injuries, that provision does

---

[168] Fiduciary breaches not only include the general fiduciary and co-fiduciary provisions, but also the prohibited transaction rules.

[169] Plans are forbidden to adopt exculpatory clauses for plan fiduciaries. ERISA § 410.

[170] 754 F.2d 1049 (2d Cir. 1985).

[171] 473 U.S. 134 (1985).

[172] As discussed in the next section, the problem with looking to Section 502(a)(3) for relief is that investment loss is unlikely to be awarded as a type of equitable relief.

[173] 552 U.S. 248 (2008).

authorize recovery for fiduciary breaches that impair the value of plan assets in a participant's individual account."[174] In other words, a loss is a loss when considering what is a "plan loss" under Section 409 in the defined contribution context. As Justice Stevens put it: "Although the record does not reveal the relative size of [the plan participant]'s account [in relation to other 401(k) account holders within the same company], the legal issue under [Section] 502(a)(2) is the same whether [the participant's] account includes 1% or 99% of the total assets [of] the [p]lan."[175] Thus, post-*LaRue*, individual relief for fiduciary breaches in the DCP/401(k) context can be had under Section 502(a)(2).[176]

[4] Claims for Equitable Relief Under the Catch-All Provision

Section 502(a)(3) is considered the catch-all provision because it is generally applicable when none of the other remedial provisions apply. Under this provision, a participant, beneficiary, or fiduciary can sue the plan or another fiduciary for "appropriate equitable relief" for violations of ERISA's provisions. In *Mertens v. Hewitt Associates*,[177] the Supreme Court interpreted "appropriate equitable relief" to mean injunctions, mandamus, or restitution, but not money damages such as compensatory or punitive damages.[178]

Even though Section 502(a)(3) remedies are limited to appropriate equitable relief, the scope of such relief is still very much in debate, and Supreme Court cases in this area have caused much controversy and confusion.[179] For instance, in cases involving claims to enforce a plan reimbursement clause,[180] the Supreme Court has

---

[174] *Id.* at 256.

[175] *Id.* at 253.

[176] Chief Justice Roberts, joined by Justice Kennedy, concurred in *LaRue* suggesting that this case was not a breach of fiduciary case at all, but a benefits case mischievously recast. As a denial of benefit case under 502(a)(1)(B), Roberts argued that the claim should be subject to exhaustion and *Firestone* discretion. Roberts therefore wrote that lower federal courts should consider whether Section 502(a)(1)(B) applies in a case like this and if so, whether there must be exhaustion of internal remedies before the Section 502(a)(2) issue is reached, if at all. It is unclear at this point to what extent lower federal courts have heeded the Chief Justice's views in this case.

[177] 508 U.S. 248 (1993).

[178] *Mertens* also stands for the proposition that a plan fiduciary may not bring a claim against a non-fiduciary plan service provider for knowingly participating in a fiduciary's breach of fiduciary duty under Section 502(a)(3). However, the Court has held that a plan fiduciary may recover equitable relief in cases where a non-fiduciary plan service provider has engaged in a prohibited transaction involving plan assets. *See* Harris Trust & Sav. Bank v. Solomon Smith Barney, 530 U.S. 238 (2000).

[179] What follows is a brief summary of the Supreme Court case law on the scope of equitable relief under Section 502(a)(3). For a more detailed discussion, see generally John H. Langbein, *What ERISA Means by "Equitable": The Supreme Court's Trail of Error in* Russell, Mertens, *and* Great-West, 103 COLUM. L. REV. 1317 (2003); Colleen E. Medill, *Resolving the Judicial Paradox of "Equitable" Relief Under ERISA Section 502(a)(3)*, 39 J. MARSHALL L. REV. 827 (2006).

[180] Plan reimbursement clauses in the self-insured health plan context are similar to subrogation clauses in the insured plan context. The difference, however, is that whereas in a subrogation claim the insurance company may sue the tortfeasor directly, in a reimbursement claim the participant must first sue and recover from the third party tortfeasor before the plan has a claim for reimbursement. *See* FMC Med. Plan v. Owens, 122 F.3d 1258, 1260 & n.1 (9th Cir. 1997).

clarified that only "equitable restitution," as opposed to "legal restitution," is permitted to be recovered under Section 502(a)(3). The existence of a claim for equitable restitution, in turn, depends on whether the funds that the plan seeks to have reimbursed are specifically identifiable funds in the possession of the participant that rightfully belong to the plan. So, in *Great-West Life & Annuity Insurance Co. v. Knudson*,[181] the plan could not seek reimbursement under Section 502(a)(3) because the funds were in a special needs trust and not in the possession of the defendant, but in *Sereboff v. Mid-Atlantic Medical Services*,[182] such funds could be recovered (under an equitable lien by agreement) because there were specifically identifiable funds in the possession of the defendant.

Other difficult issues arise when participants and beneficiaries seek individual relief for breaches of a fiduciary duty under this provision. Individual plaintiffs may seek to bring fiduciary claims for individual equitable relief under *Varity Corp. v. Howe*,[183] as long as the plaintiff cannot receive the requested relief under other remedial provisions. The forms of appropriate equitable relief permitted in these cases, however, is debatable because the *Varity* case itself included a concession by the employer that the requested remedy was equitable. More recently, the Supreme Court in *Cigna Corp. v. Amara*[184] has suggested that ERISA plaintiffs may be eligible for a monetary award to make the victims of a fiduciary breach whole through various traditional equitable remedies such as equitable estoppel, reformation of contract, or surcharge.[185] It is still unclear, however, to what extent lower federal courts will use these remedies in the Section 502(a)(3) breach of fiduciary context.[186]

---

[181] 534 U.S. 204 (2002).

[182] 547 U.S. 356 (2006). An ERISA case of the reimbursement (*Knudson/Sereboff*) variety has again made its way to the U.S. Supreme Court as of the publication of this edition. In *U.S. Airways Inc. v. McCutchen*, 663 F.3d 671 (3d Cir. 2011), *cert. granted*, 2012 U.S. LEXIS 4727 (June 25, 2012), the Court will consider whether lower courts are authorized to use equitable principles to rewrite contractual benefit plan language and refuse to order plan participants to reimburse their plan for benefits paid, even in cases in which the plan's terms give it an absolute right to full reimbursement. The appellate courts have been divided over whether ERISA Section 502(a)(3) authorizes courts to take such steps.

[183] 516 U.S. 489 (1996).

[184] 131 S. Ct. 1866 (2011).

[185] So for instance, if a plan administrator breaches their fiduciary duties by providing false and misleading information about a plan benefit, a court could utilize traditional equitable remedies like reformation of contract or equitable estoppel to reform the terms of the plan and enforce the terms of the reformed plan as a remedy. Equitable estoppel remedies, however, would require a showing of detrimental reliance on the part of the ERISA plaintiff and reformation of contract requires a showing of fraud or mistake. *See* Skinner v. Northrop Grumman Retirement Plan B, 673 F.3d 1162, 1165–66 (9th Cir. 2012). Additionally, according to the *Amara* Court, the equitable remedy of surcharge, a traditional monetary remedy against a trustee for breach of trust, could be utilized in the ERISA context to make whole a participant or beneficiary who has suffered "actual harm" because of a fiduciary breach.

[186] *See, e.g., Skinner*, 673 F.3d at 1166–76 (denying plaintiffs remedies of surcharge or reformation of contract in breach of fiduciary case under Section 502(a)(3) in light of *Amara*).

[5] Discrimination Claims Under Section 510

Section 510 prohibits discriminating against, retaliating against, or interfering with an employee for exercising his or her rights under ERISA. It protects both vested and non-vested employees and applies equally to pension and welfare benefit plans.[187] Such claims require that the plaintiff establish that the defendant has the intent to interfere with rights protected by ERISA and, thus, these cases use the proof schemes from employment discrimination law to ferret out the necessary intent from circumstantial evidence.[188] Relief for violations of Section 510 is available under Section 502(a)(3) and is limited to appropriate equitable relief, which may or may not include back pay, reinstatement, and other equitable remedies (as discussed above in relation to the recent *Amara* decision).[189]

Pension forfeiture issues are one type of claim commonly litigated under this section. In such a scenario, a participant claims the employer has interfered with his or her ability to attain pension rights under the plan by terminating her employment. For example, in *Nemeth v. Clark Equipment Co.*,[190] one of the alleged reasons the company chose to close a particular plant was because of the higher pension costs associated with workers at that plant. The court used the Title VII burden-shifting framework to determine whether pension costs were the determinative factor for closing the plant. Because the evidence did not so indicate, the court found no Section 510 violation.

In the health plan context, Section 510 does not prohibit an employer from amending a benefit plan in a manner that affects the ability of a participant to make a claim for benefits under the plan. In *McGann v. H & H Music Co.*,[191] an employer reduced the lifetime coverage amount under a health plan for HIV/AIDS from $1 million to $5,000 after it discovered that one of its employees had contracted the disease. The court reasoned that this was not a discriminatory act under Section 510 because: (1) there was no promise that the employer would keep the high coverage limit forever and the plan contemplated that it could be modified or terminated at any time, (2) the change in coverage would apply to all participants and not just to the participant who currently had the disease, and (3) ERISA does not prohibit health plan discrimination between or among different category of diseases.[192]

Nevertheless, Section 510 does appear to prohibit an employer from firing an

---

[187] *See* Inter-Modal Rail Emps. Ass'n v. Atchison, Topeka & Santa Fe Ry. Co., 520 U.S. 510 (1997).

[188] *See* McDonnell Douglas Corp. v. Green, 411 U.S. 792 (1973); *see also supra* § 12.04[B][1].

[189] There is an argument, however, that the *Great-West* decision does not permit back pay for wrongful termination as an equitable remedy under Section 502(a)(3). *See, e.g.*, Millsap v. McDonnell Douglas Corp., 368 F.3d 1246 (10th Cir. 2004) (holding that back pay as equitable relief is not available under Section 502(a)(3) for violation of Section 510).

[190] 677 F. Supp. 899 (W.D. Mich. 1987).

[191] 946 F.2d 401 (5th Cir. 1991).

[192] Although HIPAA does not disturb this last conclusion because it does not limit the employer's ability to place restrictions on benefits offered, ERISA § 702(a)(2)(B), if the case were decided today, it is possible that it might be considered actionable disability discrimination under the Americans with Disabilities Act (ADA), 42 U.S.C. §§ 12101-12232, which does not permit, with limited exceptions, disability-based distinctions in employee benefit plans.

employee because of the costs associated with the employee's health care.[193]

---

[193] *See, e.g.*, Folz v. Marriott Corp., 594 F. Supp. 1007 (W.D. Mo. 1984). It is not as clear whether refusing to hire an individual because of resulting higher medical costs violates Section 510. *Compare* Fleming v. Ayers & Assocs., 948 F.3d 993 (6th Cir. 1991) (finding a Section 510 violation), *with* Becker v. Mack Trucks, Inc., 281 F.3d 372 (3d Cir. 2002) (limiting Section 510 claims to existing employment relationships).

Chapter 15

SAFETY AND HEALTH

§ 15.01   INTRODUCTION

Laws protecting employees' health and safety represent some of the oldest workplace legislation in the United States, with many states enacting statutes throughout the 1800s. The federal government remained on the sidelines, however, until the 1960s. Following an increase in workplace injuries, Congress finally acted and passed the Occupational Safety and Health Act of 1970 (OSHAct or the Act). Although states still play some role in guaranteeing workplace safety and health,[1] the Act is by far the primary source of such protections and, therefore, serves as the focal point for most attorneys' involvement with workplace safety regulations.

§ 15.02   OCCUPATIONAL SAFETY AND HEALTH ACT (OSHA)

[A]   Coverage

The OSHAct's coverage is relatively thorough. The Act applies to most private employers and their employees.[2] Exceptions include employees covered by other statutes, such as railway workers,[3] and small farms, which are fully exempt from the Act.[4] Moreover, employers with ten or fewer employees and good safety records are exempt from regular inspections[5] and partially exempt from keeping injury and illness records.[6]

The Act also does not apply to public employers and employees.[7] However, federal agency heads are required to establish safety and health programs that are consistent with the Act.[8] States also are permitted to create their own plans under certain conditions — including the requirement that all state plans provide coverage for state and local employees.[9]

[B]   OSHA Administration

The OSHAct created four different entities, whose roles reflect the diffuse nature of the entire regulatory scheme. First is the confusingly named Occupational Safety and Health Administration, which is contained within the Department of Labor (DOL).[10] The Labor Secretary's duties include promulgating health and safety standards, conducting inspections of worksites, and prosecuting violations of the Act.

---

[1] *See infra* § 15.02[G][5].

[2] 29 U.S.C. §§ 652(6) (defining "employee" as "an employee of an employer who is employed in a business which affects commerce"), 653(a) (applying OSHAct to all "employment," save for a few exceptions).

[3] *Id.* § 653(b).

[4] Departments of Labor and Health, Education and Labor Appropriations Act of 1979, Pub. L. No. 95-480, 92 Stat. 1567 (1979).

[5] BENJAMIN W. MINTZ, OSHA: HISTORY, LAW, AND POLICY 690-92 (1984) (describing regular practice of Congress attaching inspection limitation to appropriation bills).

[6] 29 C.F.R. § 1904.1.

[7] 29 U.S.C. § 652(5) (excluding public employers, except for United States Postal Service).

[8] *Id.* § 668.

[9] *Id.* §§ 667, 672; *see infra* § 15.02[G][5].

[10] Like the statute, this agency is also referred to as "OSHA"; because it falls under the Secretary of Labor's authority, it will be referred to as the "Secretary" and the statute referred to as the "OSHAct" or "Act."

The second entity is the National Institute for Occupational Safety and Health (NIOSH), which is part of the Department of Health and Human Services (HHS).[11] NIOSH conducts research and proposes new standards — acting in large part as the research arm of the Secretary.[12] Third is the Occupational Safety and Health Review Commission (OSHRC or Commission), which is an independent unit, associated with neither the DOL nor HHS.[13] The Commission has essentially a judicial role. OSHRC administrative law judges resolve initial disputes between the Secretary and employers; those disputes can then be appealed to a three-member panel of OSHRC Commissioners, who are presidential appointees.[14] Finally, the National Advisory Committee on Occupational Safety and Health (NACOSH) is another independent agency consisting of twelve members representing management, labor, safety and health professionals, and the public.[15] NACOSH advises the DOL and HHS regarding the evaluation of proposed standards.[16] The aim of NACOSH is to act as a counterweight to prevent any single agency from gaining too much power.

[C]   General Duty Clause

The OSHAct's enforcement mechanism is fairly unique. Rather than prohibiting or mandating certain actions by employers, the Act instead imposes a "general duty" on covered employers. Under Section 5(a)(1), the general duty clause requires employers to provide a workplace "free from recognized hazards that are causing or are likely to cause death or serious physical harm."[17] Successful general duty clause claims contain four elements, which are summarized as follows:

(1)   the employer failed to furnish a workplace free of a hazard, and its employees were exposed to that hazard;

(2)   the hazard was recognized;

(3)   the hazard was causing, or was likely to cause, death or serious physical harm; and

(4)   a feasible method existed to correct the hazard.[18]

For example, in *National Realty & Construction Co. v. OSHRC*,[19] the employer was alleged to have violated the general duty clause by allowing an employee to ride on the runner of a front-end loader; the worker was killed when the front-end loader toppled on top of him. At issue was whether the employer furnished a workplace free of the hazard of riding dangerous equipment. The D.C. Circuit

---

[11] 29 U.S.C. § 671.

[12] *Id.*

[13] *Id.* § 661.

[14] *Id.*

[15] *Id.* § 656.

[16] *Id.* § 656(b).

[17] *Id.* § 654(a)(1).

[18] *See* Nat'l Realty & Constr. Co. v. OSHRC, 489 F.2d 1257, 1265 (D.C. Cir. 1973).

[19] 489 F.2d 1257 (D.C. Cir. 1973).

emphasized that a hazard must be preventable to support a violation of a general duties claim and held that the clause did not impose strict liability on an employer. No violation occurred, according to the court, because the Secretary failed to present evidence showing "the particular steps a cited employer should have taken to avoid citation, and to demonstrate the feasibility and likely utility of those measures."[20]

Depending on the facts of a particular case, successfully prosecuting a general duty claim may be no easy matter. However, under Section 5(a)(2) of the Act, employers also are required to comply with more specific standards promulgated by the Secretary.[21] If such a standard applies to the hazard in question, a Section 5(a)(1) general duty claim is typically foreclosed in favor of a claim that the employer violated the relevant standard.[22] Thus, specific requirements under the OSHAct are primarily regulatory, rather than statutory, in nature.

[D] OSHA Standards

The administrative standards permitted by the OSHAct fall under three basic schemes: interim standards, emergency temporary standards, and permanent standards. Because of peculiarities in the Act's enforcement structure, as well as political realities, the role of the standards differs from what one might expect. Interim standards, in particular, have retained far more importance than intended, while the Secretary's ability to promulgate emergency temporary standards is almost nonexistent. Finally, permanent standards have been promulgated far less frequently than initially anticipated.

[1] Promulgation of Standards

The Secretary has the duty to promulgate OSHAct standards, which currently number in the thousands.[23] Because the Secretary is bound by little more than general criteria[24] and certain administrative procedures, there is sparse guidance for the regulations. Although this vagueness gives the Secretary much leeway in promulgating regulations, it can also be a burden in that the Secretary may have less statutory support to defend its rules. This is important because, as the following discussion reveals, judicial and legislative review of OSHAct regulations has been a recurring problem for the Secretary.

---

[20] *Id.* at 1268.

[21] 29 U.S.C. § 654(a)(2).

[22] United Auto Workers v. Gen. Dynamics Land Sys. Div., 815 F.2d 1570 (D.C. Cir. 1987); *Nat'l Realty*, 489 F.2d at 1261.

[23] STEVEN L. WILLBORN ET AL., EMPLOYMENT LAW: CASES AND MATERIALS 1007 (5th ed. 2012). As will be discussed in the next section, most of these standards are interim standards.

[24] *See infra* § 15.02[D][6].

[2] Interim Standards

Under Section 6(a) of the OSHAct, the Secretary was able to issue interim standards during the two years following the Act's effective date of April 1971.[25] The interim standard rules permitted the Secretary to promulgate standards without following the normal procedures required for formal rules.[26] The purpose of these interim standards was to implement workplace safety protections much more quickly than would occur under the formal rulemaking process. The standards continue to be effective until the Secretary promulgates a formal rule revising or revoking an existing standard.

The interim standards promulgated under this authority were typically derived from established heath and safety rules — particularly from other federal standards or "national consensus studies" that were based on industry practices. One month after the Act's April 1971 effective date, the Secretary promulgated over 4,400 standards.[27] Many of these standards, however, were known as "source standards," which often were based on what the Secretary deemed "national consensus" standards that were merely advisory, rather than mandatory. Promulgating mandatory rules based solely on advisory standards was controversial, as were the costs that these often complex standards imposed on employers.[28]

The Secretary's conversion of the previously advisory standards led to problems when employers challenged its standards in court; indeed, some courts expressly relied on the change from advisory to mandatory language in invalidating certain interim standards.[29] In response to this and other types of criticism, the Secretary eliminated several hundred interim standards in 1978. However, most of the remaining interim standards still remain in effect.

[3] Emergency Temporary Standards

The Secretary also has the authority to issue emergency temporary standards under a streamlined process.[30] The Secretary may promulgate an emergency temporary standard if it finds that "employees are exposed to grave danger from exposure to substances or agents determined to be toxic or physically harmful or from new hazards" and finds that an "emergency standard is necessary to protect employees from such danger."[31] The process for an emergency standard eliminates the need for hearings or advisory committees, and the standard is effective as soon as it is published in the Federal Register.[32] However, a temporary standard expires in six months.[33]

---

[25] 29 U.S.C. § 655(a).

[26] *Id.*; *see also id.* § 655(b) (describing formal rule procedures).

[27] *See* WILLBORN ET AL., *supra* note 23, at 1007.

[28] *Id.*

[29] *See, e.g.*, Usery v. Kennecott Copper Corp., 577 F.2d 1113 (10th Cir. 1977).

[30] 29 U.S.C. § 655(c).

[31] *Id.* § 655(c)(1).

[32] *Id.*

[33] *Id.*

The Secretary has rarely — only nine times — used its authority to promulgate emergency temporary standards and only four of those standards ever went into effect.[34] The remaining standards were rejected, largely because of courts' views that the authority to promulgate emergency temporary standards was an "extraordinary power to be used only in 'limited situations' in which a grave danger exists, and then, to be 'delicately exercised.' "[35] Unless the Secretary can show how the emergency temporary standard would prevent physical harm above what full enforcement of the current standards provides, courts generally will invalidate the emergency standard.[36] As a result of this searching review in addition to their short duration — the use of emergency temporary standards has effectively disappeared.

[4] Permanent Standards

Permanent standards were intended to be the Secretary's primary means of enforcing the OSHAct. The procedures required to promulgate a permanent standard are, like the procedures to promulgate other formal administrative rules, extensive. Section 6(b) of the Act details those procedures, which include: an interested party proposing a rule, announcement of the rule in the Federal Register, comments on the proposed rule, review of the rule by the Office of Management and Budget, promulgation of rule, and review by a federal court of appeals and, perhaps, the U.S. Supreme Court.[37] Moreover, since 1996, agencies are required to send new regulations to Congress for review; Congress, subject to the President's approval, then has sixty days to reject the rule before it goes into effect.[38] In 2001, the newly elected Congress and Bush Administration used this scheme to overturn new ergonomics regulations promulgated in the final stages of the Clinton Administration.[39]

Courts are to uphold permanent standards "if supported by substantial evidence in the record considered as a whole," which is more typical for administrative adjudications than rulemaking.[40] Because the substantial evidence standard does not fit neatly with OSHAct rulemaking, courts vary in their approaches to reviewing permanent rules. Some courts have held steadfast to the substantial review standard,[41] while others have allowed the Secretary more leeway when reviewing

---

[34] WILLBORN ET AL., *supra* note 23, at 1008. Three of those standards were never challenged. *Id.*

[35] Asbestos Information Ass'n/N. Am. v. OSHA, 727 F.2d 415, 422 (5th Cir. 1984) (quoting Pub. Citizen Health Res. Group v. Auchter, 702 F.2d 1150, 1155 (D.C.Cir.1983)).

[36] *Id.* at 425-26 (holding that the Secretary must establish the grounds used to promulgate the standard).

[37] *Id.* § 655(b).

[38] 5 U.S.C. §§ 801-802 (describing "joint resolution of disapproval" of administrative rule). Congress may override a presidential veto of a joint resolution of disapproval. *Id.* § 801(a)(3).

[39] *See* WILLBORN ET AL., *supra* note 23, at 1051.

[40] 29 U.S.C. § 655(f); Indus. Union Dep't, AFL-CIO v. Am. Petro. Inst. (*Benzene* case), 448 U.S. 607, 653 (1980); *compare* 29 U.S.C. § 160(e) (requiring substantial evidence review of National Labor Relations Board decisions); Universal Camera Corp. v. NLRB, 340 U.S. 474, 488 (1951) (same), *with* 5 U.S.C. § 706(2) (Administrative Procedure Act application of "arbitrary and capricious" standard to agency rulemaking).

[41] Nat'l Grain & Feed Ass'n v. OSHA, 866 F.2d 717 (5th Cir. 1989).

determinations based on scientific policy judgments.[42]

One unusual type of rule that the Secretary has attempted, albeit with questionable success, is "generic rulemaking." This rulemaking involves the Secretary's promulgation of standards for numerous substances and hazards under a single regulation. The advantage of this type of rulemaking is that the fixed costs associated with researching and promulgating a formal standard are required only once, rather than for each regulated substance.[43] Of the Secretary's four attempts at generic rulemaking, however, only two have been successful — one requiring employers to give employees and the Secretary access to exposure and medical records,[44] and the other requiring employers to communicate with the Secretary and employees about hazardous chemicals.[45] The other two attempts, dealing with carcinogens[46] and air contaminants, failed. The judicial reaction to the Secretary's 1989 promulgation of the Air Contaminant Standard aptly shows not only the hurdles to generic rulemaking, but also the significant burden necessary to justify a permanent standard.

The Air Contaminant Standard set exposure limits for 428 toxic substances.[47] However, in *AFL-CIO v. OSHA*,[48] the Eleventh Circuit struck down the proposed rule. It is perhaps best to think of the *AFL-CIO* decision as a procedural one, because the court expressly acknowledged that the Secretary could regulate each of the 428 substances — it was the attempt to do so under one rule that was problematic.[49] The reason for this procedural shortcoming was that the Secretary did not adequately justify the standard for each substance.[50] Making general observations that applied to all substances was not sufficient; rather, the Secretary must provide evidence necessary to justify each exposure limit.[51] Thus, according to the court, the problem was not the use of a single rule for multiple substances. Instead, the Secretary erred by trying to take shortcuts in meeting its burden to justify the exposure limits for each substance.[52]

---

[42] Indus. Union Dep't v. Hodgson, 499 F.2d 467 (D.C. Cir. 1974) (concluding that the Secretary's promulgation of standards is exercise of delegated legislative authority that is entitled to significant deference).

[43] *See* AFL-CIO v. OSHA, 965 F.2d 962, 971 (11th Cir. 1992). The costs are so significant that the Secretary has only promulgated approximately 100 permanent rules since the passage of the Act in 1970. *See* WILLBORN ET AL., *supra* note 23, at 1040.

[44] 29 C.F.R. § 1910.20.

[45] The Hazard Communications Standard, 29 C.F.R. § 1910.1200.

[46] *See generally* Indus. Union Dep't, AFL-CIO v. Am. Petro. Inst., 448 U.S. 607 (1980) (striking down part of Carcinogens Policy).

[47] Air Contaminants, 54 Fed. Reg. 2332-2983 (proposed Jan. 19, 1989).

[48] 965 F.2d 962 (11th Cir. 1992).

[49] *Id.* at 972.

[50] *Id.* at 974 (holding that, although the regulation established that the substances may be associated with material impairments, the Secretary failed to meet its "responsibility to quantify or explain, at least to some reasonable degree, the risk posed by *each* toxic substance regulated"); *see also infra* § 15.02[D][6].

[51] *AFL-CIO*, 965 F.2d at 972.

[52] *Id.* at 986-87 (stating further that even calling this standard a "generic rule" was a misnomer).

In sum, the Secretary must provide adequate support for every restriction or mandate in a permanent standard because each one will almost inevitably face a time-consuming legal challenge. Given these hurdles, particularly in light of the lack of resources that the Secretary typically has at her disposal, it is little wonder that so few permanent standards are promulgated. The Secretary has had some success in creating important regulations,[53] but without more adequate funding, the regulatory authority under the Act will not be fully utilized.

[5]   Variances

Even where a standard has been held enforceable, an employer may avoid its application by seeking a variance from the Secretary. An employer may request two types of variances: temporary or permanent.

The Secretary will grant a temporary variance only where the employer establishes that (1) it is unable to comply with the standard on its effective date because of the unavailability of professional or technical workers, the unavailability of needed materials and equipment, or necessary construction to the facility cannot be completed in time;[54] (2) the employer is taking steps to protect employees against the hazards protected by the standard at issue; and (3) the employer will comply with the standard as soon as practicable.[55] Employees must have notice of an employer's application for a temporary variance, which may last for a maximum of two years.[56]

A permanent variance is appropriate where an employer convinces the Secretary that it has an alternative method to ensure the same level of workplace safety as the standard at issue.[57] As with temporary variances, employees must have notice and an opportunity to comment before the Secretary will issue a permanent variance.[58] Permanent variances must describe the alternative method of safety and may be modified or revoked at any point once six months have elapsed since their issuance.[59]

---

[53] *See, e.g.*, Bloodborne Pathogens Standard, 29 C.F.R. 1910.1030 (following congressional urging, the Secretary revised this rule to create a new Needlestick Standard). *But see* Ergonomics Program Standard, 64 Fed. Reg. 65,768-66,078; 54 Fed. Reg. 2332-2983 (proposed Nov. 23, 1999) (proposing ergonomic standards which Congress eliminated following the 2000 presidential election, as described *supra* notes 38–39 and accompanying text).

[54] 29 U.S.C. § 655(6)(A).

[55] *Id.*

[56] *Id.*

[57] *Id.* § 655(d).

[58] *Id.*

[59] *Id.*

[6]   Substantive Criteria for Evaluating and Challenging Standards

As the previous discussion of the Air Contaminant Standard in the *AFL-CIO v. OSHA* case illustrates,[60] much of the litigation surrounding the validity of OSHAct standards focuses on whether the Secretary has sufficiently justified the precise standard at issue. Two different sections may be relevant to this determination: Section 6(b)(5), which applies to toxic materials and harmful physical agents, and Section 3(8), which applies more generally to occupational safety and health standards.

Section 6(b)(5) of the Act specifies the substantive criteria for toxic materials and harmful physical agents as follows:

> The Secretary, in promulgating standards dealing with toxic materials or harmful physical agents under this subsection, shall set the standard which most adequately assures, to the extent feasible, on the basis of the best available evidence, that no employee will suffer material impairment of health or functional capacity even if such employee has regular exposure to the hazard dealt with by such standard for the period of his working life.[61]

When developing these standards, the Secretary must also attempt to attain the "highest degree" of health and safety protection, while considering the latest available scientific information, the standards' feasibility, and the Secretary's experience under the Act and other laws.[62] The standards also should be tied to objective criteria and the type of performance that the Secretary is seeking.[63]

Under Section 3(8) of the Act, an "occupational safety and health standard" is defined as a standard that "requires conditions, or the adoption or use of one or more practices, means, methods, operations, or processes reasonably necessary or appropriate to provide safe or healthful employment and places of employment."[64] Generally, the criteria used to address the validity of a standard look to its technological feasibility, economic feasibility, and benefits to employees' health or safety; at times, a cost-effectiveness analysis may also be used. These criteria primarily apply to permanent rules, yet they also are relevant to interim and emergency temporary standards as well.

[a]   Technological Feasibility

Based on the "to the extent feasible" language in Section 6(b)(5), courts have derived two different types of feasibility analyses in examining the permissibility of permanent standards: technological feasibility and economic feasibility. As to technological feasibility, the Secretary has the burden to show by substantial evidence that a standard is technologically feasible — that is, "'that modern

---

[60]   *See supra* notes 48-52 and accompanying text.

[61]   29 U.S.C. § 655(b)(5).

[62]   *Id.*

[63]   *Id.*

[64]   *Id.* § 652(8).

technology has at least conceived some industrial strategies or devices which are likely to be capable of meeting the [permissible exposure limit] and which the industries are generally capable of adopting.' "[65] Typically, the Secretary measures technological feasibility on an industry-wide basis.[66]

An example of a case that hinged on technological feasibility is *AFL-CIO v. Brennan*,[67] in which the Third Circuit addressed the Secretary's revision of its standards regarding the use of mechanical power presses. In the revision, the Secretary eliminated the prohibition against employees putting their hands in a die (which is a part of the press that cuts or forms materials). The AFL-CIO challenged the sufficiency of the Secretary's justification for the revision, particular the technological and economic feasibility findings.

The Secretary conceded that the previous "no-hands-in-die" standard was technologically impossible in certain applications and forced the elimination of certain jobs and businesses. This infeasibility was part of the Secretary's justification for eliminating the standard. Although the court recognized that the difficulties in complying with the rule was an appropriate consideration, it stressed that the OSHAct was intended to be a "technology-forcing piece of legislation."[68] Thus, a standard that is currently technologically infeasible may still be valid, but only if the "necessary technology looms on today's horizon."[69] Ultimately, however, the court agreed in this case with the Secretary's determination that the technology needed to make the "no-hands-in-die" rule was not feasible in the near future.

Brennan stressed that although the Act strives to eliminate workplace hazards, there are times when totally prohibiting a hazard is beyond present technology and does not warrant shutting down businesses or causing employees to lose their jobs.[70] The Act, in short, "did not intend to impose strict liability on employers for unavoidable occupational hazards."[71] Technological infeasibility, therefore, remains an important consideration in whether to promulgate a specific workplace standard, but the Secretary must consider advances in technology that are likely to occur in the near future.

[b]   Economic Feasibility

The Secretary's reliance on economic feasibility as a standard criterion had been unsettled for a period of time, as the OSHAct and its legislative history were murky on the issue.[72] Ultimately, courts concluded that the Act's feasibility

---

[65] AFL-CIO v. OSHA, 965 F.2d 962, 980 (11th Cir. 1992) (quoting United Steelworkers of Am. v. Marshall, 647 F.2d 1189, 1266 (D.C. Cir. 1980)).

[66] *Id.*

[67] 530 F.2d 109 (3d Cir. 1975).

[68] *Id.* at 121.

[69] *Id.*

[70] *Id.*

[71] *Id.* (citing Brennan v. OSHRC, 502 F.2d 946, 951 (3d Cir. 1974)).

[72] Indus. Union Dep't, AFL-CIO v. Hodgson, 499 F.2d 467 (D.C. Cir. 1974).

language also should include economic considerations.[73] Like technological feasibility, the Secretary has the burden to show by substantial evidence that a challenged standard is economically feasible on an industry-wide basis.[74] Economic feasibility requires the Secretary to provide "a reasonable assessment of the likely range of costs of its standard, and the likely effects of those costs on the industry, so as to demonstrate a reasonable likelihood that these costs will not threaten the existence or competitive structure of an industry."[75]

Consideration of economic feasibility does not mean that financially burdensome rules are improper; indeed, the financial ruin of some employers may be consistent with the Act's purposes.[76] Rather, economic feasibility represents industry-wide financial difficulties in complying with a rule.[77] A standard that forces lagging employers out of business is one thing, but a standard that only a few leading business can achieve is quite another.[78] Similarly, placing an entire industry at a significant disadvantage to foreign competitors may also be a relevant factor.[79]

The court in *AFL-CIO v. Brennan* applied this approach to economic feasibility and stressed that the Secretary had the authority to consider the "possibility of massive economic dislocation caused by an unreasonable standard."[80] Moreover, as the court noted, economically infeasible standards could prove impossible to enforce as employers would attempt to evade the regulations rather than go out of business. Accordingly, the court in *Brennan* upheld the new standard based on its holding that substantial evidence supported the Secretary's determination that the initial no-hands-in-die standard was both technologically and economically infeasible.

[c]   Benefit to Employees' Health and Safety

The third criterion derives from the "appropriate and necessary to provide safe or healthful employment" language in Section 3(8), and it requires the Secretary to show that a permanent standard benefits employees' health and safety. This factor focuses on scientific evidence — typically studies on the dangers associated with the hazard at issue.[81] The Secretary must be able to show that a hazard presents a

---

[73] *Id.* at 476-77 (citing S. Rep. No. 91-1282, 91st Cong., 2d Sess., at 58 (statement of Sen. Javits)).

[74] AFL-CIO v. OSHA, 965 F.2d 962, 982 (11th Cir. 1992).

[75] *Id.* (internal citations and quotation marks omitted).

[76] *Id.*; *Hodgson*, 499 F.2d at 478 (citing as an example the "economic demise of an employer who has lagged behind the rest of the industry in protecting the health and safety of employees and is consequently financially unable to comply with new standards as quickly as other employers").

[77] *AFL-CIO*, 965 F.2d at 982.

[78] *Id.*

[79] *Id.*; *see generally* Ann. P. Bartel & Lacy Glenn Thomas, *Predation Through Regulation: The Wage and Profit Effects of the Occupational Safety and Health Administration and the Environmental Protection Agency*, 30 J.L. & Econ. 239 (1987) (arguing that safety regulations could provide economic benefits to employers).

[80] *Brennan*, 530 F.2d at 123.

[81] *See* Willborn et al. *supra* note 23, at 1020–22 (discussing scientific issues with health benefit studies).

risk to employees' health and safety under current standards and that this risk will be reduced by the proposed standard.

Immediately after the Act's passage, the Secretary's need to show the health and safety benefits of its standards was even more uncertain than the feasibility factors. However, in 1980, the Supreme Court held that benefiting employees' health and safety was a necessary justification for the enforcement of a standard. In what is commonly referred to as the *Benzene* case,[82] the Court reviewed the Secretary's standard on employees' exposure to benzene, a substance that can cause leukemia at high doses. The Secretary focused solely on feasibility issues, which a Court plurality held to be inconsistent with the Act's mandate that a standard should be promulgated when "reasonably necessary or appropriate to provide safe or healthful employment and places of employment."[83] According to the Court, this statement implies that the Secretary must show that a workplace is currently not "safe," meaning that the workplace is not free of a "significant risk of harm."[84] Thus, before "promulgat[ing] *any* permanent health or safety standard, the Secretary is required to make a threshold finding that a place of employment is unsafe — in the sense that significant risks are present and can be eliminated or lessened by a change in practices."[85]

The result in the *Benzene* case was to invalidate the Secretary's standard, which presumptively assumed that any level of the substance increased the risk of cancer. The Court held that the proposed standard would give the Secretary authority to impose enormous costs with little, if any, discernable benefit.[86] Instead, under the Court's "significant risk test," the Secretary must establish that the current exposure level of a hazard presents a significant risk to employees and show, by substantial evidence, that the proposed standard would reduce that risk.[87] This significant risk test does not require the Secretary to calculate precisely the chance of harm. Instead, there must be a showing that a *significant* risk of some material impairment is present.[88] Relying on the Court's citation to a "one-in-a-thousand" risk, many courts now consider a significant risk to be present where an employee's career exposure to a substance causes a one-in-a-thousand chance of that harm occurring.[89]

---

[82] Indus. Union Dep't, AFL-CIO v. Am. Petro. Inst. (*Benzene* case), 448 U.S. 607 (1980).

[83] *Id.* at 639.

[84] *Id.* at 642.

[85] *Id.*

[86] *Id.* at 645.

[87] *Id.* at 653; *accord* United Steelworkers v. Marshall, 647 F.2d 1189 (D.C. Cir. 1980).

[88] AFL-CIO v. OSHA, 965 F.2d 962, 973–80 (11th Cir. 1992) (defining both "material impairment" and "significant risk").

[89] United Auto Workers v. Pendergrass, 878 F.2d 389 (D.C. Cir. 1989) (quoting *Benzene*, 448 U.S. at 655).

[d]   Cost-Benefit Analysis

Some also have argued that the Secretary should be required to perform a cost-benefit analysis to justify a permanent OSHA standard. Under such an analysis, the Secretary would show that the proposed standard's benefits are equal to or exceed its costs. But it is difficult to make that determination. Benefits in particular are hard to quantify — for example, how should we value a life or the effect of a workplace injury?[90]

In *American Textile Manufactures Institute v. Donovan (Cotton Dust* case),[91] the Supreme Court explored the use of cost-benefit analysis. The *Cotton Dust* case involved a standard limiting employees' exposure to cotton dust, which can cause respiratory illness. The Court held that the Secretary does *not* have to use cost-benefit analyses to justify standards promulgated under Section 6(b)(5) of the Act because in adopting that section, Congress had already implicitly undertaken that analysis "by placing the 'benefit' of worker health above all other considerations save those making attainment of this 'benefit' unachievable."[92] Instead, financial considerations are to be considered as part of the economic feasibility requirement, and that feasibility analysis should take into account that Congress intended to impose substantial costs on employers "when necessary to create a safe and healthful working environment."[93] The Court held that substantial evidence supported the Secretary's findings regarding the costs of its standard and that the Secretary properly evaluated the economic feasibility of most portions of its standard. However, the Court rejected the requirement that employers guarantee no loss of wages for employees who are transferred to eliminate their exposure to cotton dust. The Court held that the Secretary, even if it had the authority to promulgate such a rule, failed "to make the necessary determination or statement of reasons that its wage guarantee requirement is related to the achievement of a safe and healthful work environment."[94]

In the aftermath of the *Cotton Dust* case, the Secretary has used a "cost effectiveness" principle to evaluate proposed standards.[95] Under this cost-effectiveness analysis, the Secretary will choose the least expensive means to achieve a predetermined level of protection.[96] This is different than a traditional

---

[90] *See* WILLBORN ET AL., *supra* note 23, at 1020–22 (discussing economic issues with cost-benefit analyses).

[91] 452 U.S. 490 (1981).

[92] *Id.* at 509, 513. The Court left open whether cost-benefit analyses are required for *safety* standards promulgated only under Section 3(8) of the Act, or whether the Secretary is *forbidden* from using cost-benefit analyses in most instances. *Id.* at 513 nn.32 & 38.

[93] *Id.* at 520. In dissent, Chief Justice Rehnquist argued that Congress failed to choose whether the Secretary was mandated, permitted, or prohibited from performing a cost-benefit analysis under Section 6(b)(5). According to the Chief Justice, this failure to make a decision constituted an unconstitutional delegation of legislative authority. *Id.* at 545-47 (Rehnquist, C.J., dissenting).

[94] *Id.* at 537-38.

[95] *Cf.* Building & Constr. Trades Dep't v. Brock, 838 F.2d 1258, 1269 (D.C. Cir. 1988) (evaluating standard under cost-effectiveness analysis, but withholding judgment whether cost-benefit analysis is required under the Act).

[96] *Id.*

cost-benefit analysis, which looks to whether the total benefits of a standard outweigh its costs. Thus, costs remain an important consideration, but only to the extent that they impact the implementation of a necessary safety standard. It is not necessary to explicitly balance a standard's health and safety benefits against its costs.

[E] Employee Rights

The primary guarantee of employees' rights under the OSHAct — aside from the standards ensuring their health and safety — is the prohibition against retaliation. Under Section 11(c)(1) of the Act and its implementing regulations, it is unlawful for an employer to discharge or discriminate against any employee who has filed a complaint, caused the institution of a proceeding, testified in a proceeding, or exercised any rights under the Act on her or other employees' behalf.[97] However, the statute of limitations for filing a retaliation complaint is very short — only thirty days after the discriminatory act occurred.[98] Moreover, the Secretary possesses the sole enforcement authority for this provision; there is no private right of action.[99] The relief available for violations include, under appropriate conditions, reinstatement, backpay, compensatory damages, exemplary damages, and equitable relief such as expunging disciplinary records.[100]

In *Whirlpool Corp. v. Marshall*,[101] the Supreme Court addressed the validity of the Secretary's retaliation regulation. That rule protects, among other things, an employee's right to refuse work because of a reasonable fear of death or serious injury where the employee reasonably believes that no less-drastic alternatives were available.[102] The employees in *Whirlpool* refused to work with a guard screen through which another employee had fallen to his death.[103] The employer had attempted to repair the screen, but the employees refused the task because they believed that the screen was still unsafe. The regulation arguably permitted the employees' refusal, which led the employer to challenge the rule's validity. The Court rejected the employer's challenge and held that the regulation was consistent with the Act. In so doing, the Court emphasized that the rule conforms with a "fundamental objective of the Act — to prevent occupational deaths and

---

[97] 29 U.S.C. § 660(c)(1); 29 C.F.R. § 1977.12.

[98] 29 U.S.C. § 660(c)(2).

[99] *Id.*; Taylor v. Brighton Corp., 616 F.2d 256 (6th Cir. 1980).

[100] 29 U.S.C. § 660(c)(2) (providing for "all appropriate relief including rehiring or reinstatement of the employee to his former position with back pay"); Marshall v. Whirlpool Corp., 9 O.S.H. Cas. (BNA) 1038 (N.D. Ohio 1980) (ordering award of backpay in remand of Supreme Court case).

[101] 445 U.S. 1 (1980).

[102] 29 C.F.R. § 1977.12(a) (protecting employees from discrimination because of "any right afforded by" the Act), (b)(2) (stating that employee could refuse work only where "a reasonable person, under the circumstances then confronting the employee, would conclude that there is a real danger of death or serious injury and that there is insufficient time due to the urgency of the situation, to eliminate the danger through resort to regular statutory enforcement channels," and that the employee "where possible, must also have sought from his employer, and been unable to obtain, a correction of the dangerous condition").

[103] 445 U.S. at 6.

serious injuries."[104] Accordingly, employees may refuse work because of health and safety issues, but only where they reasonably believe that a hazard creates a real danger of death or serious injury, and there are no means to avoid the risk. The Secretary's burden in a refusal-to-work case, therefore, is to prove that the employee "had a reasonable and good faith belief that the conditions leading to his refusal . . . were dangerous and that defendant discharged him for that refusal."[105]

The enforcement policies of the Act, particularly the focus on employer actions, are well-illustrated by the Secretary's attempt to regulate *employees'* compliance with OSHA rules. In *Atlantic & Gulf Stevedores, Inc. v. OSHA*,[106] the Third Circuit addressed the Secretary's citation of longshoremen who refused to comply with a regulation requiring the use of protective hats — the longshoring "hardhat" standard.[107] Indeed, the longshoremen's resistance to the rule was so fierce that, in response to their employers' attempts to enforce the rule, they threatened to strike. Although they sought compliance from their employees, the employers never refused to allow an employee to work without a hardhat. Consequently, the Secretary cited the employers for violating the regulation.[108]

The Third Circuit agreed with a fractured Commission opinion that even near-total employee resistance to a rule does not relieve an employer of its duty to comply.[109] The court viewed the adjudication as another form of policymaking that can be particularly useful because the feasibility of a rule may not be discernable until employers have attempted to comply.[110] The court agreed that the employers had presented a valid economic feasibility defense, but one that would only survive if the Secretary was unable to enforce the OSHA standards against employees (if enforcement power against employees exists, then the Secretary could eliminate the threat of a strike, which was the basis for the economic feasibility argument).[111] Under its reading of the Act, the court held that its provisions could *not* be enforced against employees.[112] However, despite its acknowledgement that the threat of a strike could support an economic feasibility defense, the court deferred to the Commission's findings that the potential financial hardship of enforcing the

---

[104] *Id.* at 11 (citing 29 U.S.C. § 651(b)).

[105] Marshall v. N.L. Indus., Inc., 618 F.2d 1220, 1224 (7th Cir. 1980). The test for other rights under the OSHAct are similar — the Secretary must prove that the employer discriminated against the employee for exercising his or her rights under the Act, as defined in the regulations. *See, e.g.*, Martin v. Anslinger, Inc., 794 F. Supp. 640 (S.D. Tex.) (discussing retaliation against employee for talking to OSHA inspector, a right defined in 29 C.F.R. §§ 1977.11, 1977.12).

[106] 534 F.2d 541 (3d Cir. 1976).

[107] *Id.* at 544 (citing 29 C.F.R. § 1918.105(a)).

[108] *Id.* Virtually no employees had complied with the rule, but the fine was a total of only $455 because the violation was deemed nonserious. *Id.*

[109] *Id.* at 547 (noting that the standard of review was arbitrary, capricious, and abuse of discretion).

[110] *Id.* at 550-51. Adjudication has been approved as a administrative policymaking technique for other agencies, such as the National Labor Relations Board. *See generally* Joan Flynn, *The Costs and Benefits of "Hiding the Ball": NLRB Policymaking and the Failure of Judicial Review*, 75 B.U. L. Rev. 387, 391-93 (1995).

[111] 534 F.2d at 552.

[112] *Id.* at 554.

rule was not sufficient.[113] This holding emphasized that the Act placed the primary responsibility of enforcing its rules on employers, even in the face of employee resistance.[114]

[F] Employer Responsibilities

Most OSHA litigation involves challenges to standards or disagreements about whether a standard was violated in a particular instance. However, even when it is relatively clear that a violation has occurred, issues may still exist. For instance, there can be questions about which entities are responsible for OSHA compliance or how to classify the number of violations that occurred.

The first issue involves OSHRC's "Multi-Employer Citation Policy," which is concerned with assessing responsibility for OSHA violations where there are multiple employers at a single worksite. Under the policy, employers fall under four classifications: a "creating employer," which caused the OSHA violation; an "exposing employer," which has its own employees exposed to the unlawful hazard; a "correcting employer," which is an exposing employer with the responsibility for correcting the hazard; and a "controlling employer," which has supervisory authority over a worksite — including the authority to ensure OSHA compliance — but that did not have any of its employees exposed to the unlawful hazard. There has never been any serious dispute that creating, exposing, and correcting employers are liable for violations, but the status of controlling employers has been murkier.

In *Secretary of Labor v. Summit Contractors, Inc.*,[115] the OSHRC addressed its ability to cite controlling employers for violations. The case involved a general contractor that was overseeing a college dormitory construction site. One of the subcontractors was cited by an OSHA compliance officer for violating a scaffolding requirement; the Secretary of Labor cited the general contractor for the violation and issued a fine. The general contractor did not dispute that it was aware of the conditions cited in the violation, but argued that the relevant OSHA construction standard[116] did not permit controlling employers to be held liable. The Commission initially agreed with the general contractor, but the Eighth Circuit reversed. On remand, the Commission switched its position and concluded that controlling employers may be liable for violations.

The key issue in these cases is how to determine when an employer whose employees were not exposed to a hazard that it did not create may be considered "controlling." To answer this question, the Commission looks to whether an employer has enough supervisory authority to detect and ensure abatement of OSHA violations. In *Summit*, the Commission found that the general contractor had such authority, relying on factors such as the contract granting the general contractor "exclusive authority to manage, direct, and control" the project;

---

[113] *Id.* at 555-56.

[114] *Id.* at 555 (noting that the employer could have bargained for the right to discipline employees or for a no-strike clause).

[115] 22 O.S.H. Cas. (BNA) 1777 (2009).

[116] 29 C.F.R. § 1910.12(a).

responsibility to comply with applicable laws, supervise safety precautions, and take responsible safety precautions for all employees on the project; and discretion to terminate subcontractors that did not follow OSHA regulations. The finding that the general contractor was a controlling employer meant that it had a duty to exercise reasonable care to prevent and detect violations; however, this duty is lower than what an employer has with regard to its own employees. The general contractor violated that duty in *Summit* because it did not inform the subcontractor of the unlawful hazard at issue.

A second issue with employers' duties under OSHA is the "unit-of-prosecution" question. Take, for example, an employer with eleven employees who remove asbestos. If the employer fails to provide them with OSHA-mandated training and respirators, are there two violations or twenty-two? The Commission and appellate courts have taken different views of this issue in the past, which ultimately prompted the Secretary of Labor to promulgate a rule authorizing employee-by-employee charges under thirty-four of its standards (that is, allowing twenty-two violations in the hypothetical). However, the Secretary's Field Manual states that usually only one citation will be issued for each violated standard and employee-by-employee charges are to be used only for willful and egregious violations. After the rule's promulgation, several covered industries challenged the Secretary's authority to issue the rule. But in *National Association of Home Builders v. OSHA*, 602 F.3d 464 (D.C. Cir. 2010), the D.C. Circuit upheld the rule. The court emphasized that Congress had given the Secretary legislative-like authority to set OSHA standards, and unit-of-prosecution questions are typically a legislative responsibility.

[G] Enforcement

The Secretary possesses broad authority to enforce the various provisions of the OSHAct. Whether by regulation, inspection, or litigation, the Secretary has significant power to ensure the health and safety of workers. However, authority is not equivalent to efficacy. An unfortunate reality is that funding for the Act's enforcement has long been inadequate. Thus, despite the Secretary's statutory authority, actual enforcement of the Act is often far from ideal.

The lack of funding impacts all areas of enforcement. Resources are needed to properly research and justify regulations both at their inception and when being defended in court. Moreover, a robust litigation framework is necessary to investigate and punish violators of the Act, but such a framework requires resources. Finally, the power to inspect rings hollow if funding inadequacies mean that few employers actually face inspections. Indeed, despite having jurisdiction over approximately seven million workplaces, there are only about 1,000 federal inspectors.[117] Not surprisingly, the rate of inspections is relatively low, with only 40,648 inspections in Fiscal Year 2011.[118] That amounts to one inspection for every

---

[117] *See* WILLBORN ET AL., *supra* note 23, at 1063 (noting about 1,000 federal inspectors and less than 1,000 state inspectors); *see also* OSHA, *Commonly Used Statistics* (stating, in 2012, that there were 2,200 total federal and state inspectors), *available at* http://www.osha.gov/oshstats/commonstats.html.

[118] *See* OSHA, *Commonly Used Statistics, supra* note 117 (noting that there were 52,056 state plan inspections).

183 workplaces.

Some of this strain is alleviated by the Secretary's attempts to encourage employers to voluntarily maintain safe and healthy workplaces. For example, the Secretary has developed the Voluntary Protection Program (VPP), which allows "good" employers to avoid annual scheduled inspections.[119] Employers may qualify for VPP if they have low injury rates, internal safety programs that implement OSHA safety and health standards, and avenues for employee involvement with the internal program. In 2003, the various levels of the federal VPP involved 1,024 employers with 223,275 employees.[120]

[1] Procedures

Unlike most regulatory regimes, the OSHAct permits employers to challenge standards before they are enforced, not just during enforcement proceedings. Section 6(f) of the Act permits an employer to challenge a standard within sixty days of its promulgation.[121] If an employer does not take advantage of this pre-enforcement review, it must wait until the Secretary has cited it for a violation of the Act.[122]

An employer wanting to contest a citation has fifteen working days to do so after receiving notice of the citation.[123] A DOL attorney will litigate the challenge in a hearing before an Administrative Law Judge ("ALJ").[124] After the ALJ issues its decision, the losing party may seek review before the Commission, although the Commission need not hear the case.[125] The Commission is considered the ultimate fact-finder, but it typically will defer to the ALJ's findings of fact.[126]

Any party aggrieved by the Commission's final order may seek review in a federal court of appeals.[127] After the court of appeals decision, the losing party's

---

[119] Voluntary Protection Programs To Supplement Enforcement and To Provide Safe and Healthful Working Conditions, 47 Fed. Reg. 29,025-01 (Jul 2, 1982). The VPP was revised in 2000. *See* Revisions to the Voluntary Protection Programs To Provide Safe and Healthful Working Conditions, 65 Fed. Reg. 45,650 (July 24, 2000).

[120] *See* Orly Lobel, *Interlocking Regulatory and Industrial Relations: The Governance of Workplace Safety*, 57 ADMIN. L. REV. 1071, 1105–06 (2005) (describing different levels of VPP); *see generally* Cynthia Estlund, *Rebuilding the Law of the Workplace in an Era of Self-Regulation*, 105 COLUM. L. REV. 319 (2005) (discussing VPP as part of general analysis of workplace self-regulation). *But see* Paul M. Secunda, *Workplace Federalism: More of Less: The Limits of Minimalism and Self-Regulation*, 157 U. PA. L. REV. PENNUMBRA 28, 36 (2008) (criticizing VPP program for being too expensive, applying only to self-selecting employers with already great safety and health records, and applying only to 2,000 workplaces (in 2008) out of the approximately seven million workplaces covered by OSHA).

[121] 29 U.S.C. § 655(f).

[122] *Id.* § 659(c).

[123] *Id.* § 659(a).

[124] *Id.* § 659(c).

[125] *Id.*

[126] This treatment of fact-finding is similar to the district court/magistrate judge relationship.

[127] *Id.* § 660 (allowing case to be brought before the D.C. Circuit, any circuit court covering the geographic area where violation was alleged to have occurred, or any circuit court covering the geographic area where the employer's principal office is located).

sole recourse is the U.S. Supreme Court.

[2]   Recordkeeping and Inspections

The OSHAct requires all covered employers to make and preserve records related to workplace safety, and the Secretary must be provided access to those records.[128] The records must include reports of instances of non-minor workplace injuries and illnesses, as well as employees' exposure to potentially toxic or harmful materials.[129]

Under Section 8 of the Act, the Secretary has broad authority to inspect workplaces to ensure that employers are complying with OSHA standards.[130] Pursuant to this authority, the Secretary has established a system of inspections. Under this system, the Secretary prioritizes inspections according to the following classifications (with the first listed being the highest priority):

(1)   *Imminent Danger.* Conditions that pose a reasonable certainty of immediate death or physical harm are the highest priority for inspections.[131]

(2)   *Catastrophes and Fatal Accidents.* Investigating deaths or accidents hospitalizing three or more employees is the second priority.[132]

(3)   *Complaints and Referrals.* The next priority is investigating employee complaints and other referrals about a workplace hazard.[133]

(4)   *Programmed Inspections.* Finally, the Secretary will attempt to inspect workplaces based on the determination that special hazards exist in a given industry, workplace, or occupation.[134]

The Secretary has established rules that govern inspections. These rules include prohibitions against providing employers advanced notice of inspections in most instances.[135] The regulations also describe the types of activities permitted during inspections,[136] as well as the right of employers and employees to participate.[137]

---

[128]   *Id.* § 657(c) (allowing, alternatively, access to the Secretary of Health and Human Services); 29 C.F.R. § 1904.40.

[129]   29 U.S.C. § 657(c); 29 C.F.R. § 1904.7.

[130]   29 U.S.C. § 657(a).

[131]   29 C.F.R. § 1903.13; *OSHA Inspections*, Occupational Safety and Health Administration 3 (2002), *available at* www.osha.gov/Publications/osha2098.pdf.

[132]   *OSHA Inspections*, *supra* note 131, at 3.

[133]   29 C.F.R. § 1903.11; *OSHA Inspections*, *supra* note 131, at 4.

[134]   29 C.F.R. § 1903.3; *OSHA Inspections*, *supra* note 131, at 4.

[135]   29 C.F.R. § 1903.6 (stating that notice may be provided for circumstances such as attempts to stop imminent danger, where inspections occur after regular business hours, or if necessary to ensure presence of necessary parties).

[136]   *Id.* § 1903.7; *see also* Trinity Indus., Inc. v. OSHRC, 16 F.3d 1455 (6th Cir. 1994) (limiting inspections to scope of employee complaint); Donovan v. Fall River Foundry Co., 712 F.2d 1103 (7th Cir. 1983) (limiting inspection to separate area of workplace relevant to complaint).

[137]   29 U.S.C. § 657(e); 29 C.F.R. § 1903.8.

Moreover, the Supreme Court has held, in *Marshall v. Barlow's, Inc.*,[138] that the Secretary must obtain a warrant before it can inspect a workplace without an employer's consent. However, the probable cause required for this type of administrative search is not as substantial as the cause required for a criminal warrant. Instead, probable cause for an OSHA warrant may result from, among other things, evidence that the workplace is part of a hazardous industry; the employer was chosen for inspection as part of a general plan (like OSHA's programmed inspections); or, under certain circumstances, employee complaints.[139] In practice, the Secretary has had more success in establishing probable cause to perform programmed inspections than nonprogrammed inspections prompted by employee complaints, accident reports, and other factors.[140]

If the inspection reveals a violation, the Secretary must issue a citation to the employer that sets a reasonable time period for the employer to stop the problem.[141] An employer may contest a citation before the OSHRC, as can an employee who objects to the abatement schedule.[142] The Commission's decision may then be appealed to a federal court of appeals.[143]

[3] Penalties

Penalties for violating the OSHAct vary widely, depending on the nature of the violation. Under Section 17 of the Act, the possible penalties are as follows:

(1)	Nonserious violation:	$0-$7,000 per violation[144]
(2)	Serious violation:	$1-$7,000 per violation[145]
(3)	Repeat violation:	$0-$70,000 per violation[146]
(4)	Willful violation:	$5,000-$70,000 per violation[147]
(5)	Failure to abate:	$0-$7,000 per day[148]
(6)	Willful violation that results in death:	Criminal violation with penalties of up to $10,000 per violation and six months in jail[149]

---

[138] 436 U.S. 307 (1978).

[139] *See, e.g., In re* Establishment Inspection of Microcosm, 951 F.2d 121 (7th Cir. 1991).

[140] *See, e.g.,* Donovan v. Fed. Clearing Die Casting Co., 655 F.2d 793 (7th Cir. 1981).

[141] 29 U.S.C. § 658(a); 29 C.F.R. § 1903.14.

[142] 29 U.S.C. §§ 659(a), (c).

[143] *Id.* § 660(b).

[144] *Id.* § 666(c).

[145] *Id.* § 666(b).

[146] *Id.* § 666(a).

[147] *Id.*

[148] *Id.* § 666(d).

[149] *Id.* §§ 666(e), (f), (g).

As explained by the Fifth Circuit in *Chao v. OSHRC*[150] — a case involving an explosion that followed the tapping of an unmarked natural gas valve — a "willful" violation "is one committed voluntarily, with either intentional disregard of, or plain indifference to, OSHAct requirements."[151] Willfulness depends not upon the seriousness of the violations, but upon the employer's intent or willingness to act "in disregard of the action's legality."[152] For example, the court found that willfulness was not present in *Chao*[153] because there was no evidence of either "intentional disregard" or "plain indifference" to OSHAct requirements.[154]

Finally, when determining the proper penalty, the Commission relies on four factors: (1) the size of the employer's business, (2) the gravity of the violation, (3) the employer's good faith, and (4) the employer's history of previous violations.[155] The gravity of the violation is the most important of those factors.[156] Moreover, the Commission has significant freedom in determining a penalty, because courts will review that determination under an abuse of discretion standard.[157]

[4] Imminent Danger

Section 8(f) of the OSHAct permits employees to request an inspection if a violation of a standard threatens physical harm or there exists an "imminent danger."[158] An imminent danger is defined as a condition that creates a danger that "could reasonably be expected to cause death or serious physical harm immediately or before the imminence of such danger can be eliminated through the enforcement procedures" of the Act.[159]

The Secretary's finding that an imminent danger exists triggers several different actions. For instance, imminent dangers are given the highest priority for workplace inspections.[160] If an imminent danger is discovered, the Secretary must also inform the employer and employees of the danger and the remedies that will be sought.[161] Moreover, the Secretary may seek a temporary restraining order to force an employer to immediately abate an imminent danger or move employees from the

---

[150] 401 F.3d 355 (5th Cir. 2005).

[151] *Id.* at 367.

[152] *Id.* (citing Ga. Elec. Co. v. Marshall, 595 F.2d 309 (5th Cir. 1979) (discussing other circuits' definition of "willful")).

[153] The employer in *Chao* had also been cited for willfully violating standards requiring protective equipment for employees engaged in asbestos removal, but did not challenge that finding.

[154] *Id.* at 368; *see also* Reich v. Trinity Indus., Inc., 16 F.3d 1149 (11th Cir. 1994) (holding that employer committed a willful violation, despite its good faith belief that the workplace was safe, because it knowingly refused to comply with OSHA regulations).

[155] 29 U.S.C. § 666(j); *Chao*, 401 F.3d at 376.

[156] *Chao*, 401 F.3d at 376.

[157] *Id.*

[158] 29 U.S.C. § 657(f)(1).

[159] 29 U.S.C. § 662(a); Marshall v. Daniel Constr. Co., 563 F.2d 707, 710 n.6 (11th Cir. 1977).

[160] *See supra* note 131 and accompanying text.

[161] 29 C.F.R. § 1903.13.

location where they are exposed to that danger.[162] Interestingly, if the Secretary "arbitrarily or capriciously" fails to seek relief for an imminent danger, an employee injured as a result of that failure may sue the Secretary.[163]

[5] State Regulation of Safety and Health

The OSHAct preempts a significant portion of state safety and health measures, in large part to ensure a minimum level of protection and to minimize employers' burden in complying with health and safety laws.[164] However, Section 18 of the Act expressly permits state regulation of safety and health standards not covered by the Act.[165] Moreover, a state may seek permission from the Secretary to assume responsibility for enforcing federal occupational safety and health regulations.[166] Permission will be granted to the state if the Secretary finds, among other things, that the plan designates a state agency to administer it, provides for standards and inspections as effective as federal standards, gives adequate funding and legal authority to administer the plan, and mandates that employers provide the Secretary the same type of reports that would be required if no state plan were in place.[167] Many states and territories have taken advantage of this provision, which also provides federal funds for up to half of a state plan's operating expenses.[168]

Some states have attempted to shield from preemption what are referred to as "dual impact" statutes. These statutes have the purpose of protecting both employees and the general public. Illinois, for example, enacted laws to license hazardous waste equipment operators and workers at certain facilities.[169] These laws were challenged as being preempted by OSHA interim regulations that, like the Illinois laws, required certain levels of worker training.[170] Resolving a circuit split on the Act's preemptive effect on dual impact statutes, the Supreme Court in *Gade v. National Solid Wastes Management Association*[171] held that state laws of this type were preempted.

In *Gade*, the Court first made clear that the Act has a "field" (or "dormant") preclusive effect — that is, the Act preempts state regulation in the general field of

---

[162] 29 U.S.C. § 662(a), (b).

[163] *Id.* § 662(d).

[164] 29 U.S.C. § 667; N.J. State Chamber of Commerce v. Hughey, 774 F.2d 587 (3d Cir. 1985) (discussing preemption of state laws requiring employers to disclose information about hazardous substances under the Hazard Communication Standard, 29 C.F.R. § 1900.1200).

[165] 29 U.S.C. § 667(a).

[166] *Id.* § 667(b).

[167] *Id.* § 667(c).

[168] WILLBORN ET AL., *supra* note 23, at 1097–98. In 2010, there were 22 plans, including a plan for Puerto Rico, which covered private, state, and local employees. *Id.* at 1097. Four additional states (plus the Virgin Islands) have plans that cover only state employees. *Id.* at 1098. Finally, the vast majority of states without plans (all but three) have some type of health and safety coverage for public employees. *Id.*

[169] 225 Ill. Comp. Stat. 220/5, 220/6, 220/7, 221/5, 221/6.

[170] 29 C.F.R. § 1920.20.

[171] 505 U.S. 88 (1992).

workplace safety, even if the state law does not conflict with the Act.[172] The Court then held that this preclusive effect applied to dual impact statutes as well. Noting that Congress, in Section 18 of the Act, made explicit the requirements necessary for states to enforce their own workplace safety laws, the Court concluded that any state law that regulates in the same field as the Act is preempted, even if the state law has other objectives.[173]

The Act's preemptive effect, however, has limits. For instance, prosecutions under general state criminal law will normally not be preempted. As the Illinois Supreme Court held in *People v. Chicago Magnet Wire Corp.*,[174] to allow preemption of state criminal prosecutions would convert the Act, "which was enacted to create a safe work environment for the nation's workers, into a grant of immunity for employers responsible for serious injuries or deaths of employees."[175] Moreover, according to the *Chicago Magnet* court, federal preemption jurisprudence typically requires express preemption by Congress against traditional matters of state regulation, such as police powers.[176] Because the Act's preemption is implied, general state criminal prosecutions related to workplace safety are not preempted.[177] After *Gade*, however, it is likely that criminal penalties under state health and safety laws — in contrast to the general criminal prosecution in *Chicago Magnet* — will be preempted.[178]

Although states are significantly limited by the Act from regulating workplace health and safety, states can, and often do, exercise what authority they possess. As would be expected, the result is a patchwork of diverse state workplace safety laws. Accordingly, attorneys must not focus solely on the OSHAct when involved with a workplace safety issue; state law may be critical to the case as well and should be consulted in appropriate circumstances.

---

[172] *Id.* at 97 (citing approval requirements for state plans under 29 U.S.C. § 667(b)).

[173] *Id.* at 98.

[174] 534 N.E.2d 962 (Ill. 1989).

[175] *Id.* at 969 (discussing charges of aggravated battery and reckless conduct against officers of employer for causing injuries to forty-two workers by failing to protect them against exposure to poisonous substances).

[176] *Id.* at 966 (citing Jones v. Rath Packing Co., 430 U.S. 519 (1977)).

[177] *Id.* at 970.

[178] *See, e.g.*, Commonwealth v. College Pro Painters (U.S.) Ltd., 640 N.E.2d 777 (Mass. 1994) (holding that *Gade* preempted criminal penalties under state safety regulations).

Chapter 16

ENFORCEMENT OF EMPLOYMENT RIGHTS

SYNOPSIS

Employment rights and duties are meaningless unless there are adequate remedies available and adequate means to enforce the rights and duties. This Chapter examines remedies, enforcement through administrative agencies, and litigation through the courts.

§ 16.01   REMEDIES

Employment laws generally have two purposes: deterring employer misconduct, and compensating employees for damages they incur as a result of employer misconduct.[1] These purposes usually are consistent with each other, but occasionally may be in tension. For example, in *Balbuena v. IDR Realty LLC*,[2] an illegal alien working as a construction worker sued for injuries sustained in a workplace accident. The employer objected to the alien's claim for lost wages, arguing that the alien would be overcompensated if he received lost wages when it was unlawful for him to be working in the United States. The New York Court of Appeals, however, held that failing to award lost wages would inhibit deterrence by creating a weaker incentive for employers to comply with the applicable employment laws and with federal immigration laws.[3]

Various employment laws contain a wide array of remedies. Such remedies may include back pay (in a discharge case, pay from the date of discharge to the date of adjudication); front pay (pay from the date of adjudication forward to some future date); reinstatement (common in NLRA and union proceedings, but rare in other

---

[1] Price Waterhouse v. Hopkins, 490 U.S. 228 (1989) (O'Connor, J., concurring); Albemarle Paper Co. v. Moody, 422 U.S. 405 (1975).

[2] 845 N.E.2d 1246 (N.Y. 2006).

[3] *Compare* Hoffman Plastic Compounds, Inc. v. NLRB, 535 U.S. 137 (2002) (holding that federal immigration policy foreclosed the NLRB from awarding back pay to undocumented alien).

employment disputes); compensatory damages (usually including pain and suffering); go-and-sin-no-more injunctions or orders; attorneys' fees; and fines.

Often, the remedies (and enforcement procedures) available under various employment laws overlap or differ considerably. An example is *Bahramipour v. Citigroup Global Markets, Inc.*,[4] in which the plaintiff filed in state court a state law class action claim for violation of the federal Fair Labor Standards Act.

§ 16.02 CHOICE OF ENFORCEMENT FORUM — AGENCIES OR COURTS

Common law tort and contract claims can be brought by an aggrieved party directly to a judicial forum. Statutory rights, however, can be enforced in other ways as well. These rights may, for example, be adjudicated by an administrative agency, or an administrative agency may litigate claims (either in its own name or in the name of an aggrieved individual) in the courts.

[A] Administrative Agencies

[1] Compensation versus Fines

Administrative agencies typically are given one of two possible enforcement mechanisms. The first is to initiate an action in the name of aggrieved individuals. The Department of Labor's (DOL) Wage and Hour Division, for example, has the ability to enforce FLSA overtime requirements by filing suit on behalf of workers whom the DOL believes have been denied overtime pay to which they are entitled. If the DOL wins the case, the employer will be required to pay the employees their overtime premiums.

Not all employment statutes, however, create a remedy *for aggrieved employees*. Occupational Safety and Health Act's (OSH Act) workplace safety laws, for example, are enforceable only by the Occupational Safety and Health Administration (OSHA) *in its own name*. If an employer violates the statute, the agency may impose on the employer a fine, but the fine is payable to the agency, not to the aggrieved employee. From the employee's perspective, OSHA creates a right without a remedy. An injured worker can call the agency to complain about a workplace safety violation, but the only benefit the employee will get out of the complaint will be the satisfaction of seeing the employer fined and the problem corrected. The employee's only remedy for an injury resulting from a safety violation is through workers' compensation or, if the injury resulted from the employer's intentional misconduct, through a tort suit.

When an administrative agency, such as OSHA, serves as the exclusive enforcement mechanism for an employment statute, then the efficacy of the statute will depend primarily on two factors. The first is the severity of the penalty for noncompliance. If the penalty amounts to little more than a slap on the wrist, compliance is likely to be low because many employers will view the penalty as

---

[4] 11 Wage & Hour Cas. 2d (BNA) 498 (N.D. Cal. 2006).

nothing more than another cost of doing business.

The second factor affecting the efficacy of a statute exclusively enforced by an agency is the likelihood that a violation will be detected and penalized. Employers are more likely to comply if detection is likely than if detection is unlikely. But detection is often directly related to agency funding — a poorly-funded agency is unable to do a lot of investigating, and many workplace-related administrative agencies (such as OSHA and the EEOC) historically have been significantly underfunded.

[2]　Agency versus Court Adjudication

Some employment statutes creating administrative agencies give those agencies the power to enforce the statute by filing suit in court. The FLSA is enforced in this way by DOL. Other statutes, however, create an adjudicatory mechanism within the agency itself. Adjudications usually are presided over by an administrative law judge, then are appealable to an agency board and then to the courts. Examples include OSHA, workers' compensation, and unemployment insurance.

Agency adjudication is usually preferable to judicial adjudication when it is important that a decision be reached quickly. For example, an employee injured on the job or laid off is likely to have rent or a mortgage payment to make, medical bills to pay, and a family to feed. Workers' compensation or unemployment insurance payments are not likely to be of much help if it takes a year or more for them to be adjudicated through the judicial system.

[B]　Individual Enforcement

Many employment rights are enforced by individuals through private lawsuits. Examples include common-law tort and contract claims. The advantage of enforcing employment rights this way is that from the government's perspective it is inexpensive — no agency needs to be created or funded. There are, however, several major disadvantages as well. First, enforcement is slow — several years may elapse between the filing of a claim and final resolution. Second, transaction costs, in the form of attorneys' fees, are very high. It can easily cost upwards of $100,000 to litigate an employment claim through trial.

Third, these transaction costs make it difficult for most low- or middle-income employees to obtain enforcement. If potential damages are high, the employee will likely attract an attorney to take the case on a contingency fee basis, meaning that the attorney, instead of charging an hourly fee, will take a percentage of the verdict or settlement. But if damages are low, an attorney will not recover enough under the contingency contract to pay for the cost of litigation (under a typical 33% contingency fee contract, damages after a trial would have to exceed $300,000 just for the attorney to break even without accounting for the substantial risk that the case ultimately will be unsuccessful). Because damages in most employment cases are a function of lost wages, high-income employees are likely to have potential damage awards high enough to attract an attorney on a contingency basis, whereas middle- and low-income employees are not. And because many plaintiffs bringing employment claims have quit or been fired, they are unlikely to be in a position to pay an attorney an hourly fee out-of-pocket.

Some employment statutes (such as Title VII and ERISA) contain fee-shifting provisions that allow successful parties to recover their reasonable attorney's fees. In *Albemarle Paper Co. v. Moody*,[5] the Supreme Court held that a prevailing *plaintiff* is entitled to attorney's fees in almost all cases. In *Christiansburg Garment Co. v. EEOC*,[6] the Court held that a prevailing *defendant* is entitled to such fees only if the plaintiff's claim was "frivolous, unreasonable, or groundless, or that the plaintiff continued to litigate after it clearly became so."[7]

Fee-shifting provisions encourage some plaintiff's attorneys to accept cases in which an employee might otherwise go unrepresented. However, fees are awarded under these statutes only if the employee prevails, and the amount will not be adjusted to compensate for the possibility that the case would have been lost. This significantly decreases the incentive for plaintiff's attorneys to take cases that are not sure winners.

[C] Hybrid Enforcement

The federal antidiscrimination statutes operate under a hybrid model. An employee believing she has been the victim of unlawful discrimination initiates the enforcement process by filing a charge of discrimination with the EEOC (and/or with an allied state or local administrative agency). The EEOC or other agency then has the authority to investigate the claim and, if it chooses to do so, may file suit in its own name on behalf of the charging party. Most of the time, however, the agency does not, and instead sends the charging party a "right to sue" letter relinquishing its control over the charge and authorizing the charging party to initiate her own suit in court.

---

[5] 422 U.S. 405 (1975).

[6] 434 U.S. 412 (1978).

[7] *Id.* at 422.

Chapter 17

ARBITRATION OF EMPLOYMENT DISPUTES

SYNOPSIS

§ 17.01 ARBITRATION GENERALLY

Arbitration is a proceeding, governed by contract, in which a dispute is resolved by an impartial adjudicator, chosen by the parties, whose decision the parties have agreed to accept as final and binding.[1] It differs from mediation in that the arbitrator imposes a resolution, unlike a mediated settlement which must be agreed to by the parties. It differs from litigation because it is informal: the arbitrator is chosen by the parties rather than by the judicial system, arbitration occurs in a conference room rather than a courtroom, the rules of procedure and evidence are loosely applied, and both discovery and motion practice are limited.

Common law courts were traditionally hostile to arbitration. Congress enacted the Federal Arbitration Act of 1925 (FAA)[2] to provide a basis for enforcing commercial arbitration agreements. The U.S. Supreme Court extended the FAA to the employment context tentatively in 1991 and definitively ten years later.[3] The Court has recognized a strong federal policy favoring arbitration since the mid-1980s.[4]

---

[1] *See* Salt Lake Tribune Publ'g Co. v. Mgmt. Planning Inc., 390 F.3d 684, 689 (10th Cir.2004) ("classic arbitration" is characterized by "empower[ing] a third party to render a decision settling [the] dispute"); AMF, Inc. v. Brunswick Corp., 621 F. Supp. 456, 460 (E.D.N.Y. 1985) (the test for "arbitration" is whether the parties have agreed to submit a dispute to a third party for a decision, regardless of whether the decision is binding); Advanced Bodycare Solutions, LLC v. Thione International, Inc., 524 F.3d 1235 (11th Cir. 2008) ("arbitration" within the scope of the FAA must "produce some type of award that can be meaningfully confirmed, modified, or vacated by a court upon proper motion").

[2] 9 U.S.C. §§ 1-16.

[3] Circuit City Stores, Inc. v. Adams, 532 U.S. 105 (2001). In Gilmer v. Interstate/Johnson Lane Corp., 500 U.S. 20, 33 (1991), the Court compelled arbitration of an age discrimination case, but expressly left open the scope of the FAA's "contracts of employment" exclusion.

[4] *See, e.g.,* Mitsubishi Motors Corp. v. Soler Chrysler-Plymouth, Inc., 473 U.S. 614, 625 (1985).

Arbitration has at least three advantages over litigation. First, arbitration is much faster. Employment cases, for example, can be arbitrated in half to a third of the amount of time that they otherwise would be litigated.[5] Second, arbitration is much less expensive, because less lawyer-time is needed for discovery and motion practice. Third, arbitration is much less formal than litigation, making it easier and less time-consuming to prepare a case.

Traditionally, arbitration agreements were the product of meaningful negotiation between parties of roughly equal bargaining power, such as commercial entities entering into a contract or employers and unions entering into a collective bargaining agreement. The recent proliferation of arbitration, however, has occurred in the form of adhesive arbitration agreements imposed by a party of superior bargaining power upon a party (such as an employee or consumer) whose only alternative to acceptance is to walk away from the job or the transaction.

This has led to two concerns. The first is that adhesive arbitration agreements are "involuntary," either because the weaker party lacks adequate notice or consent (an example is an employer that gives arbitration agreements written in English to Spanish-speaking employees)[6] or because the weaker party has no meaningful alternative (because arbitration agreements now are nearly universal in credit card agreements, anyone wanting a credit card must agree to arbitration). The second concern is that controlling parties will draft lopsided adhesive arbitration agreements that "place every conceivable obstacle in the path of those seeking redress in the hope of discouraging potential claimants from pressing any actions at all."[7]

§ 17.02   A BRIEF HISTORY OF ARBITRATION IN LABOR AND EMPLOYMENT LAW

At common law, an arbitration agreement was revocable by either party any time before the arbitrator issued an award.[8] However, the FAA required courts to enforce arbitration agreements related to commerce and maritime transactions.[9] Nonetheless, in the 1953 decision of *Wilko v. Swan*,[10] the Supreme Court refused to enforce arbitration of a statutory securities claim. Lower federal courts interpreted *Wilko* as creating a FAA defense to the enforcement of arbitration agreements under the FAA when statutory claims were at issue.[11]

Only seven years after *Wilko*, in the *Steelworkers* Trilogy,[12] the Supreme Court firmly ensconced arbitration as a mechanism for resolving labor disputes arising

---

[5] *See* Alexander J.S. Colvin, *An Empirical Study of Employment Arbitration: Case Outcomes and Processes*, 8 J. EMPIRICAL LEGAL STUD. 1 (2011).

[6] *See, e.g.*, Prevot v. Phillips Petroleum Co., 133 F. Supp. 2d 937, 939-41 (S.D. Tex. 2001) (refusing to enforce arbitration agreement).

[7] Stephan Landsman, *ADR and the Cost of Compulsion*, 57 STAN. L. REV. 1593, 1612 (2005).

[8] *See, e.g.*, Vynior's Case, 77 Eng. Rep. 595 (K.B. 1609).

[9] *See* 9 U.S.C. §§ 1-16.

[10] 346 U.S. 427 (1953).

[11] *See, e.g.*, Am. Safety Equip. Corp. v. J.P. Maquire & Co., 391 F.2d 821, 827 (2d Cir. 1968).

[12] United Steelworkers of Am. v. Am. Mfg. Co., 363 U.S. 564 (1960); United Steelworkers of Am. v.

under collective bargaining agreements. The *Steelworkers* Court distinguished *Wilko* on the basis that the *Steelworkers* cases arose in the unique context of labor relations. Whereas the alternative to arbitrating statutory claims was judicial resolution of those claims "with established procedures or even special statutory safeguards," the alternative to arbitrating labor claims was, the Court explained, "industrial strife."[13]

In the 1974 case of *Alexander v. Gardner-Denver Co.*,[14] the Court held that an employee's arbitration of a discrimination claim arising under a collective bargaining agreement did not preclude later litigation of a statutory claim predicated on identical underlying facts. The Court reasoned that labor arbitrators were not competent to decide complex statutory claims, and that arbitral fact-finding procedures were inadequate to protect employees' statutory rights.[15]

Beginning in the 1980s, however, the Supreme Court abandoned its hostility toward non-labor arbitration. In the *Mitsubishi* Trilogy,[16] the Court approved arbitration of statutory claims arising under antitrust, securities, and racketeering laws. The Court interpreted the FAA as creating a presumption that statutory claims are arbitrable, and made this presumption rebuttable only upon a showing by the party opposing arbitration that Congress specifically intended otherwise. The Court predicated this new presumption of arbitrability on two assumptions. The first was that an arbitration agreement involves no waiver of substantive rights:

> By agreeing to arbitrate a statutory claim, a party does not forgo the substantive rights afforded by the statute; it only submits to their resolution in an arbitral, rather than a judicial, forum. It trades the procedures and opportunity for review of the courtroom for the simplicity, informality, and expedition of arbitration.[17]

The second new assumption was that arbitrators are capable of deciding complex statutory issues. Noting that the parties may appoint arbitrators with particular statutory expertise and that the arbitrator or the parties may employ experts, the Court concluded that "we are well past the time when judicial suspicion of the desirability of arbitration and of the competence of arbitral tribunals inhibited the development of arbitration as an alternative means of dispute resolution."[18]

Enter. Wheel & Car Corp., 363 U.S. 593 (1960); United Steelworkers of Am. v. Warrior & Gulf Navigation Co., 363 U.S. 574 (1960).

[13] *See Warrior & Gulf Navigation*, 363 U.S. at 578.

[14] 415 U.S. 36 (1974).

[15] *See id.* at 56-58.

[16] *See* Rodriquez de Quijas v. Shearson/Am. Express, Inc., 490 U.S. 477, 479, 484-85 (1989); Shearson/Am. Express, Inc. v. McMahon, 482 U.S. 220, 238, 242 (1987); Mitsubishi Motors Corp. v. Soler Chrysler-Plymouth, Inc., 473 U.S. 614, 640 (1985).

[17] *Mitsubishi*, 473 U.S. at 628.

[18] *See id.* at 626-27.

§ 17.03 EMPLOYMENT ARBITRATION LAW TODAY

The *Mitsubishi* Trilogy set the stage for the Court to apply its new pro-arbitration policy to employment law. In *Gilmer v. Interstate/Johnson Lane Corp.*,[19] the Court held for the first time that pre-dispute arbitration agreements between employers and employees are enforceable even when statutory discrimination rights are at issue. Robert Gilmer was discharged from his job as manager of financial services at Interstate/Johnson Lane Corp. He subsequently sued, alleging he had been discriminatorily fired because of his age. Interstate moved to compel arbitration pursuant to an arbitration agreement contained in Gilmer's registration agreement with the New York Stock Exchange, in which Gilmer had "agree[d] to arbitrate any dispute, claim, or controversy" between him and his employer "arising out of the employment or termination of [his] employment."[20]

The Supreme Court ordered Gilmer to arbitration. The Court began by invoking the cases of the *Mitsubishi* Trilogy, which the Court characterized as collectively standing for the proposition that the FAA makes statutory claims arbitrable. The Court also quoted with approval the language in *Mitsubishi* block-quoted above.

The Court rejected four arguments supporting Gilmer's claim that the arbitration clause should not preclude his ADEA suit. Gilmer's first argument was that an arbitral forum is inadequate to protect an employee's statutory employment rights. Gilmer argued, among other things, that arbitrators are not required to issue written opinions and that this would reduce public accountability for employer discrimination, hamper effective judicial review, and stifle development of the law. In rejecting this argument, the Court asserted, incorrectly, that NYSE arbitration rules require arbitrators to issue written opinions.[21] The Court further reasoned that courts would continue to issue judicial opinions in employment discrimination cases because not all employers and employees are likely to sign binding arbitration agreements. Finally, the Court noted that settlement agreements, which the antidiscrimination statutes encourage, similarly fail to produce written opinions.

Second, the Court rejected Gilmer's argument that arbitration was inconsistent with the statutory purposes and framework of the ADEA, and that this inconsistency rebutted the presumption of arbitrability created by the *Mitsubishi* Trilogy. The Court, in short, found arbitration sufficient to promote the social policies of the ADEA. Third, the Court rejected Gilmer's argument that courts should not enforce arbitration agreements because they often are the product of employer coercion as a result of unequal bargaining power between employers and employees. The Court found that mere inequality in bargaining power was not a sufficient reason to refuse enforcement of arbitration agreements. Fourth, the Court rejected the argument of several amici curiae that an FAA provision excluding "contracts of employment" rendered the FAA and its presumption of arbitrability inapplicable to Gilmer's case. The Court concluded that because the arbitration agreement was contained in

---

[19] 500 U.S. 20 (1991).

[20] *Id.* at 23. Because the registration agreement was with the New York Stock Exchange and not with Gilmer's employer, the registration agreement was not an employment contract.

[21] NYSE rules required only that the arbitrator issue a written *award*. Such an award merely stated who shall receive what and when the individual will receive it.

Gilmer's registration application with the NYSE and not in his employment contract with Interstate, it was not part of the "contract of employment" with his employer.

Since *Gilmer*, the Supreme Court has decided several additional cases pertinent to employment arbitration. In the 1998 decision of *Wright v. Universal Maritime Service Corp.*,[22] the Court dodged the issue of whether an arbitration clause in a collective bargaining agreement could prospectively waive an employee's right to litigate a statutory discrimination claim and held only that such a waiver, if permitted at all, must be "clear and unmistakable." In the 2000 consumer-arbitration decision of *Green Tree Financial Corp.-Alabama v. Randolph*, the Court held that where "a party seeks to invalidate an arbitration agreement on the ground that arbitration would be prohibitively expensive, . . . that party bears the burden of showing the likelihood of incurring such costs."[23] A year later in *Circuit City Stores, Inc. v. Adams*,[24] the Court resolved the "contracts of employment" issue by holding that the clause excluded only the employment contracts of those workers actually engaged in interstate transportation, like truck drivers. In the 2002 decision of *EEOC v. Waffle House*,[25] the Court held that the EEOC has the independent statutory authority to pursue in court a discrimination claim against an employer, even if the employee who filed the initial charge of discrimination had signed an arbitration agreement. In the 2003 consumer-arbitration decision of *Green Tree Financial Corp. v. Bazzle*,[26] the Court held that whether a particular arbitration agreement prohibits class-wide arbitration is a question for the arbitrator. In the 2008 case of *Hall Street Associates, L.L.C. v. Mattel, Inc.*,[27] the Court held that the statutory grounds in the FAA §§ 9-11 (which prescribe when parties to an arbitration may apply to a court for an order confirming an award, or vacating, modifying, or correcting an award) are exclusive and may not be supplemented by contract. In the 2009 case of *14 Penn Plaza v. Pyett*,[28] the Court held that a collective-bargaining agreement clearly and unmistakably requiring union members to arbitrate ADEA claims was enforceable under the FAA. In the 2010 case of *Rent-A-Center, West, Inc. v. Jackson*,[29] the Supreme Court held, 5-4, that if an arbitration agreement provides that an arbitrator will decide all issues pertaining to enforceability, an arbitrator — not a court — must decide issues of unconscionability. Finally, in the 2011 consumer case of *AT&T Mobility LLC v. Concepcion*,[30] the Supreme Court reversed a Ninth Circuit ruling that clauses in arbitration agreements waiving the right to bring a future class action are unconscionable and unenforceable. In doing so, the Court may have significantly restricted the ability

---

[22] 525 U.S. 70 (1998).

[23] 531 U.S. 79, 92 (2000).

[24] 532 U.S. 105, 119 (2001).

[25] 534 U.S. 279 (2002).

[26] 539 U.S. 444 (2003).

[27] 552 U.S. 576 (2008).

[28] 556 U.S. 247 (2009).

[29] 130 S. Ct. 2772 (2010).

[30] 131 S. Ct. 1740 (2011).

of lower courts to use unconscionability as a means of policing lopsided arbitration agreements.

§ 17.04   CURRENT ISSUES IN EMPLOYMENT ARBITRATION

Gilmer held that the FAA provides the legal authority for judicial enforcement of employment arbitration agreements. That statute, however, does not specify the scope of an arbitrator's authority or the arbitral procedures that must be used. Instead, the Supreme Court has stated consistently that these items are contractual, and therefore subject to the private agreement of the parties.[31] As a practical matter, this means that most employment arbitration agreements are drafted by employers.

Although many employers draft arbitration agreements that are scrupulously fair to employees, other employers do not. Courts generally have agreed that egregiously lopsided agreements should not be enforced, but often disagree on whether a given arbitration agreement is lopsided or not.

One set of open issues involves contract formation.[32] The FAA provides that state law governs contract-formation issues concerning arbitration agreements.[33] State-to-state variation in contract law, and legitimate disagreement over how that contract law should be applied to employment arbitration agreements, has led to widespread inconsistency in the judicial enforcement of these agreements. Courts vary, for example, on whether an employer gives employees sufficient notice of arbitration by posting an arbitration agreement on the company website.[34] Courts also vary on whether an employee has consented to arbitration if the employer pressured the employee to sign the agreement without reading it,[35] if the agreement is buried in a much longer employment agreement, if the employer misrepresented the terms of the arbitration agreement,[36] or if the employer denied the employee access to the arbitration rules when the employer presented the purported agreement to the employee. Other open contract-formation issues include whether an employer may retain the unilateral right to modify an employment arbitration agreement,[37] whether an employer may require an employee to arbitrate the employee's claims if the employer has not agreed to arbitrate its own claims against the employee, and whether the employer must give an at-will employee consideration in return for the employee's agreement to arbitration.

---

[31] *See, e.g.,* Mitsubishi Motors Corp. v. Soler Chrysler-Plymouth, Inc., 473 U.S. 614, 625 (1985).

[32] *See generally* Richard A. Bales, *Contract Formation Issues in Employment Arbitration*, 44 BRANDEIS L.J. 415 (2006).

[33] 9 U.S.C. § 2.

[34] *See, e.g.,* Campbell v. Gen. Dynamics Gov't Sys. Corp., 407 F.3d 546 (1st Cir. 2005).

[35] *See, e.g.,* Walker v. Ryan's Family Steak Houses, Inc., 400 F.3d 370 (6th Cir. 2005).

[36] *Id.*

[37] *See generally* Michael L. DeMichele & Richard A. Bales, *Unilateral-Modification Provisions in Employment Arbitration Agreements*, 24 HOFSTRA LAB. & EMPLOY. L.J. 63 (2006).

A legal doctrine related to contract formation is unconscionability. For a contract to be unenforceable on unconscionability grounds, the contract must be both substantively unconscionable (i.e., the terms of the agreement are harsh and oppressive) and procedurally unconscionable (i.e., one party has used its bargaining strength coercively or deceptively). Because unconscionability is a state-law doctrine of contract formation, it is governed by state law rather than the FAA. [However, as discussed above, the Supreme Court in *Concepcion* may have significantly limited the application of the unconscionability doctrine to arbitration agreements.]

California courts have used the substantive prong of the unconscionability doctrine to regulate employment arbitration agreements that cover public law (statutory and tort) claims. In *Little v. Auto Stiegler, Inc.*,[38] the California Supreme Court struck as unconscionable an arbitration provision permitting either party to "appeal" to a second arbitrator an arbitration award of more than $50,000. This provision, the court held, benefited only the employer, because an employer would want to appeal large damage awards and an employee would only be interested in appealing small or take-nothing awards. The court also held that arbitration agreements covering public law claims must include minimum procedural requirements. Such procedural requirements, the court explained, include the availability of punitive damages and other remedies, adequate discovery, a written arbitration agreement, judicial review of issues of law, and a fair allocation of arbitration costs.

Because most states define unconscionability more narrowly than California does, courts (both state and federal) in other states often differ on whether a given arbitration clause is sufficiently fair to warrant enforcement. A second set of open issues involves requirements that employers sometimes impose that make it difficult or impossible for employees to pursue their employment claims.[39] Examples include arbitration agreements that impose shorter statutes of limitation than those imposed by law, that impose filing or arbitration fees on employees, that forbid class actions, and that contain onerous forum selection clauses.

A third set of open issues involves arbitral provisions that may affect the process by which arbitration is conducted.[40] Examples include provisions that impede the selection of a fair and unbiased arbitrator or that unduly restrict an employee's access to discovery. Yet another open issue is whether arbitration agreements may limit the arbitrator's ability to award certain remedies, such as punitive damages or attorneys' fees.[41] For example, on the remand of *Circuit City Stores, Inc. v. Adams*, the Ninth Circuit held that the arbitration agreement at issue was unconscionable because, among other things, it limited remedies to injunctive relief, one year of back pay, two years of front pay, compensatory damages, and punitive damages of no more than the amount of back and front pay awarded or $5000, whichever is

---

[38]   63 P.3d 979 (2003).

[39]   *See generally* Richard A. Bales, *The Employment Due Process Protocol at Ten: Twenty Unresolved Issues, and a Focus on Conflicts of Interest*, 21 OHIO ST. J. DISP. RESOL. 165 (2005).

[40]   *Id.*

[41]   *Id.*

larger.[42]

§ 17.05 THE ADVANTAGES AND DISADVANTAGES OF EMPLOYMENT ARBITRATION

Arbitrating employment cases has three major advantages over litigation. First, it is much faster. Arbitrating an employment case takes, on average, less than a year, while litigating an employment case takes more than two years.[43]

Second, the transaction costs are lower. Although the parties must pay for an arbitrator whereas they would not have to pay for a judge, streamlined discovery and adjudication procedures decrease significantly the amount of attorneys' fees, and make it more realistic for a party — particularly an employee — to pursue a claim without an attorney. However, even if the total transaction costs are lower for arbitration, they may be distributed differently.[44] In litigation, the employee typically signs a contingency fee contract with an attorney; the attorney fronts the litigation expenses and does not charge an hourly fee in return for receiving a percentage of the verdict if the case is successful. An arbitrator's fees, however, typically must be paid up front, although the arbitrator may in the arbitration award redistribute the employee's share of the fee to the employer, especially if the employee's claim is successful.

The third advantage of arbitration over litigation is employee access to a dispute resolution forum. The high cost of litigation and the low provable damages in most employment cases make it impossible for most low- and moderate-income employees to pursue their claims in court, at least not with an attorney. Arbitration can provide these employees, with or without an attorney, with a forum for resolving their employment disputes.

As far as the disadvantages of arbitration, one major disadvantage is that it is often coercive. Employees often do not know what they are signing when their employer presents them with an arbitration agreement. Even if they do know what they are signing, they may feel they have little choice but to sign, especially if the employer is presenting the arbitration agreement to existing employees on a take-it-or-be-fired basis.

A second major disadvantage is that arbitration agreements are typically drafted by the employer with little or no employee input. Although some employers have drafted fair agreements with an eye toward ensuring judicial enforcement and fostering employee trust and loyalty, other employers have drafted lopsided agreements that seem designed to ensure that no employee claim — no matter how legitimate — is successful.

---

[42] Circuit City Stores, Inc. v. Adams, 279 F.3d 889 (9th Cir. 2002).

[43] *See* Colvin, *supra* note 5.

[44] *See generally* Michelle Eviston & Richard Bales, *Capping the Costs of Consumer and Employment Arbitration*, 42 U. Tol. L. Rev. 903 (2011); Mark B. Gerano & Richard Bales, *Determining the Proper Standard for Invalidating Arbitration Agreements Based on High Prohibitive Costs: A Discussion on the Varying Applications of the Case-by-Case Rule*, 14 Transactions: Tenn. J. Bus. L. ___ (forthcoming Fall 2012).

Other arguments against pre-dispute employment arbitration agreements, with counter-arguments in parenthesis, include:

- It undermines the right to trial by jury in some cases (but the right is waivable, and employees arguably waive this right by agreeing to arbitration).

- It undermines the deterrent effect of employment laws by reducing the cost of defense and liability (however, lower transaction costs benefit employees as well as employers, and empirical evidence on the relative size of arbitrated and litigated awards is equivocal).

- Unlike litigation, it is private, which further reduces the deterrent effect of employment laws (but settlement, which is how nearly all litigated cases are resolved, also is private).

- Employers as repeat-players have a built-in advantage as arbitrators may favor employers in a bid for repeat business (but repeat players also have significant advantages in litigation).[45]

- Judicial review of arbitration awards is extremely limited. The FAA permits a reviewing court to vacate an arbitration award if the arbitrator was obviously corrupt or biased. However, an arbitrator's irrational finding of fact, or error of law, generally is not a valid basis for judicial review (but this affects employers in the same way it affects employees).

It can be difficult to generalize about employment arbitration systems because they come in so many shapes and sizes. Some, for example, are individually negotiated arbitration provisions that commonly are included in the employment contract of high-ranking company executives.[46] Others are applied across-the-board to all employees on an accept-it-or-be-fired basis. Of the latter, many are simple stand-alone agreements in which both employer and employee agree to arbitrate any claims they might have against the other. Other arbitration systems contain lopsided terms indicating that the employer is treating the arbitration system as more of a claim-avoidance mechanism than the change-in-forum approach blessed by the Supreme Court in *Gilmer*.[47] Still other arbitration systems are the final step in a comprehensive, multi-step dispute resolution process that might include internal and external mediation before progressing to arbitration.[48]

---

[45] Colvin, *supra* note 5.

[46] *See* Randall Thomas et al., *Arbitration Clauses in CEO Employment Contracts: An Empirical and Theoretical Analysis*, 63 VAND. L. REV. 959 (2010).

[47] The poster child for this approach is *Hooters of America, Inc. v. Phillips*, 173 F.3d 933 (4th Cir. 1999).

[48] *See, e.g.*, RICHARD A. BALES, COMPULSORY ARBITRATION: THE GRAND EXPERIMENT IN EMPLOYMENT 102–14 (1997) (Brown & Root / Halliburton); Richard A. Bales & Jason N.W. Plowman, *Compulsory Arbitration as Part of a Broader Employment Dispute Resolution Process: The Anheuser-Busch Example*, 26 HOFSTRA LAB. & EMPLOYMENT L. J. 1 (2008) (Anheuser-Busch); Suzette M. Malveaux, *Is it the "Real Thing?" How Coke's One-Way Binding Arbitration May Bridge the Divide Between Litigation and Arbitration*, 2009 J. OF DISP. RESOL. 77 (2009) (Coca-Cola).

In any event, arbitration agreements in the employment law context will likely continue to play a large role in employment law dispute resolution for many years to come.

TABLE OF CASES

[References are to pages]

[References are to pages]

[References are to pages]

[References are to pages]

INDEX

[References are to sections.]

[References are to sections.]

[References are to sections.]

[References are to sections.]

[References are to sections.]

[References are to sections.]